FAUST ﷼﷼﷼﷼ *Sources, Works, Criticism*

HARBRACE SOURCEBOOKS

FAUST
Sources, Works, Criticism

PAUL A. BATES

Colorado State University

Under the general editorship of DAVID LEVIN, *Stanford University*

HARCOURT, BRACE & WORLD, INC.

New York / Chicago / San Francisco / Atlanta

Library of Congress Catalog Card Number: 69-11090

Printed in the United States of America

ACKNOWLEDGMENTS

The thanks of the editor go to the following for their permission to reprint material in this book:

THE DRAMA REVIEW: For " 'The Form of Faustus' Fortunes Good or Bad,' " by C. L. Barber, first published in the *Tulane Drama Review* (now *The Drama Review*), Summer 1964, Vol. 8, No. 4, T24. Copyright 1964, *Tulane Drama Review,* and 1967, *The Drama Review.* Reprinted by permission of the author and publisher.

THE JOHNS HOPKINS PRESS: For "The Comic Synthesis in Doctor Faustus," by Robert Ornstein, first published in *English Literary History,* Vol. 22, No. 3 (1955), pp. 165–72. Reprinted by permission.

METHUEN & COMPANY, LTD.: For *"Doctor Faustus,"* trans. by T. S. Dorch, from *English Tragedy Before Shakespeare* by Wolfgang Clemen. Reprinted by permission.

OXFORD UNIVERSITY PRESS, INC.: For selections from *Goethe's Faust,* Parts I and II, trans. by Louis MacNeice. Copyright 1951 by Louis MacNeice. Reprinted by permission of Oxford University Press, Inc.

PRENTICE-HALL, INC., COLUMBIA UNIVERSITY PRESS: For "Aspects of Contradictions: On Recent Criticisms of Thomas Mann," by Bernhard Blume, *Germanic Review,* Vol. XXXI (1956), pp. 175–90, copyright © 1956 by Columbia University Press, as translated by Henry Hatfield in *Thomas Mann: A Collection of Critical Essays,* Henry Hatfield, ed., © 1964. Reprinted by permission of Columbia University Press, Prentice-Hall, Inc., Englewood Cliffs, N.J., and the author and translator. For "World Without Transcendence," by Hans E. Holthusen, as translated by Henry Hatfield in *Thomas Mann: A Collection of Critical Essays,* Henry Hatfield, ed., © 1964. Reprinted by permission of Prentice-Hall, Inc., Englewood Cliffs, N.J., and the author and translator.

PRINCETON UNIVERSITY PRESS: For "Thomas Mann's *Doctor Faustus*" from *The Orbit of Thomas Mann,* by Erich Kahler, to be published by Princeton University Press in 1969. Reprinted by permission of the publisher.

RANDOM HOUSE, INC. ALFRED A. KNOPF, INC.: For "Faust's Damnation: The Morality of Knowledge," from *The Artist's Journey into the Interior* by Erich Heller. © Copyright 1959, 1964, 1965 by Erich Heller. Reprinted by permission of Random House, Inc. For "Goethe and *Faust.*" Copyright 1950 by Random House, Inc. Reprinted from the Introduction to Goethe's *Faust* by Victor Lange by permission of the publisher. For "The Progress of Faust." Copyright 1946 by Karl Shapiro. Reprinted from *Selected Poems* by Karl Shapiro by permission of Random House, Inc. Originally appeared in *The New Yorker.* For Chapter 25 from *Doctor Faustus* by Thomas Mann, trans. by H. T. Lowe-Porter. Copyright 1948 by Alfred A. Knopf, Inc. Reprinted by permission of the publisher.

ROUTLEDGE & KEGAN PAUL, LTD.: For excerpts from William Rose's edition of *The History of the Damnable Life and Deserved Death of Doctor Faustus.* Reprinted by permission.

ᔕᔕᔕᔕᔕᔕᔕᔕᔕᔕᔕᔕᔕᔕᔕᔕᔕᔕ

Introduction

From the *Faustbuch* of 1587 to the works of Thomas Mann and Paul Valéry in the twentieth century, the story of Doctor Faustus has played a major role in the literature of Europe. It has held a fascination for writers in every age because of its concern with religious and philosophical problems of universal consequence: the desire for unlimited knowledge, especially of matters beyond the reach of science; man's relationship with the forces of good and evil; his revolt against the limitations of life; and the spiritual corruption that often accompanies material gain. To understand how the Faust story became a vehicle for themes of such import, let us summarize its history.

Doctor John Faustus lived from sometime in the late fifteenth century until about 1540. The first concrete reference to him dates from 1507, and the last reference to him as a living person was in 1540. The outlines of his life are almost as uncertain as the dates that bounded it. He may even have adopted the name Faustus from an earlier magician. At any rate, a magician and conjuror called Faust did travel about Germany and other parts of Europe in the first half of the sixteenth century. A few historical records concerning this intriguing figure exist. In addition, references to him, gossip about him, and even whole manuscripts describing him circulated in the second half of the century, and legends soon accumulated around his name. Earlier stories of magicians and of people who had sold their souls to the devil, stories that had been circulating since the time of the New Testament, crystallized around the figure of Faust.

The story promptly came to play a part in the Reformation. Protestant leaders, concerned about the religious skepticism spreading through Europe, seized on the story of Faustus' sins and the rumors of his horrible death as an example to doubters. This motive is clearly evident in the first published account of Faustus' life, the *Historia von D. Johann Fausten,* issued by Johann Spies at Frankfurt am Main in 1587. The *Faustbuch,* as we shall call it, presents few facts about Faust's life, but much fantasy. Faust conjures up the devil Mephistopheles, who purchases his soul in return for twenty-four years of forbidden knowledge, devilish power, and material rewards. Various fantastic adventures of Faust are recorded, together with his final, remorseful lamentation and his horrifying death at the hands of a crew of devils.

Spies' book was quickly translated into a number of languages. In 1592, in London, one "P. F., Gentleman," published a version that he called *The Historie of the Damnable Life and Deserved Death of Doctor John Faustus.* The title clearly indicates the translator's condemnation of the heretical doctor, but the English version was less critical of him than the German original had been, perhaps because doubt and questioning were becoming more acceptable.

Christopher Marlowe (1564–93) gave the story its first major literary treatment immediately after the appearance of the English translation. His play, *The Tragicall Historie of Doctor Faustus* (first staged in 1594 and published in 1605), drawn from the more dramatic incidents in the *Faustbuch,* shows Dr. Faustus torn between his aspiration for knowledge and power and his loss of salvation.

From the time of Marlowe, the fame of the Faust story was assured. New and revised editions of the *Faustbuch* appeared periodically in Germany, culminating in the edition of 1712 by "Christlich Meynenden" ("a Christian believer"). Versions of Marlowe's play were staged on the continent by strolling players. The drama was soon adapted to the puppet stage and drew large audiences throughout the eighteenth century.

The next development in the history of the Faust theme—the salvation of Faust—was of paramount importance. The feeling that Faust deserved salvation reflected the changes in thought and society that had taken place since the days of Spies and Marlowe. Philosophical contributions by Francis Bacon (1561–1628) and René Descartes (1596–1650) had led to a scientific rationalism that undermined orthodox religious belief. In this atmosphere of the deification of reason, Faust's search for knowledge became justified, and instead of being damned, he was to find salvation. The first writer to "save" Faust was Gotthold Ephraim Lessing (1729–81), a German writer who was preoccupied with the Faust theme for twenty years. Although only a fragment of his drama survives (in his seventeenth *Literaturbrief* of 1759), he deserves the credit for rewarding Faust's search for knowledge with salvation.

The various eighteenth-century versions and the prevailing humanistic attitudes led to the greatest of all works on Faust, the two-part drama by Johann Wolfgang von Goethe (1749–1832). Goethe was concerned with the story of Faust throughout most of his long literary life. An early work, known as the *Ur-Faust*, tells for the first time the story of the seduction of Margaret by Faust. Goethe then wrote a five-act drama, *Faust*, Part I, and later a sequel, *Faust*, Part II. Like Lessing, he brings Faust to final salvation, but his work is much more complex and less optimistic than that of Lessing.

The tale of Faust and Margaret in Part I of Goethe's drama, which made the problems of good and evil concrete, had popular appeal and was soon embodied in other works. In his opera, *Faust et Marguérite* (1859), Charles Gounod gives the story of Faust and Margaret its greatest musical formulation. Other musical works based on the Faust tradition were composed by Louis Spohr (*Faust*, 1818), Arrigo Boito (*Mefistoféle*, 1868), Hector Berlioz (*La Damnation de Faust*, 1846), and Franz Liszt (*Eine Faust Symphonie*, 1857).

In addition to these adaptations, many literary versions of the Faust story poured forth in the nineteenth and twentieth centuries. The poet Heinrich Heine (1797–1856) wrote *Ist Doktor Faust, ein Tanzpoem,* or dance poem, which has occasionally been staged. In 1826 Alexander Pushkin (1799–1837) published his *Faust*. The German dramatist C. D. Grabbe (1801–36) related the story with that of Don Juan in his play *Don Juan und Faust*. A long poem by the Austrian poet Nikolaus Lenau (1802–50) dramatizes his own conflict between faith and knowledge. Ivan Turgeniev (1818–83) wrote a short novel on the Faust-Margaret theme. Paul Valéry (1871–1945) wrote a drama, *Mon Faust,* in which the intellectual knows full well that his problem is alienation and that the devil is a figment. And Anatoli Lunacharski (1873–1933), a Russian politician and literary critic, gave an optimistic Marxist version of the story in *Faust and the City,* emphasizing the concern for social improvement and service to mankind that is suggested near the end of Goethe's *Faust,* Part II.

The most impressive twentieth-century treatment of the story is the *Doctor Faustus* of the German novelist Thomas Mann (1875–1955). Mann's novel, reflecting the psychological, political, social, and moral problems of the twentieth century, is a study of the problems of the alienated German intellectual and artist in the period of the First World War and the rise of Nazism. Damnation is now a question of psychology and of the relation of the artist to society. A far more complex approach in which various personal and social themes are interwoven like musical motifs replaces the relatively optimistic attitudes of Lessing and Goethe.

Finally, the story of Faust reaches the present. The ability to orbit satellites and explode thermonuclear bombs has given men power inconceivable to Dr. Faustus. This power, neither good nor bad in itself, confronts man with the problem of directing his scientific achievements in conformity with a humanistic ethic. It is not surprising that both Erich Heller in his essay and Karl Shapiro in his poem discuss Faust in relation to the atom bomb.

This sourcebook presents materials for a study of the Faust story as it originated and evolved. It is designed for use in courses that utilize source materials and culminate in long research papers.

It should also be of value in courses in world literature, comparative literature, drama, the humanities, or literary criticism, as a primary or supplementary text. It should be especially useful in courses that combine literature and composition.

Three kinds of materials are included here. Part 1 contains the sources of the Faust story and theme: historical records and references and excerpts from the Spies' *Faustbuch,* reproduced from the English translation of 1592. These materials should enable students to distinguish between historical and fabulous elements in the story.

Part 2 includes a number of major literary treatments of the Faust story. Two are world-famous dramas that exemplify the Renaissance and early-nineteenth-century views of Faust: Marlowe's *Doctor Faustus* (complete) and Goethe's *Faust* (Part I complete and Act V of Part II, in the MacNeice translation). Students may make meaningful comparisons between these works as dramas and from them draw conclusions about the historical periods in which they originated. Finally, there is a chapter from Thomas Mann's novel *Doctor Faustus* and a poem by the American Karl Shapiro. These selections make possible a study contrasting twentieth-century attitudes toward art, knowledge, and life with those of the earlier periods. Mann modernizes and secularizes the Faust story, while the brief poem by Shapiro makes Faust a living, mythical figure traveling through space and time from sixteenth-century Germany to the salt flats of Nevada, where he witnesses the explosion of the atomic bomb. Such questions as these arise: Is this the culmination of Faust's thirst for knowledge? Has the magical power the obscure doctor sought been realized by modern science? And to what end? Is modern man still a Faust figure serving the devil?

Part 3 contains critical documents on the Faust theme and interpretations and commentaries on the various treatments of the story.

The suggestions for written assignments at the end of the book are arranged in order of increasing length and difficulty. First are short exercises on the sources and works and on certain of the critical documents, then more complex assignments involving the comparison of two or more works or critical pieces. A list of full-length research papers follows, requiring the student to draw on the various works and the criticism and form independent conclusions. Lastly, there are some suggestions for papers based on library research and others that involve consideration of the Faust tradition in music. These suggestions may of course serve also as a basis for class discussion and as guides to study.

The student may document his work directly from this volume, or he may cite the sources themselves if the instructor so directs. References to Marlowe's play may be made by act, scene, and line numbers and to Goethe's *Faust* by part and line numbers. Those to Mann's *Doctor Faustus* and the historical and critical materials may be cited by page numbers of the source, which appear directly after the last word taken from the page.

The editor is indebted to the earlier sourcebooks in the series and to Alvin Kernan of Yale University, Edgar Lohner of Stanford University, and David Levin of Stanford University, series editor, for valuable suggestions and criticism.

PAUL A. BATES

Contents

FAUST   ≈≈≈≈≈≈   *Sources, Works, Criticism*

I. Sources

The source materials provided here fall into two main parts. The first is a collection of historical records, letters, and references to a Doctor Johann Faustus that appeared in various works in Germany during the sixteenth century. They are reprinted from *The Sources of the Faust Tradition from Simon Magus to Lessing*, by Philip Mason Palmer and Robert Pattison More (New York: Oxford University Press, 1936; reissued by Octagon Books, New York, 1966), a volume that contains much of the available material concerning the historical Faustus. Each historical item is dated, and the author or source is identified. Some of these items are taken from city records; others are eyewitness accounts; still others are secondhand reports.

These historical references may be used in a variety of ways. First, one can simply attempt to establish the facts of Faust's life. Even with regard to the city records, we cannot be sure that the student who matriculated at Heidelberg University in 1509 (*The Sources of the Faust Tradition*, p. 87) is the same man referred to in the various items about a wandering magician. Both the eyewitness accounts and the secondhand reports must be evaluated in terms of the probable reliability of the person who wrote the account, the source of his information, and the inherent probability of the events reported in the account.

One can trace in these historical accounts the growth of the legend of Doctor Faustus. We begin with apparently factual accounts of a wandering, boastful magician, but we soon find suggestions that Faust has real powers beyond his trickery and then that he is allied with the devil; the final documents give lurid accounts of his death. Discrimination is needed in determining what is historically accurate, what is probable, and what is clearly legendary. This study might

be extended to a study of *euhemerism*, the theory that legends and mythology originate with actual persons.

The student can also begin to note a relationship between the Faust story and Lutheranism. The selections from the writings of Luther and Melanchthon in particular indicate an early interest in the story of Faust on the part of the Protestant leaders.

The second part of this section consists of excerpts from *The History of the Damnable Life and Deserved Death of Doctor John Faustus*, the English translation of 1592 of Spies' *Faustbuch*, modernized in spelling and punctuation by William Rose (New York: Dutton, 1925; reprinted in paperback by the University of Notre Dame Press, South Bend, Ind., 1963). The excerpts chosen for inclusion are those that have been utilized in various literary versions of the story. The complete text includes long sections of little interest to the modern student, such as a lengthy description of Faust's travels that was lifted from contemporary chronicles.

Like the historical references, the *Faustbuch* can be used in a variety of ways. It is a readable account in itself, once the tedious portions have been excised. The student can compare the full-blown legendary material with the earlier historical materials. He can compare the versions by Marlowe and Goethe with this narrative account, deciding why they chose to dramatize certain elements and to eliminate others. The relationship of Mann's novel to the *Faustbuch* is of special interest in that both narrate the life of the hero from birth to death. The student who is interested can read the complete novel and trace the various subtle relationships between the two works.

Footnotes in the section "The Historical Faustus" are based on those by Palmer and More. Footnotes to the *Faustbuch* are by Rose.

The Historical Faustus

I

Letter of Johannes Tritheim[1] to
Johannes Virdung[2]

The man of whom you wrote me, George Sabellicus, who has presumed to call himself the prince of necromancers, is a vagabond, a babbler and a rogue, who deserves to be thrashed so that he may not henceforth rashly venture to profess in public things so execrable and so hostile to the holy church. For what, other than /83/ symptoms of a very foolish and insane mind, are the titles assumed by this man, who shows himself to be a fool and not a philosopher? For thus he has formulated the title befitting him: Master George Sabellicus, the younger Faust, the chief of necromancers, astrologer, the second magus, palmist, diviner with earth and fire, second in the art of divination with water. Behold the foolish temerity of the man, the madness by which he is possessed, in that he dares to call himself the source of necromancy, when in truth, in his ignorance of all good letters, he ought to call himself a fool rather than a master. But his wickedness is not hidden from me. When I was returning last year from the Mark Brandenburg, I happened upon this same man in the town of Gelnhausen, and many silly things were told me about him at the inn,—things promised by him with great rashness on his part. As soon as he

heard that I was there, he fled from the inn and could not be persuaded to come into my presence. The description of his folly, such as he gave to you and which we have mentioned, he also sent to me through a certain /84/ citizen. Certain priests in the same town told me that he had said, in the presence of many people, that he had acquired such knowledge of all wisdom and such a memory, that if all the books of Plato and Aristotle, together with their whole philosophy, had totally passed from the memory of man, he himself, through his own genius, like another Hebrew Ezra, would be able to restore them all with increased beauty. Afterwards, while I was at Speyer, he came to Würzburg and, impelled by the same vanity, is reported to have said in the presence of many that the miracles of Christ the Saviour were not so wonderful, that he himself could do all the things which Christ had done, as often and whenever he wished. Towards the end of Lent of the present year he came to Kreuznach and with like folly and boastfulness made great promises, saying that in alchemy he was the most learned man of all times and that by his knowledge and ability, he could do whatever /85/ anyone might wish. In the meantime there was vacant in the same town the position of schoolmaster, to which he was appointed through the influence of Franz von Sickingen, the magistrate of your prince and a man very fond of mystical lore. Then he began to indulge in the most dastardly kind of lewdness with the boys and when this was suddenly discovered, he avoided by flight the punishment that awaited him. These are the things which I know through very definite evidence concerning the man whose coming you await with such anticipation. When he comes to you, you will find him to be not a philosopher but a fool with

[1]Johannes Tritheim (1462–1516), physicist, humanist, writer; abbot of the monastery at Spanheim near Kreuznach from 1485 to 1506 and later of the monastery of St. James at Würzburg. Tritheim combined great learning with an inclination to the fantastic, which led to his considerable reputation as a magician.

[2]Johannes Virdung of Hasfurt, professor at Heidelberg and mathematician and astrologer to the Elector of the Palatinate.

an overabundance of rashness.—Würzburg, the 20th day of August.

A.D. 1507. /86/

II

Letter of Conrad Mutianus Rufus[3] to Heinrich Urbanus[4]

Eight days ago there came to Erfurt a certain soothsayer by the name of George Faust, the demigod of Heidelberg, a mere braggart and fool. His claims, /87/ like those of all diviners, are idle and such physiognomy has no more weight than a water spider. The ignorant marvel at him. Let the theologians rise against him and not try to destroy the philosopher Reuchlin. I heard him babbling at an inn, but I did not reprove his boastfulness. What is the foolishness of other people to me?

October 3, 1513.

III

From the Account Book of the Bishop of Bamberg,[5] 1519–1520

The annual accounts of Hans Muller, chamberlain, from Walpurgis 1519 to Walpurgis 1520.

Entry on February 12, 1520, under the heading "Miscellaneous." /88/

10 gulden given and presented as a testimonial to Doctor Faust, the philosopher, who made for my master a horoscope or prognostication. Paid on the Sunday after Saint Scholastica's Day by the order of his reverence.

IV

From the Journal of Kilian Lieb,[6] July 1528

George Faust of Helmstet said on the fifth of June that when the sun and Jupiter are in the

same constellation prophets are born (presumably such as he). He asserted that he was the commander or preceptor of the order of the Knights of St. John at a place called Hallestein on the border of Carinthia. /89/

V

From the Records of the City of Ingolstadt

(a) Minute on the actions of the city council in Ingolstadt.

Today, the Wednesday after St. Vitus' Day, 1528. The soothsayer shall be ordered to leave the city and to spend his penny elsewhere.

(b) Record of those banished from Ingolstadt.

On Wednesday after St. Vitus' Day, 1528, a certain man who called himself Dr. George Faust of Heidelberg was told to spend his penny elsewhere and he pledged himself not to take vengeance on or make fools of the authorities for this order.

VI

Entry in the Records of the City Council of Nuremberg, May 10, 1532

Safe conduct to Doctor Faust, the great sodomite and necromancer, at Fürth refused.

The junior Burgomaster. /90/

VII

From the Waldeck Chronicle

Francis I by the grace of God, son of Philip II[7] by his second marriage, Bishop of Münster, on June 25, 1535, invested the city of Münster which had been occupied by the Anabaptists and captured it with the aid of princes of the Empire under the leadership of Hensel Hochstraten. John of Leyden,[8] the boastful pretender, who called himself King of Israel and Zion, was

---

[3]Conrad Mutianus Rufus (1471–1526), canon of the Church of St. Mary's at Gotha; a humanist and philosopher ranked by the humanists with Erasmus and Reuchlin.

[4]Heinrich Urbanus, student and later friend of Mutianus Rufus, through whom he became interested in humanism. From about 1505 he was steward of the Cistercian cloister Georgenthal at Erfurt.

[5]George Schenk of Limburg, Bishop of Bamberg from 1502 to 1522.

[6]Prior of Rebdorf in Bavaria.

[7]Philip II, Count of Waldeck.

[8]Originally a tailor, John of Leyden became a leader of the Anabaptist movement in Münster and set up there the "Kingdom of Zion," proclaiming himself king. Krechting was his chancellor, and Knipperdollinck was mayor of Münster during the Anabaptist regime.

executed together with Knipperdollinck and Krechting, their bodies being torn with red-hot pincers, enclosed in iron cages and suspended from the tower of St. Lambert's Church on the 23rd of January, 1536. It was at this time that the famous necromancer Dr. Faust, coming on the same day from Corbach, prophesied that the city of Münster would surely be captured by the Bishop on that very night. /91/

VIII

Letter of Joachim Camerarius[9] to Daniel Stibar[10]

I owe to your friend Faust the pleasure of discussing these affairs with you. I wish he had taught you something of this sort rather than puffed you up with the wind of silly superstition or held you in suspense with I know not what juggler's tricks. But what does he tell us, pray? For I know that you have questioned him diligently about all things. Is the emperor victorious? That is the way you should go about it.

Tübingen, the 13th of August, 1536

IX

From the Tischreden of Martin Luther[11]

God's word alone overcomes the fiery arrows of the devil and all his temptations. /92/

When one evening at the table a sorcerer named Faust was mentioned, Doctor Martin said in a serious tone: "The devil does not make use of the services of sorcerers against me. If he had been able to do me any harm he would have done it long since. To be sure he has often had me by the head but he had to let me go again."

X

From the Tischreden of Martin Luther[12]

Mention was made of magicians and the

magic art, and how Satan blinded men. Much was said about Faust, who called the devil his brother-in-law, and the remark was made: "If I, Martin Luther, had given him even my hand, he would have destroyed me; but I would not have been afraid of him,—with God as my protector, I would have given him my hand in the name of the Lord." /93/

XI

From the Index sanitatis of Philipp Begardi[13]

There is another well-known and important man whom I would not have mentioned were it not for the fact that he himself had no desire to remain in obscurity and unknown. For some years ago he traveled through almost all countries, principalities and kingdoms, and himself made his name known to everybody and bragged much about his great skill not only in medicine but also in chiromancy, nigromancy, physiognomy, crystal-gazing, and the like arts. And he not only bragged but confessed and signed himself as a famous and experienced master. He himself avowed and did not deny that he was and was called Faust and in addition signed himself "The philosopher of philosophers." The number of those who complained to me that they were cheated by him was very great. Now his promises were great like those of Thessalus,[14] likewise his fame /94/ as that of Theophrastus.[15] But his deeds, as I hear, were very petty and fraudulent. But in taking or—to speak more accurately—in receiving money he was not slow. And afterwards also, on his departure, as I have been informed, he left many to whistle for their money. But what is to be done about it? What's gone is gone. I will drop the subject here. Anything further is your affair.

[9]Joachim Camerarius (1500–74), called to Tübingen to reform the university in 1535.
[10]City councilman of Würzburg.
[11]Martin Luther (1483–1546), reformer and founder of the Protestant church. The Tischreden, published in Eisleben in 1566, are the comments and discussions of Luther in the informal circle of his family and friends.
[12]This quotation was taken down by Antonius Lau-

terback in 1537 and first published by E. Kroker, Luthers Tischreden in der Mathesischen Sammlung (Leipzig, 1903), p. 422.
[13]City physician in Worms. The Index sanitatis (Index to Health) is of the year 1539.
[14]Greek physician of the first century A.D., always mentioned by Galen in terms of contempt.
[15]Theophrastus (1493–1541), physician and dentist.

XII

Letter from Philipp von Hutten[16] to His Brother Moritz von Hutten

Here you have a little about all the provinces so that you may see that we are not the only ones who have been unfortunate in Venezuela up to this time; that all the abovementioned expeditions which left Sevilla before and after us perished within three months. /95/ Therefore I must confess that the philosopher Faust hit the nail on the head, for we struck a very bad year. But God be praised, things went better for us than for any of the others. God willing I shall write you again before we leave here. Take good care of our dear old mother. Give my greetings to all our neighbours and friends, especially Balthasar Rabensteiner and George von Libra, William von Hessberg and all my good comrades. Pay my respects to Herr N of Thüngen, my master's brother. Done in Coro in the Province of Venezuela on January 16th, 1540.

XIII

From the Sermones convivales *of Johannes Gast[17]*

Concerning the necromancer Faust. He puts up at night at a certain very rich monastery, intending to spend the night there. A brother places before him some ordinary wine of indifferent quality /96/ and without flavor. Faust requests that he draw from another cask a better wine which it was the custom to give to nobles. Then the brother said: "I do not have the keys, the prior is sleeping, and it is a sin to awaken him." Faust said: "The keys are lying in that corner. Take them and open that cask on the left and give me a drink." The brother objected that he had no orders from the prior to place any other wine before guests. When Faust heard this he became very angry and said: "In a short time you shall see marvels, you inhospitable

brother." Burning with rage he left early in the morning without saying farewell and sent a certain raging devil who made a great stir in the monastery by day and by night and moved things about both in the church and in the cells of the monks, so that they could not get any rest, no matter what they did. Finally they deliberated whether they should leave the monastery or destroy it altogether. And so they wrote to the Count Palatine concerning the misfortune in which they were involved. He took the monastery under his own protection and ejected the monks to whom he furnishes supplies from year to year and uses what is left for /97/ himself. It is said that to this very day, if monks enter the monastery, such great disturbances arise that those who live there can have no peace. This the devil was able to bring to pass.

Another story about Faust. At Basle I dined with him in the great college and he gave to the cook various kinds of birds to roast. I do not know where he bought them or who gave them to him, since there were none on sale at the time. Moreover I never saw any like them in our regions. He had with him a dog and a horse which I believe to have been demons and which were ready for any service. I was told that the dog at times assumed the form of a servant and served the food. However, the wretch was destined to come to a deplorable end, for he was strangled by the devil and his body on its bier kept turning face downward even though it was five times turned on its back. God preserve us lest we become slaves of the devil. /98/

XIV

From the Explicationes Melanchthoniae,[18] pars II

There [in the presence of Nero] Simon Magus tried to fly to heaven, but Peter prayed that he might fall. I believe that the Apostles had great struggles although not all are recorded. Faust

---

[16]Philipp von Hutten (1511–46), one of the leaders of the Welser troops in Venezuela, where he met his death. The letter seems to indicate that Faust had made predictions concerning the fortunes of the expedition in Venezuela.

[17]Johannes Gast (d. 1572), a Protestant clergyman at Basle. The quotation is from the second volume of his *Sermones convivales,* published in 1548.

[18]Philipp Melanchthon (1497–1560), a co-worker of Luther and after him the most important figure in the German Reformation, succeeded Luther as head of the church. The *Explicationes* were published posthumously by Pezelius, a former student of Melanchthon, beginning in 1594.

also tried this at Venice. But he was sorely dashed to the ground.

XV

From the Explicationes Melanchthoniae, pars IV

The devil is a marvellous craftsman, for he is able by some device to accomplish things which are natural but which we do not understand. For he can do more than man. Thus many strange feats of magic are recounted such as I have related elsewhere concerning the girl at Bologna. In like manner Faust, the magician, devoured at Vienna another magician who was /99/ discovered a few days later in a certain cave. The devil can perform many miracles; nevertheless the church has its own miracles. /100/

XVI

From the Locorum communium collectanea *of Johannes Manlius*[19]

I knew a certain man by the name of Faust from Kundling, which is a small town near my birthplace. When he was a student at Cracow he studied magic, for there was formerly much practice of the art in that city and in that place too there were public lectures on this art. He wandered about everywhere and talked of many mysterious things. When he wished to provide a spectacle at Venice he said he would fly to heaven. So the devil raised him up and then cast him down so that he was dashed to the ground and almost killed. However he did not die.

A few years ago this same John Faust, on the day before his end, sat very downcast in a certain village /101/ in the Duchy of Württemberg. The host asked him why, contrary to his custom and habit, he was so downcast (he was otherwise a most shameful scoundrel who led a very wicked life, so that he was again and again nigh to being killed because of his dissolute habits). Then he said to the host in the village: "Don't be frightened tonight." In the middle of the

night the house was shaken. When Faust did not get up in the morning and when it was now almost noon, the host with several others went into his bedroom and found him lying near the bed with his face turned toward his back. Thus the devil had killed him. While he was alive he had with him a dog which was the devil, just as the scoundrel[20] who wrote "De vanitate artium" likewise had a dog that ran about with him and was the devil. This same Faust escaped in this town of Wittenberg when the good prince Duke John had given orders to arrest him. Likewise in Nuremberg he escaped. He was just beginning to dine when he became restless and immediately rose and paid the host /102/ what he owed. He had hardly got outside the gate when the bailiffs came and inquired about him.

The same magician Faust, a vile beast and a sink of many devils, falsely boasted that all the victories which the emperor's armies have won in Italy had been gained by him through his magic. This was an absolute lie. I mention this for the sake of the young that they may not readily give ear to such lying men.

XVII

From the Zimmerische Chronik[21]

That the practice of such art [soothsaying] is not only godless but in the highest degree dangerous is undeniable, for experience proves it and we know what happened to the notorious sorcerer Faust. After he had practiced during his lifetime many marvels about which a special treatise could be written, he was finally killed /103/ at a ripe old age by the evil one in the seigniory of Staufen in Breisgau.

After 1539. About this time also Faust died in or not far from the town of Staufen in Breisgau. In his day he was as remarkable a sorcerer as could be found in German lands in our times. He had so many strange experiences at various times that he will not easily be forgotten for

[20]Cornelius Heinrich Agrippa von Nettesheim (1486–1535), author, physician, and philosopher. Like many others, he was suspected of being a sorcerer.

[21]A Swabian chronicle of the sixteenth century, written by Count Froben Christoph von Zimmern and his secretary, that gives the history of the Swabian noblemen and contains an invaluable store of legends and folklore.

[19]Johannes Manlius, a former student of Melanchthon, published extracts from his and other works in the *Locorum* (1563).

many years. He became an old man and, as it is said, died miserably. From all sorts of reports and conjectures many have thought that the evil one, whom in his lifetime he used to call his brother-in-law, had killed him. The books which he left behind fell into the hands of the Count of Staufen in whose territory he died. Afterwards many people tried to get these books and in doing so in my opinion were seeking a dangerous and unlucky treasure and gift. He sent a spirit into the monastery of the monks at Luxheim in the Vosges mountains which they could /104/ not get rid of for years and which bothered them tremendously,—and this for no other reason than that once upon a time they did not wish to put him up overnight. For this reason he sent them the restless guest. In like manner, it is said, a similar spirit was summoned and attached to the former abbot of St. Diesenberg by an envious wandering scholar.

XVIII

From the De praestigiis daemonum of Johannes Wier[22]

John Faust was born in the little town Kundling and studied magic in Cracow, where it was formerly taught openly; and for a few years previous to 1540 he practiced his art in various places in Germany with many lies and much fraud, to the marvel of many. There was nothing he could not do with his inane boasting and his promises. I will give one example of his art on the condition that the reader will first promise not /105/ to imitate him. This wretch, taken prisoner at Batenburg on the Maas, near the border of Geldern, while the Baron Hermann was away, was treated rather leniently by his chaplain, Dr. Johannes Dorstenius, because he promised the man, who was good but not shrewd, knowledge of many things and various arts. Hence he kept drawing him wine, by which Faust was very much exhilarated, until the vessel was empty. When Faust learned this, and

the chaplain told him that he was going to Grave, that he might have his beard shaved, Faust promised him another unusual art by which his beard might be removed without the use of a razor, if he would provide more wine. When this condition was accepted, he told him to rub his beard vigorously with arsenic, but without any mention of its preparation. When the salve had been applied, there followed such an inflammation that not only the hair but also the skin and the flesh were burned off. The chaplain himself told me of this piece of villainy more than once with much indignation. When another acquaintance of mine, whose beard was black and whose face was rather dark and showed signs of melancholy /106/ (for he was splenetic), approached Faust, the latter exclaimed: "I surely thought you were my brother-in-law and therefore I looked at your feet to see whether long curved claws projected from them": thus comparing him to the devil whom he thought to be entering and whom he used to call his brother-in-law. He was finally found dead near his bed in a certain town in the Duchy of Württemberg, with his face turned towards his back; and it is reported that during the middle of the night preceding, the house was shaken.

XIX

From the Von Gespänsten of Ludwig Lavater[23]

To this very day there are sorcerers who boast that they can saddle a horse on which they can in a short time make great journeys. The devil will give them all their reward in the long run. What wonders is the notorious sorcerer Faust said to have done in our own times. /107/

XX

From the Chronica von Thüringen und der Stadt Erffurth of Zacharias Hogel[24]

(a) It was also probably about this time

---

[22]Johannes Wier (1515–88), a Dutch physician known as an opponent of the prosecution of witches. The De praestigiis daemonum (first edition, 1563) was an appeal to the emperor and princes in Wier's campaign against superstition. The passages relating to Faust appear for the first time in the fourth edition (1568).

[23]Ludwig Lavater (1527–86), for many years a preacher in Zurich and finally head of the Protestant church there. His Von Gespänsten ("About Ghosts") (1569) was very popular.

[24]Hogel's chronicle was written in the seventeenth century, but its source was the lost Reichmann-Wam-

[1550] that those strange things happened which are said to have taken place in Erfurt in the case of the notorious sorcerer and desperate brand of hell, Dr. Faust. Although he lived in Wittenberg, yet, just as his restless spirit in other instances drove him about in the world, so he also came to the university at Erfurt, rented quarters near the large Collegium, and through his boasting brought it to pass that he was allowed to lecture publicly and to explain the Greek poet Homer to the students. When, in this connection, he had occasion to mention the king of Troy, Priam, and the heroes of the Trojan war, Hector, Ajax, Ulysses, Agamemnon, /108/ and others, he described them each as they had appeared. He was asked (for there are always inquisitive fellows and there was no question as to what Faust was) to bring it to pass through his art, that these heroes should appear and show themselves as he had just described them. He consented to this and appointed the time when they should next come to the auditorium. And when the hour had come and more students than before had appeared before him, he said in the midst of his lecture that they should now get to see the ancient Greek heroes. And immediately he called in one after the other and as soon as one was gone another came in to them, looked at them and shook his head as though he were still in action on the field before Troy. The last of them all was the giant Polyphemus, who had only a single terrible big eye in the middle of his forehead. He wore a fiery red beard and was devouring a fellow, one of

---

bach chronicle dating from the middle of the sixteenth century.

whose legs was dangling out of his mouth. The sight of him scared them so that their hair stood on end and /109/ when Dr. Faust motioned him to go out, he acted as though he did not understand but wanted to grasp a couple of them too with his teeth. And he hammered on the floor with his great iron spear so that the whole Collegium shook, and then he went away.

Not long afterward the commencement for masters was held and [at the banquet given in connection therewith], in the presence of the members of the theological faculty and of delegates from the council, the comedies of the ancient poets Plautus and Terence were discussed and regret was expressed that so many of them had been lost in times gone by, for if they were available, they could be used to good advantage in the schools. Dr. Faust listened to this and he also began to speak about the two poets and cited several quotations which were supposed to be in their lost comedies. And he offered, if it would not be held against him, and if the theologians had no objections, to bring to light again all the lost comedies and to put them at their disposal for several hours, during which time they /110/ would have to be copied quickly by a goodly number of students or clerks, if they wanted to have them. After that they would be able to use them as they pleased. The theologians and councilmen, however, did not take kindly to the proposal: for they said the devil might interpolate all sorts of offensive things into such newly found comedies. And after all, one could, even without them, learn enough good Latin from those which still existed. The conjurer accordingly could not exhibit one of his masterpieces in this connection. . . . /111/

JOHANN SPIES

ꙮꙮꙮꙮꙮꙮꙮꙮꙮꙮꙮꙮꙮ

The Faustbuch

A Discourse of the most famous Doctor John Faustus of Wittenberg in Germanie, Coniurer, and Necromancer: wherein is declared many strange things that he himselfe hath seene, and done in the earth and in the Ayre, with his bringing vp, his trauailes, studies, and last end

CHAPTER I

Of his Parentage and Birth

John Faustus, born in the town of Rhode, lying in the province of Weimer in Germanie, his father a poor husbandman, and not able well to bring him up: but having an uncle at Wittenberg, a rich man, and without issue, took this J. Faustus from his father, and made him his heir, in so much that his father was no more troubled with him, for he remained with his uncle at Wittenberg, where he was kept at the University in the same city to study Divinity. But Faustus being of a naughty mind and otherwise addicted, applied not his studies, but took himself to other exercises: the which his uncle oftentimes hearing, rebuked him for it, as Eli ofttimes rebuked his children for sinning against the Lord: even so this good man laboured to have Faustus apply his study of Divinity, that he might come to the /65/ knowledge of God and his laws. But it is manifest that many virtuous parents have wicked children, as Cain, Ruben, Absolom, and such-like have been to their parents: so this Faustus having godly parents, and seeing him to be of a toward wit, were very desirous to bring him up in those virtuous studies, namely, of Divinity: but he gave himself secretly to study Necromancy and Conjuration, in

so much that few or none could perceive his profession.

But to the purpose: Faustus continued at study in the University, and was by the Rectors and sixteen Masters afterwards examined how he had profited in his studies; and being found by them, that none for his time were able to argue with him in Divinity, or for the excellency of his wisdom to compare with him, with one consent they made him Doctor of Divinity. But Doctor Faustus within short time after he had obtained his degree, fell into such fantasies and deep cogitations, that he was marked of many, and of the most part of the Students was called the Speculator; and sometime he would throw the Scriptures from him as though he had no care of his former profession: so that he began a very ungodly life, as hereafter more at large may appear; for the old proverb saith, Who can hold that will away? so, who can hold Faustus from the Devil, that seeks after him with all his endeavour? For he accompanied himself with divers that were seen in those Devilish Arts, and that had the Chaldean, Persian, Hebrew, Arabian, and Greek tongues, using Figures, Characters, Conjurations, Incantations, with many other ceremonies belonging to these infernal Arts, /66/ as Necromancy, Charms, Soothsaying, Witchcraft, Enchantment, being delighted with their books, words, and names so well, that he studied day and night therein: in so much that he could not abide to be called Doctor of Divinity, but waxed a worldly man, and named himself an Astrologian, and a Mathematician: and for a shadow sometimes a Physician, and did great cures, namely, with herbs, roots, waters, drinks, receipts, and clysters. And without doubt he was passing wise, and excellent perfect in the holy scriptures: but he that knoweth his master's will and doth it not, is worthy to be beaten with many stripes. It is written, no man can serve two masters: and, thou shalt not tempt the Lord thy God: but Faustus threw all this in the wind, and made his soul of no estimation, regarding more his worldly pleasure than the joys to come: therefore at the day of judgment there is no hope of his redemption.

CHAPTER II

How Doctor Faustus began to practise in his Devilish Art, and how he conjured the Devil, making him to appear and meet him on the morrow at his own house

You have heard before, that all Faustus' mind was set to study the arts of Necromancy and Conjuration, the which exercise he followed day and night: and taking to him the wings of an Eagle, thought to fly over the /67/ whole world, and to know the secrets of heaven and earth; for his Speculation was so wonderful, being expert in using his Vocabula, Figures, Characters, Conjurations, and other Ceremonial actions, that in all the haste he put in practice to bring the Devil before him. And taking his way to a thick Wood near to Wittenberg, called in the German tongue Spisser Waldt: that is in English the Spissers Wood (as Faustus would oftentimes boast of it among his crew being in his jollity), he came into the same wood towards evening into a cross way, where he made with a wand a Circle in the dust, and within that many more Circles and Characters: and thus he passed away the time, until it was nine or ten of the clock in the night, then began Doctor Faustus to call for Mephostophiles the Spirit, and to charge him in the name of Beelzebub to appear there personally without any long stay: then presently the Devil began so great a rumour in the Wood, as if heaven and earth would have come together with wind, the trees bowing their tops to the ground, then fell the Devil to blare as if the whole Wood had been full of Lions, and suddenly about the Circle ran the Devil as if a thousand Wagons had been running together on paved stones. After this at the four corners of the Wood it thundered horribly,

with such lightnings as if the whole world, to his seeming, had been on fire. Faustus all this while half amazed at the Devil's so long tarrying, and doubting whether he were best to abide any more such horrible Conjurings, thought to leave his Circle and depart; whereupon the Devil made him such music of all sorts, as if the Nymphs themselves had been in /68/ [the] place: whereat Faustus was revived and stood stoutly in his circle aspecting his purpose, and began again to conjure the Spirit Mephostophiles in the name of the Prince of Devils to appear in his likeness: whereat suddenly over his head hanged hovering in the air a mighty Dragon: then calls Faustus again after his Devilish manner, at which there was a monstrous cry in the Wood, as if Hell had been open, and all the tormented souls crying to God for mercy; presently not three fathoms above his head fell a flame in manner of a lightning, and changed itself into a Globe: yet Faustus feared it not, but did persuade himself that the Devil should give him his request before he would leave: Often-times after to his companions he would boast, that he had the stoutest head (under the cope of heaven) at commandment: whereat they answered, they knew none stouter than the Pope or Emperor: but Doctor Faustus said, the head that is my servant is above all on earth, and repeated certain words out of Saint Paul to the Ephesians to make his argument good: The Prince of this world is upon earth and under heaven. Well, let us come again to his Conjuration where we left him at his fiery Globe: Faustus vexed at the Spirit's so long tarrying, used his Charms with full purpose not to depart before he had his intent, and crying on Mephostophiles the Spirit; suddenly the Globe opened and sprang up in height of a man: so burning a time, in the end it converted to the shape of a fiery man. This pleasant beast ran about the Circle a great while, and lastly appeared in manner of a gray Friar, asking Faustus what was his request. Faustus commanded that the /69/ next morning at twelve of the clock he should appear to him at his house; but the Devil would in no wise grant. Faustus began again to conjure him in the name of Beelzebub, that he should fulfil his request: whereupon the Spirit agreed, and so they departed each one his way.

CHAPTER III

*The conference of Doctor Faustus with
the Spirit Mephostophiles the morning
following at his own house*

Doctor Faustus having commanded the Spirit
to be with him, at his hour appointed he came
and appeared in his chamber, demanding of
Faustus what his desire was: then began Doctor
Faustus anew with him to conjure him that he
should be obedient unto him, and to answer him
certain Articles, and to fulfil them in all points.

1. That the Spirit should serve him and be
obedient unto him in all things that he asked of
him from that hour until the hour of his death.

2. Farther, anything that he desired of him
he should bring it to him.

3. Also, that in all Faustus his demands or In-
terrogations, the Spirit should tell him nothing
but that which is true.

Hereupon the Spirit answered and laid his
case forth, that he had no such power of himself, until /70/ he had first given his Prince (that
was ruler over him) to understand thereof, and
to know if he could obtain so much of his Lord:
therefore speak farther that I may do thy whole
desire to my Prince: for it is not in my power
to fulfil without his leave. Shew me the cause
why (said Faustus). The Spirit answered: Faustus, thou shalt understand, that with us it is even
as well a kingdom, as with you on earth: yea,
we have our rulers and servants, as I my self am
one, and we name our whole number the Legion: for although that Lucifer is thrust and
fallen out of heaven through his pride and high
mind, yet he hath notwithstanding a Legion of
Devils at his commandment, that we call the
Oriental Princes; for his power is great and infinite. Also there is an host in Meridie, in Septentrio, in Occidente: and for that Lucifer hath
his kingdom under heaven, we must change and
give ourselves unto men to serve them at their
pleasure. It is also certain, we have never as yet
opened unto any man the truth of our dwelling,
neither of our ruling, neither what our power is,
neither have we given any man any gift, or
learned him anything, except he promise to be
ours.

Doctor Faustus upon this arose where he sat,[1]

and said, I will have my request, and yet I will
not be damned. The Spirit answered, Then shalt
thou want thy desire, and yet art thou mine
notwithstanding: if any man would detain thee
it is in vain, for thine infidelity hath confounded
thee.

Hereupon spake Faustus: Get thee hence
from me, /71/ and take Saint Valentine's farewell
and Crisam[1] with thee, yet I conjure thee that
thou be here at evening, and bethink thyself on
that I have asked thee, and ask thy Prince's
counsel therein. Mephostophiles the Spirit, thus
answered, vanished away, leaving Faustus in his
study, where he sat pondering with himself how
he might obtain his request of the Devil without
loss of his soul: yet fully he was resolved in himself, rather than to want his pleasure, to do
whatsoever the Spirit and his Lord should condition upon.

CHAPTER IV

*The second time of the Spirit's appearing
to Faustus in his house, and of their parley*

Faustus continuing in his Devilish cogitations,
never moving out of the place where the Spirit
left him (such was his fervent love to the Devil)
the night approaching, this swift flying Spirit
appeared to Faustus, offering himself with all
submission to his service, with full authority
from his Prince to do whatsoever he would request, if so be Faustus would promise to be his:
this answer I bring thee, and an answer must
thou make by me again, yet will I hear what is
thy desire, because thou hast sworn me to be
here at this time. Doctor Faustus gave him this
answer, though faintly (for his soul's sake),
That his request /72/ was none other but to become a Devil, or at the least a limb of him, and
that the Spirit should agree unto these Articles
as followeth.

1. That he might be a Spirit in shape and
quality.

2. That Mephostophiles should be his servant,
and at his commandment.

3. That Mephostophiles should bring him
anything, and do for him whatsoever.

4. That at all times he should be in his house,

Page 71: 1. A mistranslation of the German text,
"entsetzt sich darob," *i.e.* "was terrified at this."

Page 72: 1. Saint Valentine's sickness is epilepsy.
Crisam is Gk. *chrisma*, a composition of oil and balm.

invisible to all men, except only to himself, and at his commandment to shew himself.

5. Lastly, that Mephostophiles should at all times appear at his command, in what form or shape soever he would.

Upon these points the Spirit answered Doctor Faustus, that all this should be granted him and fulfilled, and more if he would agree unto him upon certain Articles as followeth.

First, that Doctor Faustus should give himself to his Lord Lucifer, body and soul.

Secondly, for confirmation of the same, he should make him a writing, written with his own blood.

Thirdly, that he would be an enemy to all Christian people.

Fourthly, that he would deny his Christian belief.

Fifthly, that he let not any man change his opinion, if so be any man should go about to dissuade, or withdraw him from it.

Further, the Spirit promised Faustus to give him certain years to live in health and pleasure, and when such years were expired, that then Faustus should be fetched away, and if he should hold these Articles /73/ and conditions, that then he should have all whatsoever his heart would wish or desire; and that Faustus should quickly perceive himself to be a Spirit in all manner of actions whatsoever. Hereupon Doctor Faustus his mind was so inflamed, that he forgot his soul, and promised Mephostophiles to hold all things as he had mentioned them: he thought the Devil was not so black as they used to paint him, nor Hell so hot as the people say, *etc.*

my name is as thou sayest, Mephostophiles, and I am a prince, but servant to Lucifer: and all the circuit from Septentrio to the Meridian, I rule under him. Even at these words was this wicked wretch Faustus inflamed, to hear himself to have gotten so great a Potentate to be his servant, forgot the Lord his maker, and Christ his redeemer, /74/ became an enemy unto all mankind, yea, worse than the Giants whom the Poets feign to climb the hills to make war with the Gods: not unlike that enemy of God and his Christ, that for his pride was cast into Hell: so likewise Faustus forgot that the high climbers catch the greatest falls, and that the sweetest meat requires the sourest sauce.

After a while, Faustus promised Mephostophiles to write and make his Obligation, with full assurance of the Articles in the Chapter before rehearsed. A pitiful case, (Christian Reader), for certainly this Letter or Obligation was found in his house after his most lamentable end, with all the rest of his damnable practices used in his whole life. Therefore I wish all Christians to take an example by this wicked Faustus, and to be comforted in Christ, contenting themselves with that vocation whereunto it hath pleased God to call them, and not to esteem the vain delights of this life, as did this unhappy Faustus, in giving his Soul to the Devil: and to confirm it the more assuredly, he took a small penknife, and pricked a vein in his left hand, and for certainty thereupon, were seen on his hand these words written, as if they had been written with blood, ô HOMO FUGE: whereat the Spirit vanished, but Faustus continued in his damnable mind, and made his writing as followeth. /75/

CHAPTER V

The third parley between Doctor Faustus and Mephostophiles about a conclusion

After Doctor Faustus had made his promise to the Devil, in the morning betimes he called the Spirit before him and commanded him that he should always come to him like a Friar, after the order of Saint Francis, with a bell in his hand like Saint Anthony, and to ring it once or twice before he appeared, that he might know of his certain coming: Then Faustus demanded the Spirit, what was his name? The Spirit answered,

CHAPTER VI

How Doctor Faustus set his blood in a saucer on warm ashes, and writ as followeth

I, Johannes Faustus, Doctor, do openly acknowledge with mine own hand, to the greater force and strengthening of this Letter, that sith-thence I began to study and speculate the course and order of the Elements, I have not found through the gift that is given me from above, any such learning and wisdom, that can bring me to my desires: and for that I find, that men are unable to instruct me any farther in the matter, now have I Doctor John Faustus, unto the hellish prince of Orient and his messenger Mephostophiles, given both body and soul, upon such condition, that they shall learn me, and fulfil my desire in all things, as they have promised and vowed unto me, with due obedience unto me, according unto the Articles mentioned between us.

Further, I covenant and grant with them by these presents, that at the end of twenty-four years next ensuing the date of this present Letter, they being expired, and I in the meantime, during the said years be served of them at my will, they accomplishing my desires to the full in all points as we are agreed, that then I give them full power to do with me at their pleasure, to rule, to send, fetch, or carry me or mine, be it either body, soul, flesh, blood, or goods, into their habitation, be it wheresoever: and hereupon, I defy God and his Christ, all the host of heaven, and /76/ all living creatures that bear the shape of God, yea all that lives; and again I say it, and it shall be so. And to the more strengthening of this writing, I have written it with mine own hand and blood, being in perfect memory, and hereupon I subscribe to it with my name and title, calling all the infernal, middle, and supreme powers to witness of this my Letter and subscription.

John Faustus, approved in the Elements, and the spiritual Doctor.

CHAPTER VII

How Mephostophiles came for his writing, and in what manner he appeared, and his sights he shewed him: and how he caused him to keep a copy of his own writing

Doctor Faustus sitting pensive, having but one only boy with him, suddenly there appeared his Spirit Mephostophiles, in likeness of a fiery man, from whom issued most horrible fiery flames, in so much that the boy was afraid, but being hardened by his master, he bade him stand still and he should have no harm: the Spirit began to blare as in a singing manner. This pretty sport pleased Doctor Faustus well, but he would not call his Spirit into his Counting house, until he had seen more: anon was heard a rushing of armed men, and trampling of horses: this ceas-

ing, came a kennel of hounds, and they chased a great /77/ Hart in the hall, and there the Hart was slain. Faustus took heart, came forth, and looked upon the Hart, but presently before him there was a Lion and a Dragon together fighting, so fiercely, that Faustus thought they would have brought down the house, but the Dragon overcame the Lion, and so they vanished.

After this, came in a Peacock, with a Peahen, the cock brustling of his tail, and turning to the female, beat her, and so vanished. Afterward followed a furious Bull, that with a full fierceness ran upon Faustus, but coming near him, vanished away. Afterward followed a great old Ape, this Ape offered Faustus the hand, but he refused: so the Ape ran out of the hall again. Hereupon fell a mist in the hall, that Faustus saw no light, but it lasted not, and so soon as it was gone, there lay before Faustus two great sacks, one full of gold, the other full of silver.

Lastly, was heard by Faustus all manner Instruments of music, as Organs, Clarigolds,[1] Lutes, Viols, Citterns,[2] Waits,[3] Hornpipes, Flutes, Anomes,[4] Harps, and all manner of other Instruments, the which so ravished his mind, that he thought he had been in another world, forgot both body and soul, in so much that he was minded never to change his opinion concerning that which he had done. Hereat, came Mephostophiles into the Hall to Faustus, in apparel like unto a Friar, to whom Faustus spake, thou hast done me a wonderful pleasure in shewing me this pastime, /78/ if thou continue as thou hast begun, thou shalt win me heart and soul, yea and have it. Mephostophiles answered, this is nothing, I will please thee better: yet that thou mayest know my power and all, ask what thou wilt request of me, that shalt thou have, conditionally hold thy promise, and give me thy handwriting: at which words, the wretch thrust forth his hand, saying, hold thee, there hast thou my promise: Mephostophiles took the writing, and willing Faustus to take a copy of it, with that the perverse Faustus being resolute in his damnation, wrote a copy thereof, and gave the Devil the one, and kept in store the other. Thus

Page 78: 1. A stringed musical instrument, or clavichord.
2. A kind of guitar.
3. A wind instrument.
4. This instrument is unknown.

the Spirit and Faustus were agreed, and dwelt together: no doubt there was a virtuous house-keeping.

CHAPTER VIII

The manner how Faustus proceeded with his damnable life, and of the diligent service Mephostophiles used towards him

Doctor Faustus having given his soul to the Devil, renouncing all the powers of heaven, confirming this lamentable action with his own blood, and having already delivered his writing now into the Devil's hand, the which so puffed up his heart, that he had forgot the mind of a man, and thought rather himself to be a spirit. This Faustus dwelt in his uncle's house at Wittenberg, who died, and bequeathed it in his Testament to his Cousin Faustus. Faustus kept a /79/ boy with him that was his scholar, an unhappy wag, called Christopher Wagner, to whom this sport and life that he saw his master follow seemed pleasant. Faustus loved the boy well, hoping to make him as good or better seen in his Devilish exercise than himself; and he was fellow with Mephostophiles: otherwise Faustus had no more company in his house; but himself, his boy and his Spirit, that ever was diligent at Faustus' command, going about the house, clothed like a Friar, with a little bell in his hand, seen of none but Faustus. For his victual and other necessaries, Mephostophiles brought him at his pleasure from the Duke of Saxon, the Duke of Bavaria, and the Bishop of Saltzburg: for they had many times their best wine stolen out of their cellars by Mephostophiles. Likewise their provision for their own table, such meat as Faustus wished for, his Spirit brought him in: besides that, Faustus himself was become so cunning, that when he opened his window, what fowl soever he wished for, it came presently flying into his house, were it never so dainty. Moreover, Faustus and his boy went in sumptuous apparel, the which Mephostophiles stole from the Mercers at Norenberg, Auspurg, Franckeford, and Liptzig: for it was hard for them to find a lock to keep out such a thief. All their maintenance was but stolen and borrowed ware: and thus they lived an odious life in the sight of God, though as yet the world were unacquainted

with their wickedness. It must be so, for their fruits be none other: as Christ saith through John, where he calls the Devil a thief, and a murderer: and that found Faustus, for he stole him away both body and soul. /80/

CHAPTER IX

How Doctor Faustus would have married, and how the Devil had almost killed him for it

Doctor Faustus continued thus in his Epicurish life day and night, and believed not that there was a God, hell, or Devil: he thought that body and soul died together, and had quite forgotten Divinity or the immortality of his soul, but stood in his damnable heresy day and night. And bethinking himself of a wife, called Mephostophiles to counsel; which would in no wise agree: demanding of him if he would break the covenant made with him, or if he had forgot it. Hast not thou (quoth Mephostophiles) sworn thyself an enemy to God and all creatures? To this I answer thee, thou canst not marry; thou canst not serve two masters, God, and my Prince: for wedlock is a chief institution ordained of God, and that hast thou promised to defy, as we do all, and that hast thou also done: and moreover thou hast confirmed it with thy blood: persuade thyself, that what thou dost in contempt of wedlock, it is all to thine own delight. Therefore Faustus, look well about thee, and bethink thyself better, and I wish thee to change thy mind: for if thou keep not what thou hast promised in thy writing, we will tear thee in pieces like the dust under thy feet. Therefore sweet Faustus, think with what unquiet life, anger, strife, and debate thou shalt live in when thou takest a wife: therefore change thy mind. /81/

Doctor Faustus was with these speeches in despair: and as all that have forsaken the Lord, can build upon no good foundation: so this wretched Faustus having forsook the rock, fell in despair with himself, fearing if he should motion Matrimony any more, that the Devil would tear him in pieces. For this time (quoth he to Mephostophiles) I am not minded to marry. Then you do well, answered his Spirit. But shortly and that within two hours after, Faustus called his Spirit, which came in his old manner like a Friar. Then Faustus said unto him, I am not able to resist nor bridle my fantasy, I must and will have a wife, and I pray thee give thy consent to it. Suddenly upon these words came such a whirlwind about the place, that Faustus thought the whole house would come down, all the doors in the house flew off the hooks: after all this, his house was full of smoke, and the floor covered over with ashes: which when Doctor Faustus perceived, he would have gone up the stairs: and flying up, he was taken and thrown into the hall, that he was not able to stir hand nor foot: then round about him ran a monstrous circle of fire, never standing still, that Faustus fried as he lay, and thought there to have been burned. Then cried he out to his Spirit Mephostophiles for help, promising him he would live in all things as he had vowed in his handwriting. Hereupon appeared unto him an ugly Devil, so fearful and monstrous to behold, that Faustus durst not look on him. The Devil said, what wouldst thou have Faustus? how likest thou thy wedding? what mind art thou in now? Faustus answered, he had forgot his promise, desiring him of /82/ pardon, and he would talk no more of such things. The Devil answered, thou were best so to do, and so vanished.

After appeared unto him his Friar Mephostophiles with a bell in his hand, and spake to Faustus: It is no jesting with us, hold thou that which thou hast vowed, and we will perform as we have promised: and more than that, thou shalt have thy heart's desire of what women soever thou wilt, be she alive or dead, and so long as thou wilt, thou shalt keep her by thee.

These words pleased Faustus wonderful well, and repented himself that he was so foolish to wish himself married, that might have any woman in the whole City brought to him at his command; the which he practised and persevered in a long time.

CHAPTER X

Questions put forth by Doctor Faustus unto his Spirit Mephostophiles

Doctor Faustus living in all manner of pleasure that his heart could desire, continuing in his amorous drifts, his delicate fare, and costly apparel, called on a time his Mephostophiles to him: which being come, brought with him a book in his hand of all manner of Devilish and enchanted arts, the which he gave Faustus, saying: hold my Faustus, work now thy heart's desire: The copy of this enchanting book /84/ was afterward found by his servant Christopher Wagner. Well (quoth Faustus to his Spirit) I have called thee to know what thou canst do if I have need of thy help. Then answered Mephostophiles and said, my Lord Faustus, I am a flying spirit: yea, so swift as thought can think, to do whatsoever. Here Faustus said: but how came thy Lord and master Lucifer to have so great a fall from heaven? Mephostophiles answered: My Lord Lucifer was a fair Angel, created of God as immortal, and being placed in the Seraphims, which are above the Cherubims, he would have presumed unto the Throne of God, with intent to have thrust God out of his seat. Upon this presumption the Lord cast him down headlong, and where before he was an Angel of light, now dwells he in darkness, not able to come near his first place, without God send for him to appear before him as Raphael: but unto the lower degree of Angels that have their conversation with men he was come, but not unto the second degree of Heavens that is kept by the Archangels, namely, Michael and Gabriel, for these are called Angels of God's wonders: yet are these far inferior places to that from whence my Lord and Master Lucifer fell. And thus far Faustus, because thou art one of the beloved children of my Lord Lucifer, following and feeding thy mind in manner as he did his, I have shortly resolved thy request, and more I will do for thee at thy pleasure. I thank thee Mephostophiles (quoth Faustus) come let us now go rest, for it is night: upon this they left their communication. /85/

CHAPTER XI

How Doctor Faustus dreamed that he had seen hell in his sleep, and how he questioned with his Spirit of matters as concerning hell, with the Spirit's answer

The night following, after Faustus his communication had with Mephostophiles, as concerning the fall of Lucifer, Doctor Faustus dreamed that he had seen a part of hell: but in what manner it was, or in what place he knew not: whereupon he was greatly troubled in mind, and called unto him Mephostophiles his Spirit, saying to him, my Mephostophiles, I pray thee resolve me in this doubt: what is hell, what substance is it of, in what place stands it, and when was it made? Mephostophiles answered: my Faustus, thou shalt know, that before the fall of my Lord Lucifer there was no hell, but even then was hell ordained: it is of no substance, but a confused thing: for I tell thee, that before all Elements were made, and the earth seen, the Spirit of God moved on the waters, and darkness was over all: but when God said, let it be light, it was so at his word, and the light was on God's right hand, and God praised the light. Judge thou further: God stood in the middle, the darkness was on his left hand, in the which my Lord was bound in chains until the day of judgment: in this confused hell is nought to find but a filthy, Sulphurish, fiery, stinking mist or fog. Further, we Devils know not what substance it is of, but a confused thing. For as a /86/ bubble of water flieth before the wind, so doth hell before the breath of God. Further, we Devils know not how God hath laid the foundation of our hell, nor whereof it is: but to be short with thee Faustus, we know that hell hath neither bottom nor end.

CHAPTER XII

The second question put forth by Doctor Faustus to his Spirit, what Kingdoms there were in hell, how many, and what were their rulers' names

Faustus spake again to Mephostophiles, saying: thou speakest of wonderful things, I pray thee now tell me what Kingdoms is there in your hell, how many are there, what are they called, and who rules them: the Spirit answered him: my Faustus, know that hell is as thou wouldst think with thyself another world, in the which we have our being, under the earth, and above the earth, even to the Heavens; within the circumference whereof are contained ten Kingdoms, namely:

1. Lacus mortis.   3. Terra tenebrosa.
2. Stagnum ignis.   4. Tartarus.

5. Terra oblivionis.   8. Barathrum.
6. Gehenna.   9. Styx.
7. Herebus.   10. Acheron.

The which Kingdoms are governed by five kings, that is, Lucifer in the Orient, Beelzebub in Septentrio, /87/ Belial in Meridie, Astaroth in Occidente, and Phlegeton in the middest of them all: whose rule and dominions have none end until the day of Doom. And thus far Faustus, hast thou heard of our rule and Kingdoms.

CHAPTER XIII

Another question put forth by Doctor Faustus to his Spirit concerning his Lord Lucifer, with the sorrow that Faustus fell afterwards into

Doctor Faustus began again to reason with Mephostophiles, requiring him to tell him in what form and shape, and in what estimation his Lord Lucifer was when he was in favour with God. Whereupon his Spirit required of him three days' respite, which Faustus granted. The three days being expired, Mephostophiles gave him this answer: Faustus, my Lord Lucifer (so called now, for that he was banished out of the clear light of heaven) was at the first an Angel of God, he sat on the Cherubims, and saw all the wonderful works of God, yea he was so of God ordained, for shape, pomp, authority, worthiness, and dwelling, that he far exceeded all other the creatures of God, yea our gold and precious stones: and so illuminated, that he far surpassed the brightness of the Sun and all other Stars: wherefore God placed him on the Cherubims, where he had a kingly office, and was always before God's seat, to the end he might be the more perfect in all his beings: but when he /88/ began to be high-minded, proud, and so presumptuous that he would usurp the seat of his Majesty, then was he banished out from amongst the heavenly powers, separated from their abiding into the manner of a fiery stone, that no water is able to quench, but continually burneth until the end of the world.

Doctor Faustus, when he had heard the words of his Spirit, began to consider with himself, having diverse and sundry opinions in his head: and very pensively (saying nothing unto his

Spirit) he went into his chamber, and laid him on his bed, recording the words of Mephostophiles; which so pierced his heart, that he fell into sighing and great lamentation, crying out: alas, ah, woe is me! what have I done? Even so shall it come to pass with me: am not I also a creature of God's making, bearing his own Image and similitude, into whom he hath breathed the Spirit of life and immortality, unto whom he hath made all things living subject: but woe is me, mine haughty mind, proud aspiring stomach, and filthy flesh, hath brought my soul into perpetual damnation; yea, pride hath abused my understanding, in so much that I have forgot my maker, the Spirit of God is departed from me. I have promised the Devil my Soul: and therefore it is but a folly for me to hope for grace, but it must be even with me as with Lucifer, thrown into perpetual burning fire: ah, woe is me that ever I was born. In this perplexity lay this miserable Doctor Faustus, having quite forgot his faith in Christ, never falling to repentance truly, thereby to attain the grace and holy Spirit of God again, the which would have been able to have resisted the /89/ strong assaults of Satan: for although he had made him a promise, yet he might have remembered through true repentance sinners come again into the favour of God; which faith the faithful firmly hold, knowing they that kill the body, are not able to hurt the soul: but he was in all his opinions doubtful, without faith or hope, and so he continued.

CHAPTER XIV

Another disputation betwixt Doctor Faustus and his Spirit, of the power of the Devil, and of his envy to mankind

After Doctor Faustus had a while pondered and sorrowed with himself of his wretched estate, he called again Mephostophiles unto him, commanding him to tell him the judgment, rule, power, attempts, tyranny and temptation of the Devil, and why he was moved to such kind of living: whereupon the Spirit answered, this question that thou demandest of me, will turn thee to no small discontentment: therefore thou shouldst not have desired me of such matters, for it toucheth the secrets of our Kingdom, although I cannot deny to resolve thy request. Therefore know thou Faustus, that so soon as my Lord Lucifer fell from heaven, he became a mortal enemy both to God and man, and hath used (as now he doth) all manner of tyranny to the destruction of man, as is manifest by divers examples, one falling suddenly dead, another /90/ hangs himself, another drowns himself, others stab themselves, others unfaithfully despair, and so come to utter confusion: the first man Adam that was made perfect to the similitude of God, was by my Lord his policy, the whole decay of man: yea, Faustus, in him was the beginning and first tyranny of my Lord Lucifer used to man: the like did he with Cain, the same with the children of Israel, when they worshipped strange Gods, and fell to whoredom with strange women: the like with Saul: so did he by the seven husbands of her that after was the wife of Tobias: likewise Dagon our fellow brought to destruction thirty thousand men, whereupon the Ark of God was stolen: and Belial made David to number his men, whereupon were slain sixty thousand, also he deceived King Solomon that worshipped the Gods of the heathen: and there are such Spirits innumerable that can come by men and tempt them, drive them to sin, weaken their belief: for we rule the hearts of Kings and Princes, stirring them up to war and bloodshed; and to this intent do we spread ourselves throughout all the world, as the utter enemies of God, and his Son Christ, yea and all those that worship them: and that thou knowest by thyself Faustus, how we have dealt with thee. To this answered Faustus, why then thou didst also beguile me. Yea (quoth Mephostophiles) why should not we help thee forwards: for so soon as we saw thy heart, how thou didst despise thy degree taken in Divinity, and didst study to search and know the secrets of our Kingdom; even then did we enter into thee, giving thee divers foul and filthy cogitations, pricking thee forward in /91/ thine intent, and persuading thee that thou couldst never attain to thy desire, until thou hast the help of some Devil: and when thou wast delighted with this, then took we root in thee; and so firmly, that thou gavest thyself unto us, both body and soul the which thou (Faustus) canst not deny. Hereat answered Faustus, Thou sayest true Mephostophiles, I cannot deny it: Ah, woe is me miserable Faustus; how have I been deceived? had not I desired to know so much, I had not been in this case: for having studied the lives of the holy Saints and Prophets, and thereby thought myself to understand sufficient in heavenly matters, I thought myself not worthy to be called Doctor Faustus, if I should not also know the secrets of hell, and be associated with the furious Fiend thereof; now therefore must I be rewarded accordingly. Which speeches being uttered, Faustus went very sorrowfully away from Mephostophiles.

CHAPTER XV

How Doctor Faustus desired again of his Spirit to know the secrets and pains of hell; and whether those damned Devils and their company might ever come into the favour of God again or not

Doctor Faustus was ever pondering with himself how he might get loose from so damnable an end as he had given himself unto, both of body and soul: but his repentance was like to that of Cain and Judas, /92/ he thought his sins greater than God could forgive, hereupon rested his mind: he looked up to heaven, but saw nothing therein; for his heart was so possessed with the Devil, that he could think of nought else but of hell, and the pains thereof. Wherefore in all the haste he calleth unto him his Spirit Mephostophiles, desiring him to tell him some more of the secrets of hell, what pains the damned were in, and how they were tormented, and whether the damned souls might get again the favour of God, and so be released out of their torments or not: whereupon the Spirit answered, my Faustus, thou mayest well leave to question any more of such matters, for they will but disquiet thy mind, I pray thee what meanest thou? Thinkest thou through these thy fantasies to escape us? No, for if thou shouldst climb up to heaven, there to hide thyself, yet would I thrust thee down again; for thou art mine, and thou belongest unto our society: therefore sweet Faustus, thou wilt repent this thy foolish demand, except thou be content that I shall tell thee nothing. Quoth Faustus ragingly, I will know, or I will not live, wherefore dispatch and tell me: to whom Mephostophiles answered,

Faustus, it is no trouble unto me at all to tell thee, and therefore sith thou forcest me thereto, I will tell thee things to the terror of thy soul, if thou wilt abide the hearing. Thou wilt have me tell thee of the secrets of hell, and of the pains thereof: know Faustus, that hell hath many figures, semblances, and names, but it cannot be named nor figured in such sort unto the living that are damned, as it is unto those that are dead, and do both see and feel the torments thereof: for hell is /93/ said to be deadly, out of the which came never any to life again but one, but he is as nothing for thee to reckon upon, hell is bloodthirsty, and is never satisfied; hell is a valley, into the which the damned souls fall: for so soon as the soul is out of man's body, it would gladly go to the place from whence it came, and climbeth up above the highest hills, even to the heavens; where being by the Angels of the first Mobile denied entertainment (in consideration of their evil life spent on the earth) they fall into the deepest pit or valley which hath no bottom, into a perpetual fire, which shall never be quenched: for like as the Flint thrown into the water, loseth not his virtue, neither is his fire extinguished; even so the hellish fire is unquenchable: and even as the Flint stone in the fire being burned is red hot, and yet consumeth not: so likewise the damned souls in our hellish fire are ever burning, but their pains never diminishing. Therefore is hell called the everlasting pain, in which is neither hope nor mercy: So is it called utter darkness, in which we see neither the light of Sun, Moon, nor Star: and were our darkness like the darkness of the night, yet were there hope of mercy, but ours is perpetual darkness, clean exempt from the face of God. Hell hath also a place within it called Chasma, out of the which issueth all manner of thunders, lightnings, with such horrible shriekings and wailings, that oft-times the very Devils themselves stand in fear thereof: for one while it sendeth forth winds with exceeding snow, hail, and rain congealing the water into ice; with the which the damned are frozen, gnash their teeth, howl and cry, and yet cannot die. Otherwhiles, it /94/ sendeth forth most horrible hot mists or fogs, with flashing flames of fire and brimstone, wherein the sorrowful souls of the damned lie broiling in their reiterated torments: yea Faustus, hell is called a prison wherein the damned lie continually bound; it is also called Pernicies, and Exitium, death, destruction, hurtfulness, mischief, a mischance, a pitiful and an evil thing, world without end. We have also with us in hell a ladder, reaching of an exceeding height, as though it would touch the heavens, on which the damned ascend to seek the blessing of God; but through their infidelity, when they are at the very highest degree, they fall down again into their former miseries, complaining of the heat of that unquenchable fire: yea sweet Faustus, so must thou understand of hell, the while thou art so desirous to know the secrets of our Kingdom. And mark Faustus, hell is the nurse of death, the heat of all fire, the shadow of heaven and earth, the oblivion of all goodness, the pains unspeakable, the griefs unremovable, the dwelling of Devils, Dragons, Serpents, Adders, Toads, Crocodiles, and all manner of venomous creatures, the puddle of sin, the stinking fog ascending from the Stygian lake, Brimstone, Pitch, and all manner of unclean metals, the perpetual and unquenchable fire, the end of whose miseries was never purposed by God: yea, yea Faustus, thou sayest, I shall, I must, nay I will tell thee the secrets of our Kingdom, for thou buyest it dearly, and thou must and shalt be partaker of our torments, that (as the Lord God said) never shall cease: for hell, the woman's belly, and the earth are never satisfied; there shalt thou abide horrible /95/ torments, trembling, gnashing of teeth, howling, crying, burning, freezing, melting, swimming in a labyrinth of miseries, scalding, burning, smoking in thine eyes, stinking in thy nose, hoarseness of thy speech, deafness of thine ears, trembling of thy hands, biting thine own tongue with pain, thy heart crushed as in a press, thy bones broken, the Devils tossing firebrands upon thee, yea thy whole carcass tossed upon muckforks from one Devil to another, yea Faustus, then wilt thou wish for death, and he will fly from thee, thine unspeakable torments shall be every day augmented more and more, for the greater the sin, the greater is the punishment: how likest thou this, my Faustus, a resolution answerable to thy request?

Lastly, thou wilt have me tell thee that which belongeth only to God, which is, if it be possible for the damned to come again into the favour of God, or not: why Faustus, thou knowest that this is against thy promise, for what shouldst thou desire to know that, having already given thy soul to the Devil to have the pleasure of this world, and to know the secrets of hell? therefore art thou damned, and how canst thou then come again to the favour of God? Wherefore I directly answer, no; for whomsoever God hath forsaken and thrown into hell, must there abide his wrath and indignation in that unquenchable fire, where is no hope nor mercy to be looked for, but abiding in perpetual pains world without end: for even as much it availeth thee Faustus, to hope for the favour of God again, as Lucifer himself, who indeed although he and we all have a hope, yet is it to small avail, and taketh none effect, for out of that /96/ place God will neither hear crying nor sighing; if he do, thou shalt have as little remorse, as Dives, Cain, or Judas had: what helpeth the Emperor, King, Prince, Duke, Earl, Baron, Lord, Knight, Squire or Gentleman, to cry for mercy being there? Nothing: for if on the earth they would not be Tyrants, and self-willed, rich with covetousness; proud with pomp, gluttons, drunkards, whoremongers, backbiters, robbers, murderers, blasphemers, and such-like, then were there some hope to be looked for: therefore my Faustus, as thou comest to hell with these qualities, thou must say with Cain, My sins are greater than can be forgiven, go hang thyself with Judas: and lastly, be content to suffer torments with Dives. Therefore know Faustus, that the damned have neither end nor time appointed in the which they may hope to be released, for if there were any such hope, that they but by throwing one drop of water out of the Sea in a day, until it were all dry: or if there were an heap of sand as high as from the earth to the heavens, that a bird carrying away but one corn in a day, at the end of this so long labour; that yet they might hope at the last, God would have mercy on them, they would be comforted: but now there is no hope that God once thinks upon them, or that their howlings shall never be heard; yea, so impossible, as it is for thee to hide thyself from God, or impossible for thee to remove the mountains, or to empty the sea, or to tell the number of the drops of rain that have fallen from Heaven until this day, or to tell what there is most of in the world, yea and for a Camel to go through the eye of a needle: even so impossible it is for thee Faustus, /97/ and the rest of the damned, to come again into the favour of God. And thus Faustus hast thou heard my last sentence, and I pray thee how dost thou like it? But know this, that I counsel thee to let me be unmolested hereafter with such disputations, or else I will vex thee every limb, to thy small contentment. Doctor Faustus departed from his Spirit very pensive and sorrowful, laid him on his bed, altogether doubtful of the grace and favour of God, wherefore he fell into fantastical cogitations: fain he would have had his soul at liberty again, but the Devil had so blinded him, and taken such deep root in his heart, that he could never think to crave God's mercy, or if by chance he had any good motion, straightways the Devil would thrust him a fair Lady into his chamber, which fell to kissing and dalliance with him, through which means, he threw his godly motions in the wind, going forward still in his wicked practices, to the utter ruin both of his body and soul.

CHAPTER XVI

Another question put forth by Doctor Faustus to his Spirit Mephostophiles of his own estate

Doctor Faustus, being yet desirous to hear more strange things, called his Spirit unto him, saying: My Mephostophiles, I have yet another suit unto thee, which I pray thee deny not to resolve me of. Faustus (quoth the Spirit) I am loth to reason with /98/ thee any further, for thou art never satisfied in thy mind, but always bringest me a new. Yet I pray thee this once (quoth Faustus) do me so much favour, as to tell me the truth in this matter, and hereafter I will be no more so earnest with thee. The Spirit was altogether against it, but yet once more he would abide him: well (said the Spirit to Faustus), what demandest thou of me? Faustus said, I would gladly know of thee, if thou wert a man in manner and form as I am; what wouldest thou do to please both God and man? Whereat the Spirit smiled saying: my Faustus, if I were a man as thou art, and that God had adorned me with those gifts of nature as thou once haddest; even so long as the breath of God were by,

and within me, would I humble myself unto his Majesty, endeavouring in all that I could to keep his Commandments, praise him, glorify him, that I might continue in his favour, so were I sure to enjoy the eternal joy and felicity of his Kingdom. Faustus said, but that have not I done. No, thou sayest true (quoth Mephostophiles) thou hast not done it, but thou hast denied thy Lord and maker, which gave thee the breath of life, speech, hearing, sight, and all other thy reasonable senses that thou mightest understand his will and pleasure, to live to the glory and honour of his name, and to the advancement of thy body and soul, him I say being thy maker hast thou denied and defied, yea wickedly thou hast applied that excellent gift of thine understanding, and given thy soul to the Devil: therefore give none the blame but thine own self-will, thy proud and aspiring mind, which hath brought thee into the wrath of God and utter damna- /99/ tion. This is most true (quoth Faustus), but tell me Mephostophiles, wouldst thou be in my case as I am now? Yea, saith the Spirit (and with that fetched a great sigh) for yet would I so humble myself, that I would win the favour of God. Then (said Doctor Faustus) it were time enough for me if I amended. True (said Mephostophiles), if it were not for thy great sins, which are so odious and detestable in the sight of God, that it is too late for thee, for the wrath of God resteth upon thee. Leave off (quoth Faustus) and tell me my question to my greater comfort. /100/

CHAPTER XIX

How Doctor Faustus fell into despair with himself: for having put forth a question unto his Spirit, they fell at variance, whereupon the whole route of Devils appeared unto him, threatening him sharply

Doctor Faustus revolving with himself the speeches of his Spirit, he became so woeful and sorrowful in /104/ his cogitations, that he thought himself already frying in the hottest flames of hell, and lying in his muse, suddenly there appeared unto him his Spirit, demanding what thing so grieved and troubled his conscience, whereat Doctor Faustus gave no answer: yet the Spirit very earnestly lay upon him to know the cause; and if it were possible, he would find remedy for his grief, and ease him of his sorrows. To whom Faustus answered, I have taken thee unto me as a servant to do me service, and thy service will be very dear unto me; yet I cannot have any diligence of thee farther than thou list thyself, neither dost thou in anything as it becometh thee. The Spirit replied, my Faustus, thou knowest that I was never against thy commandments as yet, but ready to serve and resolve thy questions, although I am not bound unto thee in such respects as concern the hurt of our Kingdom, yet was I always willing to answer thee, and so I am still: therefore my Faustus say on boldly, what is thy will and pleasure? At which words, the Spirit stole away the heart of Faustus, who spake in this sort, Mephostophiles, tell me how and after what sort God made the world, and all the creatures in them, and why man was made after the Image of God?

The Spirit hearing this, answered, Faustus thou knowest that all this is in vain for thee to ask, I know that thou art sorry for that thou hast done, but it availeth thee not, for I will tear thee in thousands of pieces, if thou change not thine opinions, and hereat he vanished away. Whereat Faustus all sorrowful for that he had put forth such a question, fell to weeping and to howling bitterly, not for his sins towards /105/ God, but for that the Devil was departed from him so suddenly, and in such a rage. And being in this perplexity, he was suddenly taken in such an extreme cold, as if he should have frozen in the place where he sat, in which, the greatest Devil in hell appeared unto him, with certain of his hideous and infernal company in the most ugliest shapes that it was possible to think upon, and traversing the chamber round about where Faustus sat, Faustus thought to himself, now are they come for me though my time be not come, and that because I have asked such questions of my servant Mephostophiles: at whose cogitations, the chiefest Devil which was his Lord, unto whom he gave his soul, that was Lucifer, spake in this sort: Faustus, I have seen thy thoughts, which are not as thou hast vowed unto me, by virtue of this letter, and shewed him the Obligation that he had written with his own blood, wherefore I am come to visit thee and to shew thee some of our hellish pastimes, in hope that

will draw and confirm thy mind a little more stedfast unto us. Content quoth Faustus, go to, let me see what pastime you can make. At which words, the great Devil in his likeness sat him down by Faustus, commanding the rest of the Devils to appear in their form, as if they were in hell: first entered Belial in form of a Bear, with curled black hair to the ground, his ears standing upright: within the ear was as red as blood, out of which issued flames of fire, his teeth were a foot at least long, as white as snow, with a tail three ells long (at the least) having two wings, one behind each arm, and thus one after another they appeared to Faustus in form as they were in hell. Lucifer himself /106/ sat in manner of a man, all hairy, but of a brown colour like a Squirrel, curled, and his tail turning upwards on his back as the Squirrels use, I think he could crack nuts too like a Squirrel. After him came Beelzebub in curled hair of horse-flesh colour, his head like the head of a Bull, with a mighty pair of horns, and two long ears down to the ground, and two wings on his back, with pricking stings like thorns: out of his wings issued flames of fire, his tail was like a Cow. Then came Astaroth in form of a worm, going upright on his tail; he had no feet, but a tail like a slow-worm: under his chaps grew two short hands, and his back was coal black, his belly thick in the middle, and yellow like gold, having many bristles on his back like a Hedgehog. After him came Chamagosta, being white and gray mixed, exceeding curled and hairy: he had a head like the head of an Ass, the tail like a Cat, and Claws like an Ox, lacking nothing of an ell broad. Then came Anobis; this Devil had a head like a Dog, white and black hair in shape of a Hog, saving that he had but two feet, one under his throat, the other at his tail: he was four ells long, with hanging ears like a Bloodhound. After him came Dythycan, he was a short thief in form of a Pheasant, with shining feathers, and four feet: his neck was green, his body red, and his feet black. The last was called Brachus, with four short feet like an Hedgehog, yellow and green: the upper side of his body was brown, and the belly like blue flames of fire; the tail red, like the tail of a Monkey. The rest of the Devils were in form of insensible beasts, as Swine, Harts, Bears, Wolves, Apes, Buffs, Goats, Antelopes, Elephants, Dragons, /*107*/ Horses, Asses, Lions, Cats, Snakes, Toads, and all manner of ugly odious Serpents and Worms: yet came in such sort, that every one at his entry into the Hall, made their reverence unto Lucifer, and so took their places, standing in order as they came, until they had filled the whole Hall: wherewith suddenly fell a most horrible thunder-clap, that the house shook as though it would have fallen to the ground, upon which every monster had a muckfork in his hand, holding them towards Faustus as though they would have run a tilt at him: which when Faustus perceived, he thought upon the words of Mephostophiles, when he told him how the souls in hell were tormented, being cast from Devil to Devil upon muck-forks, he thought verily to have been tormented there of them in like sort. But Lucifer perceiving his thought, spake to him, my Faustus, how likest thou this crew of mine? Quoth Faustus, why came you not in another manner of shape? Lucifer replied, we cannot change our hellish form, we have shewed ourselves here, as we are there; yet can we blind men's eyes in such sort, that when we will we repair unto them, as if we were men or Angels of light, although our dwelling be in darkness. Then said Faustus, I like not so many of you together, whereupon Lucifer commanded them to depart, except seven of the principal, forthwith they presently vanished, which Faustus perceiving, he was somewhat better comforted, and spake to Lucifer, where is my servant Mephostophiles, let me see if he can do the like, whereupon came a fierce Dragon, flying and spitting fire round about the house, and coming towards Lucifer, made reverence, and /*108*/ then changed himself to the form of a Friar, saying, Faustus, what wilt thou? Saith Faustus, I will that thou teach me to transform myself in like sort as thou and the rest have done: then Lucifer put forth his Paw, and gave Faustus a book, saying hold, do what thou wilt, which he looking upon, straightways changed himself into a Hog, then into a Worm, then into a Dragon, and finding this for his purpose, it liked him well. Quoth he to Lucifer, and how cometh it that all these filthy forms are in the world? Lucifer answered, they are ordained of God as plagues unto men, and so shalt thou be plagued (quoth he) whereupon, came Scorpions, Wasps, Emmets, Bees, and Gnats, which fell to stinging and biting him, and all the whole house was filled with a most horrible stinking fog, in so much, that Faustus saw nothing, but still was tormented; wherefore he cried for help saying, Mephostophiles my faithful servant, where art thou, help, help, I pray thee: hereat his Spirit answered nothing, but Lucifer himself said, ho ho ho Faustus, how likest thou the creation of the world, and incontinent it was clear again, and the Devils and all the filthy Cattle were vanished, only Faustus was left alone; seeing nothing, but hearing the sweetest music that ever he heard before, at which he was so ravished with delight, that he forgot the fears he was in before: and it repented him that he had seen no more of their pastime. /*109*/

CHAPTER XX

How Doctor Faustus desired to see hell, and of the manner how he was used therein

Doctor Faustus bethinking how his time went away, and how he had spent eight years thereof, he meant to spend the rest to his better contentment, intending quite to forget any such motions as might offend the Devil any more: wherefore on a time he called his Spirit Mephostophiles, and said unto him, bring thou hither unto me thy Lord Lucifer, or Belial: he brought him (notwithstanding) one that was called Beelzebub, the which asked Faustus his pleasure. Quoth Faustus, I would know of thee if I may see hell and take a view thereof? That thou shalt (said the Devil) and at midnight I will fetch thee. Well, night being come, Doctor Faustus awaited very diligently for the coming of the Devil to fetch him, and thinking that he tarried all too long, he went to the window, where he pulled open a casement, and looking into the Element, he saw a cloud in the North more black, dark, and obscure, than all the rest of the Sky, from whence the wind blew most horrible right into Faustus his chamber, filled the whole house with smoke, that Faustus was almost smothered: hereat fell an exceeding thunder-clap, and withal came a great rugged black Bear, all curled, and upon his back a chair of beaten gold, and spake to Faustus, saying, sit up and away with me: and Doctor Faustus that had so long abode the smoke, wished rather to be in hell than there, got on the /110/ Devil, and so they went together. But mark how the Devil blinded him, and made him believe that he carried him into hell, for he carried him into the air, where Faustus fell into a sound sleep, as if he had sat in a warm water or bath: at last they came to a place which burneth continually with flashing flames of fire and brimstone, whereout issued an exceeding mighty clap of thunder, with so horrible a noise, that Faustus awaked, but the Devil went forth on his way and carried Faustus thereinto, yet notwithstanding, howsoever it burnt, Doctor Faustus felt no more heat, than as it were the glimpse of the Sun in May: there heard he all manner of music to welcome him, but saw none playing on them; it pleased him well, but he durst not ask, for he was forbidden it before. To meet the Devil and the guest that came with him, came three other ugly Devils, the which ran back again before the Bear to make them way, against whom there came running an exceeding great Hart, which would have thrust Faustus out of his chair, but being defended by the other three Devils, the Hart was put /111/ to the repulse: thence going on their way Faustus looked, and behold there was nothing but Snakes, and all manner of venomous beasts about him, which were exceeding great, unto the which Snakes came many Storks, and swallowed up all the whole multitude of Snakes, that they left not one: which when Faustus saw, he marvelled greatly: but proceeding further on their hellish voyage, there came forth of a hollow cliff an exceeding great flying Bull, the which with such a force hit Faustus his chair with his head and horns, that he turned Faustus and his Bear over and over, so that the Bear vanished away, whereat Faustus began to cry: oh, woe is me that ever I came here: for he thought there to have been beguiled of the Devil, and to make his end before his time appointed or conditioned of the Devil: but shortly came unto him a monstrous Ape, bidding Faustus be of good cheer, and said, get upon me; all the fire in hell seemed to Faustus to have been put out, whereupon followed a monstrous thick fog, that he saw nothing, but shortly it seemed to him to wax clear, where he saw two great Dragons fastened to a waggon, into the which the Ape ascended

and set Faustus therein; forth flew the Dragons into an exceeding dark cloud, where Faustus saw neither Dragon nor Chariot wherein he sat, and such were the cries of tormented souls, with mighty thunder-claps and flashing lightnings about his ears, that poor Faustus shook for fear. Upon this came they to a water, stinking and filthy, thick like mud, into the which ran the Dragons, sinking under with waggon and all; but Faustus felt no water but as it were a small mist, saving that the waves beat so sore upon him, that he /112/ saw nothing under and over him but only water, in the which he lost his Dragons, Ape, and waggon; and sinking yet deeper and deeper, he came at last as it were upon an high Rock, where the waters parted and left him thereon: but when the water was gone, it seemed to him he should there have ended his life, for he saw no way but death: the Rock was as high from the bottom as Heaven is from the earth: there sat he, seeing nor hearing any man, and looked ever upon the Rock; at length he saw a little hole, out of the which issued fire; thought he, how shall I now do? I am forsaken of the Devils, and they that brought me hither, here must I either fall to the bottom, or burn in the fire, or sit still in despair: with that in his madness he gave a leap into the fiery hole, saying: hold you infernal Hags, take here this sacrifice as my last end; the which I justly have deserved: upon this he was entered, and finding himself as yet unburned or touched of the fire, he was the better appayed,[1] but there was so great a noise as he never heard the like before, it passed all the thunder that ever he had heard; and coming down further to the bottom of the Rock, he saw a fire, wherein were many worthy and noble personages, as Emperors, Kings, Dukes, and Lords, and many thousands more of tormented souls, at the edge of which fire ran a most pleasant, clear, and cool water to behold, into the which many tormented souls sprang out of the fire to cool themselves; but being so freezing cold, they were constrained to return again into the fire, and thus wearied themselves and spent their endless torments out of /113/ one labyrinth into another, one while in heat, another while in cold: but Faustus standing thus all this while gazing on them were

Page 113: 1. i.e., pleased.

thus tormented, he saw one leaping out of the fire and screeching horribly, whom he thought to have known, wherefore he would fain have spoken unto him, but remembering that he was forbidden, he refrained speaking. Then this Devil that brought him in, came to him again in likeness of a Bear, with the chair on his back, and bade him sit up, for it was time to depart: so Faustus got up, and the Devil carried him out into the air, where he had so sweet music that he fell asleep by the way. His boy Christopher being all this while at home, and missing his master so long, thought his master would have tarried and dwelt with the Devil for ever: but whilst his boy was in these cogitations, his master came home, for the Devil brought him home fast asleep as he sat in his chair, and so he threw him on his bed, where (being thus left of the Devil) he lay until day. When he awaked, he was amazed, like a man that had been in a dark dungeon; musing with himself if it were true or false that he had seen hell, or whether he was blinded or not: but he rather persuaded himself that he had been there than otherwise, because he had seen such wonderful things: wherefore he most carefully took pen and ink, and wrote those things in order as he had seen: the which writing was afterwards found by his boy in his study; which afterwards was published to the whole city of Wittenberg in open print, for example to all Christians. /114/

CHAPTER XXI

*How Doctor Faustus was carried through
the air up to the heavens to see the
world, and how the Sky and Planets ruled:
after the which he wrote one letter to his
friend of the same to Liptzig, how he
went about the world in eight days*

This letter was found by a freeman and Citizen of Wittenberg, written with his own hand, and sent to his friend at Liptzig a Physician, named John Victor, the contents of which were as followeth.

Amongst other things (my loving friend and brother) I remember yet the former friendship had together, when we were schoolfellows and students in the University at Wittenberg, whereas you first studied Physic, Astronomy, Astrology, Geometry, and Cosmography; I to the contrary (you know) studied Divinity: notwithstanding now in any of your own studies I am seen (I am persuaded) further then your self: for sithence I began I have never erred, for (might I speak it without affecting my own praise) my Calendars and other practices have not only the commendations of the common sort, but also of the chiefest Lords and Nobles of this our Dutch Nation: because (which is chiefly to be noted) I write and presaged of matters to come, which all accord and fall out so right, as if they had been already seen before. And for that (my beloved Victori) you write to know my voyage which I made into the Heavens, the which (as you certify me you have had some suspicion of, although you partly /115/ persuaded yourself, that it is a thing impossible) no matter for that, it is as it is, and let it be as it will, once it was done, in such manner as now according unto your request I give you here to understand.

I being once laid on my bed, and could not sleep for thinking on my Calendar and practice, I marvelled with myself how it were possible that the Firmament should be known and so largely written of men, or whether they write true or false, by their own opinions, or supposition, or by due observations and true course of the heavens. Behold, being in these my muses, suddenly I heard a great noise, in so much that I thought my house would have been blown down, so that all my doors and chests flew open, whereat I was not a little astonied, for withal I heard a groaning voice which said, get up, the desire of thy heart, mind, and thought shalt thou see: at the which I answered, what my heart desireth, that would I fain see, and to make proof, if I shall see I will away with thee. Why then (quoth he) look out at thy window, there cometh a messenger for thee, that did I, and behold, there stood a Waggon, with two Dragons before it to draw the same, and all the Waggon was of a light burning fire, and for that the Moon shone, I was the willinger at that time to depart: but the voice spake again, sit up and let us away: I will, said I, go with thee, but upon this condition, that I may ask after all things that I see, hear, or think on: the voice answered, I am content for this time. Hereupon I got me into the Waggon, so that the Dragons carried me upright into the air. The Waggon had also four wheels the which rattled so, and made such a noise as if we had been all this /*116*/ while running on the stones: and round about us flew out flames of fire, and the higher that I came, the more the earth seemed to be darkened, so that methought I came out of a dungeon, and looking down from Heaven, behold, Mephostophiles my Spirit and servant was behind me, and when he perceived that I saw him, he came and sat by me, to whom I said, I pray thee Mephostophiles whither shall I go now? Let not that trouble thy mind, said he, and yet they carried us higher up. And now will I tell thee good friend and schoolfellow, what things I have seen and proved; for on the Tuesday went I out, and on Tuesday seven-nights following I came home again, that is, eight days, in which time I slept not, no not one wink came in mine eyes, and we went invisible of any man: and as the day began to appear, after our first night's journey, I said to my Spirit Mephostophiles, I pray thee how far have we now ridden, I am sure thou knowest: for methinks that we are ridden exceeding far, the World seemeth so little: Mephostophiles answered me, my Faustus believe me, that from the place from whence thou camest, unto this place where we are now, is already forty-seven leagues right in height, and as the day increased, I looked down upon the World, there saw I many kingdoms and provinces, likewise the whole world, Asia, Europa, and Africa, I had a sight of: and being so high, quoth I to my Spirit, tell me now how these Kingdoms lie, and what they are called, the which he denied not, saying, see this on our left hand is Hungaria, this is also Prussia on our left hand, and Poland, Muscovia, Tartascelesia,[1] Bohemia, Saxony: /*117*/ and here on our right hand, Spain, Portugal, France, England, and Scotland: then right out before us lie the Kingdoms of Persia, India, Arabia, the King of Alchar, and the great Cham: now are we come to Wittenberg, and are right over the town of Weim in Austria, and ere long will we be at Constantinople, Tripolie, and Jerusalem, and after will we pierce the frozen Zone, and shortly touch the Horizon, and the Zenith of

Page 117: 1. Probably a corruption of Tartary and Silesia.

Wittenberg. There looked I on the Ocean Sea, and beheld a great many of ships and Galleys ready to the battle, one against another: and thus I spent my journey, now cast I my eyes here, now there, toward South, North, East, and West, I have been in one place where it rained and hailed, and in another where the Sun shone excellent fair, and so I think that I saw the most things in and about the world, with great admiration that in one place it rained, and in another hail and snow, on this side the Sun shone bright, some hills covered with snow never consuming, others were so hot that grass and trees were burned and consumed therewith. Then looked I up to the heavens, and behold, they went so swift, that I thought they would have sprung in thousands. Likewise it was so clear and so hot, that I could not long gaze into it, it so dimmed my sight: and had not my Spirit Mephostophiles covered me as it were with a shadowing cloud, I had been burnt with the extreme heat thereof, for the Sky the which we behold here when we look up from the earth, is so fast and thick as a wall, clear and shining bright as a Crystal, in the which is placed the Sun, which casteth forth his rays or beams over the universal world, to the uttermost /*118*/ confines of the earth. But we think that the Sun is very little: no, it is altogether as big as the world. Indeed the body substantial is but little in compass, but the rays or stream that it casteth forth, by reason of the thing wherein it is placed, maketh him to extend and shew himself over the whole world: and we think that the Sun runneth his course, and that the heavens stand still: no, it is the heavens that move his course, and the Sun abideth perpetually in his place, he is permanent, and fixed in his place, and although we see him beginning to ascend in the Orient or East, at the highest in the Meridian or South, setting in the Occident or West, yet is he at the lowest in Septentrio or North, and yet he moveth not. It is the axle of the heavens that moveth the whole firmament, being a Chaos or confused thing, and for that proof, I will shew thee this example, like as thou seest a bubble made of water and soap blown forth of a quill, is in form of a confused mass or Chaos, and being in this form, is moved at pleasure of the wind, which runneth round about that Chaos, and moveth him also round: even so is the whole firmament or Chaos, wherein are placed the Sun, and the rest of the Planets turned and carried at the pleasure of the Spirit of God, which is wind. Yea Christian Reader, to the glory of God, and for the profit of thy soul, I will open unto thee the divine opinion touching the ruling of this confused Chaos, far more than any rude German Author, being possessed with the Devil, was able to utter; and to prove some of my sentence before to be true, look into Genesis unto the works of God, at the creation of the world, there shalt thou find, that the Spirit of /119/ God moved upon the waters before heaven and earth were made. Mark how he made it, and how by his word every element took his place: these were not his works, but his words; for all the words he used before, he concluded afterwards in one work, which was in making man: mark reader with patience for thy soul's health, see into all that was done by the word and work of God, light and darkness was, the firmament stood, and their great ☉ and little light ☽ in it: the moist waters were in one place, the earth was dry, and every element brought forth according to the word of God: now followeth his works he made man like his own image, how? out of the earth? The earth will shape no image without water, there was one of the elements. But all this while where was wind? all elements were at the word of God, man was made, and in a form by the work of God, yet moved not that work, before God breathed the Spirit of life into his nostrils, and made him a living soul, here was the first wind and Spirit of God out of his own mouth, which we have likewise from the same seed which was only planted by God in Adam, which wind, breath, or spirit, when he had received, he was living and moving on earth, for it was ordained of God for his habitation, but the heavens are the habitation of the Lord: and like as I shewed before of the bubble or confused Chaos made of water and soap, through the wind and breath of man is turned round, and carried with every wind; even so the firmament wherein the Sun and the rest of the Planets are fixed, moved, turned, and carried with the wind, breath, or Spirit of God, for the heavens and firmament are /120/ movable as the Chaos, but the Sun is fixed in the firmament. And farther my good schoolfellow, I was thus nigh the heavens, where methought every Planet was but as half the earth, and under the firmament ruled the Spirits in the air, and as I came down I looked upon the world and the heavens, and methought that the earth was enclosed in comparison within the firmament, as the yolk of an egg within the white, and methought that the whole length of the earth was not a span long, and the water was as if it had been twice as broad and long as the earth, even thus at the eight days end came I home again, and fell asleep, and so I continued sleeping three days and three nights together: and the first hour that I waked, I fell fresh again to my Calendar, and have made them in right ample manner as you know, and to satisfy your request, for that you writ unto me, I have in consideration of our old friendship had at the University of Wittenberg, declared unto you my heavenly voyage, wishing no worse unto you, than unto myself, that is, that your mind were as mine in all respects. Dixi.

Doctor Faustus the Astrologian. /121/

CHAPTER XXII

How Doctor Faustus made his journey through the principal and most famous lands in the world

. . . Well, forward he went to Rome, which lay, and doth yet lie, on the river Tybris, the which divideth the City in two parts: over the river are four great stone bridges, and upon the one bridge called Ponte S. Angelo is the Castle of S. Angelo, wherein are so many great cast pieces as there are days in a year, and such Pieces that will shoot seven bullets off with one fire, to this Castle cometh a privy vault from the Church and Palace of Saint Peter, through the which the Pope (if any danger be) passeth from his Palace to the Castle for safeguard; the City hath eleven gates, and a hill called Vaticinium,[1] whereon S. Peter's Church is built: in that Church the holy Fathers will hear no confession, without the penitent bring money in his hand. Adjoining to this Church, is the Campo Santo, the which Carolus Magnus built, where every day thirteen Pilgrims have their dinners served

Page 126: 1. A mistake for *Vaticanum.*

of the best: that is to say, Christ and his Twelve Apostles. Hard by this he visited the Church yard of S. Peter's, where he saw the Pyramid that Julius Cæsar brought out of Africa: it stood in Faustus his time leaning against the Church wall of Saint Peter's, but now Papa Sixtus hath erected it in the middle of S. Peter's Church yard; it is twenty-four fathoms long and at the lower end six fathoms four square, and so forth smaller upwards, on the top is a Crucifix of beaten gold, the stone /126/ standeth on four Lions of brass. Then he visited the seven Churches of Rome, that were S. Peter's, S. Paul's, S. Sebastian's, S. John Lateran, S. Laurence, S. Mary Magdalen, and S. Marie Majora: then went he without the town, where he saw the conduits of water that run level through hill and dale, bringing water into the town fifteen Italian miles off: other monuments he saw, too many to recite, but amongst the rest he was desirous to see the Pope's Palace, and his manner of service at his table, wherefore he and his Spirit made themselves invisible, and came into the Pope's Court, and privy chamber where he was, there saw he many servants attendant on his holiness, with many a flattering Sycophant carrying of his meat, and there he marked the Pope and the manner of his service, which he seeing to be so unmeasurable and sumptuous; fie (quoth Faustus), why had not the Devil made a Pope of me? Faustus saw notwithstanding in that place those that were like to himself, proud, stout, wilful, gluttons, drunkards, whoremongers, breakers of wedlock, and followers of all manner of ungodly exercises: wherefore he said to his Spirit, I thought that I had been alone a hog, or pork of the devil's, but he must bear with me yet a little longer, for these hogs of Rome are already fattened, and fitted to make his roast-meat, the Devil might do well now to spit them all and have them to the fire, and let him summon the Nuns to turn the spits: for as none must confess the Nun but the Friar, so none should turn the roasting Friar but the Nun. Thus continued Faustus three days in the Pope's Palace, and yet had no lust to his meat, but stood still in the Pope's chamber, /127/ and saw everything whatsoever it was: on a time the Pope would have a feast prepared for the Cardinal of Pavia, and for his first welcome the Cardinal was bidden to dinner: and as he sat at meat, the Pope would ever be blessing and crossing over his mouth; Faustus could suffer it no longer, but up with his fist and smote the Pope on the face, and withal he laughed that the whole house might hear him, yet none of them saw him nor knew where he was: the Pope persuaded his company that it was a damned soul, commanding a Mass presently to be said for his delivery out of Purgatory, which was done: the Pope sat still at meat, but when the latter mess came in to the Pope's board, Doctor Faustus laid hands thereon saying; this is mine: and so he took both dish and meat and fled unto the Capitol or Campadolia, calling his Spirit unto him and said: come let us be merry, for thou must fetch me some wine, and the cup that the Pope drinks of, and hereupon Monte Caval will we make good cheer in spite of the Pope and all his fat abbey lubbers. His Spirit hearing this, departed towards the Pope's chamber, where he found them yet sitting and quaffing: wherefore he took from before the Pope the fairest piece of plate or drinking goblet, and a flagon of wine, and brought it to Faustus; but when the Pope and the rest of his crew perceived they were robbed, and knew not after what sort, they persuaded themselves that it was the damned soul that before had vexed the Pope so, and that smote him on the face, wherefore he sent commandment through all the whole City of Rome, that they should say Mass in every Church, and ring all the bells for to lay the /128/ walking Spirit, and to curse him with Bell, Book, and Candle, that so invisibly had misused the Pope's holiness, with the Cardinal of Pavia, and the rest of their company: but Faustus notwithstanding made good cheer with that which he had beguiled the Pope of, and in the midst of the order of Saint Barnard's bare-footed Friars, as they were going on Procession through the market place, called Campa de fiore, he let fall his plate dishes and cup, and withal for a farewell he made such a thunder-clap and a storm of rain, as though Heaven and earth should have met together, and so he left Rome. . . . /129/

The third and last part of Doctor Faustus his merry conceits, shewing after what sort he practised Necromancy in the Courts of great Princes, and lastly of his fearful and pitiful end

CHAPTER XXIX

How the Emperor Carolus Quintus requested of Faustus to see some of his cunning, whereunto he agreed

The Emperor Carolus the fifth of that name was personally with the rest of his Nobles and gentlemen at the Town of Innsbruck where he kept his Court, unto /*150*/ the which also Doctor Faustus resorted, and being there well known of divers Nobles and gentlemen, he was invited into the Court to meat, even in the presence of the Emperor: whom when the Emperor saw, he looked earnestly on him, thinking him by his looks to be some wonderful fellow, wherefore he asked one of his Nobles whom he should be: who answered that he was called Doctor Faustus. Whereupon the Emperor held his peace until he had taken his repast, after which he called unto him Faustus, into the privy chamber, whither being come, he said unto him: Faustus, I have heard much of thee, that thou art excellent in the black Art, and none like thee in mine Empire, for men say that thou hast a familiar Spirit with thee and that thou canst do what thou list: it is therefore (saith the Emperor) my request of thee that thou let me see a proof of thine experience, and I vow unto thee by the honour of mine Imperial Crown, none evil shall happen unto thee for so doing. Hereupon Doctor Faustus answered his Majesty, that upon those conditions he was ready in anything that he could, to do his Highness' commandment in what service he would appoint him. Well, then hear what I say (quoth the Emperor). Being once solitary in my house, I called to mind mine elders and ancestors, how it was possible for them to attain unto so great a degree of authority, yea so high, that we the successors of that line are never able to come near. As, for example, the great and mighty monarch of the world, Alexander Magnus, was such a lantern and spectacle to all his successors, as the Chronicles make mention of so great riches, conquering, and subduing so many /*151*/ Kingdoms, the which I and those that follow me (I fear) shall never be able to attain

unto: wherefore, Faustus, my hearty desire is that thou wouldst vouchsafe to let me see that Alexander, and his Paramour, the which was praised to be so fair, and I pray thee shew me them in such sort that I may see their personages, shape, gesture, and apparel, as they used in their lifetime, and that here before my face; to the end that I may say I have my long desire fulfilled, and to praise thee to be a famous man in thine art and experience. Doctor Faustus answered: My most excellent Lord, I am ready to accomplish your request in all things, so far forth as I and my Spirit are able to perform: yet your Majesty shall know, that their dead bodies are not able substantially to be brought before you, but such Spirits as have seen Alexander and his Paramour alive, shall appear unto you in manner and form as they both lived in their most flourishing time: and herewith I hope to please your Imperial Majesty. Then Faustus went a little aside to speak to his Spirit, but he returned again presently, saying: now, if it please your Majesty, you shall see them, yet upon this condition that you demand no question of them, nor speak unto them, which the Emperor agreed unto. Wherewith Doctor Faustus opened the privy chamber door, where presently entered the great and mighty Emperor Alexander Magnus, in all things to look upon as if he had been alive, in proportion a strong thick-set man, of a middle stature, black hair, and that both thick and curled head and beard, red cheeks, and a broad face, with eyes like a Basilisk, he had on a complete harness burnished and graven /*152*/ exceeding rich to look upon; and so passing towards the Emperor Carolus, he made low and reverent curtsy: whereat the Emperor Carolus would have stood up to receive and greet him with the like reverence, but Faustus took hold of him and would not permit him to do it. Shortly after Alexander made humble reverence and went out again, and coming to the door his Paramour met him, she coming in, she made the Emperor likewise reverence, she was clothed in blue Velvet, wrought and embroidered with pearl and gold, she was also excellent fair like Milk and blood mixed, tall and slender, with a face round as an Apple, and thus she passed certain times up and down the house, which the Emperor marking, said to himself: now have I seen two persons, which my heart hath long wished for to behold, and sure it cannot otherwise be; said he to himself, but that the Spirits have changed themselves into these forms, and have not deceived me, calling to his mind the woman that raised the Prophet Samuel: and for that the Emperor would be the more satisfied in the matter, he thought, I have heard say, that behind her neck she had a great wart or wen, wherefore he took Faustus by the hand without any words, and went to see if it were also to be seen on her or not, but she perceiving that he came to her, bowed down her neck, where he saw a great wart, and hereupon she vanished, leaving the Emperor and the rest well contented. /153/

CHAPTER XXX

How Doctor Faustus in the sight of the Emperor conjured a pair of Hart's horns upon a Knight's head that slept out of a casement

When Doctor Faustus had accomplished the Emperor's desire in all things as he was requested, he went forth into a gallery, and leaning over a rail to look into the privy garden, he saw many of the Emperor's Courtiers walking and talking together, and casting his eyes now this way, now that way, he espied a Knight leaning out at a window of the great hall; who was fast asleep (for in those days it was hot) but the person shall be nameless that slept, for that he was a Knight, although it was done to a little disgrace of the Gentleman: it pleased Doctor Faustus, through the help of his Spirit Mephostophiles, to firm upon his head as he slept, a huge pair of Hart's horns, and as the Knight awaked thinking to pull in his head, he hit his horns against the glass that the panes thereof flew about his /154/ ears. Think here how this good Gentleman was vexed, for he could neither get backward nor forward: which when the Emperor heard all the Courtiers laugh, and came forth to see what was happened, the Emperor also when he beheld the Knight with so fair a head, laughed heartily thereat, and was therewithal well pleased: at last Faustus made him quit of his horns again, but the Knight perceived how they came, *etc.*[1]

Page 155: 1. There seems to be no explanation for the *etc.* here and at the end of the following two chapters. Cf. also end of Chapter IV.

CHAPTER XXXI

How the above-mentioned Knight went about to be revenged of Doctor Faustus

Doctor Faustus took his leave of the Emperor and the rest of the Courtiers, at whose departure they were sorry, giving him many rewards and gifts: but being a league and a half from the City he came into a Wood, where he beheld the Knight that he had jested with at the Court with others in harness, mounted on fair palfreys, and running with full charge towards Faustus, but he seeing their intent, ran towards the bushes, and before he came amongst the bushes he returned again, running as it were to meet them that chased him, whereupon suddenly all the bushes were turned into horsemen, which also ran to encounter with the Knight and his company, and coming to them, they closed the Knight and the /155/ rest, and told them that they must pay their ransom before they departed. Whereupon the Knight seeing himself in such distress, besought Faustus to be good to them, which he denied not, but let them loose, yet he so charmed them, that every one, Knight and others for the space of a whole month did wear a pair of Goat's horns on their brows, and every Palfrey a pair of Ox horns on their head: and this was their penance appointed by Faustus, *etc.* /156/

CHAPTER XXXIV

How Doctor Faustus deceived an Horse-courser

In like manner he served an Horse-courser at a fair called Pheiffring, for Doctor Faustus through his /162/ cunning had gotten an excellent fair Horse, whereupon he rid to the Fair, where he had many Chap-men that offered him money: lastly, he sold him for forty Dollars, willing him that bought him, that in any wise he should not ride him over any water, but the Horse-courser marvelled with himself that Faustus bade him ride him over no water (but quoth he), I will prove, and forthwith he rid him into the river, presently the horse vanished from under him, and he sat on a bundle of straw, in so much that the man was almost drowned. The

Horse-courser knew well where he lay that had sold him his horse, wherefore he went angrily to his Inn, where he found Doctor Faustus fast asleep, and snorting on a bed, but the Horse-courser could no longer forbear him, took him by the leg and began to pull him off the bed, but he pulled him so, that he pulled his leg from his body, in so much that the Horse-courser fell down backwards in the place, then began Doctor Faustus to cry with an open throat, he hath murdered me. Hereat the Horse-courser was afraid, and gave the flight,[1] thinking /163/ none other with himself, but that he had pulled his leg from his body; by this means Doctor Faustus kept his money.

CHAPTER XXXV

How Doctor Faustus ate a load of Hay

Doctor Faustus being in a Town of Germanie called Zwickaw, where he was accompanied with many Doctors and Masters, and going forth to walk after supper, they met with a Clown[1] that drove a load of Hay. Good even good fellow said Faustus to the Clown, what shall I give thee to let me eat my belly full of Hay? The Clown thought with himself, what a mad man is this to eat Hay, thought he with himself, thou wilt not eat much, they agreed for three farthings he should eat as much as he could: wherefore Doctor Faustus began to eat, and that so ravenously, that all the rest of his company fell a-laughing, blinding so the poor Clown, that he was sorry at his heart, for he seemed to have eaten more than the half of his Hay, wherefore the Clown began to speak him fair, for fear he should have eaten the other half also. Faustus made as though he had had pity on the Clown, and went his way. When the Clown came in place where he would be, he had his Hay again as he had before, a full load. /164/

CHAPTER XXXIX

How Doctor Faustus played a merry jest with the Duke of Anholt in his Court

Doctor Faustus on a time came to the Duke of Anholt, the which welcomed him very cour-

teously, this was in the month of January, where sitting at the table, he perceived the Duchess to be with child, and forbearing himself until the meat was taken from the table, and that they brought in the banqueting dishes, said Doctor Faustus to the Duchess, Gracious Lady, I have always heard, that the great-bellied women do always long for some dainties, I beseech therefore your Grace hide not your mind from me, but tell me what you desire to eat, she answered him, Doctor Faustus now truly I will not hide from you what my heart doth most desire, namely, that if it were now Harvest, I would eat my belly full of ripe Grapes, and other dainty fruit. Doctor Faustus answered hereupon, Gracious Lady, this is a small thing for me to do, for I can do more than this, wherefore he took a plate, and made open one of the casements of the window, /167/ holding it forth, where incontinent he had his dish full of all manner of fruits, as red and white Grapes, Pears, and Apples, the which came from out of strange Countries, all these he presented the Duchess, saying: Madame, I pray you vouchsafe to taste of this dainty fruit, the which came from a far Country, for there the Summer is not yet ended. The Duchess thanked Faustus highly, and she fell to her fruit with full appetite. The Duke of Anholt notwithstanding could not withhold to ask Faustus with what reason there were such young fruit to be had at that time of the year? Doctor Faustus told him, may it please your Grace to understand, that the year is divided into two circles over the whole world, that when with us it is Winter, in the contrary circle it is notwithstanding Summer, for in India and Saba there falleth or setteth the Sun, so that it is so warm, that they have twice a year fruit: and gracious Lord, I have a swift Spirit, the which can in the twinkling of an eye fulfil my desire in any thing, wherefore I sent him into those Countries, who hath brought this fruit as you see: whereat the Duke was in great admiration.

CHAPTER XL

How Doctor Faustus through his Charms made a great Castle in presence of the Duke of Anholt

Doctor Faustus desired the Duke of Anholt to walk a little forth of the Court with him,

Page 163: 1. *i.e.*, took to flight.
Page 164: 1. *i.e.*, peasant.

wherefore they /168/ went both together into the field, where Doctor Faustus through his skill had placed a mighty Castle: which when the Duke saw, he wondered thereat, so did the Duchess, and all the beholders, that on that hill, which was called the Rohumbuel, should on the sudden be so fair a Castle. At last Doctor Faustus desired the Duke and the Duchess to walk with him into the Castle, which they denied not. This Castle was so wonderful strong, having about it a great and deep trench of water, the which was full of Fish, and all manner of water-fowl, as Swans, Ducks, Geese, Bitterns, and suchlike. About the wall were five stone doors and two other doors: also within was a great open court, wherein were enchanted all manner of wild beasts, especially such as were not to be found in Germanie, as Apes, Bears, Buffs, Antelopes, and suchlike strange beasts. Furthermore, there were other manner of beasts, as Hart, Hind, and wild Swine, Roe, and all manner of land fowl that any man could think on, the which flew from one tree /169/ to another. After all this, he set his guests to the table, being the Duke and the Duchess with their train, for he had provided them a most sumptuous feast, both of meat and all manner of drinks, for he set nine messes of meat upon the board at once, and all this must his Wagner do, place all things on the board, the which was brought unto him by the Spirit invisibly of all things that their heart could desire, as wild fowl, and Venison, with all manner of dainty fish that could be thought on, of Wine also great plenty, and of divers sorts, as French wine, Cullin wine, Crabatsher wine, Rhenish wine, Spanish wine, Hungarian wine, Watzburg wine, Malmsey, and Sack: in the whole, there were an hundred cans standing round about the house. This sumptuous banquet the Duke took thankfully, and afterwards he departed homewards, and to their thinking they had neither eaten nor drunk, so were they blinded the whilst that they were in the Castle: but as they were in their Palace they looked towards the Castle, and behold it was all in a flame of fire, and all those that beheld it wondered to hear so great a noise, as if it were great Ordnance should have been shot off: and thus the Castle burned and consumed away clean. Which done, Doctor Faustus returned to the Duke, who gave him great thanks for shewing them of so great courtesy, giving him an hundred Dollars, and liberty to depart or use his own discretion therein. /170/

CHAPTER XLV

How Doctor Faustus shewed the fair Helena unto the Students upon the Sunday following

The Sunday following came these Students home to Doctor Faustus his own house, and brought their /177/ meat and drink with them: these men were right welcome guests unto Faustus, wherefore they all fell to drinking of wine smoothly: and being merry, they began some of them to talk of the beauty of women, and every one gave forth his verdict what he had seen and what he had heard. So one among the rest said, I never was so desirous of anything in this world, as to have a sight (if it were possible) of fair Helena of Greece, for whom the worthy town of Troie was destroyed and razed down to the ground, therefore saith he, that in all men's judgment she was more than commonly fair, because that when she was stolen away from her husband, there was for her recovery so great bloodshed.

Doctor Faustus answered: For that you are all my friends and are so desirous to see that famous pearl of Greece, fair Helena, the wife of King Menelaus, and daughter of Tindalus and Laeda, sister to Castor and Pollux, who was the fairest Lady in all Greece: I will therefore bring her into your presence personally, and in the same form of attire as she used to go when she was in her chiefest flowers and pleasantest prime of youth. The like have I done for the Emperor Carolus Quintus, at his desire I shewed him Alexander the great, and his Paramour: but (said Doctor Faustus) I charge you all that upon your perils you speak not a word, nor rise up from the Table so long as she is in your presence. And so he went out of the Hall, returning presently again, after whom immediately followed the fair and beautiful Helena, whose beauty was such that the Students were all amazed to see her, esteeming her rather to be a heavenly than an earthly /178/ creature. This Lady appeared before them in a most sumptuous gown of purple Velvet, richly embroidered, her hair hanged down loose as fair as the beaten Gold, and of such length that it reached down to her hams, with amorous coal-black eyes, a sweet and pleasant round face, her lips red as a Cherry, her cheeks of rose all colour, her mouth small, her neck as white as the Swan, tall and slender of personage, and in sum, there was not one imperfect part in her: she looked round about her with a rolling Hawk's eye, a smiling and wanton countenance, which near hand inflamed the hearts of the Students, but that they persuaded themselves she was a Spirit, wherefore such fantasies passed away lightly with them: and thus fair Helena and Doctor Faustus went out again one with another. But the Students at Doctor Faustus his entering again into the hall, requested of him to let them see her again the next day, for that they would bring with them a painter and so take her counterfeit: which he denied, affirming that he could not always /179/ raise up her Spirit, but only at certain times: yet (said he) I will give you her counterfeit, which shall be always as good to you as if your selves should see the drawing thereof, which they received according to his promise, but soon lost it again. The Students departed from Faustus' home everyone to his house, but they were not able to sleep the whole night for thinking on the beauty of fair Helena. Wherefore a man may see that the Devil blindeth and enflameth the heart with lust oftentimes, that men fall in love with Harlots, nay even with Furies, which afterward cannot lightly be removed.

CHAPTER XLVI

How Doctor Faustus conjured away the four wheels from a clown's waggon

Doctor Faustus was sent for to the Marshal of Brunswicke, who was greatly troubled with the falling sickness. Now Faustus had this use, never to ride but walk forth on foot, for he could ease himself when he list, and as he came near unto the town of Brunswicke, there overtook him a Clown with four horses and an empty waggon, to whom Doctor Faustus jestingly to try him, said: I pray thee, good fellow, let me ride a little to ease my weary legs; which the buzzardly ass denied, saying: that his horses were also weary, and he would not let him get

up. Doctor /180/ Faustus did this but to prove the buzzard, if there were any courtesy to be found in him if need were.

But such churlishness as is commonly found among clowns, was by Doctor Faustus well requited, even with the like payment: for he said unto him, Thou doltish Clown, void of all humanity, seeing thou art of so currish a disposition, I will pay thee as thou hast deserved, for the four wheels of thy Waggon thou shalt have taken from thee, let me see then how canst thou shift: hereupon his wheels were gone, his horses also fell down to the ground, as though they had been dead: whereat the Clown was sore affright, measuring it as a just scourge of God for his sins and churlishness: wherefore all troubled, and wailing, he humbly besought Doctor Faustus to be good unto him, confessing he was worthy of it, notwithstanding if it pleased him to forgive him, he would hereafter do better. Which humility made Faustus his heart to relent, answering him on this manner, well, do so no more, but when a poor weary man desireth thee, see that thou let him ride, but yet thou shalt not go altogether clear, for although thou have again thy four wheels, yet shalt thou fetch them at the four Gates of the City, so he threw dust on the horses, and revived them again, and the Clown for his churlishness was fain to fetch his wheels, spending his time with weariness, whereas before he might have done a good deed, and gone about his business quietly. /181/

CHAPTER XLVII

How four Jugglers cut one another's heau off, and set them on again; and how Doctor Faustus deceived them

Doctor Faustus came in the Lent unto Franckfort Fair, where his Spirit Mephostophiles gave him to understand that in an Inn were four Jugglers that cut one another's head off, and after their cutting off, sent them to the Barber to be trimmed, which many people saw. This angered Faustus (for he meant to have himself the only Cock in the Devil's basket), and he went to the place where they were, to behold them. And as these Jugglers were together, ready one to cut off the other's head, there stood also the Barbers ready to trim them, and by them upon the table stood likewise a glass full of distilled water, and he that was the chiefest among them stood by it. Thus they began, they smote off the head of the first, and presently there was a Lily in the glass of distilled water, where Faustus perceived this Lily as it were springing, and the chief Juggler named it the tree of life, thus dealt he with the first, making the Barber wash and comb his head, and then he set it on again, presently the Lily vanished away out of the water, hereat the man had his head whole and sound again; the like did they with the other two: and as the turn and lot came to the chief Juggler that he also should be beheaded, and that his Lily was most pleasant, fair, and flourishing green, they smote his head off, and when it came to /182/ be barbed, it troubled Faustus his conscience, in so much that he could not abide to see another do anything, for he thought himself to be the principal conjurer in the world, wherefore Doctor Faustus went to the table whereat the other Jugglers kept that Lily, and so he took a small knife and cut off the stalk of the Lily, saying to himself, none of them should blind Faustus: yet no man saw Faustus to cut the Lily, but when the rest of the Jugglers thought to have set on their master's head, they could not, wherefore they looked on the Lily, and found it a bleeding: by this means the Juggler was beguiled, and so died in his wickedness, yet not one thought that Doctor Faustus had done it.

CHAPTER XLVIII

How an old man, the neighbour of Faustus, sought to persuade him to amend his evil life, and to fall unto repentance

A good Christian an honest and virtuous old man, a lover of the holy Scriptures, who was neighbour unto Doctor Faustus: when he perceived that many Students had their recourse in and out unto Doctor Faustus, he suspected his evil life, wherefore like a friend he invited Doctor Faustus to supper unto his house, unto the which he agreed; and having ended their banquet, the old man began with these words. My loving friend and neighbour Doctor Faustus, /183/ I have to desire of you a friendly and Christian request, beseeching you that you will vouchsafe not to be angry with me, but friendly resolve me in my doubt, and take my poor inviting in good part. To whom Doctor Faustus answered: My loving neighbour, I pray you say your mind. Then began the old Patron to say: My good neighbour, you know in the beginning how that you have defied God, and all the host of heaven, and given your soul to the Devil, wherewith you have incurred God's high displeasure, and are become from a Christian far worse than a heathen person: oh consider what you have done, it is not only the pleasure of the body, but the safety of the soul that you must have respect unto: of which if you be careless, then are you cast away, and shall remain in the anger of almighty God. But yet is it time enough Doctor Faustus, if you repent and call unto the Lord for mercy, as we have example in the Acts of the Apostles, the eighth Chapter of Simon in Samaria, who was led out of the way, affirming that he was Simon homo sanctus. This man was notwithstanding in the end converted, after that he had heard the Sermon of Philip, for he was baptized, and saw his sins, and repented. Likewise I beseech you good brother Doctor Faustus, let my rude Sermon be unto you a conversion; and forget the filthy life that you have led, repent, ask mercy, and live: for Christ saith, *Come unto me all ye that are weary and heavy laden, and I will refresh you.* And in Ezechiel: *I desire not the death of a sinner, but rather that he convert and live.* Let my words good brother Faustus, pierce into your adamant heart, and /184/ desire God for his Son Christ his sake, to forgive you. Wherefore have you so long lived in your Devilish practices, knowing that in the Old and New Testament you are forbidden, and that men should not suffer any such to live, neither have any conversation with them, for it is an abomination unto the Lord; and that such persons have no part in the Kingdom of God. All this while Doctor Faustus heard him very attentively, and replied: Father, your persuasions like me wondrous well, and I thank you with all my heart for your good will and counsel, promising you so far as I may to follow your discipline: whereupon he took his leave. And being come home, he laid him very pensive on his bed, bethinking himself of the words of the good old man, and in a manner began to repent that he had given his Soul to the Devil, intending to deny all that he had promised unto Lucifer. Continuing in these cogitations, suddenly his Spirit appeared unto him clapping him upon the head, and wrung it as though he would have pulled the head from the shoulders, saying unto him, Thou knowest Faustus, that thou hast given thyself body and soul unto my Lord Lucifer, and hast vowed thyself an enemy unto God and unto all men; and now thou beginnest to hearken to an old doting fool which persuadeth thee as it were unto God, when indeed it is too late, for that thou art the Devil's, and he hath good power presently to fetch thee: wherefore he hath sent me unto thee, to tell thee, that seeing thou hath sorrowed for that thou hast done, begin again and write another writing with thine own blood, if not, then will I tear thee all to pieces. Hereat Doctor Faustus was sore /185/ afraid, and said: My Mephostophiles, I will write again what thou wilt: wherefore he sat him down, and with his own blood he wrote as followeth: which writing was afterward sent to a dear friend of the said Doctor Faustus being his kinsman.

CHAPTER XLIX

How Doctor Faustus wrote the second time with his own blood and gave it to the Devil

I, Doctor John Faustus, acknowledge by this my deed and handwriting, that sith my first writing, which is seventeen years, that I have right willingly held, and have been an utter enemy unto God and all men, the which I once again confirm, and give fully and wholly myself unto the Devil both body and soul, even unto the great Lucifer: and that at the end of seven years ensuing after the date of this letter, he shall have to do with me according as it pleaseth him, either to lengthen or shorten my life as liketh him: and hereupon I renounce all persuaders that seek to withdraw me from my purpose by the Word of God, either ghostly or bodily. And further, I will never give ear unto any man, be he spiritual or temporal, that moveth any matter for the salvation of my soul. Of all this writing, and that therein contained, be witness, my own blood, the which with mine own hands I have begun, and ended.

Dated at Wittenberg, the 25th of July. /186/

And presently upon the making of this Letter, he became so great an enemy unto the poor old man, that he sought his life by all means possible; but this godly man was strong in the Holy Ghost, that he could not be vanquished by any means: for about two days after that he had exhorted Faustus, as the poor man lay in his bed, suddenly there was a mighty rumbling in the Chamber, the which he was never wont to hear, and he heard as it had been the groaning of a Sow, which lasted long: whereupon the good old man began to jest, and mock, and said: oh what Barbarian cry is this, oh fair Bird, what foul music is this of a fair Angel, that could not tarry two days in his place? beginnest thou now to run into a poor man's house, where thou hast no power, and wert not able to keep thine own two days? With these and such-like words the Spirit departed. And when he came home Faustus asked him how he had sped with the old man: to whom the Spirit answered, the old man was harnessed, and that he could not once lay hold upon him: but he would not tell how the old man had mocked him, for the Devils can never abide to hear of their fall. Thus doth God defend the hearts of all honest Christians, that betake themselves under his tuition. /187/

CHAPTER LIV

How Doctor Faustus found a mass of money when he had consumed twenty-two of his years

To the end that the Devil would make Faustus his only heir, he shewed unto him where he should go and find a mighty huge mass of money, and that he should have it in an old Chapel that was fallen down, half a mile distant from Wittenberg, there he bade him to dig and he should find it, the which he did, and having digged reasonable deep, he saw a mighty huge serpent, the which lay on the treasure itself, the treasure itself lay like a huge light burning: but D. Faustus charmed the serpent that he crept into a hole, and when he digged deeper to get up the treasure, he found nothing but coals of fire: there also he heard and saw many that were tormented, yet notwithstanding he brought away the coals, and when he was come home, it was all turned into silver and gold, as after his death was found by his servant, the which was almost about estimation, a thousand gilders.

CHAPTER LV

How Doctor Faustus made the Spirit of fair Helena of Greece his own Paramour and bedfellow in his twenty-third year

To the end that this miserable Faustus might fill the lust of his flesh, and live in all manner of voluptuous /*193*/ pleasures, it came in his mind after he had slept his first sleep,[1] and in the twenty-third year past of his time, that he had a great desire to lie with fair Helena of Greece, especially her whom he had seen and shewed unto the Students of Wittenberg, wherefore he called unto him his Spirit Mephostophiles, commanding him to bring him the fair Helena, which he also did. Whereupon he fell in love with her, and made her his common Concubine and bedfellow, for she was so beautiful and delightful a piece, that he could not be one hour from her, if he should therefore have suffered death, she had so stolen away his heart: and to his seeming, in time she was with child, and in the end brought him a man child, whom Faustus named Justus Faustus: this child told Doctor Faustus many things that were to come, and what strange matters were done in foreign countries; but in the end when Faustus lost his life, the mother and the child vanished away both together.

CHAPTER LVI

How Doctor Faustus made his Will, in the which he named his servant Wagner to be his heir

Doctor Faustus was now in his twenty-fourth and last year, and he had a pretty stripling to his servant, the which had studied also at the University of Wittenberg: this youth was very well acquainted with his knaveries and sorceries, so that he was hated as /*194*/ well for his own knaveries, as also for his Master's: for no man

Page 194: 1. The German text has "at midnight, when he awoke."

would give him entertainment into his service, because of his unhappiness, but Faustus: this Wagner was so well beloved with Faustus, that he used him as his son: for do what he would his master was always therewith well content. And when the time drew nigh that Faustus should end, he called unto him a Notary and certain masters the which were his friends and often conversant with him, in whose presence he gave this Wagner his house and Garden. Item, he gave him in ready money one thousand six hundred gilders. Item, a Farm. Item, a gold chain, much plate, and other household stuff. This gave he all to his servant, and the rest of his time he meant to spend in Inns and Students' company, drinking and eating, with other jollity: and thus he finished his Will for that time.

CHAPTER LVII

How Doctor Faustus fell in talk with his servant touching his Testament, and the covenants thereof

Now when this Will was made, Doctor Faustus called unto him his servant, saying: I have thought upon thee in my Testament, for that thou hast been a trusty servant unto me and a faithful, and hast not opened my secrets: and yet further (said he) ask of me before I die what thou wilt, and I will give it unto thee. His servant rashly answered, I pray you let /*195*/ me have your cunning. To which Doctor Faustus answered, I have given thee all my books, upon this condition, that thou wouldst not let them be common, but use them for thine own pleasure, and study carefully in them. And dost thou also desire my cunning? That mayest thou peradventure have, if thou love and peruse my books well. Further (said Doctor Faustus) seeing that thou desirest of me this request, I will resolve thee: my Spirit Mephostophiles his time is out with me, and I have nought to command him as touching thee, yet will I help thee to another, if thou like well thereof. And within three days after he called his servant unto him, saying: art thou resolved? wouldst thou verily have a Spirit? Then tell me in what manner or form thou wouldst have him? To whom his servant answered, that he would have him in the form of an Ape: whereupon presently appeared a Spirit unto him in manner and form of an Ape, the which leaped about the house. Then said Faustus, see, there hast thou thy request, but yet he will not obey thee until I be dead, for when my Spirit Mephostophiles shall fetch me away, then shall thy Spirit be bound unto thee, if thou agree: and thy Spirit shalt thou name Akercocke, for so is he called: but all this is upon condition that thou publish my cunning, and my merry conceits, with all that I have done (when I am dead) in an history: and if thou canst not remember all, thy Spirit Akercocke will help thee: so shall the great acts that I have done be manifested unto the world. /*196*/

CHAPTER LVIII

How Doctor Faustus having but one month of his appointed time to come, fell to mourning and sorrow with himself for his devilish exercise

Time ran away with Faustus, as the hourglass, for he had but one month to come of his twenty-four years, at the end whereof he had given himself to the Devil body and soul, as is before specified. Here was the first token, for he was like a taken murderer or a thief, the which findeth himself guilty in conscience before the Judge have given sentence, fearing every hour to die: for he was grieved, and wailing spent the time, went talking to himself, wringing of his hands, sobbing and sighing, he fell away from flesh, and was very lean, and kept himself close: neither could he abide to see or hear of his Mephostophiles any more.

CHAPTER LIX

How Doctor Faustus complained that he should in his lusty time and youthful years die so miserably

This sorrowful time drawing near so troubled Doctor Faustus, that he began to write his mind, to the end he might peruse it often and not forget it, and is in manner as followeth.

Ah Faustus, thou sorrowful and woeful man, now /*197*/ must thou go to the damned company in unquenchable fire, whereas thou mightest have had the joyful immortality of the soul, the which thou now hast lost. Ah gross understanding and wilful will, what seizeth on my limbs other than a robbing of my life? Bewail with me my sound and healthful body, wit and soul, bewail with me my senses, for you have had your part and pleasure as well as I. Oh envy and disdain, how have you crept both at once into me, and now for your sakes I must suffer all these torments? Ah whither is pity and mercy fled? Upon what occasion hath heaven repaid me with this reward by sufferance to suffer me to perish? Wherefore was I created a man? The punishment that I see prepared for me of myself now must I suffer. Ah miserable wretch, there is nothing in this world to shew me comfort: then woe is me, what helpeth my wailing.

CHAPTER LX

Another complaint of Doctor Faustus

Oh poor, woeful and weary wretch: oh sorrowful soul of Faustus, now art thou in the number of the damned, for now must I wait for unmeasurable pains of death, yea far more lamentable than ever yet any creature hath suffered. Ah senseless, wilful and desperate forgetfulness! O cursed and unstable life! O blind and careless wretch, that so hast abused thy body, sense, and soul! O foolish pleasure, into what /*198*/ a weary labyrinth hast thou brought me, blinding mine eyes in the clearest day? Ah weak heart! O troubled soul, where is become thy knowledge to comfort thee? O pitiful weariness! Oh desperate hope, now shall I never more be thought upon! Oh, care upon carefulness, and sorrows on heaps: Ah grievous pains that pierce my panting heart, whom is there now that can deliver me? Would God that I knew where to hide me, or into what place to creep or fly. Ah, woe, woe is me, be where I will, yet am I taken. Herewith poor Faustus was so sorrowfully troubled, that he could not speak or utter his mind any further.

CHAPTER LXI

*How Doctor Faustus bewailed to think on
Hell, and of the miserable pains
therein provided for him*

Now thou Faustus, damned wretch, how happy wert thou if as an unreasonable beast thou mightest die without soul, so shouldst thou not feel any more doubts? But now the Devil will take thee away both body and soul, and set thee in an unspeakable place of darkness: for although others' souls have rest and peace, yet I poor damned wretch must suffer all manner of filthy stench, pains, cold, hunger, thirst, heat, freezing, burning, hissing, gnashing, and all the wrath and curse of God, yea all the creatures that God hath created are enemies to me. And now too late I remember that my Spirit Mephostophiles did once tell me, there was a /199/ great difference amongst the damned; for the greater the sin, the greater the torment: for as the twigs of the tree make greater flame than the trunk thereof, and yet the trunk continueth longer in burning: even so the more that a man is rooted in sin, the greater is his punishment. Ah thou perpetual damned wretch, now art thou thrown into the everlasting fiery lake that never shall be quenched, there must I dwell in all manner of wailing, sorrow, misery, pain, torment, grief, howling, sighing, sobbing, blubbering, running of eyes, stinking at nose, gnashing of teeth, fear to the ears, horror to the conscience, and shaking both of hand and foot. Ah that I could carry the heavens on my shoulders, so that there were time at last to quit me of this everlasting damnation! Oh who can deliver me out of these fearful tormenting flames, the which I see prepared for me? Oh there is no help, nor any man that can deliver me, nor any wailing of sins can help me, neither is there rest to be found for me day nor night. Ah woe is me, for there is no help for me, no shield, no defence, no comfort. Where is my hold? knowledge dare I not trust: and for a soul to Godwards that have I not, for I shame to speak unto him: if I do, no answer shall be made me, but he will hide his face from me, to the end that I should not behold the joys of the chosen. What mean I then to complain where no help is? No, I know no hope resteth in my groanings: I have desired that it should be so, and God hath said Amen to my misdoings: for now I must have shame to comfort me in my calamities. /200/

CHAPTER LXII

*Here followeth the miserable and
lamentable end of Doctor Faustus, by the
which all Christians may take an
example and warning*

In the twenty-fourth year Doctor Faustus his time being come, his Spirit appeared unto him, giving him his writing again, and commanding him to make preparation, for that the Devil would fetch him against a certain time appointed. Dr. Faustus mourned and sighed wonderfully, and never went to bed, nor slept wink for sorrow. Wherefore his Spirit appeared again, comforting him, and saying: My Faustus, be not thou so cowardly minded; for although that thou losest thy body, it is not long unto the day of Judgment, and thou must die at the last, although thou live many thousand years. The Turks, the Jews, and many an unchristian Emperor, are in the same condemnation: therefore (my Faustus) be of good courage, and be not discomforted, for the Devil hath promised that thou shalt not be in pains as the rest of the damned are. This and such-like comfort he gave him, but he told him false, and against the saying of the Holy Scriptures. Yet Doctor Faustus that had none other expectation but to pay his debts with his own skin, went on the same day that his Spirit said the Devil would fetch him, unto his trusty and dearest beloved brethren and companions, as Masters, and Bachelors of Arts, and other Students more the which had often visited him at his house in merriment: these he entreated /201/ that they would walk into the Village called Rimlich, half a mile from Wittenberg, and that they would there take with him for their repast part of a small banquet, the which they all agreed unto: so they went together, and there held their dinner in a most sumptuous manner. Doctor Faustus with them (dissemblingly) was merry, but not from the heart: wherefore he requested them that they would also take part of his rude supper: the which they agreed unto: for (quoth he) I must tell you what is the Victualler's due: and when they slept (for drink was in their heads) then Doctor Faustus paid and discharged the shot, and bound the Students and the Masters to go with him into another room, for he had many wonderful matters to tell them: and when they were entered the room as he requested, Doctor Faustus said unto them, as hereafter followeth.

CHAPTER LXIII

An Oration of Faustus to the Students

My trusty and well-beloved friends, the cause why I have invited you into this place is this: Forasmuch as you have known me this many years, in what manner of life I have lived, practising all manner of conjurations and wicked exercises, the which I have obtained through the help of the Devil, into whose Devilish fellowship they have brought me, the which use the like Art and practice, urged by the /202/ detestable provocation of my flesh, my stiff-necked and rebellious will, with my filthy infernal thoughts, the which were ever before me, pricking me forward so earnestly, that I must perforce have the consent of the Devil to aid me in my devices. And to the end I might the better bring my purpose to pass, to have the Devil's aid and furtherance, which I never have wanted in mine actions, I have promised unto him at the end and accomplishing of twenty-four years, both body and soul, to do therewith at his pleasure: and this day, this dismal day, those twenty-four years are fully expired, for night beginning my hour-glass is at an end, the direful finishing whereof I carefully expect: for out of all doubt this night he will fetch me, to whom I have given myself in recompense of his service both body and soul, and twice confirmed writings with my proper blood. Now have I called you my well-beloved Lords, friends, brethren, and fellows, before that fatal hour to take my friendly farewell, to the end that my departing may not hereafter be hidden from you, beseeching you herewith courteous, and loving Lords and brethren, not to take in evil part anything done by me, but with friendly commendations to salute all my friends and companions wheresoever: desiring both you and them, if ever I

have trespassed against your minds in anything, that you would all heartily forgive me: and as for those lewd practices the which this full twenty-four years I have followed, you shall hereafter find them in writing: and I beseech you let this my lamentable end to the residue of your lives be a sufficient warning, that you have God always before your eyes, praying /203/ unto him that he would ever defend you from the temptation of the Devil, and all his false deceits, not falling altogether from God, as I wretched and ungodly damned creature have done, having denied and defied Baptism, the Sacraments of Christ's body, God himself, all heavenly powers, and earthly men, yea, I have denied such a God, that desireth not to have one lost. Neither let the evil fellowship of wicked companions mislead you as it hath done me: visit earnestly and oft the Church, war and strive continually against the Devil with a good and steadfast belief on God, and Jesus Christ, and use your vocation in holiness. Lastly, to knit up my troubled Oration, this is my friendly request, that you would to rest, and let nothing trouble you: also if you chance to hear any noise, or rumbling about the house, be not therewith afraid, for there shall no evil happen unto you: also I pray you arise not out of your beds. But above all things I entreat you, if you hereafter find my dead carcass, convey it unto the earth, for I die both a good and bad Christian; a good Christian, for that I am heartily sorry, and in my heart always pray for mercy, that my soul may be delivered: a bad Christian, for that I know the Devil will have my body, and that would I willingly give him so that he would leave my soul in quiet: wherefore I pray you that you would depart to bed, and so I wish you a quiet night, which unto me notwithstanding will be horrible and fearful.

This oration or declaration was made by Doctor Faustus, and that with a hearty and resolute mind, to the end he might not discomfort them: but the /204/ Students wondered greatly thereat, that he was so blinded, for knavery, conjuration, and such-like foolish things, to give his body and soul unto the Devil: for they loved him entirely, and never suspected any such thing before he had opened his mind to them: wherefore one of them said unto him; ah, friend Faustus, what have you done to conceal this matter so long from us, we would by the help of good Divines, and the grace of God, have brought you out of this net, and have torn you out of the bondage and chains of Satan, whereas now we fear it is too late, to the utter ruin of your body and soul? Doctor Faustus answered, I durst never do it, although I often minded, to settle myself unto godly people, to desire counsel and help, as once mine old neighbour counselled me, that I should follow his learning, and leave all my conjurations, yet when I was minded to amend, and to follow that good man's counsel, then came the Devil and would have had me away, as this night he is like to do, and said so soon as I turned again to God, he would dispatch me altogether. Thus, even thus (good Gentlemen, and my dear friends) was I enthralled in that Satanical band, all good desires drowned, all piety banished, all purpose of amendment utterly exiled, by the tyrannous threatenings of my deadly enemy. But when the Students heard his words, they gave him counsel to do naught else but call upon God, desiring him for the love of his sweet Son Jesus Christ's sake, to have mercy upon him, teaching him this form of prayer. O, God, be merciful unto me, poor and miserable sinner, and enter not into judgment with me, for no flesh is able to stand before /205/ thee. Although, O Lord, I must leave my sinful body unto the Devil, being by him deluded, yet thou in mercy mayest preserve my soul.

This they repeated unto him, yet it could take no hold, but even as Cain he also said his sins were greater than God was able to forgive; for all his thought was on his writing, he meant he had made it too filthy in writing it with his own blood. The Students and the others that were there, when they had prayed for him, they wept, and so went forth, but Faustus tarried in the hall: and when the Gentlemen were laid in bed, none of them could sleep, for that they attended to hear if they might be privy of his end. It happened between twelve and one o'clock at midnight, there blew a mighty storm of wind against the house, as though it would have blown the foundation thereof out of his place. Hereupon the Students began to fear, and got out of their beds, comforting one another, but they would not stir out of the chamber: and the Host of the house ran out of doors, thinking the

house would fall. The Students lay near unto that hall wherein Doctor Faustus lay, and they heard a mighty noise and hissing, as if the hall had been full of Snakes and Adders: with that the hall door flew open wherein Doctor Faustus was, then he began to cry for help, saying: murther, murther, but it came forth with half a voice hollowly: shortly after they heard him no more. But when it was day, the Students that had taken no rest that night, arose and went into the hall in the which they left Doctor Faustus, where notwithstanding they found no Faustus, but all the hall lay besprinkled with blood, /206/ his brains cleaving to the wall: for the Devil had beaten him from one wall against another, in one corner lay his eyes, in another his teeth, a pitiful and fearful sight to behold. Then began the Students to bewail and weep for him, and sought for his body in many places: lastly they came into the yard where they found his body lying on the horse dung, most monstrously torn, and fearful to behold, for his head and all his joints were dashed in pieces.

The forenamed Students and Masters that were at his death, have obtained so much, that they buried him in the Village where he was so grievously tormented. After the which, they returned to Wittenberg, and coming into the house of Faustus, they found the servant of Faustus very sad, unto whom they opened all the matter, who took it exceedingly heavily. There found they also this history of Doctor Faustus noted, and of him written as is before declared, all save only his end, the which was after by the Students thereto annexed: further, what his servant had noted thereof, was made in another book. And you have heard that he held by him in his life the Spirit of fair Helena, the which had by him one son, the which he named Justus Faustus, even the same day of his death they vanished away, both mother and son. The house before was so dark, that scarce anybody could abide therein. The same night Doctor Faustus appeared unto his servant lively, and shewed unto him many secret things the which he had done and hidden in his lifetime. Likewise there were certain which saw Doctor Faustus look out of the window by night as they passed by the house. /207/

And thus ended the whole story of Doctor Faustus his conjuration, and other acts that he did in his life; out of the which example every Christian may learn, but chiefly the stiff-necked and high minded may thereby learn to fear God, and to be careful of their vocation, and to be at defiance with all Devilish works, as God hath most precisely forbidden, to the end we should not invite the Devil as a guest, nor give him place as that wicked Faustus hath done: for here we have a fearful example of his writing, promise, and end, that we may remember him: that we go not astray, but take God always before our eyes, to call alone upon him, and to honour him all the days of our life, with heart and hearty prayer, and with all our strength and soul to glorify his holy name, defying the Devil and all his works, to the end we may remain with Christ in all endless joy: Amen, Amen, that wish I unto every Christian heart, and God's name to be glorified. Amen.

FINIS   /208/

2. Works

Christopher Marlowe (1564–93), born the son of a shoemaker in the cathedral town of Canterbury in southern England, was a dramatist and poet second only to Shakespeare. After receiving his education at Corpus Christi College, Cambridge, Marlowe went to London, where he joined the theatrical company of the Earl of Nottingham. Little further is known of Marlowe's private life. He was, however, reputed to be an atheist, and in 1593 a warrant issued by the Privy Council ordered that he be brought before that body. Before the warrant could be served, Marlowe was killed in a brawl with dinner companions at Deptford.

Aside from *Doctor Faustus,* Marlowe's best-known works are the two-part tragedy *Tamburlaine the Great* (published in 1587); *The Famous Tragedie of the Rich Jew of Malta* (1633); *The Troublesome Reigne and Lamentable Death of Edward II, King of England* (1594); and the narrative poem *Hero and Leander* (1600). Although his plays show no great power of characterization, they reveal a vigorous and searching mind. *Tamburlaine* is a tale of heroic aspiration; Barabbas in *The Jew of Malta* seeks limitless wealth; Faustus seeks boundless knowledge in addition to wealth and power.

Most critics agree that *The Tragicall Historie of Doctor Faustus,* Marlowe's masterpiece, was written not long before his death in 1593. It was published in two editions, the first in 1604 (the A text) and the second, which contains added material, in 1616 (the B text). The relative merit of the two versions has long been a subject of controversy. In recent years the 1616 text has won favor, although some scholars still prefer the 1604 quarto. The debate revolves around whether Marlowe wrote the additions found in the 1616 text. Some discussions of the controversy can be found in the articles by Ornstein, Clemen, and Barber in Part Three. This edition is based on that of 1616. The editions of Frederick S. Boas (London: Methuen & Co., 1932) and Irving Ribner (New York: Odyssey Press, 1963) have proved most helpful.

Doctor Faustus reflects the pride in intellect that marked the Renaissance. The very movement that gave rise to works like the *Faustbuch* was of course related to the rise of the power of the cities and the growth of liberalism in thought and action. The more sympathetic portrayal of Faustus in Marlowe's play than in the Spies *Faustbuch* also reflects the growth of the new spirit.

The meaning of Marlowe's play has been much debated in recent years. That Marlowe himself was accused of atheism gives rise to several questions. The ending is obviously Christian—Faustus is carried off to hell. But does this reflect Marlowe's own ideas, or was he writing what would be acceptable to his audience? Are the thoughts of the characters to be read as the thoughts of the writer, or must we determine Marlowe's views by other means? One center of argument has been that Marlowe's poetry seems to contradict his plot: Faustus is damned for his worldly aspirations, yet the poetry reveals a sensuous delight in worldly things. In any case, the play has clearly moved beyond the simple condemnation of Faustus in the *Faustbuch*. Faustus is now a tragic hero, torn between unbounded aspiration and the limitations of human life.

Johann Wolfgang von Goethe (1749–1832), poet and dramatist, was born into a well-to-do burgher family, and his life was spent in prosperity and comfort. He studied law at Leipzig but began writing early and soon won literary fame. In 1775 he was invited to the court of Duke Karl August at Weimar, where he spent the rest of his life, except for several months of writing and study in Italy, as a prominent public official and an honored writer. Besides *Faust*, Goethe was famed for his lyrics and for such works as *The Sorrows of Young Werther* and *Wilhelm Meister's Apprenticeship*.

In his early years Goethe was part of the *Sturm und Drang*, or "storm and stress," movement, a phase of romanticism that rebelled against imitative literature and classical doctrines and instead glorified Shakespeare and the old German epics. After settling in Weimar, Goethe moved toward a more classical approach, seeking balance and serenity in life and art. These two periods in Goethe's life are reflected in the two parts of *Faust*. Goethe worked on *Faust* intermittently for fifty years. Aside from fragments, the work was first published as a whole in 1832 and reflects the evolution of Goethe's thought from youth to age. Faust struggles for perfection, often yielding to evil but never coming to love it. Faust's failure in his quest for absolute knowledge leads to despair, from which he is rescued only by a life of useful labor. Throughout the whole work, the importance of effort and struggle for salvation is central. In his speculation about the scriptures early in Part One, Faust alters the opening words of the Book of John, "In the beginning was the Word," to "In the beginning was the *Deed*." Later he exclaims: "He only earns his freedom and existence who daily conquers them anew."

In Part One of *Faust* Mephistopheles is not so much a melodramatic prince of evil as he is an element of life, the element of negation and cynicism. Faust is the more positive, active force. The Lord of the Prologue, like God in the ancient story of Job, stands above all, confident that Faust will find the right path. However Faust sins, he is destined to retain his sense of what is right and wrong and to keep striving for a better way.

Part One is largely concerned with the story of Margaret. This tale, new to the Faust tradition but destined to be the heart of later operas, enabled Goethe to make the sins of Faust concrete and dramatic. Margaret suffers a terrible fate, and Mephistopheles attempts to divert Faust from his feelings of regret and guilt. Despite the temptations of the Walpurgis Night, however, Faust cannot forget his remorse.

The opening of Part Two reveals Faust in a pleasing landscape, where various ministrations of nature heal him and salve his sense of guilt. He and Mephistopheles then engage in a series of adventures. They entertain the emperor and his court, and Faust solves the emperor's financial problems by introducing paper money. They visit the mysterious land of the Mothers, sources of all earthly forms, from which Faust brings back Helen and Paris of Troy for the delight of the emperor and his court. There is a classical Walpurgis Night in which figures from Greek mythology replace the Germanic ghosts and demons who appeared in the first part of the drama. Faust marries the peerless Helen of Troy, and, like the child of Faust and Helen in the Spies *Faustbuch*, their son, Euphorion, has mysterious powers of prophecy. After a flight like that of Icarus, Euphorion falls at the feet of his parents. A well-known figure (that of Byron, suggesting the spirit of romance) appears in place of the dead child; then all fades away. Helen vanishes, leaving her veil, robe, and lyre on the ground. Finally, Faust turns to social action, draining and clearing land to build an ideal state. In the process Mephistopheles, carrying out Faust's instruction to clear the area, causes the death of two harmless peasants, Philemon and Baucis.

The developments in this second part place Faust in the larger contexts of social and political life, cultural history, and philosophy. The incident with the paper money shows his concern for government and practical matters. The marriage with Helen and the birth of Euphorion symbolize the union of Germanic tradition with that of classical Greece. Thus, there is a mixture of good and evil to the very end of Faust's life.

The version of *Faust* included here consists of Part I (certain scenes such as that in which Mephistopheles cynically advises a student and that in which Mephistopheles takes Faust to Aurbach's Cellar are omitted) and the conclusion of Part Two. The translation is by Louis MacNeice (London: Faber and Faber, 1951).

A brief summary of the entire Part Two may be found in the article by Victor Lange, pp. 171–78.

Thomas Mann (1875–1955), a major German novelist and critic, was born in Lübeck; he moved to Munich after his father died, when he was fifteen. He registered at the university in Munich but did not complete a regular program of study. For a considerable period of time he lived in Palestrina in northern Italy, where he began work on the novel *Buddenbrooks* (1900). The saga of a merchant family of Lübeck traced through four generations of gradual decay, this novel established Mann as a writer.

Mann supported Germany in World War I but went into self-imposed exile after the Nazis took power in 1933. In 1938 he came to the United States and later became an American citizen. In 1954 he returned to Europe and settled near Zurich, where he died in 1955.

In his *Doctor Faustus: The Life of the German Composer Adrian Leverkühn as Told by a Friend* (1947), Mann adapts the Faust story to recount the life of his hero, Leverkühn, and to portray the drama of life in Germany through the end of World War II. Mann contrasts the artist and the "normal" man. Serenus Zeitblom, highly intelligent but prosaic, tells the life story of his devil-ridden friend Leverkühn, the Doctor Faustus of the title. The story begins with Leverkühn's childhood and early education. Adrian lives for a time with an uncle (as did the Doctor Faustus of the *Faustbuch*) and secretly studies music. Like Doctor Faustus, Adrian studies theology and rejects it. Adrian's fall is rooted in his pride, his intellectual arrogance that leads him to feel contempt for teachers and fellow students alike. Like so many others in the twentieth century, he feels alienated from his society. In fact, his alienation as the modern form of damnation is a major theme of the novel. His fall is given concrete form by a brief love episode with a prostitute. He contracts syphilis, which forever debars him from love and increasingly affects his brain.

As with Mann's other work, *Doctor Faustus* is woven of many themes, including the relationship of artist and society, the split between the Catholic and Protestant churches, and argumentation over theology. The portion of the book reprinted here is Chapter 25, in which the devil "actually" appears to Faustus (Leverkühn). This devil is really a projection of one side of Leverkühn's personality. The language of the chapter is archaic German, carrying the reader back in spirit to the time of the first *Faustbuch* and lending an atmosphere of reality to the appearance of the devil. The spelling of some English words has been deliberately altered to achieve an equally archaic effect in the translation.

The confrontation with the devil (Mephistopheles?) is presented as recorded by Leverkühn in an account later found by Zeitblom, the narrator. The interview takes place in Italy, where Leverkühn is staying for a time with his friend Schildknapp. The setting is reflected in the use of some Italian expressions and is also implied in some comments about the relationship between the Protestant north of Germany and Catholic Italy.

The discussion of the state of Leverkühn's mind and the devil's references to the little imps already at work inside his brain are related to his infection with syphilis, improperly treated in its early stages. The prostitute is referred to in these passages as Esmeralda. Leverkühn's madness, then, can be viewed as partly psychological and partly physical.

Leverkühn's "magic," comparable to the necromancy of the first Doctor Faustus, is his advanced, revolutionary music. The bulk of Chapter 25 is devoted to discussion of this music. Adrian is to triumph in his career as a composer through an alliance with the devil. His music will be extreme, barbaric, new. He will live a masterly life as a composer but will never know love or normal happiness. Leverkühn has always been of a cold, mathematical cast of mind, austere, remote, superior to his friends and acquaintances, conscious of his own genius. This is the essential source of his damnation. So the pact with the devil is only a formal recording of what is already a fact. Mann has utilized the old Faust story to treat some of the chief concerns of art, literature, and music in the twentieth century. The breakdown of old forms, the search for revolutionary techniques, and the widespread concern over the collapse of standards all find expression in this music.

Toward the conclusion of the novel, Leverkühn, near his end, invites friends to listen to his "Lamentation of Dr. Faustus," his last great composition. When the guests have gathered, Leverkühn tells the story of his life and his bargain with the devil. The friends conclude, of course, that Leverkühn is mentally ill, and they pack him off to the care of experts.

Mann's novel ends with Zeitblom completing his account of the life of Leverkühn as Germany lies in ruins at the end of World War II. This has often been called a "terminal" work, one which comes at the end of certain developments in western civilization, like James Joyce's *Ulysses* and Marcel Proust's *Remembrance of Things Past*. But although the novel certainly does suggest that one phase of German and European civilization is at an end, it makes equally clear that Germany and her people will go on, whatever new form their lives may take.

Chapter 25 is reprinted here from the translation of *Doctor Faustus* by H. T. Lowe-Porter (New York: Knopf, 1948).

Karl Jay Shapiro (b. 1913) is an American poet. Born in Baltimore, he was educated at the University of Virginia and Johns Hopkins University. He published his first volume of poetry in 1935. Mr. Shapiro is now teaching at the University of Nebraska.

In his "Progress of Faust" Shapiro telescopes the historical and literary versions of the Faust story, making of Faust a sort of wandering Jew who roams from Germany to England, back to Germany, and then on to an atomic testing site in the United States. Shapiro's poem is reprinted from *Poems, 1940–1953* (New York: Random House, 1953).

Footnotes to Marlowe's *Doctor Faustus* and the selection from Mann's *Doctor Faustus* are by the editor of this volume, as are the glosses in Goethe's *Faust*.

CHRISTOPHER MARLOWE

The Tragical History of the Life and Death of Doctor Faustus

CHORUS
DOCTOR JOHN FAUSTUS
WAGNER, *a student, his servant*
THREE SCHOLARS, *students under Faustus*
VALDES *and* CORNELIUS, *friends of Faustus*
AN OLD MAN
RAYMOND, *King of Hungary*
POPE ADRIAN
BRUNO, *the rival pope*
THE CARDINALS OF FRANCE *and* PADUA
THE ARCHBISHOP OF RHEIMS
THE DUKE OF SAXONY
THE DUKE OF ANHOLT
THE DUCHESS OF ANHOLT
CHARLES V, *Emperor of Germany*
MARTINO, FREDERICK, *and* BENVOLIO, *gentlemen of his court*
ROBIN, *a clown*
DICK
VINTNER, HORSE-COURSER (*horse-trader*), CARTER, *and* HOSTESS
GOOD ANGEL
BAD ANGEL
MEPHISTOPHILIS
LUCIFER
BEËLZEBUB
THE SEVEN DEADLY SINS (PRIDE, COVETOUSNESS, ENVY, WRATH, GLUTTONY, SLOTH, *and* LECHERY)
ALEXANDER THE GREAT ⎫
HIS PARAMOUR   ⎬ *spirits*
DARIUS, *King of Persia* ⎪
HELEN OF TROY   ⎭

TWO CUPIDS
DEVILS
PIPER
BISHOPS
MONKS
FRIARS
SERVANTS
SOLDIERS
ATTENDANTS

ACT I

Prologue

Enter CHORUS.

CHOR. Not marching in the fields of Trasi-
mene
Where Mars did mate the warlike Carthagens,°
Nor sporting in the dalliance of love
In courts of kings, where state is overturned,
Nor in the pomp of proud audacious deeds
Intends our Muse to vaunt his heavenly verse.
Only this, gentles: we must now perform
The form of Faustus' fortunes, good or bad.
And now to patient judgments we appeal,
And speak for Faustus in his infancy.   10
Now is he born, of parents base of stock,
In Germany, within a town called Rhode.

Act I, Prol.: 1–2. Trasimene . . . Carthagens: Hannibal won this battle. **mate** suggests "ally himself with."

At riper years to Wittenberg he went,
Whereas his kinsmen chiefly brought him up.
So much he profits in divinity,
The fruitful plot of scholarism graced,°
That shortly he was graced with doctor's name,
Excelling all, whose sweet delight disputes
In th'heavenly matters of theology,
Till swoll'n with cunning of a self-conceit,°   20
His waxen wings did mount above his reach,°
And melting, heavens conspired his overthrow;
For, falling to a devilish exercise
And glutted now with learning's golden gifts,
He surfeits upon cursèd necromancy.
Nothing so sweet as magic is to him,
Which he prefers before his chiefest bliss;
And this the man that in his study sits.   EXIT.

SCENE I

FAUSTUS in his study.

FAUST.   Settle thy studies, Faustus, and begin
To sound the depth of that thou wilt profess.
Having commenced,° be a Divine in show;
Yet level at the end of every art,
And live and die in Aristotle's works.
Sweet Analytics, 'tis thou hast ravished me!
Bene disserere est finis logices.
Is to dispute well Logic's chiefest end?
Affords this Art no greater miracle?
Then read no more; thou hast attained that
    end.   10
A greater subject fitteth Faustus' wit!
Bid <i>On cay mae on</i>° farewell; <i>Galen</i>° come.
Seeing <i>ubi desinit philosophus ibi incipit medi-
cus,</i>°
Be a physician, Faustus; heap up gold,
And be eternized for some wondrous cure.
Summum bonum, medicinae sanitas.
The end of physic is our body's health.
Why, Faustus, hast thou not attained that end?
Is not thy common talk sound aphorisms?°
Are not thy bills° hung up as monuments,   20

16. The . . . graced: He was an ornament to the fruitful garden of scholarship. 20. Till . . . self-conceit: proud of his knowledge. 21. His . . . reach: like the wings of Icarus, which melted when he flew too near the sun.
    Sc. i: 3. commenced: taken his degree. 12. On . . . on: being or not being (Aristotle). Galen: Greek physician. 13. ubi . . . medicus: where the philosopher leaves off, there the physician begins. (adapted from Aristotle). 19. sound aphorisms: reliable medical precepts. 20. bills: prescriptions.

Whereby whole cities have escaped the plague,
And divers desperate maladies been cured?
Yet art thou still but Faustus and a man.
Couldst thou make men to live eternally,
Or, being dead, raise them to life again,
Then this profession were to be esteemed.
Physic, farewell! Where is Justinian?
    [He reads.]
Si una eademque res legatus duobus,
Alter rem, alter valorem rei,</i>° etc.
A petty case of paltry legacies!   30
    [He reads.]
Exhaereditare filium non potest pater nisi—°
Such is the subject of the Institute
And universal body of the law.
This study fits a mercenary drudge
Who aims at nothing but external trash,
Too servile and illiberal for me.
When all is done, divinity is best.
Jeromè's Bible,° Faustus, view it well:
    [He reads.]
Stipendium peccati mors est. Ha! Stipendium,
    etc.
The reward of sin is death. That's hard.   40
    [He reads.]
Si peccasse negamus, fallimur
Et nulla est in nobis veritas.
If we say that we have no sin,
We deceive ourselves, and there's no truth in us.
Why then belike we must sin,
And so consequently die.
Ay, we must die, an everlasting death.
What doctrine call you this? <i>Che serà, serà:</i>
What will be, shall be! Divinity, adieu!
These metaphysics° of magicians   50
And necromantic books are heavenly.
Lines, circles, signs, letters, and characters—
Ay, these are those that Faustus most desires.
O, what a world of profit and delight,
Of power, of honor, of omnipotence
Is promised to the studious artisan!
All things that move between the quiet poles
Shall be at my command. Emperors and kings
Are but obeyed in their several provinces,

28–29. Si . . . rei: If the same thing is bequeathed to two persons, one shall have the thing itself, the other its value. 31. Exhaereditare . . . nisi: A father cannot disinherit his son except . . . . 38. Jeromè's Bible: the <i>Vulgate.</i> The sentences Faustus translates are from Rom. 6:23 and John 1:8 50. metaphysics: supernatural powers.

Nor can they raise the wind or rend the clouds,
But his dominion that exceeds in this   61
Stretcheth as far as doth the mind of man.
A sound magician is a demi-god.
Here try thy brains to get a deity!
    Enter WAGNER.
Wagner! Commend me to my dearest friends,
The German Valdes and Cornelius;
Request them earnestly to visit me.
    WAG. I will sir.   EXIT.
    FAUST. Their conference will be a greater
    help to me
Than all my labors, plod I ne'er so fast.   70
    Enter the GOOD ANGEL *and the* EVIL ANGEL.
    G. ANG. O, Faustus, lay that damnèd book
    aside,
And gaze not on it, lest it tempt thy soul
And heap God's heavy wrath upon thy head.
Read, read the Scriptures. That is blasphemy.
    BAD ANG. Go forward, Faustus, in that fa-
    mous art
Wherein all nature's treasury is contained.
Be thou on earth as Jove is in the sky,
Lord and commander of these elements.
                              EXEUNT ANGELS.
    FAUST. How am I glutted with conceit of
    this!°
Shall I make spirits fetch me what I please,   80
Resolve me of all ambiguities,
Perform what desperate enterprise I will?
I'll have them fly to India for gold,
Ransack the ocean for orient pearl,
And search all corners of the new-found world
For pleasant fruits and princely delicates.
I'll have them read me strange philosophy
And tell the secrets of all foreign kings;
I'll have them wall all Germany with brass   89
And make swift Rhine circle fair Wittenberg.
I'll have them fill the public schools with silk
Wherewith the students shall be bravely clad.
I'll levy soldiers with the coin they bring
And chase the Prince of Parma° from our land
And reign sole king of all the provinces.
Yea, stranger engines for the brunt of war
Than was the fiery keel at Antwerp's bridge°
I'll make my servile spirits to invent.

Come, German Valdes and Cornelius,
                        [*He calls within.*]
And make me blessed with your sage confer-
    ence!   100
    Enter VALDES *and* CORNELIUS.
Valdes, sweet Valdes, and Cornelius,
Know that your words have won me at the last
To practice magic and concealèd arts;
Yet not your words only, but mine own fantasy
That will receive no object, for my head
But ruminates on necromantic skill.
Philosophy is odious and obscure;
Both law and physic are for petty wits;
Divinity is basest of the three,
Unpleasant, harsh, contemptible and vile.   110
'Tis magic, magic, that hath ravished me.
Then, gentle friends, aid me in this attempt,
And I, that have with subtle syllogisms
Gravelled° the pastors of the German church,
And made the flowering pride of Wittenberg
Swarm to my problems° as th'infernal spirits
On sweet Musaeus° when he came to hell,
Will be as cunning as Agrippa° was,
Whose shadows made all Europe honor him.
    VALD. Faustus, these books, thy wit, and our
    experience   120
Shall make all nations to canonize us.
As Indian Moors° obey their Spanish lords,
So shall the spirits of every element
Be always serviceable to us three.
Like lions shall they guard us when we please,
Like Almain rutters° with their horsemen's
    staves
Or Lapland giants trotting by our sides,
Sometimes like women or unwedded maids,
Shadowing more beauty in their airy brows
Than in the white breasts of the queen of love.
From Venice shall they drag huge argosies,   131
And from America the golden fleece
That yearly stuffs old Philip's treasury,
If learnèd Faustus will be resolute.
    FAUST. Valdes, as resolute am I in this
As thou to live; therefore object it not.
    CORN. The miracles that magic will perform

79. glutted . . . this: filled with this idea. 94.
Prince of Parma: the Spanish governor general of
the Netherlands. 97. fiery . . . bridge: a fire ship
used by the Dutch to destroy a bridge.

114. Gravelled: perplexed. 116. problems: questions for argument. 117. Musaeus: legendary Greek
poet, presumed author of *Hero and Leander.* 118.
Agrippa: magician (1486–1535) said to have power
to raise the dead. 122. Indian Moors: American In-
dians. 126. Almain rutters: German troopers.

Will make thee vow to study nothing else.
He that is grounded in astrology,   139
Enriched with tongues,° well seen in minerals,
Hath all the principles magic doth require.
Then doubt not, Faustus, but to be renowned
And more frequented for this mystery
Than heretofore the Delphian oracle.
The spirits tell me they can dry the sea
And fetch the treasure of all foreign wracks,
Yea, all the wealth that our forefathers hid
Within the massy entrails of the earth.
Then tell me, Faustus, what shall we three want?

FAUST. Nothing, Cornelius. O, this cheers
    my soul!   150
Come, show me some demonstrations magical,
That I may conjure in some lusty grove
And have these joys in full possession.

VALD.   Then haste thee to some solitary grove,
And bear wise Bacon's° and Abanus'° works,
The Hebrew Psalter, and New Testament;
And whatsoever else is requisite
We will inform thee ere our conference cease.

CORN.   Valdes, first let him know the words
    of art,
And then, all other ceremonies learned,   160
Faustus may try his cunning° by himself.

VALD.   First I'll instruct thee in the rudi-
    ments,
And then wilt thou be perfecter than I.

FAUST.   Then come and dine with me, and
    after meat
We'll canvass every quiddity° thereof,
For ere I sleep I'll try what I can do.
This night I'll conjure, though I die therefore.

                            EXEUNT omnes.

SCENE II

Enter two SCHOLARS.

FIRST SCHOL.   I wonder what's become of
Faustus, that was wont to make our schools ring
with *sic probo.*°

Enter WAGNER.

SECOND SCHOL.   That shall we presently
know; here comes his boy.

---

140. tongues: especially Latin, used in calling up spirits. 155. Bacon: Roger Bacon (1214?–94). Abanus:
Pietro D'Abano (1250–1316). Both were supposed to
be magicians. 161. cunning: skill. 165. quiddity:
essential particular.
Sc. ii: 3. sic probo: thus I prove (a scholastic
formula).

FIRST SCHOL.   How now sirrah! Where's thy
master?

WAG.   God in heaven knows.

SEC. SCHOL.   Why, dost not thou know then?

WAG.   Yes, I know, but that follows not.   10

FIRST SCHOL.   Go to, sirrah! Leave your jesting and tell us where he is.

WAG.   That follows not by force of argument,
which you, being licentiates,° should stand
upon; therefore acknowledge your error and be
attentive.

SEC. SCHOL.   Then you will not tell us?

WAG.   You are deceived, for I will tell you.
Yet if you were not dunces, you would never ask
me such a question. For is he not *corpus* [20
naturale, and is not that *mobile?*° Then wherefore should you ask me such a question? But that
I am by nature phlegmatic, slow to wrath, and
prone to lechery—to love, I would say—it were
not for you to come within forty foot of the
place of execution, although I do not doubt but
to see you both hanged the next sessions. Thus
having triumphed over you, I will set my countenance like a precisian° and begin to speak
thus: Truly, my dear brethren, my master [30
is within at dinner with Valdes and Cornelius,
as this wine, if it could speak, would inform your
worships. And so, the Lord bless you, preserve
you, and keep you, my dear brethren.   EXIT.

FIRST SCHOL.   O Faustus, then I fear that
    which I have long suspected.
That thou art fall'n into that damnèd art
For which they two are infamous through the
    world.

SEC. SCHOL.   Were he a stranger, not allied
    to me,
The danger of his soul would make me mourn.
But come, let us go and inform the rector.°   40
It may be his grave counsel may reclaim him.

FIRST SCHOL.   I fear me nothing will reclaim
    him now.

SEC. SCHOL.   Yet let us see what we can do.
                                    EXEUNT.

SCENE III

Thunder. Enter [above] LUCIFER *and
four* DEVILS. *Enter* FAUSTUS *to conjure.*

---

14. licentiates: those licensed to work toward a
Master's degree. 20–21. corpus . . . mobile: a scholastic expression for the subject matter of physics.
29. precisian: puritan. 40. rector: head of the university.

FAUST.   Now that the gloomy shadow of the
   night,
Longing to view Orion's drizzling look,
Leaps from th'Antarctic world unto the sky
And dims the welkin with her pitchy breath,
Faustus begin thine incantations,
And try if devils will obey thy hest,
Seeing thou hast prayed and sacrificed to them.
Within this circle is Jehovah's name,
Forward and backward anagrammatized,
Th'abbreviated names of holy saints,   10
Figures of every adjunct to the heavens,°
And characters of signs and erring stars,°
By which the spirits are enforced to rise.
Then fear not, Faustus, to be resolute,
And try the utmost magic can perform.
                         Thunder.
Sint mihi Dei Acherontis propitii! Valeat numen
triplex Jehovae. Ignei, aerii, aquatani spiritus,
salvete! Orientis princeps, Beëlzebub, inferni ar-
dentis monarcha, et Demogorgon, propitiamus
vos, ut appareat et surgat Mephistophilis. [20
Quid tu moraris? Per Jehovam, Gehennam, et
consecratam aquam quam nunc spargo, signum-
que crucis quod nunc facio, et per vota nostra,
ipse nunc surgat nobis dicatus Mephistophilis.°
      Enter [MEPHISTOPHILIS] *a* DEVIL
I charge thee to return and change thy shape;
Thou art too ugly to attend on me.
Go, and return an old Franciscan friar;
That holy shape becomes a devil best.
                      EXIT DEVIL.
I see there's virtue in my heavenly words.
Who would not be proficient in this art?   30
How pliant is this Mephistophilis,
Full of obedience and humility.
Such is the force of magic and my spells.
      Enter MEPHISTOPHILIS
MEPH.   Now Faustus, what wouldst thou
   have me do?

FAUST.   I charge thee wait upon me whilst I
   live,
To do whatever Faustus shall command,
Be it to make the moon drop from her sphere
Or the ocean to overwhelm the world.
MEPH.   I am a servant to great Lucifer
And may not follow thee without his leave.   40
No more than he commands must we perform.
FAUST.   Did not he charge thee to appear to
   me?
MEPH.   No, I came hither of mine own ac-
   cord.
FAUST.   Did not my conjuring raise thee?
   Speak.
MEPH.   That was the cause, but yet *per ac-*
   cidens,°
For when we hear one rack the name of God,
Abjure the Scriptures and his Savior Christ,
We fly in hope to get his glorious soul;
Nor will we come unless he use such means
Whereby he is in danger to be damned.   50
Therefore the shortest cut for conjuring
Is stoutly to abjure the Trinity
And pray devoutly to the prince of hell.
FAUST.   So Faustus hath
Already done, and holds this principle:
There is no chief but only Beëlzebub,
To whom Faustus doth dedicate himself.
This word 'damnation' terrifies not me,
For I confound hell in Elysium.°
My ghost be with the old philosophers!°   60
But leaving these vain trifles of men's souls,
Tell me, what is that Lucifer thy lord?
MEPH.   Arch-regent and commander of all
   spirits.
FAUST.   Was not that Lucifer an angel once?
MEPH.   Yes Faustus, and most dearly loved of
   God.
FAUST.   How comes it then that he is prince
   of devils?
MEPH.   O, by aspiring pride and insolence,
For which God threw him from the face of
   heaven.
FAUST.   And what are you that live with Lu-
   cifer?

Sc. iii: 11. adjunct . . . heavens: every star joined
to the heavens. 12. signs . . . stars: signs of the
Zodiac and planets. 16–24. Sint . . . Mephistophilis: May the gods of Acheron be propitious to me.
Away with the threefold name of Jehovah. Hail spirits of fire, air, and water. The prince of the east,
Beëlzebub [Lucifer], monarch of burning hell, and
Demogorgon, we propitiate you that Mephistophilis
may appear and rise! Why do you delay? By Jehovah,
hell, and the holy water which I now sprinkle, and
by the sign of the cross which I now make, and by
our prayers, let Mephistophilis now rise to serve us.

45. per accidens: a scholastic term. Mephistophilis
was not raised by the conjuring directly but came
because of the insults to the name of God. 59. I
. . . Elysium: I do not believe in heaven and hell
but only an afterlife in Elysium. 60. old philosophers: who also did not believe in an eternity of reward and punishment.

MEPH.   Unhappy spirits that fell with Lucifer,
Conspired against our God with Lucifer,   71
And are for ever damned with Lucifer.
  FAUST.   Where are you damned?
  MEPH.   In hell.
  FAUST.   How comes it then that thou art out
    of hell?
  MEPH.   Why this is hell, nor am I out of it.
Think'st thou that I who saw the face of God
And tasted the eternal joys of heaven
Am not tormented with ten thousand hells
In being deprived of everlasting bliss?
O Faustus, leave these frivolous demands   80
Which strike a terror to my fainting soul.
  FAUST.   What, is great Mephistophilis so pas-
    sionate
For being deprivèd of the joys of heaven?
Learn thou of Faustus manly fortitude,
And scorn those joys thou never shalt possess.
Go bear these tidings to great Lucifer:
Seeing Faustus hath incurred eternal death
By desperate thoughts against Jove's deity,
Say he surrenders up to him his soul,
So he will spare him four and twenty years,   90
Letting him live in all voluptuousness,
Having thee ever to attend on me,
To give me whatsoever I shall ask,
To tell me whatsoever I demand,
To slay mine enemies, and aid my friends,
And always be obedient to my will.
Go, and return to mighty Lucifer,
And meet me in my study at midnight,
And then resolve me of thy master's mind.
  MEPH.   I will, Faustus.   100
                              EXIT.
  FAUST.   Had I as many souls as there be stars,
I'd give them all for Mephistophilis.
By him I'll be great emperor of the world,
And make a bridge thorough the moving air,
To pass the ocean with a band of men.
I'll join the hills that bind the Afric shore,
And make that country continent to Spain,
And both contributory to my crown.
The Emperor shall not live but by my leave,
Nor any potentate of Germany.   110
Now that I have obtained what I desire,
I'll live in speculation° of this art
Till Mephistophilis return again.   EXIT.

112. speculation: contemplation.

SCENE IV

Enter WAGNER *and* [ROBIN] *the* CLOWN.
  WAG.   Come hither, sirrah boy.
  ROB.   Boy! O disgrace to my person. Zounds,°
boy in your face! You have seen many boys with
such pickedevants,° I am sure.
  WAG.   Sirrah, hast thou no comings in?°
  ROB.   Yes, and goings out too, you may see,
sir.
  WAG.   Alas, poor slave! See how poverty jests
in his nakedness. I know the villain's out of service, and so hungry that I know he would   [10
give his soul to the devil for a shoulder of mutton, though it were blood-raw.
  ROB.   Not so neither. I had need to have it
well roasted, and good sauce to it, if I pay so
dear, I can tell you.
  WAG.   Sirrah, wilt thou be my man and wait
on me, and I will make thee go like *Qui mihi
discipulus?*°
  ROB.   What, in verse?
  WAG.   No slave; in beaten silk° and   [20
staves-acre.°
  ROB.   Staves-acre? That's good to kill vermin.
Then, belike, if I serve you I shall be lousy.
  WAG.   Why, so thou shalt be, whether thou
dost it or no; for, sirrah, if thou dost not presently bind thyself to me for seven years, I'll turn
all the lice about thee into familiars° and make
them tear thee in pieces.
  ROB.   Nay sir, you may save yourself a labor,
for they are as familiar with me as if they   [30
paid for their meat and drink, I can tell you.
  WAG.   Well, sirrah, leave your jesting and
take these guilders.°
  ROB.   Yes, marry sir, and I thank you too.
  WAG.   So, now thou art to be at an hour's
warning, whensoever and wheresoever the devil
shall fetch thee.
  ROB.   Here, take your guilders. I'll none of
'em.

Sc. iv: 2. Zounds: by God's wounds. 4. pickedevants: pointed beards. 5. comings in: earnings. 17–
18. Qui mihi discipulus: You who are my pupil (the
first words of a Latin poem by William Lyly). 20.
beaten silk: silk with metal hammered in. Wagner
suggests in a pun that he will beat Robin. 21. staves-
acre: seeds of delphinium, used for killing lice. 27.
familiars: attendant spirits. 33. guilders: Dutch coins.

WAG. Not I. Thou art pressed.° Pre- [40
pare thyself, for I will presently raise up two
devils to carry thee away. Banio! Belcher!

ROB. Belcher? And Belcher come here, I'll
belch him. I am not afraid of a devil.

Enter two DEVILS.

WAG. How now, sir? Will you serve me now?

ROB. Ay, good Wagner; take away the devil
then.

WAG. Spirits away! Now, sirrah, follow me.

ROB. I will sir. But hark you, master, will you
teach me this conjuring occupation?   [50

WAG. Ay, sirrah. I'll teach thee to turn thyself to a dog, or a cat, or a mouse, or a rat, or
any thing.

ROB. A dog, or a cat, or a mouse, or a rat!
O brave Wagner!

WAG. Villain, call me Master Wagner, and
see that you walk attentively, and let your right
eye be always diametrally° fixed upon my left
heel, that thou may'st *quasi vestigias nostras
insistere.*°   [60

ROB. Well, sir, I warrant you.   EXEUNT.

ACT II

SCENE I

Enter FAUSTUS *in his Study.*

FAUST. Now Faustus must thou needs be
    damned,
And canst thou not be saved.
What boots it then to think on God or heaven?
Away with such vain fancies, and despair;
Despair in God, and trust in Beëlzebub.
Now go not backward; Faustus, be resolute.
Why waver'st thou? O, something soundeth in
    mine ear:
'Abjure this magic; turn to God again.'
Ay, and Faustus will turn to God again!
To God? He loves thee not.   10
The God thou serv'st is thine own appetite,
Wherein is fixed the love of Beëlzebub.
To him I'll build an altar and a church,
And offer lukewarm blood of new-born babes.

Enter the two ANGELS.

B. ANG. Go forward, Faustus, in that famous
    art.

G. ANG. Sweet Faustus, leave that execrable
    art.

FAUST. Contrition, prayer, repentance—what
    of these?

G. ANG. O, they are means to bring thee unto
    heaven.

B. ANG. Rather illusions, fruits of lunacy,   19
That make men foolish that do use them most.

G. ANG. Sweet Faustus, think of heaven and
    heavenly things.

B. ANG. No Faustus; think of honor and
    wealth.   EXEUNT ANGELS.

FAUST. Wealth? Why, the signory of Em-
    den° shall be mine.
When Mephistophilis shall stand by me,
What power can hurt me? Faustus thou art safe.
Cast° no more doubts. Mephistophilis, come
And bring glad tidings from great Lucifer.
Is't not midnight? Come, Mephistophilis,
Veni, veni, Mephistophile.

Enter MEPHISTOPHILIS.

Now tell me what saith Lucifer, thy lord?   30

MEPH. That I shall wait on Faustus whilst he
    lives,
So he will buy my service with his soul.

FAUST. Already Faustus hath hazarded that
    for thee.

MEPH. But now thou must bequeath it sol-
    emnly
And write a deed of gift with thine own blood,
For that security craves great Lucifer.
If thou deny it, I must back to hell.

FAUST. Stay, Mephistophilis! Tell me what
    good
Will my soul do thy lord.

MEPH.   Enlarge his kingdom.

FAUST. Is that the reason why he tempts us
    thus?   40

MEPH. *Solamen miseris socios habuisse do-
    loris.*°

FAUST. Why, have you any pain that torture
    others?

MEPH. As great as have the human souls of
    men.
But tell me, Faustus, shall I have thy soul?
And I will be thy slave and wait on thee
And give thee more than thou hast wit to ask.

FAUST. Ay, Mephistophilis, I'll give it him.

40. pressed: hired, drafted. 58. diametrally: directly. 59–60. quasi . . . insistere: walk in my tracks.
Act II, Sc. i: 23. Emden: a great port city in
Friesland. 26. Cast: consider. 41. Solamen . . .
doloris: Misery loves company.

MEPH.   Then Faustus, stab thy arm coura-
geously,
And bind thy soul that at some certain day
Great Lucifer may claim it as his own,   50
And then be thou as great as Lucifer.
FAUST.   [*stabbing his arm*]   Lo, Mephisto, for
love of thee,
I cut mine arm, and with my proper blood
Assure my soul to be great Lucifer's,
Chief lord and regent of perpetual night.
View here this blood that trickles from mine
arm,
And let it be propitious for my wish.
MEPH.   But Faustus,
Write it in manner of a deed of gift.
FAUST.   Ay, so I do. But Mephistophilis,   60
My blood congeals, and I can write no more.
MEPH.   I'll fetch thee fire to dissolve it
straight.   EXIT.
FAUST.   What might the staying of my blood
portend?
Is it unwilling I should write this bill?
Why streams it not that I may write afresh?
'Faustus gives to thee his soul.' Ah, there it
stayed.
Why shouldst thou not? Is not thy soul thine
own?
Then write again: 'Faustus gives to thee his
soul.'
Enter MEPHISTOPHILIS *with the chafer
of fire.*
MEPH.   See Faustus, here is fire. Set it on.°
FAUST.   So. Now the blood begins to clear
again.   70
Now will I make an end immediately.
MEPH.   What will not I do to obtain his soul?
FAUST.   *Consummatum est;*° this bill is
ended,
And Faustus hath bequeathed his soul to Lucifer.
But what is this inscription on mine arm?
Homo fuge!° Whither should I fly?
If unto God, he'll throw me down to hell.
My senses are deceived; here's nothing writ.
O yes, I see it plain. Even here is writ
Homo fuge! Yet shall not Faustus fly.   80
MEPH.   I'll fetch him somewhat to delight
his mind.   EXIT.

69. Set it on: the dish of blood.   73. Consummatum est: "It is finished," the last words of Christ
on the cross. (John, 19:30).   76. Homo fuge: Man,
fly.

Enter DEVILS, *giving crowns and rich
apparel to* FAUSTUS. *They dance and then
depart. Enter* MEPHISTOPHILIS.
FAUST.   What means this show? Speak Meph-
istophilis.
MEPH.   Nothing, Faustus, but to delight thy
mind
And let thee see what magic can perform.
FAUST.   But may I raise such spirits when I
please?
MEPH.   Ay Faustus, and do greater things
than these.
FAUST.   Then, Mephistophilis, receive this
scroll,
A deed of gift of body and of soul,
But yet conditionally that thou perform
All covenants and articles between us both.   90
MEPH.   Faustus, I swear by hell and Lucifer
To effect all promises between us made.
FAUST.   Then hear me read it Mephistophilis.
*On these conditions following: First, that Faus-
tus may be a spirit in form and substance; Secondly, that Mephistophilis shall be his servant
and be at his command; Thirdly, that Mephistophilis shall do for him and bring him whatsoever; Fourthly, that he shall be in his chamber
or house invisible; Lastly, that he shall ap-* [100
*pear to the said John Faustus at all times, in
what form or shape soever he please: I, John
Faustus, of Wittenberg, doctor, by these presents,
do give both body and soul to Lucifer, Prince
of the East, and his minister, Mephistophilis;
and furthermore grant unto them that four and
twenty years being expired, the articles above
written inviolate, full power to fetch or carry the
said John Faustus, body and soul, flesh, blood, or
goods, into their habitation wheresoever.* [110
By me, John Faustus.
MEPH.   Speak Faustus. Do you deliver this as
your deed?
FAUST.   Ay, take it, and the devil give thee
good of it.
MEPH.   So now, Faustus, ask me what thou
wilt.
FAUST.   First will I question with thee about
hell.
Tell me, where is the place that men call hell?
MEPH.   Under the heavens.
FAUST.   Ay, so are all things else. But where-
abouts?
MEPH.   Within the bowels of these elements,

Where we are tortured and remain for ever.   120
Hell hath no limits, nor is circumscribed
In one self place, but where we are is hell,
And where hell is, there must we ever be.
And, to be short, when all the world dissolves
And every creature shall be purified,
All places shall be hell that is not heaven.

FAUST.   I think hell's a fable.

MEPH.   Ay, think so still, till experience
change thy mind.

FAUST.   Why, dost thou think that Faustus
shall be damned?   130

MEPH.   Ay, of necessity, for here's the scroll
In which thou hast given thy soul to Lucifer.

FAUST.   Ay, and body too. But what of that?
Think'st thou that Faustus is so fond to imagine
That after this life there is any pain?
No, these are trifles and mere old wives' tales.

MEPH.   But I am an instance to prove the
contrary,
For I tell thee I am damned and now in hell.

FAUST.   Nay, and this be hell, I'll willingly be
damned.
What? Sleeping, eating, walking and disputing?
But, leaving off this, let me have a wife,   141
The fairest maid in Germany,
For I am wanton and lascivious,
And cannot live without a wife.

MEPH.   I prithee, Faustus, talk not of a wife.

FAUST.   Nay, sweet Mephistophilis, fetch me
one, for I will have one.

MEPH.   Well, Faustus, thou shalt have a wife.
Sit there till I come.

Enter [MEPHISTOPHILIS] *with a* DEVIL
dressed like a woman, with fireworks.

FAUST.   What sight is this?

MEPH.   Now Faustus, how dost thou like thy
wife?

FAUST.   Here's a hot whore indeed! No, I'll
no wife.   150

MEPH.   Marriage is but a ceremonial toy,
And if thou lovest me, think no more of it.
I'll cull thee out the fairest courtesans
And bring them every morning to thy bed.
She whom thine eye shall like, thy heart shall
have,
Were she as chaste as was Penelope,°
As wise as Saba,° or as beautiful
As was bright Lucifer before his fall.

156. **Penelope:** wife of Ulysses in the *Odyssey*.   157.
Saba: Queen of Sheba.

Hold; take this book; peruse it thoroughly.
The iterating° of these lines brings gold;   160
The framing of this circle on the ground
Brings thunder, whirlwinds, storm and lightning.
Pronounce this thrice devoutly to thyself,
And men in harness° shall appear to thee,
Ready to execute what thou command'st.

FAUST.   Thanks, Mephistophilis, for this
sweet book.
This will I keep as chary as my life.   EXEUNT.

SCENE II

Enter FAUSTUS *in his study and* MEPH-
ISTOPHILIS.

FAUST.   When I behold the heavens, then I
repent
And curse thee, wicked Mephistophilis,
Because thou hast deprived me of those joys.

MEPH.   'Twas thine own seeking, Faustus;
thank thyself.
But think'st thou heaven is such a glorious thing?
I tell thee, Faustus, 'tis not half so fair
As thou, or any man that breathes on earth.

FAUST.   How prov'st thou that?

MEPH.   'Twas made for man; then he's more
excellent.

FAUST.   If heaven was made for man, 'twas
made for me.   10
I will renounce this magic and repent.

Enter the two ANGELS.

G. ANG.   Faustus repent; yet God will pity
thee.

B. ANG.   Thou art a spirit;° God cannot pity
thee.

FAUST.   Who buzzeth in mine ears I am a
spirit?
Be I a devil, yet God may pity me;
Yea, God will pity me if I repent.

B. ANG.   Ay, but Faustus never shall repent.

EXEUNT ANGELS.

FAUST.   My heart is hardened; I cannot re-
pent.
Scarce can I name salvation, faith, or heaven,
But fearful echoes thunder in mine ears: 20
'Faustus, thou art damned!' Then swords and
knives,
Poison, guns, halters, and envenomed steel
Are laid before me to dispatch myself;

160. **iterating:** repetition.   164. **harness:** armor.
Sc. ii: 13. spirit: devil.

And long ere this I should have done the deed,
Had not sweet pleasure conquered deep despair.
Have not I made blind Homer sing to me
Of Alexander's love and Oenon's° death?
And hath not he,° that built the walls of Thebes
With ravishing sound of his melodious harp,
Made music with my Mephistophilis?   30
Why should I die then, or basely despair?
I am resolved; Faustus shall not repent.
Come, Mephistophilis, let us dispute again
And reason of divine astrology.
Speak; are there many spheres above the moon?
Are all celestial bodies but one globe,
As is the substance of this centric earth?

    MEPH.   As are the elements, such are the
        heavens,
Even from the moon unto the empyreal orb,
Mutually folded in each others' spheres,   40
And jointly move upon one axle-tree,
Whose terminè° is termed the world's wide pole;
Nor are the names of Saturn, Mars, or Jupiter
Feigned, but are erring stars.

    FAUST.   But have they all
One motion, both *situ et tempore?*°

    MEPH.   All move from east to west in four
and twenty hours upon the poles of the world,
but differ in their motions upon the poles of the
zodiac.

    FAUST.   These slender questions Wagner can
        decide.   50
Hath Mephistophilis no greater skill?
Who knows not the double motion of the plan-
ets?
That the first is finished in a natural day?
The second thus? Saturn in thirty years?
Jupiter in twelve; Mars in four; the sun, Venus and
Mercury in a year; the moon in twenty eight days?
These are freshmen's suppositions. But tell me,
hath every sphere a dominion or *intelligentia?*°

    MEPH.   Ay.

    FAUST.   How many heavens, or spheres,   [60
are there?

    MEPH.   Nine—the seven planets, the firma-
ment, and the empyreal heaven.

27. **Alexander's . . . Oenon's:** Paris, the shepherd
lover of Oenon, later seduced Helen, wife of Menelaus. 28. **he:** Amphion, who played on the lyre so
skillfully that stones moved to build the walls of
Thebes. 42. **terminè:** end. 45. **situ et tempore:** in
position and time. Do they move in the same direction and time around the earth? 58. **intelligentia:**
angels that govern the spheres.

    FAUST.   But is there not *coelum igneum, et
crystallinum?*°

    MEPH.   No, Faustus, they be but fables.

    FAUST.   Resolve me then in this one question:
why are not conjunctions,° oppositions,° aspects,° eclipses all at one time, but in some years
we have more, in some less?   70

    MEPH.   *Per inaequalem motum respectu to-
tius.*°

    FAUST.   Well, I am answered. Now tell me
who made the world.

    MEPH.   I will not.

    FAUST.   Sweet Mephistophilis, tell me.

    MEPH.   Move° me not, Faustus.

    FAUST.   Villain, have not I bound thee to
tell me any thing?   79

    MEPH.   Ay, that is not against our kingdom.
This is. Thou art damned. Think thou of hell.

    FAUST.   Think, Faustus, upon God that made
        the world.

    MEPH.   Remember this.   EXIT.

    FAUST.   Ay, go accursèd spirit to ugly hell.
'Tis thou hast damned distressèd Faustus' soul.
Is't not too late?

        Enter the two ANGELS.

    B. ANG.   Too late.

    G. ANG.   Never too late, if Faustus will repent.

    B. ANG.   If thou repent, devils will tear thee
        in pieces.

    G. ANG.   Repent, and they shall never raze thy
        skin.   90

        EXEUNT ANGELS.

    FAUST.   O Christ, my Savior, my Savior,
Help to save distressèd Faustus' soul.

    Enter LUCIFER, BEËLZEBUB, *and* MEPH-
ISTOPHILIS.

    LUC.   Christ cannot save thy soul, for he is
        just.
There's none but I have interest in the same.

    FAUST.   O, what art thou that look'st so ter-
        ribly?

    LUC.   I am Lucifer,
And this is my companion prince in hell.

    FAUST.   O, Faustus, they are come to fetch
        thy soul.

65. **coelum . . . crystallinum:** the crystalline and
fiery spheres of Ptolemaic astronomy. 68. **conjunctions:** apparent proximities of two heavenly bodies.
oppositions: divergences of heavenly bodies. 69. **aspects:** various relative positions. 71–72. **Per . . .
totius:** because of their unequal motions in relation
to the whole. 77. **Move:** anger.

BEËL.   We are come to tell thee thou dost injure us.

LUC.   Thou call'st on Christ, contrary to thy promise.   100

BEËL.   Thou shouldst not think on God.

LUC.   Think on the devil.

BEËL.   And his dam too.

FAUST.   Nor will I henceforth. Pardon me in this,
And Faustus vows never to look to heaven,
Never to name God, or to pray to him,
To burn his Scriptures, slay his ministers,
And make my spirits pull his churches down.

LUC.   So shalt thou show thyself an obedient servant,
And we will highly gratify thee for it.   110

BEËL.   Faustus, we are come from hell in person to show thee some pastime. Sit down, and thou shalt behold the Seven Deadly Sins appear to thee in their own proper shapes and likeness.

FAUST.   That sight will be as pleasant to me as Paradise was to Adam the first day of his creation.

LUC.   Talk not of Paradise or creation, but mark the show. Go, Mephistophilis, fetch them in.   120

                    [EXIT MEPHISTOPHILIS.]

Enter the SEVEN DEADLY SINS, [*with*
MEPHISTOPHILIS, *led by a* PIPER].

BEËL.   Now Faustus, question them of their names and dispositions.

FAUST.   That shall I soon. What art thou, the first?

PRIDE.   I am Pride. I disdain to have any parents. I am like to Ovid's flea:° I can creep into every corner of a wench. Sometimes, like a periwig, I sit upon her brow. Next, like a necklace, I hang about her neck. Then, like a fan of feathers, I kiss her lips, and then, turning [130 myself to a wrought smock, do what I list.° But fie, what a smell is here! I'll not speak another word unless the ground be perfumed and covered with cloth of Arras.°

FAUST.   Thou art a proud knave indeed. What art thou, the second?

COVETOUSNESS.   I am Covetousness, begotten

of an old churl in a leather bag, and might I now obtain my wish, this house, you and all, should turn to gold, that I might lock [140 you safe into my chest. O my sweet gold!

FAUST.   And what art thou, the third?

ENVY.   I am Envy, begotten of a chimney-sweeper and an oyster-wife. I cannot read and therefore wish all books burned. I am lean with seeing others eat. O, that there would come a famine over all the world, that all might die, and I live alone; then thou shouldst see how fat I'd be. But must thou sit and I stand? Come down, with a vengeance.   150

FAUST.   Out envious wretch! But what are thou, the fourth?

WRATH.   I am Wrath. I had neither father nor mother. I leaped out of a lion's mouth when I was scarce an hour old, and ever since have run up and down the world with this case of rapiers, wounding myself when I could get none to fight withal. I was born in hell, and look to it, for some of you shall be my father.

FAUST.   And what are you, the fifth?   160

GLUTTONY.   I am Gluttony. My parents are all dead, and the devil a penny they have left me but a small pension, and that buys me thirty meals a day and ten bevers°—a small trifle to suffice nature. I come of a royal pedigree. My father was a gammon of bacon, and my mother was a hogshead of claret wine. My godfathers were these: Peter Pickled-herring and Martin Martlemas-beef.° But my godmother, O, she was a jolly gentlewoman, and well beloved in [170 every good town and city; her name was Mistress Margery March-beer.° Now Faustus, thou hast heard all my progeny; wilt thou bid me to a supper?

FAUST.   Not I. Thou wilt eat up all my victuals.

GLUTTONY.   Then the devil choke thee.

FAUST.   Choke thyself, glutton. What art thou, the sixth?

SLOTH.   Heigh ho! I am Sloth. I was [180 begotten on a sunny bank, where I have lain ever since, and you have done me great injury to bring me from thence. Let me be carried thither again by Gluttony and Lechery. Heigh

---

126. **Ovid's flea:** *Elegia de pulice,* a medieval poem, was incorrectly attributed to the Roman poet Ovid. 131. **list:** wish.   134. **cloth of Arras:** Use of such rich cloth on the floor would be characteristic of Pride.

164. **bevers:** snacks.   169. **Martlemas-beef:** meat salted on Martinmas, November 11th, for use in the winter.   172. **March-beer:** strong beer made in March.

ho! I'll not speak a word more for a king's ransom.

FAUST.   And what are you Mistress Minx, the seventh and last?

LECHERY.   Who, I, sir? I am one that loves an inch of raw mutton° better than an   [190 ell of fried stockfish,° and the first letter of my name begins with lechery.

LUC.   Away to hell! Away! On piper!

EXEUNT *the* SEVEN SINS [*and the* PIPER].

FAUST.   O, how this sight doth delight my soul!

LUC.   But Faustus, in hell is all manner of delight.

FAUST.   O, might I see hell and return again safe, how happy were I then!

LUC.   Faustus, thou shalt. At midnight   [200 I will send for thee. Meanwhile peruse this book and view it thoroughly, and thou shalt turn thyself into what shape thou wilt.

FAUST.   Thanks, mighty Lucifer.
This will I keep as chary as my life.

LUC.   Now Faustus, farewell.

FAUST.   Farewell, great Lucifer. Come, Mephistophilis.   EXEUNT, *several ways.*

SCENE III

Enter the CLOWN, [ROBIN, *holding a book*].

ROB.   What, Dick, look to the horses there till I come again. I have gotten one of Doctor Faustus' conjuring books, and now we'll have such knavery as't passes.

Enter DICK.

DICK.   What, Robin, you must come away and walk the horses.

ROB.   I walk the horses? I scorn't, 'faith. I have other matters in hand. Let the horses walk themselves and they will. [*He reads.*] *A per se a; t, h, e, the; o per se o; deny orgon,*   [10 *gorgon.* Keep further from me, O thou illiterate and unlearned hostler.

DICK.   'Snails,° what hast thou got there? A book? Why, thou canst not tell ne'er a word on't.

ROB.   That thou shalt see presently. Keep out of the circle, I say, lest I send you into the hostry° with a vengeance.

DICK.   That's like, 'faith. You had best leave your foolery, for an my master come, he'll conjure you, 'faith.   20

ROB.   My master conjure me? I'll tell thee what: an my master come here, I'll clap as fair a pair of horns° on's head as e'er thou sawest in thy life.

DICK.   Thou needst not do that, for my mistress hath done it.°

ROB.   Ay, there be of us here that have waded as deep into matters as other men, if they were disposed to talk.

DICK.   A plague take you! I thought you   [30 did not sneak up and down after her for nothing. But I prithee, tell me in good sadness, Robin, is that a conjuring book?

ROB.   Do but speak what thou'lt have me to do, and I'll do't. If thou'lt dance naked, put off thy clothes, and I'll conjure thee about presently. Or if thou'lt go but to the tavern with me, I'll give thee white wine, red wine, claret wine, sack, muscadine, malmesey and whippincrust.° Hold belly, hold, and we'll not pay one penny   [40 for it.

DICK.   O brave! Prithee let's to it presently, for I am as dry as a dog.

ROB.   Come then, let's away.   EXEUNT.

ACT III

Prologue

Enter the CHORUS.

CHOR.   Learnèd Faustus,
To find the secrets of astronomy
Graven in the book of Jove's high firmament,
Did mount him up to scale Olympus' top,
Where, sitting in a chariot burning bright
Drawn by the strength of yokèd dragons' necks,
He views the clouds, the planets, and the stars,
The tropics, zones, and quarters of the sky,
From the bright circle of the hornèd moon
Even to the height of *Primum Mobile.*°   10
And whirling round with this circumference,
Within the concave compass of the pole,

---

190. raw mutton: slang for prostitute. 191. stock-fish: dried codfish.
Sc. iii: 13. 'Snails: by God's nails. 17. hostry: hostelry, inn.

23. horns: symbol of a cuckold. 25–26. mistress . . . it: His mistress has already given his master horns, *i. e.,* committed adultery. 39. whippincrust: a humorous distortion of "hippocras," a highly spiced wine.
Act III, Prol.: 10. Primum Mobile: the outermost sphere of Ptolemaic astronomy, which gave motion to the others.

From east to west his dragons swiftly glide
And in eight days did bring him home again.
Not long he stayed within his quiet house
To rest his bones after his weary toil,
But new exploits do hale him out again,
And mounted then upon a dragon's back,
That with his wings did part the subtle air,
He now is gone to prove cosmography,   20
That measures coasts and kingdoms of the earth,
And, as I guess, will first arrive at Rome
To see the Pope and manner of his court
And take some part of holy Peter's feast,
The which this day is highly solemnized.

                                        EXIT.

SCENE I

Enter FAUSTUS *and* MEPHISTOPHILIS.

FAUST.   Having now, my good Mephistophi-
lis,
Passed with delight the stately town of Trier,
Environed round with airy mountain tops,
With walls of flint, and deep entrenchèd lakes,°
Not to be won by any conquering prince;
From Paris next, coasting the realm of France,
We saw the river Main fall into Rhine,
Whose banks are set with groves of fruitful vines;
Then up to Naples, rich Campania,   9
Whose buildings fair and gorgeous to the eye,
The streets straight forth and paved with finest
    brick,
Quarters the town in four equivalents.
There saw we learnèd Maro's° golden tomb,
The way he cut, an English mile in length,
Through a rock of stone in one night's space.°
From thence to Venice, Padua, and the rest,
In midst of which a sumptuous temple stands,
That threats the stars with her aspiring top,
Whose frame is paved with sundry colored
    stones,
And roofed aloft with curious work in gold.   20
Thus hitherto hath Faustus spent his time.
But tell me now, what resting-place is this?
Hast thou, as erst I did command,
Conducted me within the walls of Rome?
    MEPH.   I have, my Faustus, and for proof
    thereof

This is the goodly palace of the Pope;
And 'cause we are no common guests,
I choose his privy chamber for our use.
    FAUST.   I hope his holiness will bid us wel-
    come.
    MEPH.   All's one, for we'll be bold with his
    venison.   30
But now, my Faustus, that thou may'st perceive
What Rome contains for to delight thine eyes,
Know that this city stands upon seven hills
That underprop the groundwork of the same.
Just through the midst runs flowing Tiber's
    stream,
With winding banks that cut it in two parts,
Over the which four stately bridges lean,
That make safe passage to each part of Rome.
Upon the bridge called Ponte Angelo
Erected is a castle passing strong,   40
Where thou shalt see such store of ordinance
As that the double cannons, forged of brass,
Do match the number of the days contained
Within the compass of one complete year;
Beside° the gates and high pyramidès°
That Julius Caesar brought from Africa.
    FAUST.   Now, by the kingdoms of infernal
    rule,
Of Styx, of Acheron, and the fiery lake
Of ever-burning Phlegethon, I swear
That I do long to see the monuments   50
And situation of bright-splendent Rome.
Come, therefore, let's away.
    MEPH.   Nay, stay my Faustus. I know you'd
    see the Pope
And take some part of holy Peter's feast,
The which, in state and high solemnity,
This day is held through Rome and Italy
In honor of the Pope's triumphant victory.
    FAUST.   Sweet Mephistophilis, thou pleasest
    me.
Whilst I am here on earth, let me be cloyed
With all things that delight the heart of man.
My four and twenty years of liberty   60
I'll spend in pleasure and in dalliance,
That Faustus' name, whilst this bright frame
    doth stand,
May be admirèd through the furthest land.

Sc. i: **4. lakes:** moats.   **13. Maro's:** Virgil's.   **14–15.
The . . . space:** In the Middle Ages Virgil was reputed to have been a magician.

45. Beside: besides. **pyramidès:** The obelisk that the
emperor Caligula brought from Heliopolis in the first
century A.D. still stands before the gates of St. Peter's.

MEPH. 'Tis well said, Faustus. Come then,
    stand by me
And thou shalt see them come immediately.
    FAUST. Nay, stay, my gentle Mephistophilis,
And grant me my request, and then I go.
Thou know'st within the compass of eight days
We viewed the face of heaven, of earth, and
    hell.   70
So high our dragons soared into the air,
That looking down, the earth appeared to me
No bigger than my hand in quantity.
There did we view the kingdoms of the world,
And what might please mine eye I there beheld.
Then in this show let me an actor be,
That this proud Pope may Faustus' cunning see.
    MEPH. Let it be so, my Faustus. But, first
    stay
And view their triumphs as they pass this way,
And then devise what best contents thy mind
By cunning in thine art to cross the Pope   81
Or dash the pride of this solemnity,
To make his monks and abbots stand like apes
And point like antics at his triple crown,
To beat the beads about the friars' pates
Or clap huge horns upon the cardinals' heads,
Or any villainy thou canst devise,
And I'll perform it, Faustus. Hark, they come.
This day shall make thee be admired in Rome.
        Enter the CARDINALS *and* BISHOPS, *some*
        bearing crosiers, some the pillars; MONKS
        and FRIARS *singing their procession. Then*
        the POPE, *and* RAYMOND, *King of Hungary,*
        with BRUNO, *led in chains.*
    POPE. Cast down our footstool.
    RAY.   Saxon Bruno, stoop,   90
Whilst on thy back his holiness ascends
Saint Peter's chair and state pontifical.
    BRUN. Proud Lucifer, that state belongs to
    me,
But thus I fall to Peter, not to thee.
    POPE. To me and Peter shalt thou grovelling
    lie
And crouch before the papal dignity.
Sound trumpets then, for thus Saint Peter's heir
From Bruno's back ascends Saint Peter's chair.
        A flourish while he ascends.
Thus, as the gods creep on with feet of wool
Long ere with iron hands they punish men,   100
So shall our sleeping vengeance now arise
And smite with death thy hated enterprise.
Lord Cardinals of France and Padua,

Go forthwith to our holy consistory,°
And read amongst the Statutes Decretal°
What, by the holy council held at Trent,°
The sacred synod hath decreed for him
That doth assume the papal government
Without election and a true consent.
Away, and bring us word with speed.   110
    FIRST CARD. We go my Lord.
                        EXEUNT CARDINALS.
    POPE. Lord Raymond.
                        [*They talk apart.*]
    FAUST. Go, haste thee, gentle Mephistophilis,
Follow the cardinals to the consistory,
And as they turn their superstitious books,
Strike them with sloth and drowsy idleness,
And make them sleep so sound that in their
    shapes
Thyself and I may parley with this Pope,
This proud confronter of the Emperor,
And in despite of all his holiness   120
Restore this Bruno to his liberty
And bear him to the states of Germany.
    MEPH. Faustus, I go.
    FAUST. Dispatch it soon.
The Pope shall curse that Faustus came to
    Rome.
        EXEUNT FAUSTUS *and* MEPHISTOPHILIS.
    BRUN. Pope Adrian, let me have some right
    of law.
I was elected by the Emperor.°
    POPE. We will depose the Emperor for that
    deed
And curse the people that submit to him.
Both he and thou shalt stand excommunicate
And interdict from church's privilege   131
And all society of holy men.
He grows too proud in his authority,
Lifting his lofty head above the clouds,
And like a steeple over-peers the church.
But we'll pull down his haughty insolence,
And as Pope Alexander, our progenitor,
Trod on the neck of German Frederick,
Adding this golden sentence to our praise,
'That Peter's heirs should tread on emperors
And walk upon the dreadful adder's back,   140
Treading the lion and the dragon down

---

104. consistory: the meeting place of the papal
senate. 105. Statutes Decretal: ecclesiastical law.
106. council . . . Trent: This council met between
1545 and 1563. 127. Emperor: Charles V, Holy
Roman Emperor from 1519 to 1556.

And fearless spurn the killing basilisk,'°
So will we quell that haughty schismatic,
And by authority apostolical
Depose him from his regal government.

BRUN.   Pope Julius swore to princely Sigis-
mond,
For him and the succeeding popes of Rome,
To hold the emperors their lawful lords.

POPE.   Pope Julius did abuse the church's
rites,   149
And therefore none of his decrees can stand.
Is not all power on earth bestowed on us?
And therefore, though we would, we cannot err.
Behold this silver belt, whereto is fixed
Seven golden keys fast sealed with seven seals
In token of our sevenfold power from heaven,
To bind or loose, lock fast, condemn or judge,
Resign, or seal, or whatso pleaseth us.
Then he and thou and all the world shall stoop,
Or be assurèd of our dreadful curse
To light as heavy as the pains of hell.   160

    Enter FAUSTUS *and* MEPHISTOPHILIS,
    like the CARDINALS.

MEPH.   Now tell me, Faustus, are we not
fitted well?

FAUST.   Yes, Mephistophilis, and two such
cardinals
Ne'er served a holy pope as we shall do.
But whilst they sleep within the consistory,
Let us salute his reverend fatherhood.

RAY.   Behold, my lord, the cardinals are returned.

POPE.   Welcome, grave fathers. Answer pres-
ently:
What have our holy council there decreed
Concerning Bruno and the Emperor,
In quittance of their late conspiracy   170
Against our state and papal dignity?

FAUST.   Most sacred patron of the church of
Rome,
By full consent of all the synod
Of priests and prelates it is thus decreed:
That Bruno and the German Emperor
Be held as Lollards° and bold schismatics
And proud disturbers of the church's peace.
And if that Bruno by his own assent,
Without enforcement of the German peers,

Did seek to wear the triple diadem   180
And by your death to climb Saint Peter's chair,
The Statutes Decretal have thus decreed:
He shall be straight condemned of heresy
And on a pile of fagots burned to death.

POPE.   It is enough. Here, take him to your
charge,
And bear him straight to Ponte Angelo,
And in the strongest tower enclose him fast.
Tomorrow, sitting in our consistory
With all our college of grave cardinals,
We will determine of his life or death.   190
Here, take his triple crown along with you,
And leave it in the church's treasury.
Make haste again, my good lord cardinals,
And take our blessing apostolical.

MEPH.   So, so. Was never devil thus blessed
before.

FAUST.   Away, sweet Mephistophilis, be gone.
The cardinals will be plagued for this anon.

    EXEUNT FAUSTUS *and* MEPHISTOPHILIS
                          [*with* BRUNO].

POPE.   Go presently and bring a banquet
forth,
That we may solemnize Saint Peter's feast, 199
And with Lord Raymond, King of Hungary,
Drink to our late and happy victory.

                                    EXEUNT.

                    SCENE II

    *A sennet [is sounded] while the banquet
    is brought in; and then enter* FAUSTUS
    and MEPHISTOPHILIS *in their own shapes.*

MEPH.   Now, Faustus, come, prepare thyself
for mirth.
The sleepy cardinals are hard at hand
To censure Bruno, that is posted hence,
And on a proud-paced steed, as swift as thought,
Flies o'er the Alps to fruitful Germany,
There to salute the woeful Emperor.

FAUST.   The Pope will curse them for their
sloth today,
That slept both Bruno and his crown away.
But now, that Faustus may delight his mind
And by their folly make some merriment,   10
Sweet Mephistophilis, so charm me here
That I may walk invisible to all
And do whate'er I please unseen of any.

MEPH.   Faustus, thou shalt. Then kneel down
presently:

142. basilisk: a mythical reptile that kills by its
looks.   176. Lollards: adherents of the English reformer, John Wycliffe (1320?–84).

Whilst on thy head I lay my hand
And charm thee with this magic wand.
First wear this girdle; then appear
Invisible to all are here.
The planets seven, the gloomy air,
Hell and the Furies' forkèd hair,°   20
Pluto's blue fire, and Hecate's tree,
With magic spells so compass thee
That no eye may thy body see.
So Faustus. Now, for all their holiness,
Do what thou wilt, thou shalt not be discerned.
  FAUST. Thanks, Mephistophilis. Now friars
take heed
Lest Faustus make your shaven crowns to bleed.
  MEPH. Faustus, no more. See where the car-
dinals come.
  Enter POPE *and all the* LORDS. *Enter the*
CARDINALS *with a book.*
  POPE. Welcome, lord cardinals. Come, sit
down.
Lord Raymond, take your seat. Friars attend,
And see that all things be in readiness,   31
As best beseems this solemn festival.
  FIRST CARD. First, may it please your sacred
holiness
To view the sentence of the reverend synod
Concerning Bruno and the Emperor?
  POPE. What needs this question? Did I not
tell you
Tomorrow we would sit i' th' consistory
And there determine of his punishment?
You brought us word even now; it was decreed
That Bruno and the cursèd Emperor   40
Were by the holy council both condemned
For loathèd Lollards and base schismatics.
Then wherefore would you have me view that
book?
  FIRST CARD. Your grace mistakes. You gave
us no such charge.
  RAY. Deny it not. We all are witnesses
That Bruno here was late delivered you,
With his rich triple crown to be reserved
And put into the church's treasury.
  BOTH CARDS. By holy Paul, we saw them not.
  POPE. By Peter, you shall die   50
Unless you bring them forth immediately.
Hale them to prison. Lade their limbs with
gyves.°
False prelates, for this hateful treachery

Cursed be your souls to hellish misery.
  [EXEUNT *the two* CARDINALS *with* ATTENDANTS.]
  FAUST. So, they are safe. Now, Faustus, to
the feast.
The Pope had never such a frolic guest.
  POPE. Lord Archbishop of Rheims, sit down
with us.
  ARCHBISHOP. I thank your holiness.
  FAUST. Fall to. The devil choke you an you
spare.   59
  POPE. Who's that spoke? Friars look about.
  FRIAR. Here's nobody, if it like your holiness.°
  POPE. Lord Raymond, pray fall to. I am be-
holding
To the Bishop of Milan for this so rare a present.
  FAUST. I thank you, sir.
        [He snatches the dish.]
  POPE. How now? Who snatched the meat
from me?
Villains, why speak you not?
My good Lord Archbishop, here's a most dainty
dish
Was sent me from a cardinal in France.
  FAUST. I'll have that too.
        [He snatches the dish.]
  POPE. What Lollards do attend our holiness,
That we receive such great indignity?   71
Fetch me some wine.
  FAUST. Ay, pray do, for Faustus is a-dry.
  POPE. Lord Raymond, I drink unto your
grace.
  FAUST. I pledge your grace.
        [He snatches the cup.]
  POPE. My wine gone too? Ye lubbers, look
about
And find the man that doth this villainy,
Or by our sanctitude, you all shall die.
I pray, my lords, have patience at this
Troublesome banquet.   80
  ARCH. Please it your holiness, I think it be
some ghost crept out of purgatory, and now is
come unto your holiness for his pardon.
  POPE. It may be so.
Go then, command our priests to sing a dirge
To lay the fury of this same troublesome ghost.
      [EXIT *an* ATTENDANT.]
Once again, my lord, fall to.
    The POPE *crosseth himself.*
  FAUST. How now?

Sc. ii: 20. forkèd hair: the serpents that made up
the hair of the Furies. **52. gyves:** shackles.

61. Here's . . . holiness: 1604 text.

Must every bit be spicèd with a cross?
Nay then, take that.   90
[He strikes the POPE.]
POPE. O I am slain. Help me, my lords.
O come and help to bear my body hence.
Damned be this soul for ever for this deed.
EXEUNT *the* POPE *and his train.*
MEPH. Now, Faustus, what will you do now?
For I can tell you you'll be cursed with bell,
book, and candle.°
FAUST. Bell, book, and candle; candle, book,
    and bell,
Forward and backward, to curse Faustus to hell.
Enter the FRIARS *with bell, book, and
candle for the dirge.*
FIRST FRIAR. Come, brethren, let's about our
business with good devotion.   100
[They chant.]
*Cursed be he that stole his holiness' meat from
    the table.*
Maledicat Dominus!°
*Cursed be he that struck his holiness a blow on
    the face.*
Maledicat Dominus!
*Cursed be he that struck Friar Sandelo a blow
    on the pate.*
Maledicat Dominus!
Cursed be he that disturbeth our holy dirge.
Maledicat Dominus!
Cursed be he that took away his holiness' wine.
*Maledicat Dominus! Et omnes sancti.
    Amen.*   110
[FAUSTUS *and* MEPHISTOPHILIS] *beat the*
FRIARS, *fling fireworks among them, and*
EXEUNT.

SCENE III

Enter [ROBIN,] *the* CLOWN, *and* DICK,
with a cup.
DICK. Sirrah Robin, we were best look that
your devil can answer the stealing of this same
cup, for the vintner's boy follows us at the hard
heels.
ROB. 'Tis no matter. Let him come. An he
follow us, I'll so conjure him as he was never

95–96. **bell . . . candle:** The tolling of a bell, the
closing of a book, and the extinguishing of a candle
marked the end of a form of excommunication. **102.
Maledicat Dominus:** May the Lord curse him.

conjured in his life, I warrant him. Let me see
the cup.
Enter VINTNER.
DICK. Here 'tis. Yonder he comes. Now,
Robin, now or never show thy cunning.   10
VINT. O, are you here? I am glad I have
found you. You are a couple of fine compan-
ions. Pray, where's the cup you stole from the
tavern?
ROB. How, how? We steal a cup? Take heed
what you say. We look not like cup stealers, I
can tell you.
VINT. Never deny't, for I know you have it,
and I'll search you.
ROB. Search me? Ay, and spare not. [20
Hold the cup, Dick. *[Aside to* DICK.] Come,
come, search me, search me.
[The VINTNER *searches* ROBIN.]
VINT. [*to* DICK] Come on, sirrah, let me
search you now.
DICK. Ay, ay, do, do. Hold the cup, Robin.
[Aside to ROBIN.] I fear not your searching. We
scorn to steal your cups, I can tell you.
[The VINTNER *searches* DICK.]
VINT. Never outface me for the matter, for
sure the cup is between you two.
ROB. Nay, there you lie. 'Tis beyond us   [30
both.
VINT. A plague take you! I thought 'twas
your knavery to take it away. Come, give it me
again.
ROB. Ay, much. When? Can you tell? Dick,
make me a circle, and stand close at my back,
and stir not for thy life. Vintner, you shall have
your cup anon. Say nothing, Dick, *O per se, O
Demogorgon, Belcher and Mephistophilis.*
Enter MEPHISTOPHILIS. [EXIT *the* VINT-
NER, *in fright.*]
MEPH. Monarch of hell, under whose black
    survey   40
Great potentates do kneel with awful fear,
Upon whose altars thousand souls do lie,°
How am I vexèd by these villains' charms!
From Constantinople have they brought me
    now,
Only for pleasure of these damnèd slaves.
ROB. By Lady, sir, you have had a shrewd
journey of it. Will it please you to take a shoul-

Sc. iii: 40–42: Monarch . . . lie: 1604 text.

der of mutton to supper and a tester° in your
purse, and go back again?

DICK.   Ay, I pray you heartily, sir, for   [50
we called you but in jest, I promise you.

MEPH.   To purge the rashness of this cursèd
deed,
First be thou turnèd to this ugly shape,
For apish deeds transformèd to an ape.

ROB.   O brave, an ape! I pray sir, let me
have the carrying of him about to show some
tricks.

MEPH.   And so thou shalt. Be thou transformed to a dog, and carry him upon thy back.
Away, be gone!   60

ROB.   A dog? That's excellent. Let the maids
look well to their porridge pots, for I'll into the
kitchen presently. Come, Dick, come.

EXEUNT [ROBIN and DICK,] the two CLOWNS.

MEPH.   Now with the flames of ever-burning
fire,
I'll wing myself and forthwith fly amain
Unto my Faustus, to the great Turk's court.

EXIT.

ACT IV

Prologue

Enter CHORUS.

CHOR.   When Faustus had with pleasure ta'en
the view
Of rarest things and royal courts of kings,
He stayed his course and so returnèd home;
Where such as bare his absence but with grief—
I mean his friends and nearest companions—
Did gratulate his safety with kind words,
And in their conference of what befell,
Touching his journey through the world and air,
They put forth questions of astrology,
Which Faustus answered with such learnèd skill
As they admired and wondered at his wit.   11
Now is his fame spread forth in every land.
Amongst the rest, the Emperor is one—
Carolus the fifth—at whose palace now
Faustus is feasted 'mongst his noblemen.
What there he did in trial of his art
I leave untold; your eyes shall see performed.

EXIT.

SCENE I

Enter MARTINO *and* FREDERICK, *at several doors.*

MART.   What ho, officers, gentlemen,
Hie to the presence to attend the Emperor.
Good Frederick, see the rooms be voided straight;
His majesty is coming to the hall.
Go back, and see the state in readiness.

FRED.   But where is Bruno, our elected Pope,
That on a fury's back came post from Rome?
Will not his grace consort the Emperor?

MART.   O yes, and with him comes the Ger-
man conjurer,
The learnèd Faustus, fame of Wittenberg,   10
The wonder of the world for magic art;
And he intends to show great Carolus
The race of all his stout progenitors,
And bring in presence of his majesty
The royal shapes and warlike semblances
Of Alexander and his beauteous paramour.

FRED.   Where is Benvolio?

MART.   Fast asleep, I warrant you.
He took his rouse° with stoups of Rhenish wine
So kindly yesternight to Bruno's health   20
That all this day the sluggard keeps his bed.

FRED.   See, see, his window's ope. We'll call
to him.

MART.   What ho, Benvolio!

Enter BENVOLIO *above at a window, in
his nightcap, buttoning.*

BENV.   What a devil ail you two?

MART.   Speak softly, sir, lest the devil hear
you,
For Faustus at the court is late arrived,
And at his heels a thousand furies wait
To accomplish whatsoever the doctor please.

BENV.   What of this?

MART.   Come, leave thy chamber first, and
thou shalt see   30
This conjurer perform such rare exploits
Before the Pope and royal Emperor
As never yet was seen in Germany.

BENV.   Has not the Pope enough of conjuring
yet?
He was upon the devil's back late enough,
And if he be so far in love with him,
I would he would post with him to Rome again.

Act IV, sc. i: 19. **took his rouse**: had a drinking
party.

48. **tester**: sixpence.

FRED. Speak, wilt thou come and see this sport?

BENV.   Not I.

MART. Wilt thou stand in thy window and see it then?

BENV. Ay, and I fall not asleep i' th' mean-time.   40

MART. The Emperor is at hand, who comes to see
What wonders by black spells may compassed be.

BENV. Well, go you attend the Emperor. I am content for this once to thrust my head out at a window, for they say if a man be drunk over-night the devil cannot hurt him in the morning. If that be true, I have a charm in my head shall control him as well as the conjurer, I warrant you.

EXIT [FREDERICK, *with* MARTINO. BENVOLIO *remains at the window above*].

SCENE II

A sennet [is sounded. Enter] CHARLES, *the German* EMPEROR, BRUNO, [*the Duke of*] SAXONY, FAUSTUS, MEPHISTOPHILIS, FREDERICK, MARTINO, *and* ATTENDANTS.

EMP. Wonder of men, renownèd magician.
Thrice-learnèd Faustus, welcome to our court.
This deed of thine, in setting Bruno free
From his and our professèd enemy,
Shall add more excellence unto thine art
Than if by powerful necromantic spells
Thou couldst command the world's obedience.
Forever be beloved of Carolus,
And if this Bruno thou hast late redeemed°
In peace possess the triple diadem   10
And sit in Peter's chair despite of chance,
Thou shalt be famous through all Italy
And honored of the German Emperor.

FAUST. These gracious words, most royal Carolus,
Shall make poor Faustus to his utmost power
Both love and serve the German Emperor
And lay his life at holy Bruno's feet.
For proof whereof, if so your grace be pleased,
The doctor stands prepared by power of art
To cast his magic charms that shall pierce through   20
The ebon gates of ever-burning hell,
And hale the stubborn Furies from their caves

Sc. ii: 9. redeemed: freed.

To compass whatsoe'er your grace commands.

BENV. [*above*] Blood,° he speaks terribly, but for all that, I do not greatly believe him. He looks as like a conjurer as the Pope to a coster-monger.°

EMP. Then, Faustus, as thou late did'st promise us,
We would behold that famous conqueror,
Great Alexander, and his paramour   30
In their true shapes and state majestical,
That we may wonder at their excellence.

FAUST. Your majesty shall see them pres-ently.
Mephistophilis, away,
And with a solemn noise of trumpets' sound
Present before this royal Emperor,
Great Alexander and his beauteous paramour.

MEPH. Faustus, I will.   [EXIT.]

BENV. Well, master doctor, an your devils come not away quickly, you shall have [40 me asleep presently. Zounds, I could eat myself for anger to think I have been such an ass all this while, to stand gaping after the devil's gov-ernor and can see nothing.

FAUST. I'll make you feel something anon, if my art fail me not.
My lord, I must forewarn your majesty
That when my spirits present the royal shapes
Of Alexander and his paramour,
Your grace demand no questions of the king,
But in dumb silence let them come and go.   50

EMP. Be it as Faustus please; we are content.

BENV. Ay, ay, and I am content too. And thou bring Alexander and his paramour before the Emperor, I'll be Actæon and turn myself to a stag.°

FAUST. And I'll play Diana and send you the horns presently.

[*A*] *sennet [is sounded]. Enter at one [door] the* EMPEROR ALEXANDER, *at the other* DARIUS.° *They meet [in combat].* DARIUS *is thrown down;* ALEXANDER *kills him, takes off his crown, and, offering to go out,* HIS PARAMOUR *meets him. He em-braceth her and sets* DARIUS' *crown upon*

24. Blood: by God's blood. 27. costermonger: a hawker of fish, vegetables, fruit, etc. 54–55. Actaeon . . . stag: When Actaeon saw the goddess Diana bathing, she changed him into a stag, and his own dogs tore him to pieces. 57ff. Darius: Darius III of Persia, defeated in 334 B.C. by Alexander the Great.

*her head; and coming back, both salute
the* EMPEROR, *who, leaving his state, offers
to embrace them, which* FAUSTUS *seeing,
suddenly stays him. Then trumpets cease
and music sounds.*
My gracious lord, you do forget yourself.
These are but shadows, not substantial.
  EMP. O pardon me. My thoughts are so rav-
    ishèd
With sight of this renownèd emperor,   60
That in mine arms I would have compassed
  him.
But, Faustus, since I may not speak to them,
To satisfy my longing thoughts at full,
Let me this tell thee: I have heard it said
That this fair lady, whilst she lived on earth,
Had on her neck a little wart or mole;
How may I prove that saying to be true?
  FAUST. Your majesty may boldly go and see.
  EMP. Faustus, I see it plain,
And in this sight thou better pleasest me   70
Than if I gained another monarchy.
  FAUST. Away! Be gone!   EXIT *show.*
See, see, my gracious lord, what strange beast is
yon, that thrusts his head out at window?
  EMP. O wondrous sight! See, Duke of Sax-
    ony,
Two spreading horns most strangely fastenèd
Upon the head of young Benvolio.
  SAX. What? Is he asleep or dead?
  FAUST. He sleeps, my lord, but dreams not of
    his horns.
  EMP. This sport is excellent. We'll call and
    wake him.   80
What ho, Benvolio!
  BENV. A plague upon you! Let me sleep a
    while.
  EMP. I blame thee not to sleep much, having
such a head of thine own.
  SAX. Look up, Benvolio; 'tis the Emperor
calls.
  BENV. The Emperor? Where? O zounds, my
head!°
  EMP. Nay, and thy horns hold, 'tis no matter
for thy head, for that's armed sufficiently.   91
  FAUST. Why, how now, sir knight! What,
hanged by the horns? This is most horrible. Fie,
fie, pull in your head for shame. Let not all the
world wonder at you.

89. **my head:** his horns hold his head in the window.

  BENV. Zounds, doctor, is this your villainy?
  FAUST. O say not so, sir. The doctor has no
    skill,
No art, no cunning, to present these lords
Or bring before this royal Emperor
The mighty monarch, warlike Alexander.   100
If Faustus do it, you are straight resolved
In bold Actæon's shape to turn a stag.
And therefore, my lord, so please your majesty,
I'll raise a kennel of hounds shall hunt him so
As all his footmanship shall scarce prevail
To keep his carcass from their bloody fangs.
Ho, Belimote, Argiron, Asterote!
  BENV. Hold, hold! Zounds, he'll raise up a
kennel of devils, I think, anon. Good, my lord,
entreat for me. 'Sblood, I am never able to en-
dure these torments.   111
  EMP. Then, good master doctor,
Let me entreat you to remove his horns.
He has done penance now sufficiently.
  FAUST. My gracious lord, not so much for
injury done to me, as to delight your majesty
with some mirth, hath Faustus justly requited
this injurious knight; which being all I desire,
I am content to remove his horns. Mephistophilis, transform him. [MEPHISTOPHILIS *re-* [120
moves the horns.] And hereafter, sir, look you
speak well of scholars.
  BENV. [*aside*] Speak well of ye? 'Sblood, and
scholars be such cuckold makers to clap horns
of honest men's heads o' this order, I'll ne'er
trust smooth faces and small ruffs° more. But
an I be not revenged for this, would I might be
turned to a gaping oyster and drink nothing but
salt water.   [EXIT BENVOLIO *above.*]
  EMP. Come, Faustus. While the Emperor
lives,   130
In recompense of this thy high desert,
Thou shalt command the state of Germany
And live beloved of mighty Carolus.   EXEUNT.

SCENE III

Enter BENVOLIO, MARTINO, FREDERICK,
and SOLDIERS.
  MART. Nay, sweet Benvolio, let us sway thy
    thoughts
From this attempt against the conjurer.

126. **smooth . . . ruffs:** beardless scholars in academic garb.

BENV.   Away! You love me not to urge me thus.
Shall I let slip so great an injury,
When every servile groom jests at my wrongs
And in their rustic gambols proudly say,
'Benvolio's head was graced with horns today'?
O, may these eyelids never close again
Till with my sword I have that conjurer slain.
If you will aid me in this enterprise,   10
Then draw your weapons and be resolute.
If not, depart. Here will Benvolio die,
But Faustus' death shall quit° my infamy.
   FRED.   Nay, we will stay with thee, betide what may,
And kill that doctor if he come this way.
   BENV.   Then, gentle Frederick, hie thee to the grove,
And place our servants and our followers
Close in an ambush there behind the trees.
By this, I know, the conjurer is near.   19
I saw him kneel and kiss the Emperor's hand
And take his leave, laden with rich rewards.
Then, soldiers, boldly fight. If Faustus die,
Take you the wealth; leave us the victory.
   FRED.   Come, soldiers. Follow me unto the grove.
Who kills him shall have gold and endless love.
            EXIT FREDERICK *with the* SOLDIERS.
   BENV.   My head is lighter than it was by th'horns,
But yet my heart's more ponderous than my head
And pants until I see that conjurer dead.
   MART.   Where shall we place ourselves, Benvolio?
   BENV.   Here will we stay to bide the first assault.   30
O, were that damnèd hell-hound but in place,
Thou soon shouldst see me quit my foul disgrace.
            Enter FREDERICK.
   FRED.   Close, close, the conjurer is at hand
And all alone comes walking in his gown.
Be ready then, and strike the peasant down.
   BENV.   Mine be that honor then. Now, sword, strike home.
For horns he gave I'll have his head anon.
            Enter FAUSTUS *with the false head.*
   MART.   See, see, he comes.
   BENV.   No words! This blow ends all.

Sc. iii: **13 quit:** pay for.

Hell take his soul; his body thus must fall.
            [*He stabs* FAUSTUS.]
   FAUST. [*falling*] Oh!   40
   FRED.   Groan you, master doctor?
   BENV.   Break may his heart with groans! Dear Frederick, see,
Thus will I end his griefs immediately.
   MART.   Strike with a willing hand. His head is off.
      [BENVOLIO *strikes off* FAUSTUS' *false head.*]
   BENV.   The devil's dead. The Furies now may laugh.
   FRED.   Was this that stern aspèct, that awful frown,
Made the grim monarch of infernal spirits
Tremble and quake at his commanding charms?
   MART.   Was this that damnèd head whose heart conspired
Benvolio's shame before the Emperor?   50
   BENV.   Ay, that's the head, and here the body lies,
Justly rewarded for his villainies.
   FRED.   Come, let's devise how we may add more shame
To the black scandal of his hated name.
   BENV.   First, on his head, in quittance of my wrongs,
I'll nail huge forkèd horns and let them hang
Within the window where he yoked me first,
That all the world may see my just revenge.
   MART.   What use shall we put his beard to?
   BENV.   We'll sell it to a chimney-sweeper. [60
It will wear out ten birchen brooms, I warrant you.
   FRED.   What shall eyes do?
   BENV.   We'll put out his eyes, and they shall serve for buttons to his lips to keep his tongue from catching cold.
   MART.   An excellent policy! And now, sirs, having divided him, what shall the body do?
            [FAUSTUS *rises.*]
   BENV.   Zounds, the devil's alive again.
   FRED.   Give him his head, for God's sake.   70
   FAUST.   Nay, keep it. Faustus will have heads and hands,
Ay, all your hearts, to recompense this deed.
Knew you not, traitors, I was limited
For four-and-twenty years to breathe on earth?
And had you cut my body with your swords,
Or hewed this flesh and bones as small as sand,
Yet in a minute had my spirit returned,

And I had breathed a man made free from
    harm.
But wherefore do I dally my revenge?
Asteroth, Belimoth, Mephistophilis!   80
    Enter MEPHISTOPHILIS *and other* DEV-
    ILS.
Go, horse these traitors on your fiery backs,
And mount aloft with them as high as heaven;
Thence pitch them headlong to the lowest hell.
Yet stay. The world shall see their misery,
And hell shall after plague their treachery.
Go, Belimoth, and take this caitiff hence,
And hurl him in some lake of mud and dirt.
Take thou this other; drag him through the
    woods
Amongst the pricking thorns and sharpest briars,
Whilst with my gentle Mephistophilis   90
This traitor flies unto some steepy rock
That, rolling down, may break the villain's bones
As he intended to dismember me.
Fly hence. Dispatch my charge immediately.
    FRED.   Pity us, gentle Faustus. Save our lives.
    FAUST.   Away!
    FRED.   He must needs go that the devil drives.°
            EXEUNT SPIRITS *with the* KNIGHTS.
        Enter the ambushed SOLDIERS.
    FIRST SOLD.   Come, sirs, prepare yourselves
    in readiness.
Make haste to help these noble gentlemen;
I heard them parley with the conjurer.   100
    SEC. SOLD.   See where he comes. Dispatch
    and kill the slave.
    FAUST.   What's here? An ambush to betray
    my life?
Then, Faustus, try thy skill. Base peasants, stand,
For lo, these trees remove at my command
And stand as bulwarks 'twixt yourselves and me,
To shield me from your hated treachery.
Yet to encounter this your weak attempt,
Behold an army comes incontinent.°
    FAUSTUS *strikes the door, and enter a*
    DEVIL *playing on a drum, after him an-*
    other bearing an ensign, and divers with
    weapons, MEPHISTOPHILIS *with fireworks.*
    They set upon the SOLDIERS *and drive*
    them out. [EXIT FAUSTUS.]

97. He . . . drives: a popular proverb.   **108. in-**
continent: immediately.

SCENE IV

Enter at several doors BENVOLIO, FRED-
ERICK, *and* MARTINO, *their heads and faces*
bloody and besmeared with mud and dirt,
all having horns on their heads.
    MART.   What ho, Benvolio!
    BENV.   Here! What, Frederick, ho!
    FRED.   O help me, gentle friend. Where is
    Martino?
    MART.   Dear Frederick, here,
Half smothered in a lake of mud and dirt,
Through which the Furies dragged me by the
    heels.
    FRED.   Martino, see! Benvolio's horns again.
    MART.   O misery! How now, Benvolio?
    BENV.   Defend me, heaven. Shall I be
    haunted° still?
    MART.   Nay, fear not man; we have not
    power to kill.   10
    BENV.   My friends transformèd thus! O hellish
    spite!
Your heads are all set with horns.
    FRED.   You hit it right.
It is your own you mean. Feel on your head.
    BENV.   Zounds, horns again!
    MART.   Nay, chafe not man. We all are sped.°
    BENV.   What devil attends this damned magi-
    cian,
That, spite of spite, our wrongs are doublèd?
    FRED.   What may we do, that we may hide
    our shames?
    BENV.   If we should follow him to work re-
    venge,   19
He'd join long asses' ears to these huge horns,
And make us laughing-stocks to all the world.
    MART.   What shall we then do, dear Ben-
    volio?
    BENV.   I have a castle joining near these
    woods,
And thither we'll repair and live obscure
Till time shall alter these our brutish shapes.
Sith black disgrace hath thus eclipsed our fame,
We'll rather die with grief than live with shame.
                            EXEUNT *omnes.*

SCENE V

Enter FAUSTUS *and* MEPHISTOPHILIS.

Sc. iv: 9. haunted: bewitched, with a pun on
"hunted."   **15. sped:** provided (with horns).

FAUST. Now, Mephistophilis, the restless course
That time doth run with calm and silent foot,
Shortening my days and thread of vital life,
Calls for the payment of my latest years.
Therefore, sweet Mephistophilis, let us
Make haste to Wittenberg.

MEPH. What, will you go on horseback, or on foot?

FAUST. Nay, till I am past this fair and pleasant green,
I'll walk on foot.   [EXIT MEPHISTOPHILIS.]
          Enter a HORSE-COURSER.

HORSE-C. I have been all this day seek- [10
ing one Master Fustian. Mass, see where he is.
God save you, master doctor.

FAUST. What, horse-courser! You are well met.

HORSE-C. I beseech your worship, accept of these forty dollars.

FAUST. Friend, thou canst not buy so good a horse for so small a price. I have no great need to sell him, but if thou likest him for ten dollars more, take him, because I see thou hast a [20 good mind to him.

HORSE-C. I beseech you, sir, accept of this. I am a very poor man and have lost very much of late by horse-flesh, and this bargain will set me up again.

FAUST. Well, I will not stand° with thee. Give me the money.

          [*The* HORSE-COURSER *gives* FAUST *money.*]
Now, sirrah, I must tell you that you may ride him o'er hedge and ditch, and spare him not. But, do you hear? In any case, ride him [30 not into the water.

HORSE-C. How sir? Not into the water? Why, will he not drink of all waters?

FAUST. Yes, he will drink of all waters, but ride him not into the water—o'er hedge and ditch, or where thou wilt, but not into the water. Go, bid the hostler deliver him unto you, and remember what I say.

HORSE-C. I warrant you, sir. O joyful day! Now am I a man made forever.   40
          EXIT.

FAUST. What art thou, Faustus, but a man condemned to die?
Thy fatal time draws to a final end.

Despair doth drive distrust into my thoughts.
Confound these passions with a quiet sleep.
Tush! Christ did call the thief upon the cross;
Then rest thee, Faustus, quiet in conceit.
          He sits to sleep [*in his chair*].
          Enter the HORSE-COURSER, *wet.*

HORSE-C. O what a cozening doctor was this? I riding my horse into the water, thinking some hidden mystery had been in the horse, I had nothing under me but a little straw [50 and had much ado to escape drowning. Well, I'll go rouse him and make him give me my forty dollars again. Ho, sirrah doctor, you cozening scab!° Master doctor, awake and rise, and give me my money again, for your horse is turned to a bottle of hay. Master doctor!

          He [*tries to wake* FAUSTUS, *and in doing so*] *pulls off his leg.*
Alas, I am undone! What shall I do? I have pulled off his leg.

          [FAUSTUS *awakes.*]

FAUST. O, help, help! The villain hath murdered me.   60

HORSE-C. Murder or not murder, now he has but one leg, I'll outrun him and cast this leg into some ditch or other.

FAUST. Stop him, stop him, stop him! Ha, ha, ha, Faustus hath his leg again, and the horse-courser a bundle of hay for his forty dollars.

          Enter WAGNER.
How now, Wagner, what news with thee?

WAG. If it please you, the Duke of Anholt doth earnestly entreat your company and hath sent some of his men to attend you with [70 provision fit for your journey.

FAUST. The Duke of Anholt's an honorable gentleman, and one to whom I must be no niggard of my cunning. Come away.   EXEUNT.

SCENE VI

          Enter [ROBIN, *the*] CLOWN, DICK, [*the*]
          HORSE-COURSER, *and a* CARTER.

CART. Come, my masters, I'll bring you to the best beer in Europe. What ho, hostess! Where be these whores?
          Enter HOSTESS.

HOSTESS. How now, what lack you? What, my old guests, welcome.

Sc. v: 26. **stand:** haggle.

54. **scab:** rascal.

ROB. Sirrah, Dick, dost thou know why I stand so mute?

DICK. No, Robin; why is't?

ROB. I am eighteen pence on the score.° But say nothing; see if she have forgotten me.   10

HOSTESS. Who's this that stands so solemnly by himself? What, my old guest?

ROB. O hostess, how do you? I hope my score stands still.

HOSTESS. Ay, there's no doubt of that, for methinks you make no haste to wipe it out.

DICK. Why, hostess, I say, fetch us some beer.

HOSTESS. You shall presently. Look up into th'hall there, ho!   EXIT.

DICK. Come, sirs, what shall we do now [20 till mine hostess come?

CART. Marry, sir, I'll tell you the bravest tale how a conjurer served me. You know Doctor Fauster?

HORSE-C. Ay, a plague take him. Here's some on's have cause to know him. Did he conjure thee too?

CART. I'll tell you how he served me. As I was going to Wittenberg t'other day with a load of hay, he met me and asked me what he [30 should give me for as much hay as he could eat. Now, sir, I thinking that a little would serve his turn, bade him take as much as he would for three farthings. So he presently gave me my money and fell to eating; and as I am a cursen° man, he never left eating till he had eat up all my load of hay.

ALL. O monstrous! Eat a whole load of hay!

ROB. Yes, yes, that may be, for I have heard of one that has eat a load of logs.   40

HORSE-C. Now, sirs, you shall hear how villainously he served me. I went to him yesterday to buy a horse of him, and he would by no means sell him under forty dollars. So, sir, because I knew him to be such a horse as would run over hedge and ditch and never tire, I gave him his money. So when I had my horse, Doctor Fauster bade me ride him night and day and spare him no time; but, quoth he, in any case ride him not into the water. Now sir, I thinking the horse [50 had had some rare quality that he would not have me know of, what did I but rid him into a great river, and when I came just in the midst,

my horse vanished away, and I sat straddling upon a bottle of hay.

ALL. O brave doctor!

HORSE-C. But you shall hear how bravely I served him for it. I went me home to his house, and there I found him asleep. I kept a hallooing and whooping in his ears, but all could not [60 wake him. I seeing that, took him by the leg and never rested pulling till I had pulled me his leg quite off, and now 'tis at home in mine hostry.

ROB. And has the doctor but one leg then? That's excellent, for one of his devils turned me into the likeness of an ape's face.

CART. Some more drink, hostess.

ROB. Hark you, we'll into another room and drink a while, and then we'll go seek out the doctor.   70

EXEUNT.

SCENE VII

Enter the DUKE OF ANHOLT, HIS DUCHESS, FAUSTUS, *and* MEPHISTOPHILIS, [SERVANTS *and* ATTENDANTS].

DUKE. Thanks, master doctor, for these pleasant sights. Nor know I how sufficiently to recompense your great deserts in erecting that enchanted castle in the air, the sight whereof so delighted me, as nothing in the world could please me more.

FAUST. I do think myself, my good lord, highly recompensed in that it pleaseth your grace to think but well of that which Faustus hath performed. But, gracious lady, it may [10 be that you have taken no pleasure in those sights. Therefore, I pray you, tell me what is the thing you most desire to have; be it in the world, it shall be yours. I have heard that great-bellied women do long for things are rare and dainty.

DUCH. True, master doctor, and since I find you so kind, I will make known unto you what my heart desires to have. And were it now summer, as it is January, a dead time of the winter, I would request no better meat° than a [20 dish of ripe grapes.

FAUST. This is but a small matter. Go, Mephistophilis, away!   EXIT MEPHISTOPHILIS. Madam I will do more than this for your content.

Sc. vi: 9. on the score: in debt.   35. cursen: Christian, with a pun on "cursed."

Sc. vii: 20. meat: food.

Enter MEPHISTOPHILIS *again with the grapes.*
Here; now taste ye these. They should be good,
for they come from a far country, I can tell you.

DUKE.   This makes me wonder more than all
the rest, that at this time of year, when every tree
is barren of his fruit, from whence you had   [30
these ripe grapes.

FAUST.   Please it, your grace, the year is divided into two circles over the whole world, so
that when it is winter with us, in the contrary
circle it is likewise summer with them, as in
India, Saba, and such countries that lie far east,
where they have fruit twice a year. From
whence, by means of a swift spirit that I have,
I had these grapes brought, as you see.

DUCH.   And trust me, they are the sweet-   [40
est grapes that e'er I tasted.

The CLOWN[S, ROBIN, DICK, *the* CARTER,
and the HORSE-COURSER,] *bounce at the*
gate within.

DUKE.   What rude disturbers have we at the
gate?
Go, pacify their fury. Set it ope,
And then demand of them what they would
have.
                    [EXIT *a* SERVANT.]
They knock again and call out to talk with
                                    FAUSTUS.
                    [*Enter* SERVANT *to them.*]

SERV.   Why, how now, masters, what a coil
is there?
What is the reason you disturb the duke.

DICK.   We have no reason for it; therefore a
fig for him.

SERV.   What, saucy varlets, dare you be so
bold?

HORSE-C.   I hope, sir, we have wit enough to
be more bold than welcome.   50

SERV.   It appears so. Pray be bold elsewhere,
And trouble not the duke.

DUKE.   What would they have?

SERV.   They all cry out to speak with Doctor
Faustus.

CART.   Ay, and we will speak with him.

DUKE.   Will you, sir? Commit the rascals.

DICK.   Commit with us!° He were as good
commit with his father as commit with us.

56. **Commit with us:** Dick changes the meaning
from "commit to prison" to "have intercourse with."

FAUST.   I do beseech your grace, let them
        come in;
They are good subject for a merriment.   59

DUKE.   Do as thou wilt, Faustus. I give thee
leave.

FAUST.   I thank your grace.

Enter ROBIN, DICK, CARTER, *and* HORSE-
COURSER.
                    Why, how now, my good friends?
'Faith you are too outrageous, but come near;
I have procured your pardons. Welcome all!

ROB.   Nay, sir, we will be welcome for our
money, and we will pay for what we take. What
ho! Give's half a dozen of beer here, and be
hanged.

FAUST.   Nay, hark you; can you tell me   [70
where you are?

CART.   Ay, marry can I: we are under heaven.

SERV.   Ay, but sir sauce-box, know you in
what place?

HORSE-C.   Ay, ay, the house is good enough
to drink in. Zounds, fill us some beer, or we'll
break all the barrels in the house and dash out
all your brains with your bottles.

FAUST.   Be not so furious. Come, you shall
        have beer.
My lord, beseech you give me leave a while: 80
I'll gage my credit, 'twill content your grace.

DUKE.   With all my heart, kind doctor. Please
        thyself;
Our servants and our court's at thy command.

FAUST.   I humbly thank your grace. Then
        fetch some beer.

HORSE-C.   Ay, marry, there spake a doctor
indeed, and 'faith, I'll drink a health to thy
wooden leg for that word.

FAUST.   My wooden leg? What dost thou
mean by that?

CART.   Ha, ha, ha! Dost hear him, Dick?   [90
He has forgot his leg.

HORSE-C.   Ay, ay, he does not stand much
upon that.

FAUST.   No, faith; not much upon a wooden
leg.

CART.   Good lord, that flesh and blood should
be so frail with your worship! Do not you remember a horse-courser you sold a horse to?

FAUST.   Yes, I remember I sold one a horse.

CART.   And do you remember you bid   [100
he should not ride into the water?

FAUST.   Yes, I do very well remember that.

CART.   And do you remember nothing of your leg?

FAUST.   No, in good sooth.

CART.   Then, I pray, remember your courtesy.

FAUST.   I thank you, sir.

CART.   'Tis not so much worth. I pray you, tell me one thing.

FAUST.   What's that?   110

CART.   Be both your legs bedfellows every night together?

FAUST.   Wouldst thou make a Colossus° of me, that thou askest me such questions?

CART.   No, truly, sir. I would make nothing of you, but I would fain know that.

Enter HOSTESS *with drink.*

FAUST.   Then, I assure thee, certainly they are.

CART.   I thank you; I am fully satisfied.

FAUST.   But wherefore dost thou ask?   120

CART.   For nothing, sir. But methinks you should have a wooden bedfellow of one of 'em.

HORSE-C.   Why, do you hear, sir; did not I pull off one of your legs when you were asleep?

FAUST.   But I have it again, now I am awake. Look you here, sir.

ALL.   O horrible! Had the doctor three legs?

CART.   Do you remember, sir, how you cozened me and ate up my load of—

FAUSTUS *charms him dumb.*

DICK.   Do you remember how you made   [130 me wear an ape's—

[FAUSTUS *charms him dumb.*]

HORSE-C.   You whoreson conjuring scab, do you remember how you cozened me with a ho—

[FAUSTUS *charms him dumb.*]

ROB.   Ha' you forgotten me? You think to carry it away with your *hey-pass* and *re-pass;* do you remember the dog's fa—

[FAUSTUS *charms him dumb.*] EXEUNT CLOWNS.

HOSTESS.   Who pays for the ale? Hear you, master doctor, now you have sent away my guests, I pray who shall pay me for my a—

[FAUSTUS *charms her dumb.*] EXIT HOSTESS.

DUCH.   My lord,   140 We are much beholding to this learnèd man.

DUKE.   So are we, madam, which we will recompense

113. **Colossus:** The legs of the Colossus of Rhodes straddled the entrance to the harbor.

With all the love and kindness that we may. His artful sport drives all sad thoughts away.

EXEUNT.

ACT V

SCENE I

Thunder and Lightning. Enter DEVILS *with covered dishes.* MEPHISTOPHILIS *leads them into* FAUSTUS' *study. Then enter* WAGNER.

WAG.   I think my master means to die shortly. He has made his will and given me his wealth, His house, his goods, and store of golden plate, Besides two thousand ducats ready coined. I wonder what he means. If death were nigh, He would not frolic thus. He's now at supper With the scholars, where there's such belly-cheer As Wagner in his life ne'er saw the like. And see where they come; belike the feast is
        done.   EXIT.

Enter FAUSTUS, MEPHISTOPHILIS, *and two or three* SCHOLARS.

FIRST SCHOL.   Master Doctor Faustus, [10 since our conference about fair ladies, which was the beautifulest in all the world, we have determined with ourselves that Helen of Greece was the admirablest lady that ever lived. Therefore, master doctor, if you will do us so much favor as to let us see that peerless dame of Greece, whom all the world admires for majesty, we should think ourselves much beholding unto you.

FAUST.   Gentlemen,   20 For that I know your friendship is unfeigned, And Faustus' custom is not to deny The just requests of those that wish him well, You shall behold that peerless dame of Greece, No otherwise for pomp and majesty Than when Sir Paris crossed the seas with her And brought the spoils to rich Dardania.° Be silent then, for danger is in words.

Music sounds. MEPHISTOPHILIS *brings in* HELEN; *she passeth over the stage.*

SEC. SCHOL.   Was this fair Helen, whose admirèd worth Made Greece with ten years war afflict poor
        Troy?   30 Too simple is my wit to tell her praise,

Act V, sc. i: 27. **Dardania:** Troy.

Whom all the world admires for majesty.

THIRD SCHOL.   No marvel though the angry
  Greeks pursued
With ten years' war the rape of such a queen,
Whose heavenly beauty passeth all compare.

FIRST SCHOL.   Since we have seen the pride
  of nature's works
And only paragon of excellence,
We'll take our leaves, and for this blessèd sight
Happy and blest be Faustus evermore.

FAUST.   Gentlemen, farewell; the same wish
  I to you.   40

EXEUNT SCHOLARS.

Enter an OLD MAN.

OLD MAN.   O gentle Faustus, leave this
  damnèd art,
This magic that will charm thy soul to hell
And quite bereave thee of salvation.
Though thou hast now offended like a man,
Do not persevere in it like a devil.
Yet, yet, thou hast an amiable soul,
If sin by custom grow not into nature.
Then, Faustus, will repentance come too late;
Then thou art banished from the sight of heaven.
No mortal can express the pains of hell.   50
It may be this my exhortation
Seems harsh and all unpleasant; let it not,
For, gentle son, I speak it not in wrath
Or envy of thee,° but in tender love
And pity of thy future misery.
And so have hope that this my kind rebuke,
Checking thy body, may amend thy soul.

FAUST.   Where art thou, Faustus? Wretch,
  what hast thou done?
Damned art thou, Faustus, damned; despair and
  die!   59
Hell claims his right, and with a roaring voice
Says, 'Faustus, come; thine hour is almost come';
And Faustus now will come to do thee right.

MEPHISTOPHILIS *gives him a dagger.*

OLD MAN.   O stay, good Faustus, stay thy des-
  perate steps.
I see an angel hovers o'er thy head,
And with a vial full of precious grace
Offers to pour the same into thy soul.
Then call for mercy and avoid despair.

FAUST.   Ah, my sweet friend, I feel thy words
To comfort my distressèd soul.
Leave me a while to ponder on my sins.   70

OLD MAN.   Faustus, I leave thee, but with
  grief of heart,
Fearing the enemy of thy hapless soul.   EXIT.

FAUST.   Accursèd Faustus, where is mercy
  now?
I do repent, and yet I do despair.
Hell strives with grace for conquest in my breast.
What shall I do to shun the snares of death?

MEPH.   Thou traitor, Faustus, I arrest thy
  soul
For disobedience to my sovereign lord.
Revolt, or I'll in piecemeal tear thy flesh.

FAUST.   I do repent I e'er offended him.   80
Sweet Mephistophilis, entreat thy lord
To pardon my unjust presumption,
And with my blood again I will confirm
The former vow I made to Lucifer.

MEPH.   Do it then, Faustus, with unfeignèd
  heart,
Lest greater dangers do attend thy drift.°

[FAUSTUS *stabs his arm and writes on a paper*
  with his blood.]

FAUST.   Torment, sweet friend, that base and
  agèd man
That durst dissuade me from thy Lucifer,
With greatest torment that our hell affords.

MEPH.   His faith is great; I cannot touch his
  soul,   90
But what I may afflict his body with
I will attempt, which is but little worth.

FAUST.   One thing, good servant, let me
  crave of thee
To glut the longing of my heart's desire—
That I may have unto my paramour
That heavenly Helen which I saw of late,
Whose sweet embracings may extinguish clear
Those thoughts that do dissuade me from my
  vow,
And keep mine oath I made to Lucifer.

MEPH.   This, or what else my Faustus shall
  desire,   100
Shall be performed in twinkling of an eye.

Enter HELEN *again, passing over* [*the*
  stage] *between two* CUPIDS.

FAUST.   Was this the face that launched a
  thousand ships
And burnt the topless towers of Ilium?°
Sweet Helen, make me immortal with a kiss.

[*She kisses him.*]

---

54. envy of thee: ill will towards you.

86. drift: purpose.   **103. Ilium:** Troy.

Her lips suck forth my soul. See where it flies!
Come, Helen, come, give me my soul again.
Here will I dwell, for heaven is in these lips,
And all is dross that is not Helena.

[Enter the OLD MAN.]

I will be Paris, and for love of thee
Instead of Troy shall Wittenberg be sacked; 110
And I will combat with weak Menelaus°
And wear thy colors on my plumèd crest.
Yea, I will wound Achilles in the heel
And then return to Helen for a kiss.
O, thou art fairer than the evening's air,
Clad in the beauty of a thousand stars.
Brighter art thou than flaming Jupiter
When he appeared to hapless Semele,°
More lovely than the monarch of the sky
In wanton Arethusa's° azured arms, 120
And none but thou shalt be my paramour.

EXEUNT [*all but the* OLD MAN].

OLD MAN. Accursèd Faustus, miserable man,
That from thy soul exclud'st the grace of heaven
And fliest the throne of his tribunal seat!

Enter the DEVILS.

Satan begins to sift me with his pride.
As in this furnace God shall try my faith,
My faith, vile hell, shall triumph over thee.
Ambitious fiends, see how the heavens smiles
At your repulse and laughs your state to scorn.
Hence hell, for hence I fly unto my God. 130

EXEUNT.

SCENE II

Thunder. Enter [above] LUCIFER, BEËL-
ZEBUB, *and* MEPHISTOPHILIS.

LUC. Thus from infernal Dis° do we ascend
To view the subjects of our monarchy,
Those souls which sin seals the black sons of hell,
'Mong which as chief, Faustus, we come to thee,
Bringing with us lasting damnation
To wait upon thy soul. The time is come
Which makes it forfeit.

MEPH. And this gloomy night,
Here in this room will wretched Faustus be.

BEËL. And here we'll stay
To mark him how he doth demean himself. 10

MEPH. How should he, but in desperate lunacy?

111. **Menelaus:** husband of Helen of Troy. **117–18.
Jupiter . . . Semele:** Jupiter visited Semele in the
form of lightning. **120. Arethusa:** Greek nymph for
whom various fountains were named.
Sc. ii: 1. Dis: Hades.

Fond worldling, now his heart-blood dries with
grief;
His conscience kills it, and his laboring brain
Begets a world of idle fantasies
To over-reach the devil. But all in vain;
His store of pleasures must be sauced with pain.
He and his servant, Wagner, are at hand.
Both come from drawing Faustus' latest will.
See where they come.

Enter FAUSTUS *and* WAGNER.

FAUST. Say, Wagner, thou hast perused my
will; 20
How dost thou like it?

WAG. Sir, so wondrous well
As in all humble duty I do yield
My life and lasting service for your love.

Enter the SCHOLARS.

FAUST. Gramercies,° Wagner. Welcome, gentlemen. [EXIT WAGNER.]

FIRST SCHOL. Now, worthy Faustus, methinks
your looks are changed.

FAUST. Ah, gentlemen!

SEC. SCHOL. What ails Faustus?

FAUST. Ah, my sweet chamber-fellow, [30
had I lived with thee, then had I lived still, but
now must die eternally. Look, sirs; comes he not?
Comes he not?

FIRST SCHOL. O my dear Faustus, what im-
ports this fear?

SEC. SCHOL. Is all our pleasure turned to
melancholy?

THIRD SCHOL. He is not well with being
over-solitary.

SEC. SCHOL. If it be so, we'll have phy- [40
sicians, and Faustus shall be cured.

THIRD SCHOL. 'Tis but a surfeit sir; fear
nothing.

FAUST. A surfeit of deadly sin that hath
damned both body and soul.

SEC. SCHOL. Yet Faustus, look up to heaven,
and remember mercy is infinite.

FAUST. But Faustus' offence can ne'er be
pardoned. The serpent that tempted Eve may
be saved, but not Faustus. Ah gentlemen, [50
hear me with patience and tremble not at my
speeches. Though my heart pants and quivers to
remember that I have been a student here these
thirty years, O, would I had never seen Wittenberg, never read book. And what wonders I have

24. Gramercies: from Fr., many thanks.

done, all Germany can witness—yea, all the world—for which Faustus hath lost both Germany and the world, yea heaven itself, heaven the seat of God, the throne of the blessed, the kingdom of joy, and must remain in hell [60 for ever. Hell, ah hell for ever! Sweet friends, what shall become of Faustus, being in hell for ever?

SEC. SCHOL.   Yet Faustus, call on God.

FAUST.   On God, whom Faustus hath abjured? On God, whom Faustus hath blasphemed? Ah, my God, I would weep, but the devil draws in my tears. Gush forth blood instead of tears, yea life and soul. O, he stays my tongue! I would lift up my hands, but see, [70 they hold 'em; they hold 'em.

ALL.   Who, Faustus?

FAUST.   Why, Lucifer and Mephistophilis. Ah, gentlemen, I gave them my soul for my cunning.

ALL.   God forbid!

FAUST.   God forbade it indeed, but Faustus hath done it. For the vain pleasure of four and twenty years hath Faustus lost eternal joy and felicity. I writ them a bill with mine own [80 blood. The date is expired. This is the time, and he will fetch me.

FIRST SCHOL.   Why did not Faustus tell us of this before, that divines might have prayed for thee?

FAUST.   Oft have I thought to have done so, but the devil threatened to tear me in pieces if I named God, to fetch me, body and soul, if I once gave ear to divinity. And now 'tis too late. Gentlemen away, lest you perish with me. [90

SEC. SCHOL.   O, what may we do to save Faustus?

FAUST.   Talk not of me, but save yourselves and depart.

THIRD SCHOL.   God will strengthen me; I will stay with Faustus.

FIRST SCHOL.   Tempt not God, sweet friend, but let us into the next room and there pray for him.

FAUST.   Ay, pray for me, pray for me; [100 and what noise soever you hear, come not unto me, for nothing can rescue me.

SEC. SCHOL.   Pray thou, and we will pray that God may have mercy upon thee.

FAUST.   Gentlemen, farewell. If I live till morning, I'll visit you; if not, Faustus is gone to hell.

ALL.   Faustus, farewell.

EXEUNT SCHOLARS.

MEPH. [*above*]   Ay, Faustus, now thou hast no hope of heaven;

Therefore despair. Think only upon hell,   110
For that must be thy mansion, there to dwell.

FAUST.   O thou bewitching fiend, 'twas thy temptation

Hath robbed me of eternal happiness.

MEPH.   I do confess it, Faustus, and rejoice.
'Twas I, that when thou wert i' the way to heaven,

Damned up thy passage. When thou took'st the book

To view the Scriptures, then I turned the leaves
And led thine eye.

What, weep'st thou? 'Tis too late. Despair! Farewell!

Fools that will laugh on earth must weep in hell.   120

EXIT.

Enter the GOOD ANGEL *and the* BAD ANGEL *at several doors.*

G. ANG.   Ah, Faustus, if thou hadst given ear to me,

Innumerable joys had followed thee;
But thou didst love the world.

B. ANG.   Gave ear to me,
And now must taste hell's pains perpetually.

G. ANG.   O what will all thy riches, pleasures, pomps

Avail thee now?

B. ANG.   Nothing but vex thee more,
To want in hell, that had on earth such store.

Music while the throne descends.

G. ANG.   O, thou hast lost celestial happiness,
Pleasures unspeakable, bliss without end.
Hadst thou affected sweet divinity,   130
Hell or the devil had had no power on thee.
Hadst thou kept on that way, Faustus, behold
In what resplendent glory thou hadst sat
In yonder throne, like those bright shining saints,
And triumphed over hell. That hast thou lost,
And now, poor soul, must thy good angel leave thee.

[*The throne ascends.*]

The jaws of hell are open to receive thee.

EXIT.

Hell is discovered.

B. ANG.   Now, Faustus, let thine eyes with horror stare
Into that vast perpetual torture-house.
There are the Furies tossing damnèd souls   140
On burning forks; their bodies boil in lead.
There are live quarters broiling on the coals,
That ne'er can die. This ever-burning chair
Is for o'er-tortured souls to rest them in.
These that are fed with sops of flaming fire
Were gluttons and loved only delicates
And laughed to see the poor starve at their gates.
But yet all these are nothing; thou shalt see
Ten thousand tortures that more horrid be.   149
FAUST.   O, I have seen enough to torture me.
B. ANG.   Nay, thou must feel them, taste the smart of all.
He that loves pleasure must for pleasure fall.
And so I leave thee, Faustus, till anon;
Then wilt thou tumble in confusion.   EXIT.
    [*Hell disappears.*] *The clock strikes eleven.*
FAUST.   Ah Faustus,
Now hast thou but one bare hour to live,
And then thou must be damned perpetually.
Stand still, you ever-moving spheres of heaven,
That time may cease and midnight never come.
Fair nature's eye, rise, rise again, and make   160
Perpetual day; or let this hour be but
A year, a month, a week, a natural day,
That Faustus may repent and save his soul.
O lente, lente currite noctis equi!°
The stars move still; time runs; the clock will strike;
The devil will come, and Faustus must be damned.
O, I'll leap up to my God! Who pulls me down?
See, see, where Christ's blood streams in the firmament!
One drop would save my soul, half a drop! Ah, my Christ!   169
Rend not my heart for naming of my Christ!
Yet will I call on him. O, spare me, Lucifer!
Where is it now? 'Tis gone. And see where God
Stretcheth out his arm and bends his ireful brows.
Mountains and hills, come, come, and fall on me,

And hide me from the heavy wrath of God.
No, no!
Then will I headlong run into the earth.
Earth, gape! O no, it will not harbor me!
You stars that reigned at my nativity,   179
Whose influence hath allotted death and hell,
Now draw up Faustus like a foggy mist
Into the entrails of yon laboring cloud,
That when you vomit forth into the air,
My limbs may issue from your smoky mouths,
So that my soul may but ascend to heaven.
            The watch strikes.
Ah, half the hour is past; 'twill all be past anon.
O God,
If thou wilt not have mercy on my soul,
Yet for Christ's sake, whose blood hath ransomed me,
Impose some end to my incessant pain.   190
Let Faustus live in hell a thousand years,
A hundred thousand, and at last be saved.
O, no end is limited° to damnèd souls.
Why wert thou not a creature wanting soul?
Or why is this immortal that thou hast?
Ah, Pythagoras' *metempsychosis,*° were that true,
This soul should fly from me and I be changed
Into some brutish beast. All beasts are happy,
For, when they die
Their souls are soon dissolved in elements,   200
But mine must live still to be plagued in hell.
Cursed be the parents that engendered me!
No, Faustus, curse thyself, curse Lucifer
That hath deprived thee of the joys of heaven.
            The clock strikes twelve.
O, it strikes, it strikes! Now, body, turn to air,
Or Lucifer will bear thee quick to hell.
O soul, be changed to little water-drops,
And fall into the ocean, ne'er be found!
        Thunder, and enter the DEVILS.
My God, my God, look not so fierce on me!
Adders and serpents, let me breathe a while!
Ugly hell, gape not! Come not, Lucifer!   211
I'll burn my books! Ah, Mephistophilis!
        EXEUNT [FAUSTUS *and* DEVILS].

SCENE III

Enter the SCHOLARS.

164. O . . . equi: Oh slowly, slowly run, horses of night (a quotation from a love poem by Ovid).   193. limited: fixed.   196. Pythagoras' metempsychosis: Pythagoras of Samos was the reputed author of the belief in transmigration of souls.

FIRST SCHOL. Come, gentlemen, let us go
  visit Faustus,
For such a dreadful night was never seen
Since first the world's creation did begin.
Such fearful shrieks and cries were never heard.
Pray heaven the doctor have escaped the danger.
  SEC. SCHOL. O help us, heaven! See, here are
    Faustus' limbs,
All torn asunder by the hand of death.
  THIRD SCHOL. The devils whom Faustus
    served have torn him thus;
For 'twixt the hours of twelve and one, me-
  thought
I heard him shriek and call aloud for help,   10
At which self time the house seemed all on fire
With dreadful horror of these damnèd fiends.
  SEC. SCHOL. Well, gentlemen, though Faus-
    tus' end be such
As every Christian heart laments to think on,
Yet for he was a scholar, once admired
For wondrous knowledge in our German schools,

We'll give his mangled limbs due burial;
And all the students, clothed in mourning black,
Shall wait upon his heavy funeral.   EXEUNT.

Epilogue

Enter CHORUS.

  CHOR. Cut is the branch that might have
    grown full straight,
And burnèd is Apollo's laurel bough
That sometime grew within this learnèd man.
Faustus is gone. Regard his hellish fall,
Whose fiendful fortune may exhort the wise
Only to wonder at unlawful things,
Whose deepness doth entice such forward wits
To practise more than heavenly power permits.
                                        [EXIT.]
Terminat hora diem; terminat auctor opus.°

Epil.: 9. Terminat . . . opus: The hour ends the
day, the author ends his work.

JOHANN WOLFGANG VON GOETHE

Faust

Prologue in Heaven

The LORD. *The* HEAVENLY HOSTS. MEPH-
ISTOPHELES *following. The* THREE ARCH-
ANGELS *step forward.*

RAPHAEL.   The chanting sun, as ever, rivals
The chanting of his brother spheres
And marches round his destined circuit—
A march that thunders in our ears.
His aspect cheers the Hosts of Heaven
Though what his essence none can say;
These inconceivable creations
Keep the high state of their first day.

GABRIEL.   And swift, with inconceivable swift-
ness,
The earth's full splendour rolls around,   10
Celestial radiance alternating
With a dread night too deep to sound;
The sea against the rocks' deep bases
Comes foaming up in far-flung force,
And rock and sea go whirling onward
In the swift spheres' eternal course.

MICHAEL.   And storms in rivalry are raging
From sea to land, from land to sea,
In frenzy forge the world a girdle
From which no inmost part is free.   20
The blight of lightning flaming yonder
Marks where the thunder-bolt will play;
And yet Thine envoys, Lord, revere
The gentle movement of Thy day.

CHOIR OF ANGELS.   Thine aspect cheers the
Hosts of Heaven
Though what Thine essence none can say,
And all Thy loftiest creations
Keep the high state of their first day.

Enter MEPHISTOPHELES.

MEPH.   Since you, O Lord, once more approach and ask

If business down with us be light or heavy—   30
And in the past you've usually welcomed me—
That's why you see me also at your levee.
Excuse me, I can't manage lofty words—
Not though your whole court jeer and find me
low;
My pathos certainly would make you laugh
Had you not left off laughing long ago.
Your suns and worlds mean nothing much to
me;
How men torment themselves, that's all I see.
The little god of the world, one can't reshape,
reshade him;
He is as strange to-day as that first day you made
him.   40
His life would be not so bad, not quite,
Had you not granted him a gleam of Heaven's
light;
He calls it Reason, uses it not the least
Except to be more beastly than any beast.
He seems to me—if your Honour does not
mind—
Like a grasshopper—the long-legged kind—
That's always in flight and leaps as it flies along
And then in the grass strikes up its same old
song.
I could only wish he confined himself to the
grass!
He thrusts his nose into every filth, alas.   50

LORD.   Mephistopheles, have you no other
news?
Do you always come here to accuse?
Is nothing ever right in your eyes on earth?

MEPH.   No, Lord! I find things there as
downright bad as ever.
I am sorry for men's days of dread and dearth;

Poor things, *my* wish to plague 'em isn't fervent.
LORD.   Do you know Faust?
MEPH.   The Doctor?
LORD.   Aye, my servant.
MEPH.   Indeed! He serves you oddly enough,
   I think.
The fool has no earthly habits in meat and
   drink.
The ferment in him drives him wide and far,   60
That he is mad he too has almost guessed;
He demands of heaven each fairest star
And of earth each highest joy and best,
And all that is new and all that is far
Can bring no calm to the deep-sea swell of his
   breast.
   LORD.   Now he may serve me only gropingly,
Soon I shall lead him into the light.
The gardener knows when the sapling first turns
   green
That flowers and fruit will make the future
   bright.
   MEPH.   What do you wager? You will lose
   him yet,   70
Provided *you* give *me* permission
To steer him gently the course I set.
   LORD.   So long as he walks the earth alive,
So long you may try what enters your head;
Men make mistakes as long as they strive.
   MEPH.   I thank you for that; as regards the
   dead,
The dead have never taken my fancy.
I favour cheeks that are full and rosy-red;
No corpse is welcome to my house;
I work as the cat does with the mouse.   80
   LORD.   Very well; you have my full permis-
   sion.
Divert this soul from its primal source
And carry it, if you can seize it,
Down with you upon your course—

And stand ashamed when you must needs admit:
A good man with his groping intuitions
Still knows the path that is true and fit.
   MEPH.   All right—but it won't last for long.
I'm not afraid my bet will turn out wrong.
And, if my aim prove true and strong,   90
Allow me to triumph wholeheartedly.
Dust shall be eat—and greedily—
Like my cousin the Snake renowned in tale and
   song.
   LORD.   That too you are free to give a trial;
I have never hated the likes of you.
Of all the spirits of denial
The joker is the last that I eschew.
Man finds relaxation too attractive—
Too fond too soon of unconditional rest;
Which is why I am pleased to give him a com-
   panion   100
Who lures and thrusts and must, as devil, be
   active.
But ye, true sons of Heaven, it is your duty
To take your joy in the living wealth of beauty.
The changing Essence which ever works and
   lives
Wall you around with love, serene, secure!
And that which floats in flickering appearance
Fix ye it firm in thoughts that must endure.
   CHOIR OF ANGELS.   Thine aspect cheers the
   Hosts of Heaven
Though what Thine essence none can say,
And all Thy loftiest creations   110
Keep the high state of their first day.
         Heaven closes.
   MEPH.   (*alone*)   I like to see the Old One
   now and then
And try to keep relations on the level.
It's really decent of so great a person
To talk so humanely even to the Devil.

The First Part of the Tragedy

NIGHT

In a high-vaulted narrow Gothic room
FAUST, *restless, in a chair at his desk.*
FAUST.   Here stand I, ach, Philosophy

Behind me and Law and Medicine too
And, to my cost, Theology—
All these I have sweated through and through
And now you see me a poor fool
As wise as when I entered school!

They call me Master, they call me Doctor,
Ten years now I have dragged my college
Along by the nose through zig and zag
Through up and down and round and round   10
And this is all that I have found—
The impossibility of knowledge!
It is this that burns away my heart;
Of course I am cleverer than the quacks,
Than master and doctor, than clerk and priest,
I suffer no scruple or doubt in the least,
I have no qualms about the devil or burning,
Which is just why all joy is torn from me,
I cannot presume to make use of my learning,
I cannot presume I could open my mind   20
To proselytize and improve mankind.

Besides, I have neither goods nor gold,
Neither reputation nor rank in the world;
No dog would choose to continue so!
Which is why I have given myself to Magic
To see if the Spirit may grant me to know
Through its force and its voice full many a se-
   cret,
May spare the sour sweat that I used to pour
   out
In talking of what I know nothing about,
May grant me to learn what it is that girds   30
The world together in its inmost being,
That the seeing its whole germination, the seeing
Its workings, may end my traffic in words.

O couldst thou, light of the full moon,
Look now thy last upon my pain,
Thou for whom I have sat belated
So many midnights here and waited
Till, over books and papers, thou
Didst shine, sad friend, upon my brow!
O could I but walk to and fro   40
On mountain heights in thy dear glow
Or float with spirits round mountain eyries
Or weave through fields thy glances glean
And freed from all miasmal theories
Bathe in thy dew and wash me clean!

Oh! Am I still stuck in this jail?
This God-damned dreary hole in the wall
Where even the lovely light of heaven
Breaks wanly through the painted panes!
Cooped up among these heaps of books   50
Gnawed by worms, coated with dust,
Round which to the top of the Gothic vault
A smoke-stained paper forms a crust.
Retorts and canisters lie pell-mell
And pyramids of instruments,

The junk of centuries, dense and mat—
Your world, man! World? They call it that!

And yet you ask why your poor heart
Cramped in your breast should feel such fear,
Why an unspecified misery   60
Should throw your life so out of gear?
Instead of the living natural world
For which God made all men his sons
You hold a reeking mouldering court
Among assorted skeletons.

Away! There is a world outside!
And this one book of mystic art
Which Nostradamus wrote himself,
Is this not adequate guard and guide?
By this you can tell the course of the stars,   70
By this, once Nature gives the word,
The soul begins to stir and dawn,
A spirit by a spirit heard.
In vain your barren studies here
Construe the signs of sanctity.
You Spirits, you are hovering near;
If you can hear me, answer me!

He opens the book and perceives
the sign of the Macrocosm.

Ha! What a river of wonder at this vision
Bursts upon all my senses in one flood!
And I feel young, the holy joy of life   80
Glows new, flows fresh, through nerve and blood!
Was it a god designed this hieroglyph to calm
The storm which but now raged inside me,
To pour upon my heart such balm,
And by some secret urge to guide me
Where all the powers of Nature stand unveiled
   around me?
Am I a God? It grows so light!
And through the clear-cut symbol on this page
My soul comes face to face with all creating
   Nature.
At last I understand the dictum of the sage: 90
'The spiritual world is always open,
Your mind is closed, your heart is dead;
Rise, young man, and plunge undaunted
Your earthly breast in the morning red.'

He contemplates the sign.

Into one Whole how all things blend,
Function and live within each other!
Passing gold buckets to each other
How heavenly powers ascend, descend!
The odour of grace upon their wings,   99
They thrust from heaven through earthly things
And as all sing so *the* All sings!

What a fine show! Aye, but only a show!
Infinite Nature, where can I tap thy veins?
Where are thy breasts, those well-springs of all
    life
On which hang heaven and earth,
Towards which my dry breast strains?
They well up, they give drink, but I feel drought
    and dearth.

*He turns the pages and perceives
the sign of the* EARTH SPIRIT.

How differently this new sign works upon me!
Thy sign, thou Spirit of the Earth, 'tis thine
And thou art nearer to me.   110
At once I feel my powers unfurled,
At once I glow as from new wine
And feel inspired to venture into the world,
To cope with the fortunes of earth benign or
    malign,
To enter the ring with the storm, to grapple and
    clinch,
To enter the jaws of the shipwreck and never
    flinch.
Over me comes a mist,
The moon muffles her light,
The lamp goes dark.
The air goes damp. Red beams flash   120
Around my head. There blows
A kind of a shudder down from the vault
And seizes on me.
It is thou must be hovering round me, come at
    my prayers!
Spirit, unveil thyself!
My heart, oh my heart, how it tears!
And how each and all of my senses
Seem burrowing upwards towards new light,
    new breath!
I feel my heart has surrendered, I have no more
    defences.   129
Come then! Come! Even if it prove my death!

*He seizes the book and solemnly pro-
nounces the sign of the* EARTH SPIRIT.
There is a flash of red flame and the SPIRIT
appears in it.

SPIRIT.   Who calls upon me?
FAUST.   Appalling vision!
SPIRIT.   You have long been sucking at my
    sphere,
Now by main force you have drawn me here
And now—
FAUST.   No! Not to be endured!

SPIRIT.   With prayers and with pantings you
    have procured
The sight of my face and the sound of my
    voice—
Now I am here. What a pitiable shivering
Seizes the Superman. Where is the call of your
    soul?   140
Where the breast which created a world in itself
And carried and fostered it, swelling up, joy-
    fully quivering,
Raising itself to a level with Us, the Spirits?
Where are you, Faust, whose voice rang out to
    me,
Who with every nerve so thrust yourself upon
    me?
Are you the thing that at a whiff of my breath
Trembles throughout its living frame,
A poor worm crawling off, askance, askew?
FAUST.   Shall I yield to Thee, Thou shape of
    flame?
I am Faust, I can hold my own with Thee.   150
SPIRIT.   In the floods of life, in the storm of
    work,
In ebb and flow,
In warp and weft,
Cradle and grave,
An eternal sea,
A changing patchwork,
A glowing life,
At the whirring loom of Time I weave
The living clothes of the Deity.
FAUST.   Thou who dost rove the wide world
    round,   160
Busy Spirit, how near I feel to Thee!
SPIRIT.   You are like that Spirit which you
    can grasp,
Not me!

The SPIRIT *vanishes.*

FAUST.   Not Thee!
Whom then?
I who am Godhead's image,
Am I not even like Thee!

A knocking on the door.

Death! I know who that is. My assistant!
So ends my happiest, fairest hour.
The crawling pedant must interrupt   170
My visions at their fullest flower!

WAGNER *enters in dressing-gown and
nightcap, a lamp in his hand.*

WAG.   Excuse me but I heard your voice declaiming—
A passage doubtless from those old Greek plays.
That is an art from which I would gladly profit,
It has its advantages nowadays.
And I've often heard folk say it's true
A preacher can learn something from an actor.
    FAUST.   Yes, when the preacher is an actor too;
Which is a not uncommon factor.
    WAG.   Ah, when your study binds up your whole existence   180
And you scarcely can see the world on a holiday
Or through a spyglass—and always from a distance—
How can your rhetoric make it walk your way?
    FAUST.   Unless you feel it, you cannot gallop it down,
Unless it thrust up from your soul
Forcing the hearts of all your audience
With a primal joy beyond control.
Sit there for ever with scissors and paste!
Gather men's leavings for a rehash
And blow up a little paltry flicker   190
Out of your own little heap of ash!
It will win you claps from apes and toddlers—
Supposing your palate welcome such—
But heart can never awaken a spark in heart
Unless your own heart keep in touch.
    WAG.   However, it is the delivery wins all ears
And I know that I am still far, too far, in arrears.
    FAUST.   Win your effects by honest means,
Eschew the cap and bells of the fool!
True insight and true sense will make   200
Their point without the rhetoric school
And, given a thought that must be heard,
Is there such need to chase a word?
Yes, your so glittering purple patches
In which you make cat's cradles of humanity
Are like the foggy wind which whispers in the autumn
Through barren leaves—a fruitless vanity.
    WAG.   Ah God, we know that art
Is long and short our life!
Often enough my analytical labours   210
Pester both brain and heart.
How hard it is to attain the means
By which one climbs to the fountain head;
Before a poor devil can reach the halfway house,

Like as not he is dead.
    FAUST.   Your manuscript, is that your holy well
A draught of which for ever quenches thirst?
You have achieved no true refreshment
Unless you can tap your own soul first.
    WAG.   Excuse me—it is considerable gratification   220
To transport oneself into the spirit of times past,
To observe what a wise man thought before our days
And how we now have brought his ideas to consummation.
    FAUST.   Oh yes, consummated in heaven!
There is a book, my friend, and its seals are seven—
The times that have been put on the shelf.
Your so-called spirit of such times
Is at bottom merely the spirit of the gentry
In whom each time reflects itself,
And at that it often makes one weep   230
And at the first glance run away,
A lumber-room and a rubbish heap,
At best an heroic puppet play
With excellent pragmatical Buts and Yets
Such as are suitable to marionettes.
    WAG.   And yet the world! The heart and spirit of men!
We all would wish to understand the same.
    FAUST.   Yes, what is known as understanding—
But who dare call the child by his real name?
The few who have known anything about it,
Whose hearts unwisely overbrimmed and spake,
Who showed the mob their feelings and their visions,   242
Have ended on the cross or at the stake.
My friend, I beg you, the night is now far gone;
We must break off for this occasion.
    WAG.   I'd have been happy sitting on and on
To continue such a learned conversation.
To-morrow however, as it is Easter Day,
I shall put you some further questions if I may.
Having given myself to knowledge heart and soul   250
I have a good share of it, now I would like the whole.
                                        EXIT WAGNER.
    FAUST. (alone) To think this head should still bring hope to birth

Sticking like glue to hackneyed rags and tags,
Delving with greedy hand for treasure
And glad when it finds an earthworm in the
    earth!
    That such a human voice should here intrude
Where spiritual fulness only now enclosed me!
And yet, my God, you poorest of all the sons
Of earth, this time you have earned my grati-
    tude.
For you have snatched me away from that de-
    spair   260
Which was ripe and ready to destroy my mind;
Beside that gigantic vision I could not find
My normal self; only a dwarf was there.
    I, image of the Godhead, who deemed myself
        but now
On the brink of the mirror of eternal truth and
        seeing
My rapturous fill of the blaze of clearest Heaven,
Having stripped off my earthly being;
I, more than an angel, I whose boundless urge
To flow through Nature's veins and in the act
        of creation   269
To revel it like the gods—what a divination,
What an act of daring—and what an expiation!
One thundering word has swept me over the
        verge.
    To boast myself thine equal I do not dare.
Granted I owned the power to draw thee down,
I lacked the power to hold thee there.
In that blest moment I felt myself,
Felt myself so small, so great;
Cruelly thou didst thrust me back
Into man's uncertain fate.
Who will teach me? What must I shun?   280
Or must I go where that impulse drives?
Alas, our very actions like our sufferings
Put a brake upon our lives.
Upon the highest concepts of the mind
There grows an alien and more alien mould;
When we have reached what in this world is
        good
That which is better is labelled a fraud, a blind.
What gave us life, feelings of highest worth,
Go dead amidst the madding crowds of earth.
    Where once Imagination on daring wing   290
Reached out to the Eternal, full of hope,
Now, that the eddies of time have shipwrecked
        chance on chance,
She is contented with a narrow scope.

Care makes her nest forthwith in the heart's
        deep places,
And there contrives her secret sorrows,
Rocks herself restlessly, destroying rest and joy;
And always she is putting on new faces,
Will appear as your home, as those that you love
        within it,
As fire or water, poison or steel;   299
You tremble at every blow that you do not feel
And what you never lose you must weep for
        every minute.
    I am not like the gods—that I too deeply
        feel—
No, I am like the worm that burrows through
        the dust
Which, as it keeps itself alive in the dust,
Is annulled and buried by some casual heel.
    Is it not dust that on a thousand shelves
Narrows this high wall round me so?
The junk that with its thousandfold tawdriness
In this moth world keeps me so low?
Shall I find here what I require?   310
Read maybe in a thousand books how men
Have in the general run tortured themselves,
With but a lucky one now and then?
Why do you grin at me, you hollow skull?
To point out that your brain was once, like
        mine, confused
And looked for the easy day but in the difficult
        dusk,
Lusting for truth was led astray and abused?
You instruments, I know you are mocking me
With cog and crank and cylinder.   319
I stood at the door, you were to be the key;
A key with intricate wards—but the bolt de-
        clines to stir.
    Mysterious in the light of day
Nature lets none unveil her; if she refuse
To make some revelation to your spirit
You cannot force her with levers and with
        screws.
You ancient gear I have never used, it is only
Because my father used you that I retain you.
You ancient scroll, you have been turning black
Since first the dim lamp smoked upon this desk
        to stain you.   329
Far better to have squandered the little I have
Than loaded with that little to stay sweating
        here.
Whatever legacy your fathers left you,

To own it you must earn it dear.
The thing that you fail to use is a load of lead;
The moment can only use what the moment it-
self has bred.
    But why do my eyes fasten upon that spot?
Is that little bottle a magnet to my sight?
Why do I feel of a sudden this lovely illumina-
tion
As when the moon flows round us in a dark
wood at night?
    Bottle, unique little bottle, I salute you   340
As now I devoutly lift you down. In you
I honour human invention and human skill.
You, the quintessence of all sweet narcotics,
The extract of all rare and deadly powers,
I am your master—show me your good will!
I look on you, my sorrow is mitigated,
I hold you and my struggles are abated,
The flood-tide of my spirit ebbs away, away.
The mirroring waters glitter at my feet,
I am escorted forth on the high seas,   350
Allured towards new shores by a new day.
A fiery chariot floats on nimble wings
Down to me and I feel myself upbuoyed
To blaze a new trail through the upper air
Into new spheres of energy unalloyed.
Oh this high life, this heavenly rapture! Do *you*
Merit this, you, a moment ago a worm?
Merit it? Aye—only turn your back on the sun
Which enchants the earth, turn your back and
be firm!   359
And brace yourself to tear asunder the gates
Which everyone longs to shuffle past if he can;
Now is the time to act and acting prove
That God's height need not lower the merit of
Man;
Nor tremble at that dark pit in which our fancy
Condemns itself to torments of its own framing,
But struggle on and upwards to that passage
At the narrow mouth of which all hell is flam-
ing.
Be calm and take this step, though you should
fall
Beyond it into nothing—nothing at all.   369
    And you, you loving-cup of shining crystal—
I have not given a thought to you for years—
Down you come now out of your ancient chest!
You glittered at my ancestors' junketings
Enlivening the serious guest
When with you in his hand he proceeded to
toast his neighbour—

But to-day no neighbour will take you from my
hand.
Here is a juice that makes one drunk in a wink;
It fills you full, you cup, with its brown flood.
It was I who made this, I who had it drawn;
So let my whole soul now make my last drink
A high and gala greeting, a toast to the dawn!
            He raises the cup to his mouth. There
                is an outburst of bells and choirs.
    CHORUS OF ANGELS. Christ is arisen!   382
Joy to mortality
Whom its own fatally
Earth-bound morality
Bound in a prison.
    FAUST. What a deep booming, what a ring-
ing tone
Pulls back the cup from my lips—and with such
power!
So soon are you announcing, you deep bells,
Easter Day's first festive hour?   390
You choirs, do you raise so soon the solacing
hymn
That once round the night of the grave rang out
from the seraphim
As man's new covenant and dower?
    CHOR. OF WOMEN. With balm and with spices
'Twas we laid him out,
We who tended him,
Faithful, devout;
We wound him in linen,
Made all clean where he lay,
Alas—to discover   400
Christ gone away.
    CHOR. OF ANG. Christ is arisen!
The loving one! Blest
After enduring the
Grievous, the curing, the
Chastening test.
    FAUST. You heavenly music, strong as you
are kind,
Why do you search me out in the dust?
Better ring forth where men have open hearts!
I hear your message, my faith it is that lags be-
hind;   410
And miracle is the favourite child of faith.
Those spheres whence peals the gospel of for-
giving,
Those are beyond what I can dare,
And yet, so used am I from childhood to this
sound,
It even now summons me back to living.

Once I could feel the kiss of heavenly love
Rain down through the calm and solemn Sab-
   bath air,
Could find a prophecy in the full-toned bell,
A spasm of happiness in a prayer.
An ineffably sweet longing bound me   420
To quest at random through field and wood
Where among countless burning tears
I felt a world rise up around me.
This hymn announced the lively games of youth,
   the lovely
Freedom of Spring's own festival;
Now with its childlike feelings memory holds me
   back
From the last and gravest step of all.
But you, sweet songs of heaven, keep sounding
   forth!
My tears well up, I belong once more to earth.
   CHOR. OF DISCIPLES.   Now has the Buried
      One,   430
Lowliness ended,
Living in lordliness,
Lordly ascended;
He in the zest of birth
Near to creating light;
We on the breast of earth
Still in frustrating night!
He left us, his own ones,
Pining upon this spot,
Ah, and lamenting,   440
Master, thy lot.
   CHOR. OF ANG.   Christ is arisen
From the womb of decay!
Burst from your prison,
Rejoice in the day!
Praising him actively,
Practising charity,
Giving alms brotherly,
Preaching him wanderingly,
Promising sanctity,   450
You have your Master near,
You have him here!

EASTER HOLIDAY

*Holidaymakers of all kinds come out
through the city gate.*
   FIRST   STUDENT.   Lord,   these   strapping
      wenches they go a lick!
Hurry up, brother, we must give 'em an escort.
My programme for to-day is a strong ale,

A pipe of shag and a girl who's got up chic.
   FIRST GIRL.   Look! Will you look at the hand-
      some boys!
Really and truly it's degrading;
They could walk out with the best of us   459
And they have to run round scullery-maiding!
   SEC. STUD.   Hold on, hold on! There are two
      coming up behind
With a very pretty taste in dress;
One of those girls is a neighbour of mine,
She appeals to me, I must confess.
You see how quietly they go
And yet in the end they'll be taking *us* in tow.
   BEGGAR. (*singing*)   Good gentlemen and lovely
      ladies,
Rosy of cheek and neat of dress,
Be kind enough to look upon me
And see and comfort my distress.   470
Leave me not here a hopeless busker!
Only the giver can be gay.
A day when all the town rejoices,
Make it for me a harvest day.
   FIRST BURGHER.   I know nothing better on
      Sundays or on holidays
Than to have a chat about war and warlike
      pother
When far away, in Turkey say,
The peoples are socking one another.
One stands at the window, drinks one's half of
      mild,
And sees the painted ships glide down the wa-
      terways;   480
Then in the evening one goes happily home
And blesses peace and peaceful days.
   SEC. BURG.   Yes indeed, neighbour! That is
      all right with me.
They can break heads if they like it so
And churn up everything topsyturvy.
But at home let us keep the status quo.
   OLD WOMAN.   Eh, but how smart they look!
      Pretty young things!
Whoever saw you should adore you!
But not so haughty! It's all right—
Tell me your wish and I can get it for you.   490
   FIRST GIRL.   Come, Agatha! Such witches I
      avoid
In public places—it's much wiser really;
It's true, she helped me on St. Andrew's night
To see my future sweetheart clearly.
   SEC. GIRL.   Yes, mine she showed me in a
      crystal,

A soldier type with dashing chaps behind him;
I look around, I seek him everywhere
And yet—and yet I never find him.

SOLDIERS. (*singing*)   Castles with towering
Walls to maintain them,   500
Girls who have suitors
But to disdain them,
Would I could gain them!
Bold is the venture,
Lordly the pay.
   Hark to the trumpets!
They may be crying
Summons to gladness,
Summons to dying.
Life is a storming!   510
Life is a splendour!
Maidens and castles
Have to surrender.
Bold is the venture,
Lordly the pay;
Later the soldiers
Go marching away.

          FAUST *and* WAGNER *are now walking*
               off on the road to the village.
   FAUST.   River and brook are freed from ice
By the lovely enlivening glance of spring   519
And hope grows green throughout the dale;
Ancient winter, weakening,
Has fallen back on the rugged mountains
And launches thence his Parthian shafts
Which are merely impotent showers of hail
Streaking over the greening mead;
But the sun who tolerates nothing white
Amidst all this shaping and stirring of seed,
Wants to enliven the world with colour
And, flowers being lacking, in their lieu
Takes colourful crowds to mend the view.   530
Turn round and look back from this rise
Towards the town. From the gloomy gate
Look, can you see them surging forth—
A harlequin-coloured crowd in fête!
Sunning themselves with one accord
In homage to the risen Lord
For they themselves to-day have risen:
Out of the dismal room in the slum,
Out of each shop and factory prison,
Out of the stuffiness of the garret,   540
Out of the squash of the narrow streets,
Out of the churches' reverend night—
One and all have been raised to light.
Look, only look, how quickly the gardens

And fields are sprinkled with the throng,
How the river all its length and breadth
Bears so many pleasure-boats along,
And almost sinking from its load
How this last dinghy moves away.
Even on the furthest mountain tracks   550
Gay rags continue to look gay.
Already I hear the hum of the village,
Here is the plain man's real heaven—
Great and small in a riot of fun;
Here I'm a man—and dare be one.
   WAG.   Doctor, to take a walk with you
Is a profit and a privilege for me
But I wouldn't lose my way alone round here,
Sworn foe that I am of all vulgarity.
This fiddling, screaming, skittle-playing,   560
Are sounds I loathe beyond all measure;
They run amuck as if the devil were in them
And call it music, call it pleasure.

               They have now reached the village.
   OLD PEASANT.   Doctor, it is most good of you
Not to look down on us to-day
And, pillar of learning that you are,
To mill around with folk at play.
So take this most particular jug
Which we have filled for you at the tap,
This is a pledge and I pray aloud   570
That it quench your thirst and more mayhap:
As many drops as this can give,
So many days extra may you live.
   FAUST.   Thank you for such a reviving beer
And now—good health to all men here.
               The people collect round him.
   OLD PEAS.   Of a truth, Doctor, you have done
      rightly
To appear on this day when all are glad,
Seeing how in times past you proved
Our own good friend when days were bad.
Many a man stands here alive   580
Whom your father found in the grip
Of a raging fever and tore him thence
When he put paid to the pestilence.
You too—you were a youngster then—
Where any was ill you went your round,
Right many a corpse left home feet first
But you came out of it safe and sound,
From many a gruelling trial—Aye,
The helper got help from the Helper on high.
   CROWD.   Health to the trusty man. We pray
He may live to help us many a day.   589
   FAUST.   Kneel to the One on high, our friend

Who teaches us helpers, who help can send.

FAUST *and* WAGNER *leave the crowd and move on.*

WAG.   You great man, how your heart must leap
To be so honoured by the masses!
How happy is he who has such talents
And from them such a crop can reap!
The father points you out to his boy,
They all ask questions, run and jostle,
The fiddles and the dancers pause   600
And, as you pass, they stand in rows
And caps go hurtling in the sky;
They almost kneel to you as though
The eucharist were passing by.

FAUST.   Only a few steps more up to that stone!
Here, after our walk, we will take a rest.
Here I have often sat, thoughtful, alone,
Torturing myself with prayer and fast.
Rich in hope and firm in faith,
With tears and sighs to seven times seven   610
I thought I could end that epidemic
And force the hand of the Lord of Heaven.
But now the crowd's applause sounds to me like derision.
O could you only read in my inmost heart
How little father and son
Merited their great reputation!
My father was a worthy man who worked in the dark,
Who in good faith but on his own wise
Brooded on Nature and her holy circles
With laborious whimsicalities;   620
Who used to collect the connoisseurs
Into the kitchen and locked inside
Its black walls pour together divers
Ingredients of countless recipes;
Such was our medicine, the patients died
And no one counted the survivors.
And thus we with our hellish powders
Raged more perniciously than the plague
Throughout this district—valley and town.   629
Myself I have given the poison to thousands;
They drooped away, *I* must live on to sample
The brazen murderers' renown.

WAG.   How can you let that weigh so heavily?
Does not a good man do enough
If he works at the art that he has received
Conscientiously and scrupulously?
As a young man you honour your father,

What he can teach, you take with a will;
As a man you widen the range of knowledge
And your son's range may be wider still.   640

FAUST.   Happy the man who swamped in this sea of Error
Still hopes to struggle up through the watery wall;
What we don't know is exactly what we need
And what we know fulfils no need at all.
But let us not with such sad thoughts
Make this good hour an hour undone!
Look how the cottages on the green
Shine in the glow of the evening sun!
He backs away, gives way, the day is overspent,
He hurries off to foster life elsewhere.   650
Would I could press on his trail, on his trail for ever—
Alas that I have no wings to raise me into the air!
Then I should see in an everlasting sunset
The quiet world before my feet unfold,
All of its peaks on fire, all of its vales becalmed,
And the silver brook dispersed in streams of gold.
Not the wild peaks with all their chasms
Could interrupt my godlike flight;
Already the bays of the sea that the sun has warmed
Unfurl upon my marvelling sight.   660
But in the end the sungod seems to sink away,
Yet the new impulse sets me again in motion,
I hasten on to drink his eternal light,
With night behind me and before me day,
Above me heaven and below me ocean.
A beautiful dream—yet the sun leaves me behind.
Alas, it is not so easy for earthly wing
To fly on level terms with the wings of the mind.
Yet born with each of us is the instinct
That struggles upwards and away   670
When over our heads, lost in the blue,
The lark pours out her vibrant lay;
When over rugged pine-clad ranges
The eagle hangs on outspread wings
And over lake and over plain
We see the homeward-struggling crane.

WAG.   I myself have often had moments of fancifulness
But I never experienced yet an urge like this.
Woods and fields need only a quick look
And *I* shall never envy the bird its pinions.   680

How differently the joys of the mind's domin-
ions
Draw us from page to page, from book to book.
That's what makes winter nights lovely and
snug—
The blissful life that warms you through your
body—
And, ah, should you unroll a worthwhile manu-
script,
You bring all heaven down into your study.

FAUST.   You are only conscious of one im-
pulse. Never
Seek an acquaintance with the other.
Two souls, alas, cohabit in my breast,
A contract one of them desires to sever.   690
The one like a rough lover clings
To the world with the tentacles of its senses;
The other lifts itself to Elysian Fields
Out of the mist on powerful wings.
Oh, if there be spirits in the air,
Princes that weave their way between heaven
and earth,
Come down to me from the golden atmosphere
And carry me off to a new and colourful life.
Aye, if I only had a magic mantle
On which I could fly abroad, a-voyaging,   700
I would not barter it for the costliest raiment,
Not even for the mantle of a king.

WAG.   Do not invoke the notorious host
Deployed in streams upon the wind,
Preparing danger in a thousand forms
From every quarter for mankind.
Thrusting upon you from the North
Come fanged spirits with arrow tongues;
From the lands of morning they come parching
To feed themselves upon your lungs;   710
The South despatches from the desert
Incendiary hordes against your brain
And the West a swarm which first refreshes,
Then drowns both you and field and plain.
They are glad to listen, adepts at doing harm,
Glad to obey and so throw dust in our eyes;
They make believe that they are sent from
heaven
And lisp like angels, telling lies.
But let us move! The world has already gone
grey,   719
The air is beginning to cool and the mist to fall.
It's in the evening one really values home—
But why do you look so astonished, standing
there, staring that way?

What's there to see in the dusk that's worth the
trouble?
FAUST.   The black dog, do you mark him
ranging through corn and stubble?
WAG.   I noticed him long ago; he struck me
as nothing much.
FAUST.   Have a good look at the brute. What
do you take him for?
WAG.   For a poodle who, as is the way of
such,
Is trailing his master, worrying out the scent.
FAUST.   But don't you perceive how in wide
spirals around us   729
He is getting nearer and nearer of set intent?
And, unless I'm wrong, a running fire
Eddies behind him in his wake.
WAG.   I can see nothing but a black poodle;
It must be your eyes have caused this mistake.
FAUST.   He is casting, it seems to me, fine
nooses of magic
About our feet as a snare.
WAG.   *I* see him leaping round us uncertainly,
timidly,
Finding instead of his master two strangers there.
FAUST.   The circle narrows; now he is near.
WAG.   Just a dog, you see; no phantoms here.
He growls and hesitates, grovels on the green
And wags his tail. Pure dog routine.   742
FAUST.   Heel, sir, heel! Come, fellow, come!
WAG.   He is a real poodle noodle.
Stand still and he'll sit up and beg;
Speak to him and he's all over you;
Lose something and he'll fetch it quick,
He'll jump in the water after your stick.
FAUST.   I think you're right, I cannot find a
trace   749
Of a spirit here; it is all a matter of training.
WAG.   If a dog is well brought up, a wise
man even
Can come to be fond of him in such a case.
Yes, he fully deserves your name upon his collar,
He whom the students have found so apt a
scholar.

FAUST'S STUDY

He enters with the poodle.

FAUST.   I have forsaken field and meadow
Which night has laid in a deep bed,
Night that wakes our better soul

With a holy and foreboding dread.
Now wild desires are wrapped in sleep
And all the deeds that burn and break,   760
The love of Man is waking now,
The love of God begins to wake.

Poodle! Quiet! Don't run hither and thither!
Leave my threshold! Why are you snuffling
    there?
Lie down behind the stove and rest.
Here's a cushion; it's my best.
Out of doors on the mountain paths
You kept us amused by running riot;
But as my protégé at home
You'll only be welcome if you're quiet.   770

Ah, when in our narrow cell
The lamp once more imparts good cheer,
Then in our bosom—in the heart
That knows itself—then things grow clear.
Reason once more begins to speak
And the blooms of hope once more to spread;
One hankers for the brooks of life,
Ah, and for life's fountainhead.

Don't growl, you poodle! That animal sound
Is not in tune with the holy music   780
By which my soul is girdled round.
We are used to human beings who jeer
At what they do not understand,
Who grouse at the good and the beautiful
Which often causes them much ado;
But must a dog snarl at it too?

But, ah, already, for all my good intentions
I feel contentment ebbing away in my breast.
Why must the stream so soon run dry
And we be left once more athirst?   790
I have experienced this so often;
Yet this defect has its compensation,
We learn to prize the supernatural
And hanker after revelation,
Which burns most bright and wins assent
Most in the New Testament.
I feel impelled to open the master text
And this once, with true dedication,
Take the sacred original
And make in my mother tongue my own trans-
    lation.   800

He opens a Bible.

It is written: In the beginning was the Word.
Here I am stuck at once. Who will help me on?
I am unable to grant the Word such merit,
I must translate it differently
If I am truly illumined by the spirit.

It is written: In the beginning was the Mind.
But why should my pen scour
So quickly ahead? Consider that first line well.
Is it the Mind that effects and creates all things?
It *should* read: In the beginning was the Power.
Yet, even as I am changing what I have writ,
Something warns me not to abide by it.   812
The spirit prompts me, I see in a flash what I
    need,
And write: In the beginning was the Deed!

Dog! If we two are to share this room,
Leave off your baying,
Leave off your barking!
I can't have such a fellow staying
Around me causing all this bother.
One of us or the other   820
Will have to leave the cell.
Well?
I don't really like to eject you so
But the door is open, you may go.

But what? What do I see?
Can this really happen naturally?
Is it a fact or is it a fraud?
My dog is growing so long and broad!
He raises himself mightily,
That is not a dog's anatomy!   830
What a phantom have I brought to my house!
He already looks like a river horse
With fiery eyes and frightful jaws—
Aha! But I can give you pause!
For such a hybrid out of hell
Solomon's Key is a good spell.

SPIRITS *are heard in the passage.*

SPIRITS.   Captured within there is one of us!
Wait without, follow him none of us!
Like a fox in a snare
An old hell-cat's trembling there.   840
But on the alert!
Fly against and athwart,
To starboard and port,
And he's out with a spurt!
If help you can take him,
Do not forsake him!
For often, to earn it, he
Helped our fraternity.

FAUST.   First, to confront the beast,
Be the Spell of the Four released: 850
Salamander shall glow,
Undine shall coil,
Sylph shall vanish
And gnome shall toil.

One without sense
Of the elements,
Of their force
And proper course,
The spirits would never
Own him for master.   860
　Vanish in flames,
Salamander!
Commingle in babble of streams,
Undine!
Shine meteor-like and majestic,
Sylph!
Bring help domestic,
Lubber-fiend! Lubber-fiend!
Step out of him and make an end!
　None of the Four   870
Is the creature's core.
He lies quite quiet and grins at me,
I have not yet worked him injury.
To exorcise you
I'll have to chastise you.
　Are you, rapscallion,
A displaced devil?
This sign can level
Each dark battalion;
Look at this sign!   880
　He swells up already with bristling spine.
　You outcast! Heed it—
This name! Can you read it?
The unbegotten one,
Unpronounceable,
Poured throughout Paradise,
Heinously wounded one?
　Behind the stove, bound by my spells,
Look, like an elephant it swells,
Filling up all the space and more,   890
It threatens to melt away in mist.
Down from the ceiling! Down before—!
Down at your master's feet! Desist!
You see, I have not proved a liar;
I can burn you up with holy fire!
　Do not await
The triply glowing light!
Do not await
My strongest brand of necromancy!
　The mist subsides and MEPHISTOPHELES
comes forward from behind the stove,
dressed like a travelling scholar.
　MEPH.　What is the noise about? What might
　the gentleman fancy?   900

FAUST.　So that is what the poodle had in-
　side him!
A travelling scholar? That casus makes me laugh.
　MEPH.　My compliments to the learned gen-
　tleman.
You have put me in a sweat—not half!
　FAUST.　What is your name?
　MEPH.　The question strikes me as petty
For one who holds the Word in such low repute,
Who, far withdrawn from all mere surface,
Aims only at the Essential Root.
　FAUST.　With you, you gentry, what is essen-
　tial   910
The name more often than not supplies,
As is indeed only too patent
When they call you Fly-God, Corrupter, Father
　of Lies.
All right, who are you then?
　MEPH.　A part of that Power
Which always wills evil, always procures good.
　FAUST.　What do you mean by this conun-
　drum?
　MEPH.　I am the Spirit which always denies.
And quite rightly; whatever has a beginning
Deserves to have an undoing;   920
It would be better if nothing began at all.
Thus everything that you call
Sin, destruction, Evil in short,
Is my own element, my resort.
　FAUST.　You call yourself a part, yet you
　stand before me whole?
　MEPH.　This is the unassuming truth.
Whereas mankind, that little world of fools,
Commonly takes itself for a whole—
I am a part of the Part which in the beginning
　was all,   929
A part of the darkness which gave birth to light,
To that haughty light which is struggling now
　to usurp
The ancient rank and realm of its mother Night,
And yet has no success, try as it will,
Being bound and clamped by bodies still.
It streams from bodies, bodies it beautifies,
A body clogs it when it would run,
And so, I hope, it won't be long
Till, bodies and all, it is undone.
　FAUST.　Ah, now I know your honourable
　profession!
You cannot destroy on a large scale,   940
So you are trying it on a small.

MEPH.   And, candidly, not getting far at all.
That which stands over against the Nothing,
The Something, I mean this awkward world,
For all my endeavours up to date
I have failed to get it under foot
With waves, with storms, with earthquakes,
  fire—
Sea and land after all stay put.
And this damned stuff, the brood of beasts and
  men,
There is no coming to grips with them;   950
I've already buried heaps of them!
And always new blood, fresh blood, circulates
  again.
So it goes on, it's enough to drive one crazy.
A thousand embryos extricate themselves
From air, from water and from earth
In wet and dry and hot and cold.
Had I not made a corner in fire
I should find myself without a berth.
  FAUST.   So you when faced with the ever
    stirring,
The creative force, the beneficent,   960
Counter with your cold devil's fist
Spitefully clenched but impotent.
You curious son of Chaos, why
Not turn your hand to something else?
  MEPH.   We will give it our serious attention—
But more on that subject by and by.
Might I for this time take my leave?
  FAUST.   Why you ask I cannot see.
I have already made your acquaintance;
When you feel like it, call on me.   970
Here is the window, here is the door—
And a chimney too—if it comes to that.
  MEPH.   I must confess; there's a slight im-
    pediment
That stops me making my exit pat,
The pentagram upon your threshold—
  FAUST.   So the witch's foot is giving you
    trouble?
Then tell me, since you're worried by that spell,
How did you ever enter, child of Hell?
How was a spirit like you betrayed?
  MEPH.   You study that sign! It's not well
    made;   980
One of its corners, do you see,
The outside one's not quite intact.
  FAUST.   A happy accident in fact!
Which means you're in my custody?

I did not intend to set a gin.
  MEPH.   The dog—he noticed nothing, jump-
    ing in;
The case has now turned round about
And I, the devil, can't get out.
  FAUST.   Then why not leave there by the
    window?
  MEPH.   It is a law for devils and phantoms
    all: 990
By the way that we slip in by the same we must
    take our leave.
One's free in the first, in the second one's a
    thrall.
  FAUST.   So Hell itself has its regulations?
That's excellent; a contract in that case
Could be made with you, you gentry—and defi-
    nite?
  MEPH.   What we promise, you will enjoy
    with no reservations,
Nothing will be nipped off from it.
But all this needs a little explaining
And will keep till our next heart-to-heart;
But now I beg and doubly beg you: 1000
Let me, just for now, depart.
  FAUST.   But wait yet a minute and consent
To tell me first some news of moment.
  MEPH.   Let me go now! I'll soon be back
To be questioned to your heart's content.
  FAUST.   It was not I laid a trap for you,
You thrust your own head in the noose.
A devil in the hand's worth two in hell!
The second time he'll be longer loose.
  MEPH.   If you so wish it, I'm prepared   1010
To keep you company and stay;
Provided that by my arts the time
Be to your betterment whiled away.
  FAUST.   I am in favour, carry on—
But let your art be a pleasing one.
  MEPH.   My friend, your senses will have more
Gratification in this hour
Than in a year's monotony.
What the delicate spirits sing to you
And the beauties that they bring to you   1020
Are no empty, idle wizardry.
You'll have your sense of smell delighted,
Your palate in due course excited,
Your feelings rapt enchantingly.
Preparation? There's no need,
We are all here. Strike up! Proceed!
                    The SPIRITS *sing.*

SPIRITS.   Vanish, you darkling
Arches above him,
That a more witching
Blue and enriching   1030
Sky may look in!
If only the darkling
Clouds were unravelled!
Small stars are sparkling,
Suns are more gently
Shining within!
Spiritual beauty
Of the children of Heaven
Swaying and bowing
Floats in the air,   1040
Leanings and longings
Follow them there;
And ribbons of raiment
The breezes have caught
Cover the country,
Cover the arbour
Where, drowning in thought,
Lovers exchange their
Pledges for life.
Arbour on arbour!   1050
Creepers run rife!
Grapes in great wreathing
Clusters are poured into
Vats that are seething,
Wines that are foaming
Pour out in rivulets
Rippling and roaming
Through crystalline stones,
Leaving the sight of
The highlands behind them,   1060
Widening to lakes
Amid the delight of
Green-growing foothills.
And the winged creatures
Sipping their ecstasy,
Sunwards they fly,
Fly to discover
The glittering islands
Which bob on the wave-tops
Deceiving the eye.   1070
There we can hear
Huzzaing in chorus,
A landscape of dancers
Extending before us,
All in the open,
Free as the air.
Some of them climbing

Over the peaks,
Some of them swimming
Over the lakes,   1080
Or floating in space—
All towards existence,
All towards the distance
Of stars that will love them,
The blessing of grace.

   MEPH.   He is asleep. That's fine, you airy,
     dainty youngsters
You have sung him a real cradle song.
For this performance I am in your debt.
You are not yet the man to hold the devil for
     long.   1089
Play round him with your sweet dream trickeries
And sink him in a sea of untruth!
But to break the spell upon this threshold
What I need now is a rat's tooth.
And I needn't bother to wave a wand,
I can hear one rustling already, he'll soon re-
     spond.
The lord of rats, the lord of mice,
Of flies, frogs, bugs and lice,
Commands you to come out of that
And gnaw away this threshold, rat,
While he takes oil and gives it a few—   1100
So there you come hopping? Quick on your cue!
Now get on the job! The obstructing point
Is on the edge and right in front.
One bite more and the work's done.
Now, Faust, till we meet again, dream on!
   FAUST. (*waking*)   Am I defrauded then once
     more?
Does the throng of spirits vanish away like fog
To prove that the devil appeared to me in a
     dream
But what escaped was only a dog?

The same room. Later.

   FAUST.   Who's knocking? Come in! *Now*
     who wants to annoy me?   1110
   MEPH. (*outside door*)   It's I.
   FAUST.   Come in!
   MEPH. (*outside door*)   You must say "Come
     in" three times.
   FAUST.   Come in then!
   MEPH. (*entering*)   Thank you; you over-
     joy me.
We two, I hope, we shall be good friends;
To chase those megrims of yours away
I am here like a fine young squire to-day,
In a suit of scarlet trimmed with gold

And a little cape of stiff brocade,
With a cock's feather in my hat
And at my side a long sharp blade,
And the most succinct advice I can give   1120
Is that you dress up just like me,
So that uninhibited and free
You may find out what it means to live.

FAUST.   The pain of earth's constricted life,
I fancy,
Will pierce me still, whatever my attire;
I am too old for mere amusement,
Too young to be without desire.
How can the world dispel my doubt?
You must do without, you must do without!
That is the everlasting song   1130
Which rings in every ear, which rings,
And which to us our whole life long
Every hour hoarsely sings.
I wake in the morning only to feel appalled,
My eyes with bitter tears could run
To see the day which in its course
Will not fulfil a wish for me, not one;
The day which whittles away with obstinate
carping
All pleasures—even those of anticipation,   1139
Which makes a thousand grimaces to obstruct
My heart when it is stirring in creation.
And again, when night comes down, in anguish
I must stretch out upon my bed
And again no rest is granted me,
For wild dreams fill my mind with dread.
The God who dwells within my bosom
Can make my inmost soul react;
The God who sways my every power
Is powerless with external fact.
And so existence weighs upon my breast   1150
And I long for death and life—life I detest.

MEPH.   Yet death is never a wholly welcome
guest.

FAUST.   O happy is he whom death in the
dazzle of victory
Crowns with the bloody laurel in the battling
swirl!
Or he whom after the mad and breakneck dance
He comes upon in the arms of a girl!
O to have sunk away, delighted, deleted,
Before the Spirit of the Earth, before his might!

MEPH.   Yet I know someone who failed to
drink
A brown juice on a certain night.   1160

FAUST.   Your hobby is espionage—is it not?

MEPH.   Oh I'm not omniscient—but I know
a lot.

FAUST.   Whereas that tumult in my soul
Was stilled by sweet familiar chimes
Which cozened the child that yet was in me
With echoes of more happy times,
I now curse all things that encompass
The soul with lures and jugglery
And bind it in this dungeon of grief
With trickery and flattery.   1170
Cursed in advance be the high opinion
That serves our spirit for a cloak!
Cursed be the dazzle of appearance
Which bows our senses to its yoke!
Cursed be the lying dreams of glory,
The illusion that our name survives!
Cursed be the flattering things we own,
Servants and ploughs, children and wives!
Cursed be Mammon when with his treasures
He makes us play the adventurous man   1180
Or when for our luxurious pleasures
He duly spreads the soft divan!
A curse on the balsam of the grape!
A curse on the love that rides for a fall!
A curse on hope! A curse on faith!
And a curse on patience most of all!

The invisible SPIRITS *sing again.*

SPIRITS.   Woe! Woe!
You have destroyed it,
The beautiful world;
By your violent hand   1190
'Tis downward hurled!
A half-god has dashed it asunder!
From under
We bear off the rubble to nowhere
And ponder
Sadly the beauty departed.
Magnipotent
One among men,
Magnificent
Build it again,   1200
Build it again in your breast!
Let a new course of life
Begin
With vision abounding
And new songs resounding
To welcome it in!

MEPH.   These are the juniors
Of my faction.

Hear how precociously they counsel
Pleasure and action.   1210
Out and away
From your lonely day
Which dries your senses and your juices
Their melody seduces.
   Stop playing with your grief which battens
Like a vulture on your life, your mind!
The worst of company would make you feel
That you are a man among mankind.
Not that it's really my proposition
To shove you among the common men;   1220
Though I'm not one of the Upper Ten,
If you would like a coalition
With me for your career through life,
I am quite ready to fit in,
I'm yours before you can say knife.
I am your comrade;
If you so crave,
I am your servant, I am your slave.
   FAUST.   And what have I to undertake in
    return?
   MEPH.   Oh it's early days to discuss what that
    is.   1230
   FAUST.   No, no, the devil is an egoist
And ready to do nothing gratis
Which is to benefit a stranger.
Tell me your terms and don't prevaricate!
A servant like you in the house is a danger.
   MEPH.   I will bind myself to your service in
    this world,
To be at your beck and never rest nor slack;
When we meet again on the other side,
In the same coin you shall pay me back.
   FAUST.   The other side gives me little trou-
    ble;   1240
First batter this present world to rubble,
Then the other may rise—if that's the plan.
This earth is where my springs of joy have
    started,
And this sun shines on me when broken-hearted;
If I can first from them be parted,
Then let happen what will and can!
I wish to hear no more about it—
Whether there too men hate and love
Or whether in those spheres too, in the future,
There is a Below or an Above.   1250
   MEPH.   With such an outlook you can risk it.
Sign on the line! In these next days you will get
Ravishing samples of my arts;

I am giving you what never man saw yet.
   FAUST.   Poor devil, can *you* give anything
    ever?
Was a human spirit in its high endeavour
Even once understood by one of your breed?
Have you got food which fails to feed?
Or red gold which, never at rest,   1259
Like mercury runs away through the hand?
A game at which one never wins?
A girl who, even when on my breast,
Pledges herself to my neighbour with her eyes?
The divine and lovely delight of honour
Which falls like a falling star and dies?
Show me the fruits which, before they are
    plucked, decay
And the trees which day after day renew their
    green!
   MEPH.   Such a commission doesn't alarm me,
I have such treasures to purvey.
But, my good friend, the time draws on when
    we   1270
Should be glad to feast at our ease on something
    good.
   FAUST.   If ever I stretch myself on a bed of
    ease,
Then I am finished! Is that understood?
If ever your flatteries can coax me
To be pleased with myself, if ever you cast
A spell of pleasure that can hoax me—
Then let *that* day be my last!
That's my wager!
   MEPH.   Done!
   FAUST.   Let's shake!
If ever I say to the passing moment
"Linger a while! Thou art so fair!"   1280
Then you may cast me into fetters,
I will gladly perish then and there!
Then you may set the death-bell tolling,
Then from my service you are free,
The clock may stop, its hand may fall,
And that be the end of time for me!
   MEPH.   Think what you're saying, we shall
    not forget it.
   FAUST.   And you are fully within your rights;
I have made no mad or outrageous claim.
If I stay as I am, I am a slave—   1290
Whether yours or another's, it's all the same.
   MEPH.   I shall this very day at the College
    Banquet
Enter your service with no more ado,

But just one point—As a life-and-death insur-
ance
I must trouble you for a line or two.
    FAUST.   So you, you pedant, you too like
things in writing?
Have you never known a man? Or a man's
word? Never?
Is it not enough that my word of mouth
Puts all my days in bond for ever?   1299
Does not the world rage on in all its streams
And shall a promise hamper *me?*
Yet this illusion reigns within our hearts
And from it who would be gladly free?
Happy the man who can inwardly keep his word;
Whatever the cost, he will not be loath to pay!
But a parchment, duly inscribed and sealed,
Is a bogey from which all wince away.
The word dies on the tip of the pen
And wax and leather lord it then.
What do you, evil spirit, require?   1310
Bronze, marble, parchment, paper?
Quill or chisel or pencil of slate?
You may choose whichever you desire.
    MEPH.   How can you so exaggerate
With such a hectic rhetoric?
Any little snippet is quite good—
And you sign it with one little drop of blood.
    FAUST.   If that is enough and is some use,
One may as well pander to your fad.
    MEPH.   Blood is a very special juice.   1320
    FAUST.   Only do not fear that I shall break
this contract.
What I promise is nothing more
Than what all my powers are striving for.
I have puffed myself up too much, it is only
Your sort that really fits my case.
The great Earth Spirit has despised me
And Nature shuts the door in my face.
The thread of thought is snapped asunder,
I have long loathed knowledge in all its fashions.
In the depths of sensuality   1330
Let us now quench our glowing passions!
And at once make ready every wonder
Of unpenetrated sorcery!
Let us cast ourselves into the torrent of time,
Into the whirl of eventfulness,
Where disappointment and success,
Pleasure and pain may chop and change
As chop and change they will and can;
It is restless action makes the man.   1339
    MEPH.   No limit is fixed for you, no bound;

If you'd like to nibble at everything
Or to seize upon something flying round—
Well, may you have a run for your money!
But seize your chance and don't be funny!
    FAUST.   I've told you, it is no question of
happiness.
The most painful joy, enamoured hate, enliven-
ing
Disgust—I devote myself to all excess.
My breast, now cured of its appetite for knowl-
edge,
From now is open to all and every smart,   1349
And what is allotted to the whole of mankind
That will I sample in my inmost heart,
Grasping the highest and lowest with my spirit,
Piling men's weal and woe upon my neck,
To extend myself to embrace all human selves
And to founder in the end, like them, a wreck.
    MEPH.   O believe *me,* who have been chew-
ing
These iron rations many a thousand year,
No human being can digest
This stuff, from the cradle to the bier.
This universe—believe a devil—   1360
Was made for no one but a god!
He exists in eternal light
But *us* he has brought into the darkness
While *your* sole portion is day and night.
    FAUST.   I will all the same!
    MEPH.   That's very nice.
There's only one thing I find wrong;
Time is short, art is long.
You could do with a little artistic advice.
Confederate with one of the poets
And let him flog his imagination   1370
To heap all virtues on your head,
A head with such a reputation:
Lion's bravery,
Stag's velocity,
Fire of Italy,
Northern tenacity.
Let *him* find out the secret art
Of combining craft with a noble heart
And of being in love like a young man,
Hotly, but working to a plan.   1380
Such a person—*I'd* like to meet him;
"Mr. Microcosm" is how I'd greet him.
    FAUST.   What am I then if fate must bar
My efforts to reach that crown of humanity
After which all my senses strive?

MEPH.   You are in the end . . . what you
    are.
You can put on full-bottomed wigs with a mil-
    lion locks,
You can put on stilts instead of your socks,
You remain for ever what you are.
    FAUST.   I feel my endeavours have not been
      worth a pin   1390
When I raked together the treasures of the hu-
    man mind,
If at the end I but sit down to find
No new force welling up within.
I have not a hair's breadth more of height,
I am no nearer the Infinite.
    MEPH.   My very good sir, you look at things
Just in the way that people do;
We must be cleverer than that
Or the joys of life will escape from you.
Hell! You have surely hands and feet,   1400
Also a head and you-know-what;
The pleasures I gather on the wing,
Are they less mine? Of course they're not!
Suppose I can afford six stallions,
I can add that horse-power to my score
And dash along and be a proper man
As if my legs were twenty-four.
So good-bye to thinking! On your toes!
The world's before us. Quick! Here goes!
I tell you, a chap who's intellectual   1410
Is like a beast on a blasted heath
Driven in circles by a demon
While a fine green meadow lies round beneath.
    FAUST.   How do we start?
    MEPH.   We just say go—and skip.
But please get ready for this pleasure trip.
                             EXIT FAUST.
Only look down on knowledge and reason,
The highest gifts that men can prize,
Only allow the spirit of lies
To confirm you in magic and illusion,
And then I have you body and soul.   1420
Fate has given this man a spirit
Which is always pressing onwards, beyond con-
    trol,
And whose mad striving overleaps
All joys of the earth between pole and pole.
Him shall I drag through the wilds of life
And through the flats of meaninglessness,
I shall make him flounder and gape and stick
And to tease his insatiableness

Hang meat and drink in the air before his wa-
    tering lips;   1429
In vain he will pray to slake his inner thirst,
And even had he not sold himself to the devil
He would be equally accursed.
              Re-enter FAUST.
    FAUST.   And now, where are we going?
    MEPH.   Wherever you please.
The small world, then the great for us.
With what pleasure and what profit
You will roister through the syllabus!
    FAUST.   But I, with this long beard of mine,
I lack the easy social touch,
I know the experiment is doomed;   1439
Out in the world I never could fit in much.
I feel so small in company
I'll be embarrassed constantly.
    MEPH.   My friend, it will solve itself, any
      such misgiving;
Just trust yourself and you'll learn the art of
    living.
    FAUST.   Well, then, how do we leave home?
Where are your grooms? Your coach and horses?
    MEPH.   We merely spread this mantle wide,
It will bear us off on airy courses.
But do not on this noble voyage
Cumber yourself with heavy baggage.   1450
A little inflammable gas which I'll prepare
Will lift us quickly into the air.
If we travel light we shall cleave the sky like a
    knife.
Congratulations on your new course of life!

THE WITCH'S KITCHEN[1]

*Every sort of witch prop. A large caul-
dron hangs over the fire.* MONKEYS *sit
around it, seen through the fumes.*
    MEPH.   Look, what a pretty species of mon-
      key!
She is the kitchen-maid, he is the flunkey.
It seems your mistress isn't at home?
    MONKEYS.   Out at a rout!
Out and about!
By the chimney spout!   1460
    MEPH.   How long does she keep it up at night?
    MONKEYS.   As long as we warm our paws at
      this fire.

[1]Certain transpositions have been made in this scene.

MEPH. How do you like these delicate ani-
mals?

FAUST. I never saw such an outré sight.
I find it nauseating, this crazy witchcraft!
Do you promise me that I shall improve
In this cesspit of insanity?
Do I need advice from an old hag?
And can this filthy brew remove
Thirty years from my age? O vanity, 1470
If you know nothing better than this!
My hope has already vanished away.
Surely Nature, surely a noble spirit
Has brought some better balm to the light of
day?

MEPH. My friend, you once more talk to the
point.
There is also a natural means of rejuvenation;
But that is written in another book
And is a chapter that needs some explanation.

FAUST. I want to know it.

MEPH. Right. There is a means requires
No money, no physician, and no witch: 1480
Away with you this moment back to the land,
And there begin to dig and ditch,
Confine yourself, confine your mind,
In a narrow round, ever repeating,
Let your diet be of the simplest kind,
Live with the beasts like a beast and do not
think it cheating
To use your own manure to insure your crops
are weighty!
Believe me, that is the best means
To keep you young till you are eighty. 1489

FAUST. I am not used to it, I cannot change
My nature and take the spade in hand.
The narrow life is not my style at all.

MEPH. Then it's a job for the witch to arrange.

FAUST. The hag—but why do we need just
her?
Can you yourself not brew the drink?

MEPH. A pretty pastime! I'd prefer
To build a thousand bridges in that time.
It is not only art and science
That this work needs but patience too.
A quiet spirit is busy at it for years 1500
And time but fortifies the subtle brew.
And the most wonderful ingredients
Go into it— you couldn't fake it!

The devil taught it it her, I admit;
The devil, however, cannot make it.
Tell me, you monkeys, you damned puppets,
What are you doing with that great globe?

HE-MONKEY. This is the world:
It rises and falls
And rolls every minute; 1510
It rings like glass—
But how soon it breaks!
And there's nothing in it.
It glitters here
And here still more:
I am alive!
O my son, my dear,
Keep away, keep away!
You are bound to die!
The shards are sharp, 1520
It was made of clay.

FAUST *has meanwhile been gazing in a mirror.*

FAUST. What do I see in this magic mirror?
What a heavenly image to appear!
O Love, lend me the swiftest of your wings
And waft me away into her sphere!
But, alas, when I do not keep this distance,
If to go nearer I but dare
I can see her only as if there were mist in the
air—
The fairest image of a woman!
But can Woman be so fair? 1530
In that shape in the mirror must I see the quin-
tessence
Of all the heavens—reclining there?
Can such a thing be found on earth?

MEPH. Naturally, when a God works six days
like a black
And at the end of it slaps himself on the back,
Something should come of it of some worth.
For this occasion look your fill.
I can smell you out a sweetheart as good as this,
And happy the man who has the luck
To bear her home to wedded bliss. 1540

The WITCH *enters down the chimney—
violently.*

WITCH. What goes on here?
Who are you two?
What d'you want here?
Who has sneaked through?
May the fever of fire
Harrow your marrow!

MEPH.   Don't you know me, you bag of
bones? You monster, you!
Don't you know your lord and master?
What prevents me striking you
And your monkey spirits, smashing you up like
plaster?   1550
Has my red doublet no more claim to fame?
Can you not recognize the cock's feather?
Have I concealed my countenance?
Must I myself announce my name?
WITCH.   My lord, excuse this rude reception.
It is only I miss your cloven foot.
And where is your usual brace of ravens?
MEPH.   I'll forgive you this once, as an ex-
ception;
Admittedly some time has pass't
Since we two saw each other last.   1560
Culture too, which is licking the whole world
level,
Has latterly even reached the devil.
The Nordic spook no longer commands a sale;
Where can you see horns, claws or tail?
And as regards the foot, which is my *sine qua
non,*
It would prejudice me in the social sphere;
Accordingly, as many young men have done,
I have worn false calves this many a year.
WITCH.   Really and truly I'm knocked flat
To see Lord Satan here again!   1570
MEPH.   Woman, you must not call me that!
WITCH.   Why! What harm is there in the
name?
MEPH.   Satan has long been a myth without
sense or sinew;
Not that it helps humanity all the same,
They are quit of the Evil One but the evil ones
continue.
You may call me the Noble Baron, that should
do;
I am a cavalier among other cavaliers,
You needn't doubt my blood is blue—
                    He makes an indecent gesture.
WITCH.   Ha! Ha! Always true to type!   1579
You still have the humour of a guttersnipe!
MEPH.   Observe my technique, my friend—
not a single hitch;
This is the way to get round a witch.
WITCH.   Now tell me, gentlemen, what do
you want?
MEPH.   A good glass of your well-known
juice.

And please let us have your oldest vintage;
When it's been kept it's twice the use.
WITCH.   Delighted! Why, there's some here
on the shelf—
I now and then take a nip myself—
And, besides, this bottle no longer stinks;
You're welcome while I've a drop to give.   1590
(*aside*) But, if this man is unprepared when he
drinks,
You very well know he has not an hour to live.
MEPH.   He's a good friend and it should set
him up;
I'd gladly grant him the best of your kitchen,
So draw your circle and do your witching
And give the man a decent cup.
                    The WITCH *begins her conjuration.*
FAUST.   But, tell me, how will this mend my
status?
These lunatic gestures, this absurd apparatus,
This most distasteful conjuring trick—
I've known it all, it makes me sick.   1600
MEPH.   Pooh, that's just fooling, get it in
focus,
And don't be such a prig for goodness' sake!
As a doctor she must do her hocus-pocus
So that when you have drunk your medicine it
will take.
WITCH.   The lofty power
That is wisdom's dower,
Concealed from great and clever,
Don't use your brain
And that's your gain—
No trouble whatsoever.   1610
FAUST.   What nonsense is she saying to us?
My head is splitting; I've the sensation
Of listening to a hundred thousand
Idiots giving a mass recitation.
MEPH.   Enough, enough, you excellent Sibyl!
Give us your drink and fill the cup
Full to the brim and don't delay!
This draught will do my friend no injury;
He is a man of more than one degree
And has drunk plenty in his day.   1620
                    The WITCH *gives* FAUST *the cup.*
Now lower it quickly. Bottoms up!
And your heart will begin to glow and perk.
Now out of the circle! You mustn't rest.
WITCH.   I hope the little drink will work.
MEPH.   (*to* WITCH)   And you, if there's any-
thing you want, all right;

Just mention it to me on Walpurgis Night.
(*to* FAUST) Come now, follow me instantly!
You've got to perspire, it's necessary,
That the drug may pervade you inside and out.
I can teach you later to value lordly leisure 1630
And you soon will learn with intensest pleasure
How Cupid stirs within and bounds about.
    FAUST. Just one more look, one quick look, in the mirror!
That woman was too fair to be true.
    MEPH. No, no! The paragon of womanhood
Will soon be revealed in the flesh to you.
(*aside*) With a drink like this in you, take care—
You'll soon see Helens everywhere.

IN THE STREET

    FAUST *accosts* GRETCHEN *as she passes.*
    FAUST. My pretty young lady, might I venture
To offer you my arm and my escort too? 1640
    GRET. I'm not a young lady nor am I pretty
And I can get home without help from you.
        She releases herself and goes off.
    FAUST. By Heaven, she's beautiful, this child!
I have never seen her parallel.
So decorous, so virtuous,
And just a little pert as well.
The light of her cheek, her lip so red,
I shall remember till I'm dead!
The way that she cast down her eye
Is stamped on my heart as with a die; 1650
And the way that she got rid of me
Was a most ravishing thing to see!
        Enter MEPHISTOPHELES.
Listen to me! Get me that girl!
    MEPH. Which one?
    FAUST. The one that just went past.
    MEPH. She? She was coming from her priest,
Absolved from her sins one and all;
I'd crept up near the confessional.
An innocent thing. Innocent? Yes!
At church with nothing to confess!
Over that girl I have no power. 1660
    FAUST. Yet she's fourteen if she's an hour.
    MEPH. Why, you're talking like Randy Dick
Who covets every lovely flower
And all the favours, all the laurels,
He fancies are for him to pick;
But it doesn't always work out like that.

    FAUST. My dear Professor of Ancient Morals,
Spare me your trite morality!
I tell you straight—and hear me right—
Unless this object of delight 1670
Lies in my arms this very night,
At midnight we part company.
    MEPH. Haven't you heard: more haste less speed?
A fortnight is the least I need
Even to work up an occasion.
    FAUST. If I had only seven hours clear,
I should not need the devil here
To bring *this* quest to consummation.
    MEPH. It's almost French, your line of talk;
I only ask you not to worry. 1680
Why make your conquest in a hurry?
The pleasure is less by a long chalk
Than when you first by hook and by crook
Have squeezed your doll and moulded her,
Using all manner of poppycock
That foreign novels keep in stock.
    FAUST. I am keen enough without all that.
    MEPH. Now, joking apart and without aspersion,
You cannot expect, I tell you flat,
This beautiful child in quick reversion. 1690
Immune to all direct attack—
We must lay our plots behind her back.
    FAUST. Get me something of my angel's!
Carry me to her place of rest!
Get me a garter of my love's!
Get me a kerchief from her breast!
    MEPH. That you may see the diligent fashion
In which I shall abet your passion,
We won't let a moment waste away,
I will take you to her room to-day. 1700
    FAUST. And shall I see her? Have her?
    MEPH. No!
She will be visiting a neighbour.
But you in the meanwhile, quite alone,
Can stay in her aura in her room
And feast your fill on joys to come.
    FAUST. Can we go now?
    MEPH. It is still too soon.
    FAUST. Then a present for her! Get me one!
        EXIT FAUST.
    MEPH. Presents already? Fine. A certain hit!
I know plenty of pretty places
And of long-buried jewel-cases; 1710
I must take stock of them a bit.

GRETCHEN'S ROOM

GRET. (*alone, doing her hair*)   I'd give a lot
   to be able to say
Who the gentleman was to-day.
He cut a fine figure certainly
And is sprung from the nobility;
His face showed that—Besides, you see,
He'd otherwise not have behaved so forwardly.
   She goes out; then MEPHISTOPHELES
   and FAUST *enter.*
MEPH.   Come in—very quietly—Only come
   in!
FAUST. (*after a silence*)   I ask you: please
   leave me alone!   1719
MEPH.   Not all girls keep their room so clean.
FAUST. (*looking around*)   Welcome, sweet
   gleaming of the gloaming
That through this sanctuary falls aslope!
Seize on my heart, sweet fever of love
That lives and languishes on the dews of hope!
What a feeling of quiet breathes around me,
Of order, of contentedness!
What fulness in this poverty,
And in this cell what blessedness!
   Here I could while away hour after hour.
It was here, O Nature, that your fleeting dreams
Brought this born angel to full flower.   1731
Here lay the child and the warm life
Filled and grew in her gentle breast,
And here the pure and holy threads
Wove a shape of the heavenliest.
   And you! What brought you here to-day?
Why do I feel this deep dismay?
What do you want here? Why is your heart so
   sore?
Unhappy Faust! You are Faust no more.
   Is this an enchanted atmosphere?   1740
To have her at once was all my aim,
Yet I feel my will dissolve in a lovesick dream.
Are we the sport of every current of air?
   And were she this moment to walk in,
You would pay for this outrage, how you would
   pay!
The big man, now, alas, so small,
Would lie at her feet melted away.
MEPH.   Quick! I can see her coming below.
FAUST.   Out, yes out! I'll never come back!
MEPH.   Here is a casket, it's middling heavy,
I picked it up in a place I know.   1751
Only put it at once here in the cupboard,

I swear she won't believe her eyes;
I put some nice little trinkets in it
In order to win a different prize.
Still child is child and a game's a game.
FAUST.   I don't know; shall I?
MEPH.   You ask? For shame!
Do you perhaps intend to keep the spoil?
Then I advise Your Lustfulness
To save these hours that are so precious   1760
And save me any further toil.
I hope you aren't avaricious.
After scratching my head so much and twisting
   my hands—
         He puts the casket in the cupboard.
Now quick! We depart!
In order to sway the dear young thing
To meet the dearest wish of your heart;
And *you* assume
A look that belongs to the lecture room,
As if Physics and Metaphysics too
Stood grey as life in front of you!   1770
Come on!
   They go out; then GRETCHEN *reappears.*
GRET.   It is so sultry, so fusty here,
And it's not even so warm outside.
I feel as if I don't know what—
I wish my mother would appear.
I'm trembling all over from top to toe—
I'm a silly girl to get frightened so.
         She sings as she undresses.
   There was a king in Thule
Was faithful to the grave,
To whom his dying lady   1780
A golden winecup gave.
   He drained it at every banquet—
A treasure none could buy;
Whenever he filled and drank it
The tears o'erflowed his eye.
   And when his days were numbered
He numbered land and pelf;
He left his heir his kingdom,
The cup he kept himself.
   He sat at the royal table   1790
With his knights of high degree
In the lofty hall of his fathers
In the castle on the sea.
   There stood the old man drinking
The last of the living glow,
Then threw the sacred winecup
Into the waves below.
   He saw it fall and falter

And founder in the main;
His eyelids fell, thereafter   1800
He never drank again.

*She opens the cupboard to put away
her clothes and sees the casket.*

How did this lovely casket get in here?
I locked the cupboard, I'm quite sure.
But what can be in it? It's very queer.
Perhaps someone left it here in pawn
And my mother gave him a loan on it.
Here's a little key tied on with tape—
I've a good mind to open it.
What is all this? My God! But see!
I have never come across such things.   1810
Jewels—that would suit a countess
At a really grand festivity.
To whom can these splendid things belong?

*She tries on the jewels and
looks in the looking-glass.*

If only the ear-rings belonged to me!
They make one look quite differently.
What is the use of looks and youth?
That's all very well and fine in truth
But people leave it all alone,
They praise you and pity you in one;
Gold is their sole   1820
Concern and goal.
Alas for us who have none!

Elsewhere and later. MEPHISTOPHELES
joins FAUST.

MEPH.   By every despised love! By the ele-
  ments of hell!
I wish I knew something worse to provide a
  curse as well!
FAUST.   What's the trouble? What's biting
  you?
I never saw such a face in my life.
MEPH.   I would sell myself to the devil this
  minute
If only I weren't a devil too.
FAUST.   What is it? Are you mad? Or sick?
It suits you to rage like a lunatic!   1830
MEPH.   Imagine! The jewels that Gretchen
  got,
A priest has gone and scooped the lot!
Her mother got wind of it and she
At once had the horrors secretly.
That woman has a nose beyond compare,
She's always snuffling in the Book of Prayer,
And can tell by how each object smells

If it is sacred or something else;
So the scent of the jewels tells her clear
There's nothing very blessed here.   1840
"My child," she cries, "unrighteous wealth
Invests the soul, infects the health.
We'll dedicate it to the Virgin
And *she'll* make heavenly manna burgeon!"
Gretchen's face, you could see it fall;
She thought: "It's a gift-horse after all,
And he *can't* be lacking in sanctity
Who brought it here so handsomely!"
The mother had a priest along
And had hardly started up her song   1850
Before he thought things looked all right
And said: "Very proper and above board!
Self-control is its own reward.
The Church has an excellent appetite,
She has swallowed whole countries and the
  question
Has never arisen of indigestion.
Only the Church, my dears, can take
Ill-gotten goods without stomach-ache!"
FAUST.   That is a custom the world through,
A Jew and a king observe it too.   1860
MEPH.   So brooch, ring, chain he swipes at
  speed
As if they were merely chicken-feed,
Thanks them no more and no less for the casket
Than for a pound of nuts in a basket,
Promises Heaven will provide
And leaves them extremely edified.
FAUST.   And Gretchen?
MEPH.   Sits and worries there,
Doesn't know what to do and doesn't care,
Thinks day and night on gold and gem,   1869
Still more on the man who presented them.
FAUST.   My sweetheart's grief distresses me.
Get her more jewels instantly!
The first lot barely deserved the name.
MEPH.   So the gentleman thinks it all a nurs-
  ery game!
FAUST.   Do what I tell you and get it right;
Don't let her neighbour out of your sight.
And don't be a sloppy devil; contrive
A new set of jewels. Look alive!

                                EXIT FAUST.

MEPH.   Yes, my dear sir, with all my heart.
This is the way that a fool in love   1880
Puffs away to amuse his lady
Sun and moon and the stars above.

MARTHA'S HOUSE

MARTHA (*alone*). My dear husband, God
    forgive him,
His behaviour has *not* been without a flaw!
Careers away out into the world
And leaves me alone to sleep on straw.
And yet I never trod on his toes,
I loved him with all my heart, God knows.
                      Sobs.

Perhaps he is even dead—O fate!
If I'd only a death certificate!   1890
      GRETCHEN *enters.*
    GRET.   Frau Martha!
    MARTHA.   Gretelchen! What's up?
    GRET.   My legs are sinking under me,
I've just discovered in my cupboard
Another casket—of ebony,
And things inside it, such a store,
Far richer than the lot before.
    MARTHA.   You mustn't mention it to your
      mother;
She'd take it straight to the priest—like the
    other.
    GRET.   But only look! Just look at this!
    MARTHA.   O you lucky little Miss!   1900
    GRET.   I daren't appear in the street, I'm
    afraid,
Or in church either, thus arrayed.
    MARTHA.   Just you visit me often here
And put on the jewels secretly!
Walk up and down for an hour in front of my
    glass
And that will be fun for you and me;
And then an occasion may offer, a holiday,
Where one can let them be seen in a gradual
    way;
A necklace to start with, then a pearl ear-ring;
    your mother
Most likely won't see; if she does one can think
    up something or other.   1910
    GRET.   But who brought these two cases, who
    could it be?
It doesn't seem quite right to me.
                 Knocking.
My God! My mother? Is that her?
    MARTHA.   It is a stranger. Come in, sir!
      Enter MEPHISTOPHELES.
    MEPH.   I have made so free as to walk
    straight in;
The ladies will pardon me? May I begin

By inquiring for a Frau Martha Schwerdtlein?
    MARTHA.   That's me. What might the gentle-
    man want?
    MEPH. (*aside to* MARTHA).   Now I know who
    you are, that's enough for me;
You have very distinguished company.   1920
Forgive my bursting in so soon;
I will call again in the afternoon.
    MARTHA.   Imagine, child, in the name of
    Piety!
The gentleman takes you for society.
    GRET.   I'm a poor young thing, not at all re-
    fined;
My God, the gentleman is too kind.
These jewels and ornaments aren't my own.
    MEPH.   Oh, it's not the jewellery alone;
She has a presence, a look so keen—
How delighted I am that I may remain.   1930
    MARTHA.   What is your news? I cannot wait—
    MEPH.   I wish I'd a better tale to relate.
I trust this will not earn me a beating:
Your husband is dead and sends his greeting.
    MARTHA.   Dead? The good soul? Oh why!
    Oh why!
My husband is dead! Oh I shall die!
    GRET.   Oh don't, dear woman, despair so.
    MEPH.   Listen to my tale of woe!
    GRET.   Now, while I live, may I never love;
Such a loss would bring me to my grave.   1940
    MEPH.   Joy must have grief, grief must have
    joy.
    MARTHA.   How was his end? Oh tell it me.
    MEPH.   He lies buried in Padua
At the church of Holy Anthony,
In properly consecrated ground
Where he sleeps for ever cool and sound.
    MARTHA.   Have you nothing else for me? Is
    that all?
    MEPH.   Yes, a request; it's heavy and fat.
You must have three hundred masses said for his
    soul.
My pockets are empty apart from that.   1950
    MARTHA.   What! Not a trinket? Not a token?
What every prentice keeps at the bottom of his
    bag
And saves it up as a souvenir
And would sooner starve and sooner beg—
    MEPH.   Madam, you make me quite heart-
    broken.
But, really and truly, he didn't squander his
    money.

And, besides, he repented his mistakes,
Yes, and lamented still more his unlucky breaks.
   GRET.   Alas that men should be so unlucky!
Be assured I shall often pray that he may find
   rest above.   1960
   MEPH.   *You* deserve to be taken straight to
   the altar;
You are a child a man could love.
   GRET.   No, no, it's not yet time for that.
   MEPH.   Then, if not a husband, a lover will
   do.
It's one of the greatest gifts of Heaven
To hold in one's arms a thing like you.
   GRET.   That is not the custom of our race.
   MEPH.   Custom or not, it's what takes place.
   MARTHA.   But tell me!
   MEPH.   His deathbed, where I stood,
Was something better than a dungheap—   1970
Half-rotten straw; however, he died like a Christian
And found he had still a great many debts to
   make good.
How thoroughly, he cried, I must hate myself
To leave my job and my wife like that on the
   shelf!
When I remember it, I die!
If only she would forgive me here below!
   MARTHA.   Good man! I have forgiven him
   long ago.
   MEPH.   All the same, God knows, she was
   more at fault than I.
   MARTHA.   That's a lie! To think he lied at
   the point of death!
   MEPH.   He certainly fibbed a bit with his last
   breath,   1980
If I'm half a judge of the situation.
I had no need, said he, to gape for recreation;
First getting children, then getting bread to feed
   'em—
And bread in the widest sense, you know—
And I couldn't even eat my share in peace.
   MARTHA.   So all my love, my loyalty, went for
   naught,
My toiling and moiling without cease!
   MEPH.   Not at all; he gave it profoundest
   thought.
When I left Malta—that was how he began—
I prayed for my wife and children like one de-
   mented   1990
And Heaven heard me and consented
To let us capture a Turkish merchantman,

With a treasure for the Sultan himself on board.
Well, bravery got its due reward
And I myself, as was only fit,
I got a decent cut of it.
   MARTHA.   Eh! Eh! How? Where? Has he
   perhaps buried it?
   MEPH.   Who knows where the four winds
   now have carried it?
As he lounged round Naples, quite unknown,
A pretty lady made him her friend,   2000
She was so fond of him, so devoted,
He wore her colours at his blessed end.
   MARTHA.   The crook! The robber of his chil-
   dren!
Could no misery, no poverty,
Check the scandalous life he led!
   MEPH.   You see! That is just why he's dead.
However, if I were placed like you,
I would mourn him modestly for a year
While looking round for someone new.   2009
   MARTHA.   Ah God! My first one was so dear,
His like in this world will be hard to discover.
There could hardly be a more sweet little fool
   than mine.
It was only he was too fond of playing the rover,
And of foreign women and foreign wine,
And of the God-damned gaming-table.
   MEPH.   Now, now, he might have still got by
If he on his part had been able
To follow your suit and wink an eye.
With that proviso, I swear, I too
Would give an engagement ring to you.   2020
   MARTHA.   The gentleman is pleased to be
   witty.
   MEPH. (*aside*).   I had better go while the
   going's good;
She'd hold the devil to his word, she would!
And how is it with *your* heart, my pretty?
   GRET.   What does the gentleman mean?
   MEPH. (*aside*).   Good, innocent child!
Farewell, ladies!
   GRET.   Farewell!
   MARTHA.   O quickly! Tell me;
I'd like to have the evidence filed
Where, how and when my treasure died and was
   buried.
I have always liked things orderly and decent
And to read of his death in the weeklies would
   be pleasant.   2030
   MEPH.   Yes, Madam, when two witnesses are
   agreed,

The truth, as we all know, is guaranteed;
And I have a friend, an excellent sort,
I'll get him to swear you this in court.
I'll bring him here.
    MARTHA.   O yes! Please do!
    MEPH. And the young lady will be here too?
He's an honest lad. He's been around,
His politeness to ladies is profound.
    GRET. I'll be all blushes in his presence.
    MEPH. No king on earth should so affect
    you.   2040
    MARTHA. Behind the house there—in my
    garden—
This evening—both of you—we'll expect you.

IN THE STREET

    FAUST. How is it? Going ahead? Will it
    soon come right?
    MEPH. Excellent! Do I find you all on fire?
Gretchen is yours before many days expire.
You will see her at Martha's, her neighbour's
    house to-night
And that's a woman with a special vocation,
As it were, for the bawd-cum-gipsy occupation.
    FAUST. Good!   2049
    MEPH. But there is something *we* must do.
    FAUST. One good turn deserves another.
    True.
    MEPH. It only means the legal attesting
That her husband's played-out limbs are resting
At Padua in consecrated ground.
    FAUST. Very smart! I suppose we begin by
    going to Padua!
    MEPH. There's no need for that. What a
    simple lad you are!
Only bear witness and don't ask questions.
    FAUST. The scheme's at an end if you have
    no better suggestions.
    MEPH. Oh there you go! What sanctity!
Is this the first time in your life   2060
You have committed perjury?
God and the world and all that moves therein,
Man and the way his emotions and thoughts
    take place,
Have you not given downright definitions
Of these with an iron breast and a brazen face?
And if you will only look below the surface,
You must confess you knew as much of these
As you know to-day of Herr Schwerdtlein's late
    decease.

    FAUST. You are and remain a sophist and a
    liar.
    MEPH. Quite so—if that is as deep as you'll
    inquire.   2070
Won't you to-morrow on your honour
Befool poor Gretchen and swear before her
That all your soul is set upon her?
    FAUST. And from my heart.
    MEPH.   That's nice of you!
And your talk of eternal faith and love,
Of one single passion enthroned above
All others—will that be heartfelt too?
    FAUST. Stop! It will! If I have feeling, if I
Feel this emotion, this commotion,
And can find no name to call it by;   2080
If then I sweep the world with all my senses
    casting
Around for words and all the highest titles
And call this flame which burns my vitals
Endless, everlasting, everlasting,
Is that a devilish game of lies?
    MEPH. I'm right all the same.
    FAUST.   Listen! Mark this well,
I beg you, and spare me talking till I'm hoarse:
The man who *will* be right, provided he has a
    tongue,
Why, he'll be right of course.   2089
But come, I'm tired of listening to your voice;
You're right, the more so since I have no choice.

MARTHA'S GARDEN

They are walking in pairs: MARTHA *with*
MEPHISTOPHELES, GRETCHEN *on* FAUST'S
arm.
    GRET. The gentleman's only indulging me, I
    feel,
And condescending, to put me to shame.
You travellers are all the same,
You put up with things out of sheer good will.
I know too well that my poor conversation
Can't entertain a person of your station.
    FAUST. One glance from you, one word, en-
    tertains me more
Than all this world's wisdom and lore.
    He kisses her hand.
    GRET. Don't go to such inconvenience! How
    could you kiss my hand?   2100
It is so ugly, it is so rough.
I have had to work at Heaven knows what!
My mother's exacting, true enough.

They pass on.

MARTHA.   And you, sir, do you always move round like this?

MEPH.   Oh, business and duty keep us up to the minute!
With what regret one often leaves a place
And yet one cannot ever linger in it.

MARTHA.   That may go in one's salad days—
To rush all over the world at random;
But the evil time comes on apace   2110
And to drag oneself to the grave a lonely bachelor
Is never much good in any case.

MEPH.   The prospect alarms me at a distant glance.

MARTHA.   Then, worthy sir, be wise while you have the chance.

They pass on.

GRET.   Yes, out of sight, out of mind!
You are polite to your finger-ends
But you have lots of clever friends
Who must leave *me* so far behind.

FAUST.   Believe me, dearest, what the world calls clever
More often is vanity and narrowness.

GRET.   What? 2120

FAUST.   Alas that simplicity, that innocence,
Cannot assess itself and its sacred value ever!
That humility, lowliness, the highest gifts
That living Nature has shared out to men—

GRET.   Only think of *me* one little minute,
I shall have time enough to think of you again.

FAUST.   You are much alone, I suppose?

GRET.   Yes, our household's only small,
But it needs running after all.
We have no maid; I must cook and sweep and knit   2130
And sew and be always on the run,
And my mother looks into every detail—
Each single one.
Not that she has such need to keep expenses down;
We could spread ourselves more than some others do;
My father left us a decent property,
A little house with a garden outside town.
However, my days at the present are pretty quiet;
My brother's in the army,
My little sister is dead.   2140

The child indeed had worn me to a thread;
Still, all that trouble, I'd have it again, I'd try it,
I loved her so.

FAUST.   An angel, if she was like you!

GRET.   I brought her up, she was very fond of me.
She was born after my father died,
We gave my mother up for lost,
Her life was at such a low, low tide,
And she only got better slowly, bit by bit;
The poor little creature, she could not even
Think for a minute of suckling it;   2150
And so I brought her up quite alone
On milk and water; so she became my own.
On my own arm, on my own knee,
She smiled and kicked, grew fair to see.

FAUST.   You felt, I am sure, the purest happiness.

GRET.   Yes; and—be sure—many an hour of distress.
The little one's cradle stood at night
Beside my bed; she could hardly stir
But I was awake,
Now having to give her milk, now into my bed with her,   2160
Now, if she went on crying, try to stop her
By getting up and dandling her up and down the room,
And then first thing in the morning stand at the copper;
Then off to the market and attend to the range,
And so on day after day, never a change.
Living like that, one can't always feel one's best;
But food tastes better for it, so does rest.

They pass on.

MARTHA.   No, the poor women don't come out of it well,
A *vieux garçon* is a hard nut to crack.   2169

MEPH.   It only rests with you and your like
To put me on a better tack.

MARTHA.   Tell me, sir: have you never met someone you fancy?
Has your heart been nowhere involved among the girls?

MEPH.   The proverb says: A man's own fireside
And a good wife are gold and pearls.

MARTHA.   I mean, have you never felt any inclination?

MEPH.   I've generally been received with all consideration.

MARTHA. What I wanted to say: has your heart never been serious?

MEPH. To make a joke to a woman is always precarious.

MARTHA. Oh you don't understand me!

MEPH.   Now *that* I really mind!   2180
But I do understand—that you are very kind.
                              They pass on.

FAUST. You knew me again, you little angel,
As soon as you saw me enter the garden?

GRET. Didn't you see me cast down my eyes?

FAUST. And the liberty that I took you pardon?
The impudence that reared its head
When you lately left the cathedral door.

GRET. I was upset; it had never happened before;
No one could ever say anything bad of me—
Oh can he, I thought, have seen in my behaviour   2190
Any cheekiness, any impropriety?
The idea, it seemed, had come to you pat:
"I can treat this woman just like that."
I must admit I did not know what it was
In my heart that began to make me change my view,
But indeed I was angry with myself because
I could not be angrier with you.

FAUST. Sweet love!

GRET.   Wait a moment!
                    *She plucks a flower and starts
                         picking off the petals.*

FAUST.   What is that? A bouquet?

GRET. No, only a game.

FAUST.   A what?

GRET.   You will laugh at me. Go away!
                         GRETCHEN *murmurs.*

FAUST. What are you murmuring?   2199

GRET.   Loves me—Loves me not—

FAUST. You flower from Heaven's garden plot!

GRET. Loves me—Not—Loves me—Not—
Loves me!

FAUST. Yes, child. What this flower has told you
Regard it as God's oracle. He loves you!
Do you know the meaning of that? He loves you!
                         He takes her hands.

GRET. Oh I feel so strange.

FAUST. Don't shudder. Let this look,
Let this clasp of the hand tell you

What mouth can never express:
To give oneself up utterly and feel   2210
A rapture which must be everlasting.
Everlasting! Its end would be despair.
No; no end! No end!
          *She breaks away from him and runs off.
          After a moment's thought he follows her.*

MARTHA (*approaching*). The night's coming on.

MEPH.   Yes—and we must go.

MARTHA. I would ask you to remain here longer
But this is a terrible place, you know.
It's as if no one were able to shape at
Any vocation or recreation
But must have his neighbour's comings and goings to gape at
And, whatever one does, the talk is unleashed, unfurled.   2220
And our little couple?

MEPH.   Carefree birds of summer!
Flown to the summerhouse.

MARTHA.   He seems to like her.

MEPH. And vice versa. That is the way of the world.

A SUMMERHOUSE

GRETCHEN *runs in and hides behind the door.*

GRET.   He comes!

FAUST. (*entering*). You rogue! Teasing me so!
I've caught you!
                              He kisses her.

GRET.   Dearest! I love you so!
                    MEPHISTOPHELES *knocks.*

FAUST. Who's there?

MEPH.   A friend.

FAUST.   A brute!

MEPH.   It is time to part, you know.

MARTHA (*joining them*). Yes, it is late, sir.

FAUST.   May I not see you home?

GRET. My mother would—Farewell!

FAUST.   I must go then?
Farewell!

MARTHA. Adieu!

GRET.   Let us soon meet again!
                    FAUST *and* MEPHISTOPHELES *leave.*

Dear God! A man of such a kind,   2230
What things must go on in his mind!

I can only blush when he talks to me;
Whatever he says, I must agree.
Poor silly child, I cannot see
What it is he finds in me.

FOREST AND CAVERN

FAUST (*alone*).   Exalted Spirit, you gave me,
    gave me all
I prayed for. Aye, and it is not in vain
That you have turned your face in fire upon me.
You gave me glorious Nature for my kingdom
With power to feel her and enjoy her. Nor   2240
Is it a mere cold wondering glance you grant me
But you allow me to gaze into her depths
Even as into the bosom of a friend.
Aye, you parade the ranks of living things
Before me and you teach me to know my broth-
    ers
In the quiet copse, in the water, in the air.
And when the storm growls and snarls in the
    forest
And the giant pine falls headlong, bearing away
And crushing its neighbours, bough and bole
    and all,   2249
With whose dull fall the hollow hill resounds,
Then do you carry me off to a sheltered cave
And show me myself, and wonders of my own
    breast
Unveil themselves in their deep mystery.
And now that the clear moon rises on my eyes
To soften things, now floating up before me
From walls of rock and from the dripping covert
Come silver forms of the past which soothe and
    temper
The dour delight I find in contemplation.
    That nothing perfect falls to men, oh now
I feel that true. In addition to the rapture   2260
Which brings me near and nearer to the gods
You gave me that companion whom already
I cannot do without, though cold and brazen
He lowers me in my own eyes and with
One whispered word can turn your gifts to noth-
    ing.
He is always busily fanning in my breast
A fire of longing for that lovely image.
So do I stagger from desire to enjoyment
And in enjoyment languish for desire.
        MEPHISTOPHELES *enters.*

MEPH.   Haven't you yet had enough of this
    kind of life?   2270
How can it still appeal to you?
It is all very well to try it once,
Then one should switch to something new.
    FAUST.   I wish you had something else to do
On my better days than come plaguing me.
    MEPH.   Now, now! I'd gladly leave you alone;
You needn't suggest it seriously.
So rude and farouche and mad a friend
Would certainly be little loss.
One has one's hands full without end!   2280
One can never read in the gentleman's face
What he likes or what should be left alone.
    FAUST.   That is exactly the right tone!
He must be thanked for causing me ennui.
    MEPH.   Poor son of earth, what sort of life
Would you have led were it not for me?
The flim-flams of imagination,
I have cured you of those for many a day.
But for me, this terrestrial ball   2289
Would already have seen you flounce away.
Why behave as an owl behaves
Moping in rocky clefts and caves?
Why do you nourish yourself like a toad that sips
From moss that oozes, stone that drips?
A pretty pastime to contrive!
The doctor in you is still alive.
    FAUST.   Do you comprehend what a new and
    vital power
This wandering in the wilderness has given me?
Aye, with even an inkling of such joy,   2299
You would be devil enough to grudge it me.
    MEPH.   A supernatural gratification!
To lie on the mountain tops in the dark and dew
Rapturously embracing earth and heaven,
Swelling yourself to a godhead, ferreting through
The marrow of the earth with divination,
To feel in your breast the whole six days of cre-
    ation,
To enjoy I know not what in arrogant might
And then, with the Old Adam discarded quite,
To overflow into all things in ecstasy;
After all which your lofty intuition   2310
        He makes a gesture.
Will end—hm—unmentionably.
    FAUST.   Shame on you!
    MEPH.   Am I to blame?
You have the right to be moral and cry shame!
One must not mention to the modest ear

What the modest heart is ever agog to hear.
And, in a word, you are welcome to the pleasure
Of lying to yourself in measure;
But this deception will not last.
Already overdriven again,
If this goes on you must collapse,   2320
Mad or tormented or aghast.
Enough of this! Back there your love is sitting
And all her world seems sad and small;
You are never absent from her mind,
Her love for you is more than all.
At first your passion came overflowing
Like a brook that the melted snows have bol-
    stered high;
You have poured your passion into her heart
And now your brook once more is dry.
I think, instead of lording it here above   2330
In the woods, the great man might think fit
In view of that poor ninny's love
To make her some return for it.
She finds the time wretchedly long;
She stands at the window, watches the clouds
As over the old town walls they roll away.
"If I had the wings of a dove"—so runs her song
Half the night and all the day.
Now she is cheerful, mostly low,
Now has spent all her tears,   2340
Now calm again, it appears,
But always loves you so.

FAUST.   You snake! You snake!
MEPH. (aside).   Ha! It begins to take!
FAUST.   You outcast! Take yourself away
And do not name that lovely woman.
Do not bring back the desire for her sweet body
Upon my senses that are half astray.
MEPH.   Where's this to end? She thinks you
    have run off,
And so you have—about half and half.   2350
FAUST.   I am still near her and, though far
    removed,
Her image must be always in my head;
I already envy the body of the Lord
When her lips rest upon the holy bread.
MEPH.   Very well, my friend. I have often en-
    vied you
Those two young roes that are twins, I mean her
    two—
FAUST.   Pimp! Get away!
MEPH.   Fine! So you scold? I must laugh.
The God who created girl and boy

Knew very well the high vocation
Which facilitates their joy.   2360
But come, this is a fine excuse for gloom!
You should take the road to your sweetheart's
    room,
Rather than that to death, you know.
FAUST.   What is the joy of heaven in her
    arms?
Even when I catch fire upon her breast
Do I not always sense her woe?
Am I not the runaway? The man without a
    home?
The monster restless and purposeless
Who roared like a waterfall from rock to rock
    in foam
Greedily raging towards the precipice?   2370
And she on the bank in childlike innocence
In a little hut on the little alpine plot
And all her little household world
Concentrated in that spot.
And I, the loathed of God,
I was not satisfied
To seize and crush to powder
The rocks on the river side!
Her too, her peace, I must undermine as well!
This was the sacrifice I owed to Hell!   2380
Help, Devil, to shorten my time of torment!
What must be, must be; hasten it!
Let her fate hurtle down with mine,
Let us go together to the pit!
MEPH.   How it glows again, how it boils
    again!
Go in and comfort her, my foolish friend!
When such a blockhead sees no outlet
He thinks at once it is the end.
Long live the man who does not flinch!   2389
But you've a devil in you, somewhere there.
I know of nothing on earth more unattractive
Than your devil who feels despair.

GRETCHEN'S ROOM

GRETCHEN is alone, singing at the spinning-wheel.

GRET.   My peace is gone,
My heart is sore,
I shall find it never
And never more.

    He has left my room
An empty tomb,

He has gone and all
My world is gall.   2400
  My poor head
Is all astray,
My poor mind
Fallen away.
  My peace is gone,
My heart is sore,
I shall find it never
And never more.
  'Tis he that I look through
The window to see,   2410
He that I open
The door for—he!
  His gait, his figure,
So grand, so high!
The smile of his mouth,
The power of his eye,
  And the magic stream
Of his words—what bliss!
The clasp of his hand
And, ah, his kiss!   2420
  My peace is gone,
My heart is sore,
I shall find it never
And never more.
  My heart's desire
Is so strong, so vast;
Ah, could I seize him
And hold him fast
  And kiss him for ever
Night and day—   2430
And on his kisses
Pass away!

MARTHA'S GARDEN

GRET. Promise me, Heinrich!
FAUST.   If I can!
GRET. Tell me: how do you stand in regard
  to religion?
You are indeed a good, good man
But I think you give it scant attention.
FAUST. Leave that, my child! You feel what
  I feel for you;
For those I love I would give my life and none
Will I deprive of his sentiments and his church.
GRET. That is not right; one must believe
  thereon.   2440
FAUST. Must one?
GRET.   If only I had some influence!

Nor do you honour the holy sacraments.
FAUST. I honour them.
GRET.   Yes, but not with any zest.
When were you last at mass, when were you last
  confessed?
Do you believe in God?
FAUST.   My darling, who dare say:
I believe in God?
Ask professor or priest,
Their answers will make an odd
Mockery of you.
GRET.   You don't believe, you mean?
FAUST. Do not misunderstand me, my love,
  my queen!   2450
Who can name him?
Admit on the spot:
I believe in him?
And who can dare
To perceive and declare:
I believe in him not?
The All-Embracing One,
All-Upholding One,
Does he not embrace, uphold,
You, me, Himself?   2460
Does not the Heaven vault itself above us?
Is not the earth established fast below?
And with their friendly glances do not
Eternal stars rise over us?
Do not my eyes look into yours,
And all things thrust
Into your head, into your heart,
And weave in everlasting mystery
Invisibly, visibly, around you?
Fill your heart with *this,* great as it is,   2470
And when this feeling grants you perfect bliss,
Then call it what you will—
Happiness! Heart! Love! God!
I have no name for it!
Feeling is all;
Name is mere sound and reek
Clouding Heaven's light.
GRET. That sounds quite good and right;
And much as the priest might speak,
Only not word for word.   2480
FAUST. It is what all hearts have heard
In all the places heavenly day can reach,
Each in his own speech;
Why not I in mine?
GRET. I could almost accept it, you make it
  sound so fine,
Still there is something in it that shouldn't be;

For you have no Christianity.
FAUST.   Dear child!
GRET.   It has long been a grief to me
To see you in such company.
FAUST.   You mean?   2489
GRET.   The man who goes about with you,
I hate him in my soul, right through and through.
And nothing has given my heart
In my whole life so keen a smart
As that man's face, so dire, so grim.
FAUST.   Dear poppet, don't be afraid of him!
GRET.   My blood is troubled by his presence.
All other people, I wish them well;
But much as I may long to see you,
He gives me a horror I cannot tell,
And I think he's a man too none can trust.   2500
God forgive me if I'm unjust.
FAUST.   Such queer fish too must have room
to swim.
GRET.   I wouldn't live with the like of him!
Whenever that man comes to the door,
He looks in so sarcastically,
Half angrily,
One can see he feels no sympathy;
It is written on his face so clear
There is not a soul he can hold dear.
I feel so cosy in your arms,   2510
So warm and free from all restraint,
And his presence ties me up inside.
FAUST.   You angel, with your wild alarms!
GRET.   It makes me feel so ill, so faint,
That, if he merely happens to join us,
I even think I have no more love for you.
Besides, when he's there, I could never pray,
And that is eating my heart away;
You, Heinrich, you must feel it too.
FAUST.   You suffer from an antipathy.   2520
GRET.   Now I must go.
FAUST.   Oh, can I never rest
One little hour hanging upon your breast,
Pressing both breast on breast and soul on soul?
GRET.   Ah, if I only slept alone!
I'd gladly leave the door unlatched for you to-
night;
My mother, however, sleeps so light
And if she found us there, I own
I should fall dead upon the spot.
FAUST.   You angel, there is no fear of that.
Here's a little flask. Three drops are all   2530
It needs—in her drink—to cover nature
In a deep sleep, a gentle pall.

GRET.   What would I not do for your sake!
I hope it will do her no injury.
FAUST.   My love, do you think that of me?
GRET.   Dearest, I've only to look at you
And I do not know what drives me to meet your
will.
I have already done so much for you
That little more is left me to fulfil.
She goes out—and MEPHISTOPHELES *enters.*
MEPH.   The monkey! Is she gone?   2539
FAUST.   Have you been spying again?
MEPH.   I have taken pretty good note of it,
The doctor has been catechised—
And much, I hope, to his benefit;
The girls are really keen to be advised
If a man belongs to the old simple-and-pious
school.
"If he stand that," they think, "he'll stand *our*
rule."
FAUST.   You, you monster, cannot see
How this true and loving soul
For whom faith is her whole
Being and the only road   2550
To beatitude, must feel a holy horror
Having to count her beloved lost for good.
MEPH.   You supersensual, sensual buck,
Led by the nose by the girl you court!
FAUST.   O you abortion of fire and muck!
MEPH.   And she also has skill in physiognomy;
In my presence she feels she doesn't know what,
She reads some hidden sense behind my little
mask,
She feels that I am assuredly a genius—
Maybe the devil if she dared to ask.   2560
Now: to-night—
FAUST.   What is to-night to you?
MEPH.   I have my pleasure in it too.

AT THE WELL

GRETCHEN *and* LIESCHEN *with pitchers.*
LIES.   Haven't you heard about Barbara?
Not what's passed?
GRET.   Not a word. I go out very little.
LIES.   It's true, Sibylla told me to-day:
She has made a fool of herself at last.
So much for her fine airs!
GRET.   Why?
LIES.   It stinks!
Now she feeds two when she eats and drinks.
GRET.   Ah!   2569

LIES.   Yes; she has got her deserts in the end.
What a time she's been hanging on her friend!
Going the rounds
To the dances and the amusement grounds,
She had to be always the first in the line,
He was always standing her cakes and wine;
She thought her looks so mighty fine,
She was so brazen she didn't waver
To take the presents that he gave her.
Such cuddlings and such carryings on—
But now the pretty flower is gone.   2580
    GRET.   Poor thing!
    LIES.   Is that the way you feel?
When we were at the spinning-wheel
And mother kept us upstairs at night,
She was below with her heart's delight;
On the bench or in the shady alley
They never had long enough to dally.
But now she must grovel in the dirt,
Do penance in church in a hair shirt.
    GRET.   But surely he will marry her.   2589
    LIES.   He'd be a fool! A smart young chap
Has plenty of other casks to tap.
Besides he's gone.
    GRET.   That's not right.
    LIES.   If she hooks him she won't get off light!
The boys will tear her wreath in half
And we shall strew her door with chaff.
                    LIESCHEN *goes off*.
    GRET. (*going home*).   What scorn I used to
        pour upon her
When a poor maiden lost her honour!
My tongue could never find a name
Bad enough for another's shame!
I thought it black and I blackened it,   2600
It was never black enough to fit,
And I blessed myself and acted proud—
And now I too am under a cloud.
Yet, God! What drove me to this pass,
It was all so good, so dear, alas!

RAMPARTS

*In a niche in the wall is an image of the
Mater Dolorosa. In front of it* GRETCHEN
is putting fresh flowers in the pots.
    GRET.   Mary, bow down,
Beneath thy woeful crown,
Thy gracious face on me undone!
The sword in thy heart,
Smart upon smart,   2610

Thou lookest up to thy dear son;
Sending up sighs
To the Father which rise
For His grief and for thine own.
Who can gauge
What torments rage
Through the whole of me and how—
How my poor heart is troubled in me,
How fears and longings undermine me?
Only thou knowest, only thou!   2620
Wherever I may go,
What woe, what woe, what woe
Is growing beneath my heart!
Alas, I am hardly alone,
I moan, I moan, I moan
And my heart falls apart.
The flower-pots in my window
I watered with tears, ah me,
When in the early morning
I picked these flowers for thee.   2630
Not sooner in my bedroom
The sun's first rays were shed
Than I in deepest sorrow
Sat waking on my bed.
Save me from shame and death in one!
Ah, bow down
Thou of the woeful crown,
Thy gracious face on me undone.

NIGHT SCENE AT GRETCHEN'S DOOR

VALENTINE.   When I was at some drinking
        bout
Where big talk tends to blossom out,   2640
And my companions raised their voice
To praise the maidens of their choice
And drowned their praises in their drink,
Then I would sit and never blink,
Propped on my elbow listening
To all their brags and blustering.
Then smiling I would stroke my beard
And raise the bumper in my hand
And say: "Each fellow to his taste!
But is there one in all the land   2650
To hold a candle to my own
Dear sister, Gretchen? No, there's none!"
Hear! Hear! Kling! Klang! It went around;
Some cried: "His judgment is quite sound,
She is the pearl of womanhood!"
That shut those boasters up for good.

And now! It would make one tear one's hair
And run up walls in one's despair!
Each filthy fellow in the place
Can sneer and jeer at my disgrace!   2660
And I, like a man who's deep in debt,
Every chance word must make me sweat.
I could smash their heads for them if I tried—
I could not tell them that they lied.

FAUST *and* MEPHISTOPHELES *enter.*

VAL.   Who comes there, slinking? Who comes
   there?
If I mistake not, they're a pair.
If it's he, I'll scrag him on the spot;
He'll be dead before he knows what's what!

FAUST.   How from the window of the sacristy
   there   2669
The undying lamp sends up its little flicker
Which glimmers sideways weak and weaker
And round it presses the dark air.
My heart too feels its night, its noose.

MEPH.   And I feel like a tom-cat on the loose,
Brushing along the fire escape
And round the walls, a stealthy shape;
Moreover I feel quite virtuous,
Just a bit burglarious, a bit lecherous.
You see, I'm already haunted to the marrow
By the glorious Walpurgis Night.   2680
It returns to us the day after to-morrow,
Then one knows why one's awake all right.

FAUST.   I'd like some ornament, some ring,
For my dear mistress. I feel sad
To visit her without anything.

MEPH.   It's really nothing to regret—
That you needn't pay for what you get.
Now that the stars are gems on heaven's bro-
   cade,
You shall hear a real masterpiece.
I will sing her a moral serenade   2690
That her folly may increase.

He sings to the guitar.

MEPH.   Catherine, my dear,
What? Waiting here
At your lover's door
When the stars of the night are fading?
Oh don't begin!
When he lifts the pin,
A maid goes in—
But she won't come out a maiden.
So think aright!   2700
Grant him delight

And it's good night,
You poor, poor things—Don't linger!
A girl who's wise
Will hide her prize
From robber's eyes—
Unless she's a ring on her finger.

VALENTINE *comes forward.*

VAL.   Damn you! Who're you seducing here?
You damned pied piper! You magician!
First to the devil with your guitar!   2710
Then to the devil with the musician!

MEPH.   The guitar is finished. Look, it's
   broken in two.

VAL.   Now then, to break your heads for you!

MEPH.   Doctor! Courage! All you can muster!
Stick by me and do as I say!
Quick now, draw your feather duster!
I'll parry his blows, so thrust away!

VAL.   Then parry that!

MEPH.   Why not, why not?

VAL.   And that!

MEPH.   Of course.

VAL.   Is he the devil or what?
What's this? My hand's already lamed.   2720

MEPH.   Strike, you!

VAL.   Oh!

VALENTINE *falls.*

MEPH.   Now the lout is tamed!
But we must go! Vanish in the wink of an eye!
They're already raising a murderous hue and
   cry.

MARTHA (*at the window*).   Come out! Come
   out!

GRET. (*at the window*).   Bring a light!

MARTHA. (*as before*).   There's a row and a
   scuffle, they're having a fight.

MAN.   Here's one on the ground; he's dead.

MARTHA (*coming out*).   The murderers, have
   they gone?

GRET. (*coming out*).   Who's here?

MAN.   Your mother's son.

GRET.   O God! What pain! O God!

VAL.   I am dying—that's soon said   2730
And sooner done, no doubt.
Why do you women stand howling and wailing?
Come round and hear me out.

They all gather round him.

Look, my Gretchen, you're young still,
You have not yet sufficient skill,
You bungle things a bit.

Here is a tip—you need no more—
Since you are once for all a whore,
Then make a job of it!

    GRET. My brother? O God! Is it I you
      blame!   2740

    VAL. Leave our Lord God out of the game!
What is done I'm afraid is done,
As one starts one must carry on.
You began with one man on the sly,
There will be more of them by and by,
And when a dozen have done with you
The whole town will have you too.

    When Shame is born, she first appears
In this world in secrecy,
And the veil of night is drawn so tight   2750
Over her head and ears;
Yes, people would kill her and forget her.
But she grows still more and more
And brazenly roams from door to door
And yet her appearance grows no better.
The more her face creates dismay,
The more she seeks the light of day.
Indeed I see the time draw on
When all good people in this town
Will turn aside from you, you tart,   2760
As from a corpse in the plague cart.
Then your heart will sink within you,
When they look you in the eye!
It's good-bye to your golden chains!
And church-going and mass—good-bye!
No nice lace collars any more
To make you proud on the dancing floor!
No, in some dark and filthy nook
You'll hide with beggars and crippled folk
And, if God pardon you, he may;   2770
You are cursed on earth till your dying day.

    MARTHA. Commend your soul to the mercy
    of God!
Will you add slander to your load?

    VAL. If I could get at your withered body,
You bawd, you sinner born and hardened!
Then I should hope that all my sins
And in full measure might be pardoned.

    GRET. My brother! O hell's misery!

    VAL. I tell you: let your weeping be.
When you and your honour came to part,   2780
It was you that stabbed me to the heart.
I go to God through the sleep of death,
A soldier—brave to his last breath.

                      He dies.

CATHEDRAL

Organ and anthem. GRETCHEN *in the
congregation. An* EVIL SPIRIT *whispers to
her over her shoulder.*

EVIL SPIRIT. How different it all was
Gretchen, when you came here
All innocent to the altar,
Out of the worn-out little book
Lisping your prayers,
Half a child's game,
Half God in the heart!   2790
Gretchen!
How is your head?
And your heart—
What are its crimes?
Do you pray for your mother's soul, who thanks
    to you
And your sleeping draught overslept into a long,
    long pain?
And whose blood stains your threshold?
Yes, and already under your heart
Does it not grow and quicken
And torture itself and you   2800
With its foreboding presence?

    GRET. Alas! Alas!
If I could get rid of the thoughts
Which course through my head hither and
    thither
Despite me!

    CHOIR. Dies irae, dies illa
Solvet saeclum in favilla.

                   The organ plays.

EVIL SPIRIT. Agony seizes you!
The trumpet sounds!
The graves tremble   2810
And your heart
From its ashen rest
To fiery torment
Comes up recreated
Trembling too!

    GRET. Oh to escape from here!
I feel as if the organ
Were stifling me,
And the music dissolving
My heart in its depths.   2820

    CHOIR. Judex ergo cum sedebit,
Quidquid latet adparebit,
Nil inultum remanebit.

    GRET. I cannot breathe!
The pillars of the walls

Are round my throat!
The vaulted roof
Chokes me!—Air!
   EVIL SPIRIT. Hide yourself! Nor sin nor
    shame
Remains hidden.   2830
Air? Light?
Woe to you!
   CHOIR. Quid sum miser tunc dicturus?
Quem patronum rogaturus?
Cum vix justus sit securus.
   EVIL SPIRIT. The blessed turn
Their faces from you.
The pure shudder
To reach out their hands to you.
Woe!   2840
   CHOIR. Quid sum miser tunc dicturus?
   GRET. Neighbour! Help! Your smelling bot-
   tle!

She faints.

WALPURGIS NIGHT

   FAUST *and* MEPHISTOPHELES *making
their way through the Hartz Mountains.*
   MEPH. A broomstick—don't you long for
   such a conveyance?
I'd find the coarsest he-goat some assistance.
Taking this road, our goal is still in the distance.
   FAUST. No, so long as my legs are not in
   abeyance,
I can make do with this knotted stick.
What is the use of going too quick?
To creep along each labyrinthine valley,   2849
Then climb this scarp, downwards from which
The bubbling spring makes its eternal sally,
This is the spice that makes such journeys rich.
Already the spring is weaving through the
   birches,
Even the pine already feels the spring;
Should not our bodies too give it some purchase?
   MEPH. Candidly—*I* don't feel a thing.
In my body all is winter,
I would prefer a route through frost and snow.
How sadly the imperfect disc
Of the red moon rises with belated glow   2860
And the light it gives is bad, at every step
One runs into some rock or tree!
Permit me to ask a will o' the wisp.
I see one there, he's burning heartily.

Ahoy, my friend! Might I call on you to help
   us?
Why do you blaze away there to no purpose?
Be so good as to light us along our road.
   WILL O' THE WISP. I only hope my sense of
   your mightiness
Will control my natural flightiness;
A zigzag course is our accustomed mode.   2870
   MEPH. Ha! Ha! So it's men you want to
   imitate.
In the name of the Devil you go straight
Or I'll blow out your flickering, dickering light!
   WILL. You're the head of the house, I can
   see that all right,
You are welcome to use me at your convenience.
But remember, the mountain is magic-mad to-
   day
And, if a will o' the wisp is to show you the way,
You too must show a little lenience.
   FAUST, MEPH., WILL. *(singing successively).*
   Into realms of dreams and witchcraft
We, it seems, have found an ingress.   2880
Lead us well and show your woodcraft,
That we may make rapid progress
Through these wide and desert spaces.
   Trees on trees—how each one races,
Pushing past—how each one hastens!
And the crags that make obeisance!
And the rocks with long-nosed faces—
Hear them snorting, hear them blowing!   2890
   Through the stones and lawns are flowing
Brook and brooklet, downward hustling.
Is that song—or is it rustling?
Sweet, sad notes of love—a relic—
Voices from those days angelic?
Thus we hope, we love—how vainly!
Echo like an ancient rumour
Calls again, yes, calls back plainly.
   Now—Tu-whit!—we near the purlieu
Of—Tu-whoo!—owl, jay and curlew;
Are they all in waking humour?   2900
In the bushes are those lizards—
Straggling legs and bloated gizzards?
And the roots like snakes around us
Coil from crag and sandy cranny,
Stretch their mad and strange antennae
Grasping at us to confound us;
Stretch from gnarled and living timber
Towards the passer-by their limber
Polyp-suckers!

And in legions
Through these mossy, heathy regions   2910
Mice, all colours, come cavorting!
And above, a serried cohort,
Fly the glow-worms as our escort—
More confusing than escorting.
    Tell me what our real case is!
Are we stuck or are we going?
Rocks and trees, they all seem flying
Round and round and making faces,
And the will o' the wisps are blowing
Up so big and multiplying.   2920
    MEPH.   Hold my coat-tails, hold on tight!
Standing on this central height
Marvelling see how far and wide
Mammon lights the peaks inside.
    FAUST.   How strangely through the mountain
        hollows
A sad light gleams as of morning-red
And like a hound upon the scent
Probes the gorges' deepest bed!
Here fumes arise, there vapours float,
Here veils of mist catch sudden fire   2930
Which creeps along, a flimsy thread,
Then fountains up, a towering spire.
Here a whole stretch it winds its way
With a hundred veins throughout the glen,
And here in the narrow neck of the pass
Is suddenly one strand again.
There, near by, are dancing sparks
Sprinkled around like golden sand.
But look! The conflagration climbs
The crags' full height, hand over hand.   2940
    MEPH.   Does not Sir Mammon light his
        palace
In splendid style for this occasion?
You are lucky to have seen it;
Already I sense the noisy guests' invasion.
    FAUST.   How the Wind Hag rages through
        the air!
What blows she rains upon the nape of my
        neck!
    MEPH.   You must clamp yourself to the an-
        cient ribs of the rock
Or she'll hurl you into this gorge, to find your
        grave down there.
A mist is thickening the night.
Hark to the crashing of the trees!   2950
The owls are flying off in fright.
And the ever-green palaces—
Hark to their pillars sundering!

Branches moaning and breaking!
Tree-trunks mightily thundering!
Roots creaking and yawning!
Tree upon tree in appalling
Confusion crashing and falling,
And through the wreckage on the scarps
The winds are hissing and howling.   2960
Do you hear those voices in the air?
Far-off voices? Voices near?
Aye, the whole length of the mountain side
The witch-song streams in a crazy tide.
    WITCHES (*in chorus*).   The witches enter the
        Brocken° scene,
The stubble is yellow, the corn is green.
There assembles the mighty horde,
Urian sits aloft as lord.
So we go—over stock and stone—
Farting witch on stinking goat.   2970
    A VOICE.   But ancient Baubo comes alone,
She rides on a mother sow—take note.
    CHOR.   So honour to whom honour is due!
Let Mother Baubo head the queue!
A strapping sow and Mother on top
And we'll come after, neck and crop.
    The way is broad, the way is long,
How is this for a crazy throng?
The pitchfork pricks, the broomstick pokes,
The mother bursts and the child chokes.   2980
    VOICE FROM ABOVE.   Come along, come along,
        from Felsensee!
    VOICES FROM BELOW.   We'd like to mount
        with you straight away.
We wash ourselves clean behind and before
But we are barren for evermore.
    CHOR.   The wind is silent, the star's in flight,
The sad moon hides herself from sight.
The soughing of the magic choir
Scatters a thousand sparks of fire.
    VOICE FROM BELOW.   Wait! Wait!
    VOICE FROM ABOVE.   Who calls there from the
        cleft in the rock?   2990
    VOICE FROM BELOW.   Don't leave me behind!
        Don't leave me behind!
Three hundred years I've been struggling up
And I can never reach the top;
I want to be with my own kind.
    CHOR.   Ride on a broom or ride on a stick,
Ride on a fork or a goat—but quick!
Who cannot to-night achieve the climb
Is lost and damned till the end of time.

2965. Brocken: the highest peak in the Harz Mountains.

HALF-WITCH. So long, so long, I've been on the trot;
How far ahead the rest have got!   3000
At home I have neither peace nor cheer
And yet I do not find it here.
   CHOR. Their ointment makes the witches hale,
A rag will make a decent sail
And any trough a ship for flight;
You'll never fly, if not to-night.
Once at the peak, you circle round
And then you sweep along the ground
And cover the heath far and wide—
Witchhood in swarms on every side.   3010
                The WITCHES *land.*
   MEPH. What a push and a crush and a rush and a clatter!
How they sizzle and whisk, how they babble and batter!
Kindle and sparkle and blaze and stink!
A true witch-element, I think.
Only stick to me or we shall be swept apart!
Where are you?
   FAUST.   Here!
   MEPH.   What! Carried so far already!
I must show myself the master on this ground.
Room! Here comes Voland!° Room, sweet rabble! Steady!
Here, Doctor, catch hold of me. Let's make one bound
Out of this milling crowd and so get clear.   3020
Even for the likes of me it's *too* mad here.
There's something yonder casting a peculiar glare,
Something attracts me towards those bushes.
Come with me! We will slip in there.
   FAUST. You spirit of contradiction! Go on though! I'll follow.
You have shown yourself a clever fellow. Quite!
We visit the Brocken on Walpurgis Night
To shut ourselves away in this lonely hollow!
   MEPH. Only look—what motley flames!
It's a little club for fun and games   3030
One's not alone with a few, you know.
   FAUST. I'd rather be above there though.
Already there's fire and whorls of smoke.
The Prince of Evil is drawing the folk;
Many a riddle must there be solved.
   MEPH. And many a new one too evolved.

Let the great world, if it likes, run riot;
We will set up here in quiet.
It is a custom of old date
To make one's own small worlds within the great.   3040
I see young witches here, bare to the buff,
And old ones dressed—wisely enough.
If only for my sake, do come on;
It's little trouble and great fun.
I hear some music being let loose too.
What a damned clack! It's what one must get used to.
   Come along! Come along! You have no choice.
I'll lead the way and sponsor you
And you'll be obliged to me anew.
What do you say? This milieu isn't small.   3050
Just look! You can see no end to it at all.
A hundred fires are blazing in a row;
They dance and gossip and cook and drink and court—
Tell me where there is better sport!
   FAUST. Do you intend, to introduce us here,
To play the devil or the sorcerer?
   MEPH. I am quite accustomed to go incognito
But one wears one's orders on gala days, you know.
I have no garter for identification   3059
But my cloven foot has here some reputation.
See that snail? Creeping up slow and steady?
Her sensitive feelers have already
Sensed out something odd in me.
Here I could *not* hide my identity.
But come! Let us go the round of the fires
And I'll play go-between to your desires.
   COSTER-WITCH.° Gentlemen, don't pass me by!
Don't miss your opportunity!
Inspect my wares with careful eye;
I have a great variety.   3070
And yet there is nothing on my stall
Whose like on earth you could not find,
That in its time has done no small
Harm to the world and to mankind.
No dagger which has not drunk of blood,
No goblet which has not poured its hot and searing
Poison into some healthy frame,

3018. **Voland:** "Evil Spirit," another name for the devil.

3067. **Coster-witch:** a witch that sells things.

No gewgaw which has not ruined some endear-
ing
Woman, no sword which has not been used to
hack   3079
A bond in two and stab a partner in the back.
   MEPH.   Auntie! You are behind the times.
Past and done with! Past and done!
You must go in for novelties!
You'll lose our custom if you've none.
   FAUST.   I mustn't go crazy unawares!
This is a fair to end all fairs.
   MEPH.   The whole crowd's forcing its way
above;
You find you're shoved though you may think
you shove.
   FAUST.   Who then is that?
   MEPH.   Look well at Madam;
That's Lilith.
   FAUST.   Who?
   MEPH.   First wife of Adam.   3090
Be on your guard against her lovely hair,
That shining ornament which has no match;
Any young man whom those fair toils can catch,
She will not quickly loose him from her snare.
   FAUST.   Look, an old and a young one, there
they sit.
They have already frisked a bit.
   MEPH.   No rest to-night for 'em, not a chance.
They're starting again. Come on! Let's join the
dance.
            FAUST *dances with a young witch.*
   FAUST.   A lovely dream once came to me
In which I saw an apple tree,   3100
On which two lovely apples shine,
They beckon me, I start to climb.
   YOUNG WITCH.   Those little fruit you long
for so
Just as in Eden long ago.
Joy runs through me, through and through;
My garden bears its apples too.
           FAUST *breaks away from the dance.*
   MEPH.   Why did you let that lovely maiden
go
Who danced with you and so sweetly sang?
   FAUST.   Ugh, in the middle of it there sprang
Out of her mouth a little red mouse.   3110
   MEPH.   Why complain? That's nothing out
of the way;
You should be thankful it wasn't grey.
In an hour of love! What a senseless grouse!
   FAUST.   And then I saw—

   MEPH.   What?
   FAUST.   Mephisto, look over there!
Do you see a girl in the distance, pale and fair?
Who drags herself, only slowly, from the place?
And seems to walk with fetters on her feet?
I must tell you that I think I see
Something of dear Gretchen in her face.
   MEPH.   That can do no one good! Let it
alone! Beware!   3120
It is a lifeless phantom, an image of air.
It is a bad thing to behold;
Its cold look makes the blood of man run cold,
One turns to stone almost upon the spot;
You have heard of Medusa, have you not?
   FAUST.   Indeed, they are the eyes of one who
is dead,
Unclosed by loving hands, left open, void.
That is the breast which Gretchen offered me,
And that is the sweet body I enjoyed.
   MEPH.   That is mere magic, you gullible
fool! She can   3130
Appear in the shape of his love to every man.
   FAUST.   What ravishment! What pain! Oh
stay!
That look! I cannot turn away!
How strange that that adorable neck
In one red thread should be arrayed
As thin as the back of a knife-blade.
   MEPH.   You are quite correct! I see it too.
She can also carry her head under her arm,
Perseus has cut it off for her.
Always this love of things untrue!   3140
           A choir is heard, pianissimo.
   CHOIR.   Drifting cloud and gauzy mist
Brighten and dissever.
Breeze on the leaf and wind in the reeds
And all is gone for ever.

           Dreary day—open country
   FAUST.   In misery! In despair! Long on the
earth a wretched wanderer, now a prisoner! A
criminal cooped in a dungeon for horrible torments, that dear and luckless creature! To end
so! So! Perfidious, worthless spirit—and this you
have kept from me!   3150
Stand, Just stand there! Roll your devilish
eyes spitefully round in your head! Stand and
brave me with your unbearable presence! A prisoner! In irremediable misery! Abandoned to evil
spirits, to judging, unfeeling man! And I in
the meantime—you lull me with stale diversions,

you hide her worsening plight from me, you abandon her to perdition!

MEPH.   She is not the first.

FAUST.   Dog! Loathsome monster! [3160 Change him, Thou eternal Spirit! Change this serpent back to his shape of a dog, in which he often delighted to trot before me at night—to roll about at the feet of the harmless wanderer and, as he tripped, to sink his teeth in his shoulders. Change him back to his fancy-shape that he may crouch in the sand on his belly before me, that I may trample over his vileness!

Not the first, you say! O the pity of it!   [3170 What human soul can grasp that more than one creature has sunk to the depth of this misery, that the first did not pay off the guilt of all the rest, writhing and racked in death before the eyes of the Ever-Pardoning! It pierces me to my marrow and core, the torment of this one girl—and you grin calmly at the fate of thousands!

MEPH.   Now we're already back at our wits' end—the point where your human intel-   [3180 ligence snaps. Why do you enter our company, if you can't carry it through? So you want to fly—and have no head for heights? Did we force ourselves on you—or you on us?

FAUST.   Do not bare at me so those greedy fangs of yours! You sicken me! O great and glorious Spirit, Thou who didst deign to appear to me, Thou who knowest my heart and my soul, why fetter me to this odious partner who grazes on mischief and laps up destruction?   [3190

MEPH.   Have you finished?

FAUST.   Save her! Or woe to you! The most withering curse upon you for thousands of years!

MEPH.   I cannot undo the avenger's bonds, his bolts I cannot open. Save her! Who was it plunged her into ruin? I or you?

FAUST *looks wildly around.*

MEPH.   Are you snatching at the thunder? Luckily, that is forbidden you wretched mortals. To smash to pieces his innocent critic,   3200 that is the way the tyrant relieves himself when in difficulties.

FAUST.   Bring me to her! She shall be free!

MEPH.   And what of the risk you will run? Let me tell you; the town is still tainted with blood-guilt from your hand. Over the site of the murder there float avenging spirits who await the returning murderer.

FAUST.   That too from *you?* Murder and death of a world on your monstrous head!   3210 Take me to her, I tell you; set her free!

MEPH.   I will take you, and what I *can* do—listen! Am I omnipotent in heaven and earth? I will cast a cloud on the gaoler's senses; do you get hold of the keys and carry her out with your own human hands. I meanwhile wait, my magic horses are ready, I carry you off. That much I can manage.

FAUST.   Away! Away!

NIGHT

FAUST *and* MEPHISTOPHELES *fly past on black horses.*

FAUST.   What do they weave round the Gallows Rock?   3220

MEPH.   Can't tell what they're cooking and hatching.

FAUST.   Floating up, floating down, bending, descending.

MEPH.   A witch corporation.

FAUST.   Black mass, black water.

MEPH.   Come on! Come on!

DUNGEON

FAUST *with a bunch of keys and a lamp, in front of an iron door.*

FAUST.   A long unwonted trembling seizes me,
The woe of all mankind seizes me fast.
It is here she lives, behind these dripping walls,
Her crime was but a dream too good to last!
And *you,* Faust, waver at the door?   3230
You fear to see your love once more?
Go in at once—or her hope of life is past.

He tries the key. GRETCHEN
starts singing inside.

GRET.   My mother, the whore,
Who took my life!
My father, the rogue,
Who ate my flesh!
My little sister
My bones did lay
In a cool, cool glen;
And there I turned to a pretty little wren;   3240

Fly away! Fly away!

> FAUST *opens the lock.*

FAUST.   She does not suspect that her lover
is listening—
To the chains clanking, the straw rustling.

> *He enters.*

GRET.   Oh! They come! O death! It's hard!
Hard!

FAUST.   Quiet! I come to set you free.

> *She throws herself at his feet.*

GRET.   If you are human, feel my misery.

FAUST.   Do not cry out—you will wake the
guard.

> *He takes hold of the chains to unlock them.*

GRET. (*on her knees*).   Who has given you
this power,
Hangman, so to grieve me?
To fetch me at this midnight hour!   3250
Have pity! Oh reprieve me!
Will to-morrow not serve when the bells are
rung?

> *She gets up.*

I am still so young, I am still so young!
Is my death so near?
I was pretty too, that was what brought me here.
My lover was by, he's far to-day;
My wreath lies torn, my flowers have been
thrown away.
Don't seize on me so violently!
What have I done to you? Let me be!
Let me not vainly beg and implore;   3260
You know I have never seen you before.

FAUST.   Can I survive this misery?

GRET.   I am now completely in your power.
Only let me first suckle my child.
This night I cherished it, hour by hour;
To torture me they took it away
And now I murdered it, so they say.
And I shall never be happy again.
People make ballads about me—the heartless
crew!
An old story ends like this—   3270
Must mine too?

> FAUST *throws himself on the ground.*

FAUST.   Look! At your feet a lover lies
To loose you from your miseries.

> GRETCHEN *throws herself beside him.*

GRET.   O, let us call on the saints on bended
knee!
Beneath these steps—but see—
Beneath this sill

The cauldron of Hell!
And within,
The Evil One in his fury
Raising a din!   3280

FAUST.   Gretchen! Gretchen!

GRET.   That was my lover's voice!

> *She springs up: the chains fall off.*

I heard him calling. Where can he be?
No one shall stop me. I am free!
Quick! My arms round his neck!
And lie upon his bosom! Quick!
He called "Gretchen!" He stood at the door.
Through the whole of Hell's racket and roar,
Through the threats and jeers and from far be-
yond
I heard that voice so sweet, so fond.   3290

FAUST.   It is I!

GRET.   It's you? Oh say so once again!

> *She clasps him.*

It is! It is! Where now is all my pain?
And where the anguish of my captivity?
It's you; you have come to rescue me!
I am saved!
The street is back with me straight away
Where I saw you that first day,
And the happy garden too
Where Martha and I awaited you.

FAUST.   Come! Come!   3299

GRET.   Oh stay with me, oh do!
Where *you* stay, I would like to, too.

FAUST.   Hurry!
If you don't,
The penalty will be sore.

GRET.   What! Can you kiss no more?
So short an absence, dear, as this
And you've forgotten how to kiss!
Why do I feel so afraid, clasping your neck?
In the old days your words, your looks,
Were a heavenly flood I could not check   3310
And you kissed me as if you would smother me—
Kiss me now!
Or I'll kiss you!

> *She kisses him.*

Oh your lips are cold as stone!
And dumb!
What has become
Of your love?
Who has robbed me of my own?

> *She turns away from him.*

FAUST.   Come! Follow me, my love! Be bold!

I will cherish you after a thousandfold.   3320
Only follow me now! That is all I ask of you.

GRET.   And is it you then? Really? Is it true?

FAUST.   It is! But come!

GRET.   You are undoing each chain,
You take me to your arms again.
How comes it you are not afraid of me?
Do you know, my love, *whom* you are setting
    free?

FAUST.   Come! The deep night is passing by
    and beyond.

GRET.   My mother, I have murdered her;
I drowned my child in the pond.
Was it not a gift to you and me?   3330
To you too—You! Are you what you seem?
Give me your hand! It is not a dream!
Your dear hand—but, oh, it's wet!
Wipe it off! I think
There is blood on it.
Oh God! What have you done?
Put up your sword,
I beg you to.

FAUST.   Let what is gone be gone!
You are killing me.   3340

GRET.   No! *You* must live on!
I will tell you about the graves—
You must get them put right
At morning light;
Give the best place to my mother,
The one next door to my brother,
Me a shade to the side—
A gap, but not too wide.
And the little one on my right breast.
No one else shall share my rest.   3350
When it was you, when I could clasp you,
That was a sweet, a lovely day!
But I no longer can attain it,
I feel I must use force to grasp you,
As if you were thrusting me away.
And yet it's you and you look so kind, so just.

FAUST.   If you feel it's I, then come with me!
    You must!

GRET.   Outside there?

FAUST.   Into the air!

GRET.   If the grave is there
And death on the watch, then come!   3360
Hence to the final rest of the tomb
And not a step beyond—
You are going now? O Heinrich, if *I* could too!

FAUST.   You can! The door is open. Only
    respond!

GRET.   I dare not go out; for me there is no
    more hope.
They are lying in wait for me; what use is
    flight?
To have to beg, it is so pitiable
And that with a conscience black as night!
So pitiable to tramp through foreign lands—
And in the end I must fall into their hands!

FAUST.   I shall stay by you.   3371

GRET.   Be quick! Be quick!
Save your poor child!
Go! Straight up the path—
Along by the brook—
Over the bridge—
Into the wood—
Left where the plank is—
In the pond!
Catch hold of it quickly!   3380
It's trying to rise,
It's kicking still!
Save it! Save it!

FAUST.   Collect yourself!
One step—just one—and you are free.

GRET.   If only we were past the hill!
There sits my mother on a stone—
My brain goes cold and dead—
There sits my mother on a stone—
And wags and wags her head.   3390
No sign, no nod, her head is such a weight.
She'll wake no more, she slept so late.
She slept that we might sport and play.
What a time that was of holiday!

FAUST.   If prayer and argument are no re-
    source,
I will risk saving you by force.

GRET.   No! I will have no violence! Let me
    go!
Don't seize me in that murderous grip!
I have done everything else for you, you know.

FAUST.   My love! My love! The day is dawn-
    ing!   3400

GRET.   Day! Yes, it's growing day! The last
    day breaks on me!
My wedding day it was to be!
Tell no one you had been before with Gretchen.
Alas for my garland!
There's no more chance!
We shall meet again—
But not at the dance.
The people are thronging—but silently;
Street and square

Cannot hold them there.   3410
The bell tolls—it tolls for *me*.
How they seize me, bind me, like a slave!
Already I'm swept away to the block.
Already there jabs at every neck,
The sharp blade which jabs at mine.
The world lies mute as the grave.
    FAUST. I wish I had never been born!
      MEPHISTOPHELES *appears outside.*
    MEPH. Away! Or you are lost.
Futile wavering! Waiting and prating!
My horses are shivering,   3420
The dawn's at the door.
    GRET. What rises up from the floor?
It's he! Send him away! It's he!
What does he want in the holy place?

It is I he wants!
    FAUST.   You shall live!
    GRET. Judgment of God! I have given my-
    self to Thee!
    MEPH. (*to* FAUST). Come! Or I'll leave you
    both in the lurch.
    GRET. O Father, save me! I am Thine!
You angels! Hosts of the Heavenly Church,
Guard me, stand round in serried line!   3430
Heinrich! I shudder to look at you.
    MEPH. She is condemned!
    VOICE FROM ABOVE.   Redeemed!
    MEPH. Follow me!
                 He vanishes with FAUST.
    VOICE (*from within, dying away*). Heinrich!
    Heinrich!

The Second Part of the Tragedy

ACT V

OPEN COUNTRY

    WANDERER. Aye! It's they, the shady lindens
Grown so old and yet so strong.
And I chance again to find them
After wandering so long!
Aye, it is the old place, truly;
There's the hut which sheltered me
Tossed upon those sand-dunes yonder
By the storm-distracted sea.
Worthy couple, quick to help me,
I would bless my hosts again.   10
Talk of meeting me to-day!
They were old already then.
Ah, but they were pious people!
Shall I knock? Or call? Well met,
If to-day, still hospitable,
They delight in good works yet!
    BAUCIS (*a very old woman*). Oh dear stran-
    ger! Softly! Softly!
Quiet! For my husband's sake!
Long sleep helps him to be active
In the short time he's awake.   20
    WAND. Mother, tell me, is it really

You? At last can man and wife
Now be thanked for what they once
Did to save a young man's life?
Are you Baucis, then so busy
To fill a half-dead mouth with food?
               Her husband appears.
    Are *you* Philemon, then so sturdy
To save my treasures from the flood?
Yours the quickly kindled beacon,
Yours the silver-sounding bell,   30
The issue of that dread adventure
Was your trust—you bore it well.
    And now let me walk out yonder,
Look upon the boundless sea—
There to kneel and pray; my heart
Feels so full, it troubles me.
          He walks forward on to the dunes.
    PHILEMON (*to* BAUCIS). Hurry now and lay
    the table
Where the garden flowers are bright.
Let him run and scare himself
When he can't believe his sight.   40
              Joining the WANDERER.
That which savaged you so fiercely—
Waves on waves in foaming spleen—
Here you see become a garden,

Altered to a heavenly scene.
Old by then, I could not lend
A helping hand as on a day,
And my powers had waned already
When the waves were far away.
Clever people's daring servants
Dug their dykes and dammed them high,   50
Whittling down the sea's dominion
To usurp its mastery.
Look! Green meadow after meadow,
Pasture, garden, village, wood.
But the sun is almost setting,
Come and eat—you'll find it good.
Aye, far off there sails are moving
Towards sure harbour for the night.
Birds, you know, they know their nest—
That is now the harbour site.   60
Gazing now into the distance
First you find the sea's blue seam—
All the spaces left and right
Thick with folk and houses teem.
  BAUC. Aye, it *is* a marvel happened;
It still gives me qualms to-day.
For the way it all was done—
It was not a proper way.
  PHIL. Can the Emperor have sinned
Granting him that fief of strand?   70
Did a herald with a trumpet
Not proclaim it round the land?
Their first foothold it was planted
Near our dunes, not far from here,
Tents and huts—but soon a palace
In green meadows must appear!
  BAUC. In vain the workmen's daily racket—
Pick and shovel, slog and slam;
Where the flames by *night* were swarming,
Stood next day a brand new dam.   80
Human victims must have bled,
Night resounded with such woe—
Fireflakes flowing to the sea;
Morning a canal would show.
Godless man he is, he covets
This our cabin and our wood;
To this overweening neighbour
Everyone must be subdued.
  PHIL. All the same we have his offer—
Fine new property elsewhere.   90
  BAUC. Do not trust that water-surface;
On your upland—stand you there!
  PHIL. Let us move on to the chapel,
There to watch the last of day.

Trusting in our father's God
Let us ring the bell and pray!

PALACE

*Extensive formal garden; broad canal,
straight as a ruler.* FAUST, *in the depths of
old age, walking about and brooding.*
  LYNCEUS THE WATCHMAN (*through a mega-
phone*). The sun is sinking, the last ships
Are sailing blithely into port.
A fair-sized bark on the canal
Will reach us soon, its way is short.   100
Her coloured pennants flutter gaily,
Ready to dock her masts are bare;
On you the skipper rests his hopes
And luck now answers all your prayer.
            The little bell rings out on the dunes.
  FAUST (*with a start*). Oh that damned ring-
ing! All too shameful
It wounds me like a stab in the back;
Before my eyes my realm is endless,
Behind—I'm vexed by what I lack,
Reminding me with spiteful ringing
My great possessions are not sound.   110
The linden plot, the wooden cabin,
The crumbling church are not my ground.
And, should I wish to rest me yonder,
Strange shadows fill my heart with fear—
Thorn in the eyes and thorn in the foot;
Oh were I far away from here!
  LYNC. (*as above*). The gay-rigged bark, how
merrily
A sharp breeze bears it to the quay!
How, as it speeds, it towers on high—
Chests, crates and sacks to reach the sky!   120
    *The ship docks, laden with foreign
    merchandise.* MEPHISTOPHELES *and* THE
    THREE MIGHTY MEN *lead the chorus.*
  SAILORS' CHOR. Here we land!
  Oh here we are!
Luck to the owner
  From afar!
  They come ashore and the goods are unloaded.
  MEPH. You see how we have earned our
bays!
Content to win the owner's praise.
We went out with two ships, no more,
And we're in harbour with a score.
Our cargo'll prove, to those who doubt,
What great things we have brought about.   130

The free sea makes the spirit free;
Who thinks of thinking on the sea?
The sea demands quick nerve and grip,
You catch a fish, you catch a ship,
And starting in command of three
You hook a fourth one presently.
Ill omen for the fifth ship? Quite.
Given the might, you have the right.
One asks the What and skips the How.
No need to know much navigation;   140
War, trade and piracy are one
Inseparable combination.
    THREE MEN. Not thank nor greet!
Not greet nor thank!
As if he found
Our cargo stank!
He makes a most
Offensive face;
Our royal freight
Is in disgrace.   150
    MEPH. You need not wait for
More reward!
You had your share
While still on board.
    THREE MEN. Oh that was but
To lighten toil,
We all demand
An equal spoil.
    MEPH. First, room by room.
Arrange up there   160
The precious cargo—
Nothing spare!
When Faust comes in
To such a sight
And reckons all,
Of it aright,
He'll surely not
Be stingy then,
He'll feast the fleet
And feast again.   170
    To-morrow the painted birds are due,
I'll see the best results ensue.
                The cargo is removed.
    MEPH. (*to* FAUST). With brow austere, with
    frowning glance
You greet your latest vast advance.
Crowning your high sagacity,
Your shore is reconciled to sea;
The sea agrees to take your ships
Out from your shore on rapid trips;
Admit then: from your palace here

Your arms embrace the earthly sphere.   180
From here we started on this track,
Here stood your first poor wooden shack;
A little ditch was scratched in dirt
Where now the busy rudders spurt.
Your lofty mind, your navvies' worth,
Obtained for prize the sea and earth.
From here moreover—
    FAUST.   This damned Here!
It's that which makes my spirits drear.
I must confess to you, the expert,
It sears my heart with flame on flame,   190
I find I can no more endure it!
And, while I say so, I feel shame.
That aged couple should have yielded,
I want the lindens in my grip,
Since these few trees that are denied me
Undo my world-wide ownership.
Yonder I planned a panorama,
A platform built from bough to bough,
To grant my eye a distant prospect
Of all that I have done till now,   200
Whence I could see at once aligned
The masterpiece of human mind,
Which energizes skilfully
The peoples' lands reclaimed from sea.
    Hence is our soul upon the rack
Who feel, midst plenty, what we lack.
That clanging bell, that linden-scent,
Are like a tomb—I feel so pent.
The omnipotence of random will
Is broken on this sandy hill.   210
How to shake off this thing which binds me!
The bell rings out—and fury blinds me.
    MEPH. Naturally. Such a nagging pain
Must fill your life with gall, it's plain
To everyone. Your cultured ear
Must find this tinkling vile to hear.
And that damned ding-dong rising high
Befogs the happy evening sky,
Mingling in all things that befall
From baptism to burial,   220
As if between that ding and dong
Life were a dream that had gone wrong.
    FAUST. That obstinacy, all-perverse,
Makes all one's finest gains a curse,
So that, though gnawed at heart, one must
At last grow tired of being just.
    MEPH. Why then these scruples? Your voca-
    tion
Has long meant shifts of population.

FAUST.   Then go and shift them me at once!
You know the pretty little place   230
That I envisaged in their case.

    MEPH.   One takes them out and dumps them
    —Why,
Before one knows, they're up and spry;
A fine new homestead, in due course,
Atones them for our use of force.

    He whistles shrilly. The THREE *re-enter.*
The owner's orders! Come! Don't sorrow,
For there's a seamen's feast to-morrow.

    THREE MEN.   The old man welcomed us like
    beasts;
It's what he owes us—he-men's feasts!

    MEPH. (*to the audience*).   A tale long past
    is told again;   240
There was a Naboth's vineyard then.

DEEP NIGHT

    LYNC. (*singing on the watch-tower*).   For see-
    ing begotten,
My sight my employ,
And sworn to the watch-tower,
The world gives me joy.
I gaze in the distance,
I mark in the near
The moon and the planets,
The woods and the deer.
So find I in all things   250
Eternal delight,
The more that they please me
Am pleased to have sight.
Oh eyes, what has reached you,
So gladly aware,
Whatever its outcome,
At least it was fair.

    But not only to have pleasure
Am I posted on this tower;
What a gruesome horror threatens   260
From the world at this dark hour!
Glancing sparks I see in fountains
Through the lindens' double night.
Burrowing onward, fanned by breezes,
Ever stronger glows the light.
Ah! The hut, once damp and mossy,
Flames within it pave and lave it;
There's a call for quick assistance,
No one is at hand to save it.
Ah, that aged decent couple,   270
Once so careful about fire,

Smothered now in smoke and cinders!
What an end! How strange! How dire!
Blaze on blaze and glowing red
Stands that black and lichened frame;
Could the good folk but escape
From that hell of crazy flame!
Little lightnings, tonguing, twisting,
Climb through leaf and bough, insisting;
Dried-up branches burn and flicker—   280
One quick flare and down they fall.
Must my eyes bear this? Must I be
So far-sighted after all?
Now the little church collapses
Under falling bough on bough.
In a swirl of pointed flames
The tree-tops are on fire by now.
To their roots the hollow tree-trunks
Glow, empurpled in their glow.

                Long pause. Chanting.
That which once enticed my vision—   290
Gone like ages long ago!

    FAUST. (*on the balcony, towards the dunes*).
    What is this whimpering above me?
Both words and burden are too late.
My watchman wails; my heart resents
An action so precipitate.
Yet, though the lindens' life be ended
In half-charred trunks, a thing to dread,
One soon can build there a gazebo
To gaze on the unlimited.
There I see too that fine new dwelling   300
Which will enfold that aged pair,
Who grateful for my generous forethought
Can spend their last days blithely there.

    MEPH. *and* THREE MIGHTY MEN (*below*).   At
    a full gallop, riding strong,
Excuse us if our task went wrong.
We knocked and beat upon the door
But no one opened it the more;
We went on knocking, rattled it,
The rotten door gave way and split;
We shouted angry threats at once   310
But still we met with no response.
And, as in such a case holds good
They could have heard us if they would;
But we refused to make delay,
We quickly dragged them both away.
The pain they felt was only slight,
They fell down dead at once from fright.
A stranger hidden in the hut,
Who wished to fight, we knocked him out.

And in that short but savage fight   320
The scattered fire-coals set alight
Some straw. And that unbridled fire
Now gives all three one funeral pyre.
   FAUST.   Did you then turn deaf ears to me?
I meant exchange, not robbery.
That random stroke, so wild, perverse—
I curse it; you can share the curse.
   CHOR.   The word rings out, the ancient word:
When violence speaks, she's gladly heard.
Only be brave and tough, then take   330
House, goods—and self—and lay your stake.
          They go out.
   FAUST. (*on the balcony*).   The stars conceal
their light and now
The fire sinks down and glimmers low;
A shivery breeze still fanning it
Covers me here with smoke and grit.
Quickly required, too quickly done—
What shadowy shapes come drifting on?

MIDNIGHT

Four GREY WOMEN *approach.*
WANT.   They call me Want.
DEBT.   They call me Debt.
CARE.   They call me Care.
NEED.   They call me Need.
DEBT.   The door is locked and we cannot get
in.   340
NEED.   Nor do we want to, there's wealth
within.
WANT.   That makes me a shadow.
DEBT.   That makes me naught.
NEED.   The pampered spare me never a
thought.
CARE.   My sisters, you cannot and may not
get in.
But the keyhole there lets Care creep in.
          CARE *vanishes.*
WANT.   Come, grey sisters, away from here!
DEBT.   Debt at your side as close as fear.
NEED.   And Need at your heels as close as
breath.
THE THREE.   Drifting cloud and vanishing
star!
Look yonder, look yonder!
         From far, from far,   350
He's coming, our brother, he's coming . . .
         Death.

FAUST (*in the palace*).   Where four came
hither, but three go hence;
I heard them speak, I could not catch the sense.
An echoing word resembling "breath"—
And a dark rhyme-word followed: "Death."
A hollow, muffled, spectral sound to hear.
Not yet have I fought my way out to the air.
All magic—from my path if I could spurn it,
All incantation—once for all unlearn it,
To face you, Nature, as one man of men—   360
It would be worth it to be human then.
As I was once, before I probed the hidden,
And cursed my world and self with words forbidden.
But now such spectredom so throngs the air
That none knows how to dodge it, none knows
where.
Though one day greet us with a rational gleam,
The night entangles us in webs of dream.
We come back happy from the fields of spring—
And a bird croaks. Croaks what? Some evil
thing.
Enmeshed in superstition night and morn,   370
It forms and shows itself and comes to warn.
And we, so scared, stand without friend or kin,
And the door creaks—and nobody comes in.
Anyone here?
   CARE.   The answer should be clear.
   FAUST.   And you, who *are* you then?
   CARE.   I am just here.
   FAUST.   Take yourself off!
   CARE.   This is where I belong.
     FAUST *is first angry, then recovers himself.*
   FAUST (*to himself*).   Take care, Faust, speak
no magic spell, be strong.
   CARE.   Though to me no ear would hearken,
Echoes through the heart must darken;
Changing shape from hour to hour   380
I employ my savage power.
On the road or on the sea,
Constant fearful company,
Never looked for, always found,
Cursed—but flattered by the sound.
   Care? Have you never met with Care?
   FAUST.   I have only galloped through the
world
And clutched each lust and longing by the hair;
What did not please me, I let go,
What flowed away, I let it flow.   390
I have only felt, only fulfilled desire,
And once again desired and thus with power

Have stormed my way through life; first great
    and strong,
Now moving sagely, prudently along.
This earthly circle I know well enough.
Towards the Beyond the view has been cut off;
Fool—who directs that way his dazzled eye,
Contrives himself a double in the sky!
Let him look round him here, not stray beyond;
To a sound man this world must needs respond.
To roam into eternity is vain!   401
What he perceives, he can attain.
Thus let him walk along his earthlong day;
Though phantoms haunt him, let him go his way,
And, *moving on,* to weal and woe assent—
He, at each moment ever discontent!
    CARE.   Whomsoever I possess,
    Finds the world but nothingness;
Gloom descends on him for ever,
Seeing sunrise, sunset, never;   410
Though his senses are not wrong,
Darknesses within him throng,
Who—of all that he may own—
Never owns himself alone.
Luck, ill luck, become but fancy;
Starving in the midst of plenty,
Be it rapture, be it sorrow,
He postpones it till to-morrow,
Fixed upon futurity,
Can never really come to be.   420
    FAUST.   Stop! You cannot touch me so!
Such nonsense I refuse to hear.
Away! Your evil tale of woe
Could fog a wise man's brain, however clear.
    CARE.   Let him come or go—he'll find
    That he can't make up his mind;
Half-way down his destined way
Starts to stumble, grope and sway,
Ever deeper lost and thwarted,
Seeing all things more distorted,   430
Burden to himself and others,
Who takes breath and, breathing, smothers;
If not smothered, yet not living,
Not revolted, not self-giving.
Endless round—he must pursue it:
Painful Leave-it, hateful Do-it,
Freedom now, now harsh constraint,
Broken sleep that leaves him faint,
Bind him to his one position
And prepare him for perdition.   440
    FAUST.   You outcast phantoms! Thus a thou-
    sand times

You lead the human race into illusion;
Even indifferent days you thus transform
To nets of torment, nightmares of confusion.
Demons, I know, are hardly shaken off,
Their ghostly gripping bonds man cannot sever;
But you, O Care, your power that creeps and
    grows—
I shall not recognize it ever.
    CARE.   Then feel it now! As, leaving you,
    This final curse on you I cast.   450
The human race are blind their whole life
    through;
Now, Faust, let *you* be blind at last.
                    She breathes upon him.
    FAUST (*blinded*).   The night seems pressing
    in more thickly, thickly,
Yet in my inmost heart a light shines clear;
What I have planned, I must complete it
    quickly;
Only the master's word is weighty here.
Up and to work, my men! Each man of you!
And bring my bold conception to full view.
Take up your tools and toil with pick and spade!
What has been outlined must at once be *made.*
Good order, active diligence,   461
Ensure the fairest recompense;
That this vast work completion find,
A thousand hands need but one mind.

GREAT FORECOURT OF THE PALACE

Torches

    MEPH. (*leading the way, as foreman*).   Come
    on, come on! Come in, come in!
You gangling gang of Lemurs,
You half-alives patched up with thin
Sinews and skulls and femurs.
    LEMURS (*in chorus*).   You call us, here we
    are at hand;
And, as we understand it,   470
We stand to win a stretch of land
Intended as our mandate.
    Our pointed staves we have them here,
Our chain to measure sections,
But why you called on us, we fear,
Has slipped our recollections.
    MEPH.   Artistic efforts we can spare;
And just let each one's nature guide him!
Let now the longest lie his length down there,
You others prise away the turf beside him;   480

As for your forebears long asleep,
Dig you an oblong, long and deep.
To narrow house from palace hall
Is such a stupid way to end it all.

The LEMURS *begin to dig,*
with mocking gestures.

LEM.   When I was young and lived and
    loved,
Methought it was passing sweet;
In the merry route and roundabout
There would I twirl my feet.

  But sneaking Age has upped his crutch
And downed me unaware;   490
I stumbled over the door of the grave—
Why was it open *there?*

  FAUST (*groping his way from the palace*).
    Oh how this clink of spades rejoices me!
For that is my conscripted labour,
The earth is now her own good neighbour
And sets the waves a boundary—
Confinement strict and strenuous.

  MEPH. (*aside*).   And yet you've only toiled
    for *us*
With all your damming, all your dyking—
Spreading a feast to Neptune's liking   500
To glut that water-demon's maw.
In all respects you're lost and stranded,
The elements with us have banded—
Annihilation is the law.

  FAUST.   Foreman!

  MEPH.   Here!

  FAUST.   Use every means you can;
Bring all your gangs up and exhort them—
Threaten them if you like or court them—
But pay or woo or force each man!
And day by day send word to me, assessing   509
How my intended earthworks are progressing.

  MEPH. (*half aloud*).   The word to-day, from
    what I've heard,
Is not "intended" but "interred."

  FAUST.   A swamp along the mountains' flank
Makes all my previous gains contaminate;
My deeds, if I could drain this sink,
Would culminate as well as terminate:
To open to the millions living space,
Not danger-proof but free to run their race.
Green fields and fruitful; men and cattle hiving
Upon this newest earth at once and thriving,
Settled at once beneath this sheltering hill   519
Heaped by the masses' brave and busy skill.
With such a heavenly land behind this hedge,

The sea beyond may bluster to its edge
And, as it gnaws to swamp the work of masons,
To stop the gap one common impulse hastens.
Aye! Wedded to this concept like a wife,
I find this wisdom's final form:
He only earns his freedom and his life
Who takes them every day by storm.   530
And so a man, beset by dangers here,
As child, man, old man, spends his manly year.
Oh to see such activity,
Treading free ground with people that are free!
Then could I bid the passing moment:
"Linger a while, thou art so fair!"
The traces of my earthly days can never
Sink in the aeons unaware.
And I, who feel ahead such heights of bliss,
At last enjoy my highest moment—this.   540

FAUST *sinks back; the* LEMURS *seize*
him and lay him on the ground.

  MEPH.   By no joy sated, filled by no success,
Still whoring after shapes that flutter past,
This last ill moment of sheer emptiness—
The poor man yearns to hold it fast.
He who withstood me with such strength,
Time masters him and here he lies his length.
The clock stands still—

  CHOR.   Stands still! Like mid-
    night . . . silent . . . stilled.
Its hand drops down.

  MEPH.   Drops down; it is fulfilled.

  LEMS.   It is gone by.

  MEPH.   Gone by! A stupid phrase.
Why say gone by?   550
Gone by—pure naught—complete monotony.
What use these cycles of creation!
Or snatching off the creatures to negation!
"It is gone by!"—and we can draw the infer-
    ence:
If it had *not* been, it would make no difference;
The wheel revolves the same, no more, no less.
I should prefer eternal emptiness.

INTERMENT

  LEM. SOLO.   Oh who has built the house so
    ill
With spade and shovel rough?

  LEM. CHOR.   For you, dull guest in hempen
    garb,   560
Yon house is fine enough.

LEM. SOLO.   No chair or table in the hall—
Who's furnished it so meagre?
LEM. CHOR.   The loan was only for a time;
The creditors are eager.
MEPH.   Here lies the corpse and if the soul
would flee
At once I show the bond, the blood-signed scroll;
Though now, alas, they have so many means
To cheat the devil of a soul.
Our old procedure gives offence,   570
Our new has not yet found endorsement;
Once I'd have managed it alone,
Now I must look for reinforcement.
Come up, you devils! Make it double quick!
You straight-horned peers and crooked-horned
as well,
You old and sterling devil-stock,
Come up—and bring with you the jaws of Hell!
The Jaws of Hell open upon the left.
The eye-teeth gape; the throat's enormous vault
Spews forth a raging fiery flow   579
And through the smoking cyclone of the gullet
I see the infernal city's eternal glow.
You do right well to make the sinner quake;
And yet they think it all a dream, a fake.
Now, devils, watch this body! How does it seem?
See if you see a phosphorescent gleam.
That is the little soul, Psyche with wings—
Pull out her wings and it's a noisome worm;
With my own seal I'll set my stamp upon her,
Then forth with her into the fiery storm!
Come, claw and comb the air, strain every
nerve   590
To catch her though she flutter, though she
swerve.
To stay in her old lodging gives her pain;
The genius is about to leave the brain.
Glory, from above, on the right.
THE HOST OF HEAVEN.   Fly, as directed,
Heaven's elected,
Serenely whereby
Sin shall have pardon,
Dust become garden;
Stay your progression,
Make intercession,   600
Trace for all natures
A path to the sky.
MEPH.   Discords I hear, a filthy strumming
tumbling
Down from the sky with the unwelcome day;
That is the angels' boyish-girlish fumbling,

Their canting taste *likes* it to sound that way.
You know how we, in hours of deep damnation,
Have schemed annihilation for mankind;
Those angels use for adoration
The greatest stigma we could find.   610
They come so fawningly, the milksops!
They've kidnapped many souls before our eyes,
They fight us back with our own weapons;
They too are devils—in disguise.
Defeat to-day would mean disgrace eternal;
So stand around the grave and stand infernal!
CHOR. OF ANGELS (*scattering roses*).   Roses,
you glowing ones,
Balsam-bestowing ones!
Fluttering peaceably,
Healing invisibly,   620
Spraylets to glide upon,
Budlets unspied upon,
Hasten to bloom!
Green and empurpled,
Spring must have room;
Carry your heaven
Into the tomb!
MEPH. (*to the* SATANS).   Why duck and
squirm? Is that our wont in hell?
Stand fast and let them strew their roses!
Each gawk to his post and guard it well!   630
With such small flowers the enemy proposes
To snow up overheated devils;
Why, at your breath it melts and shrivels.
Now puff, you blow-fiends!
                              . . . Here! Stop! Stop!
Your reek is bleaching the whole flight crop.
Don't blow so hard! Muzzle your chops and
noses!
I'll swear you've *over*blown those roses!
You never know when you have passed the turn!
They're more than shrunk—they're browned,
they're dry, they *burn!*
Bright flames of poison pelt on us already;   640
In close formation, devils! Steady! Steady!
What! All your valour gone! Your strength
burns low!
The devils sense a strange insidious glow.
CHOR. OF ANGELS.   Blooms of pure blessed-
ness,
Flames of pure joyfulness,
Love is their ministry,
Rapture their legacy,
All we could pray.
Hosts of eternity

Find in such verity   650
Heavens of clarity,
Aeons of day!
    MEPH.   A curse upon these louts! How scurvy!
My Satans are all topsy-turvy
And turning cartwheels in their path
And tumbling arse-up into Hell.
I hope you like your well-earned sulphur bath!
I stand my ground and wish you well.
        He beats off the roses falling around him.
    CHOR. OF ANGELS.   What is not right for you
You must beware it,   660
What does despite to you
You may not bear it.
Lightnings may dart on us,
We must have heart in us.
Lovers can only be
Rescued by love.
    MEPH.   My head's aflame! Liver and heart
        aflame!
A super-devilish element!
Hell's fires to this are damped and tame.
That's why you make such wild lament,   670
You luckless folk in love, despised alas,
Who sprain your necks to watch your sweet-
        hearts pass.
    Me too! What draws my head in that direc-
        tion?
I, their sworn enemy! Is this defection?
To see them once was agony or worse.
Has something alien entered me completely?
To see their flower of youth affects me now so
        sweetly;
I want to curse them—but what chokes the
        curse?
And, if I let them now befool me,
Whom can the future call a fool?   680
These dashing fellows, though I hate them,
Inspire a longing that I cannot rule.
Beautiful children, must I not infer
That you like me are kin to Lucifer?
With every look you seem more fair, more fair.
Oh come near, angels, glance on me! Come near!
    ANGEL.   See, we approach—why do you
        shrink away?
We come; if you can face us—why, then, stay!
    The ANGELS, *closing in, occupy all the space.*
    CHOIR OF ANGELS.   Flames of dear feeling,
Rise beyond seeing!   690
Self-condemned being—
Truth be its healing!

Blessed transition
Forth from perdition,
Into Eternity,
Into the One!
    MEPH.   (*collecting himself*). Look! The
        damned flames are out that caused my fall.
Now I become myself and curse you one and all!
    CHOIR OF ANGELS.   Light of Creation!
Whom it embraces   700
Finds all the graces
Found in salvation.
Praising in unison
Rise to your goal!
Purged is the air now—
Breathe now the soul!
        *They soar up, carrying away
        the immortal part of* FAUST.
    MEPH.   (*looking around him*). But how is
        this? Where have they moved away to?
You juveniles, to take me by surprise!
Flying off heavenwards—and with my prey too;
They nibbled at this grave to win this prize.   710
Wresting from me a great and matchless treas-
        ure,
That noble soul which gave me right of seizure
They've filched by throwing rose-dust in my
        eyes.
Who is there now to lend an ear to
My wrong, restore my hard-earned right?
You have been hoaxed—so late in your career
        too—
It's your own fault, you're in a lurid plight.
Such gross mismanagement—outrageous!
Such a great outlay squandered! Oh the shame!
Erotic folly, vulgar lust, contagious   720
To an old devil at the game!
Experience has indulged its appetite
On such a childish-foolish level;
When all is said, the folly is not slight
Which in the end has seized the devil.

MOUNTAIN GORGES

Forest, Rock, Wilderness. HOLY ANCHO-
RITES, *disposed here and there, at different
heights among the chasms.*
    CHOR. AND ECHO.   Woods clamber trem-
        blingly,
Crags bear down weightily,
Roots cling tenaciously,
Trunks make a density;

Spurting of wave on wave—   730
Deep lies our hermits' cave.
Lions around in dumb
Friendliness gently come,
Honour our sanctuary,
Love's holy privacy.
    PATER ECSTATICUS (*floating up and down*).
      Rapture which yearns ever,
Love-bond which burns ever,
Pain in me seething up,
Love of God foaming up.
Arrows, pierce through me and,   740
Lances, subdue me and,
Clubs, leave no form in me,
Thunderstorms, storm in me!
That now the Nothingness
Drown all in emptiness,
One constant star must shine,
Kernel of love divine.
    PATER PROFUNDUS (*from the depths*).   As at
      my feet a craggy chasm
Weighs on a deeper chasm's prop,
As streams in thousands flow and sparkle   750
Towards the dread rapids' foaming drop,
As with its own strong urge the tree-trunk
Climbs up the air, erect and tall,
Even so is that almighty love
Which all things forms and fosters all.
    Around me here a frantic rushing
Makes wood and cleft a stormy sea,
Yet full of love the water's fullness
Roars as it plumbs the cavity,
Ordained to straightway feed the valley;   760
The thunderbolt which crashed in flame
To cleanse the air which bore within it
Poison and evil mists, these same
    Are messengers of love, announcing
What round us ever moves and makes.
May that light kindle too within me
Where the cold spirit gropes and quakes,
Self-racked in body's bonds of dullness,
Riveted fast in chains that smart.
O God, have mercy on my thoughts,   770
Give light to my impoverished heart!
    PATER SERAPHICUS (*at a middle height.*)
      What a morning cloudlet hovers
Through the pine-trees' waving hair!
I divine what lives within it—
Newborn souls are gathered there.
    CHOR. OF BLESSED BOYS.   Tell us, Father,
      where we wander,

Tell us, good one, who we are!
All of us are happy, living
In a state that naught can mar.   779
    PAT. SER.   Innocents—who, born at midnight
With half-opened soul and brain,
Were at once your parents' loss,
Were at once the angels' gain.
That a living man is present,
That you feel, so draw you near!
Though earth's rugged ways are barred you,
Alien to your happy sphere.
Climb up then into my eyes—
Organ matching world and earth;
See this region, using mine   790
For the eyes you lost at birth.
                  He takes them into himself.
Those are trees—and those are crags—
See that river plunging deep,
Which with its enormous welter
Delves a passage, short though deep.
    BLESS. BOYS (*from inside him*).   Yes, that is
      a mighty prospect—
But too sad this world below,
Shaking us with fear and horror.
Reverend father, let us go!
    PAT. SER.   Aye. Ascend to higher circles,   800
Ever grow invisibly
As God's presence makes you stronger
Through eternal purity.
It is this which feeds the spirit,
Rules the heights of revelation:
Window into love eternal
Opening upon salvation.
    BLESS. BOYS (*circling round the highest peak*).
      Joyfully gyring
Dance ye in union,
Hands linked and choiring   810
Blessed communion!
Pattern before you,
Godly, to cheer you,
Whom you adore, you
Soon shall see near you.
    ANGELS (*floating in the higher air, carrying
      the immortal part of* FAUST).   Saved, saved
      now is that precious part
Of our spirit world from evil:
"Should a man strive with all his heart,
Heaven can foil the devil."
And if love also from on high   820
Has helped him through his sorrow,

The hallowed legions of the sky
Will give him glad good morrow.
   THE YOUNGER ANGELS. Ah those roses, *their* donation—
Loving-holy penitent women—
Helped us to defeat Apollyon,
Brought our work to consummation,
To this priceless spirit's capture.
Devils, as we scattered rapture,
Struck by roses, fled in panic,   830
Feeling not their pains Satanic
But the pains of love's disaster;
Even that old Satan-master
Felt a torment arrowed, marrowed.
Alleluia! Hell is harrowed.
   THE MORE PERFECT ANGELS. This scrap of earth, alas,
We must convoy it;
Were it asbestos, yet
Earth would alloy it.
When soul's dynamic force   840
Has drawn up matter
Into itself, then no
Angel could shatter
The bonds of that twoness—
The oneness that tied it;
Eternal love alone
Knows to divide it.
   YOUNGER ANGELS. Close, round the mountain top,
To my perceiving
Moves like a mist a   850
Spiritual living.
Those clouds are turning bright,
I see a sainted flight:
Children unmeshed from
Meshes of earth, they
Fly in a ring,
Being refreshed from
Heaven's rebirth they
Bask in its spring.
Faust, to begin to rise   860
Towards highest Paradise,
With them must wing.
   BLESS. BOYS. Gladly receiving this
Chrysalid entity,
Now we achieve, in this,
Angels' identity.
Let the cocoon which is
Round him be broken!
Great! Fair! How soon he is

Heaven-awoken!   870
   DOCTOR MARIANUS (*in the highest, purest cell*).
   Here is the prospect free,
Spirit-uplifting.
Yonder go women's shapes
Over me drifting;
And, wreathed in her seven
Bright stars, they attend her—
The high queen of Heaven;
I gaze on her splendour.
              Entranced.
   Highest empress of the world,
Let these blue and sacred   880
Tents of heaven here unfurled
Show me now thy secret!
Sanction that which in man's breast
Soft and strong prepares him—
Love which joyful, love which blest
Towards thy presence bears him.
   Thine august commands are such,
Nothing can subdue us—
Fires burn gentler at thy touch
Should thy peace imbue us.   890
Virgin, pure as none are pure,
Mother, pearl of honour,
Chosen as our queen, the sure
Godhead stamped upon her!
   Light clouds enlacing
Circle her splendour—
These are the penitent
Women, a tender
Race. At thy knee,
Sipping the air, they   900
Call upon thee.
   Thou, albeit immaculate,
It is of thy fashion
That the easily seduced
Sue to thy compassion.
   Such whom frailty reft, are hard,
Hard to save, if ever;
Who can burst the bonds of lust
Through his own endeavour?
Do not sliding gradients cause   910
Sudden slips? What maiden
Is not fooled by flattering glance,
Tokens flattery-laden?
   (*The* MATER GLORIOSA *floats into vision.*)
   CHOR. OF PENITENT WOMEN. Mary, in soaring
To kingdoms eternal,
Hear our imploring

Thou beyond rival!
Fount of survival!
   MAGNA PECCATRIX. By my love which min-
   gled tears with
Balm to bathe His feet, revering   920
Him thy son, now God-transfigured,
When the Pharisees were jeering;
By that vessel which so sweetly
Spilt its perfumed wealth profusely,
By my hair which dried those holy
Limbs, around them falling loosely—
   MULIER SAMARITANA. By the well where Fa-
   ther Abram
Watered once his flocks when marching,
By the bucket once allowed to   929
Touch and cool Christ's lips when parching;
By that pure and generous source which
Now extends its irrigation,
Overbrimming, ever-crystal,
Flowing through the whole creation—
   MARIA AEGYPTIACA. By that more than sacred
   garden
Where they laid the Lord to rest,
By the arm which from the portal
Thrust me back with stern behest;
By my forty years' repentance
Served out in a desert land,   940
By the blessed word of parting
Which I copied in the sand—
   THE THREE. Thou who to most sinning
   women
Thy dear presence ne'er deniest,
Raising us repentant women
To eternities the highest,
Make to *this* good soul concession—
Only once misled by pleasure
To a never-dreamt transgression;
Grant her pardon in her measure.   950
   ONE OF THE PENITENTS (*formerly named*
   GRETCHEN). Uniquely tender,
Thou queen of splendour,
Thy visage render
Benign towards my felicity!
My love of old, he

Is now consoled, he
Comes back to me.
   BLESS. BOYS (*approaching, flying in circles*).
   Passing beyond us
So soon in resplendence,
He will make ample   960
Return for our tendance;
Early we left the
Terrestrial chorus;
He will instruct us,
Instructed before us.
   THE SINGLE PENITENT (*formerly named*
   GRETCHEN). By choirs of noble souls sur-
   rounded
This new one scarcely feels his soul,
Can scarcely sense this life unbounded,
Yet fills at once his heavenly role.
See how he sheds the earthly leaven,   970
Tears off each shroud of old untruth,
And from apparel woven in heaven
Shines forth his pristine power of youth!
Mary, grant me to instruct him,
Dazzled as yet by this new day.
   MATER GLORIOSA. Come then! To higher
   spheres conduct him!
Divining *you,* he knows the way.
   DOC. MAR. (*bowing in adoration*). All you
   tender penitents,
Gaze on her who saves you—
Thus you change your lineaments   980
And salvation laves you.
To her feet each virtue crawl,
Let her will transcend us;
Virgin, Mother, Queen of All,
Goddess, still befriend us!
   CHOR. MYSTICUS. All that is past of us
Was but reflected;
All that was lost in us
Here is corrected;
All indescribables   990
Here we descry;
Eternal Womanhead
Leads us on high.

FINIS

THOMAS MANN

Doctor Faustus

CHAPTER 25

Whist, mum's the word. And certes I schal be mum, will hold my tunge, were it sheerly out of shame, to spare folkes feelings, for social considerations forsooth! Am firmly minded to keep fast hold on reason and decency, not giving way even up till the end. But seen Him I have, at last, at last! He was with me, here in this hall, He sought me out; unexpected, yet long expected. I held plenteous parley with Him, and now thereafter I am vexed but sith I am not certain whereat I did shake all the whole time: an 'twere at the cold, or at Him. Did I beguile myself, or He me, that it was cold, so I might quake and thereby certify myself that He was there, Himself in person? For verily no man but knows he is a fool which quaketh at his proper brain-maggot; for sooner is such welcome to him and he yieldeth without or shaking or quaking thereunto. Mayhap He did but delude me, making out by the brutish cold I was no fool and He no figment, since I a fool did quake before Him? He is a wily-pie.

Natheles[1] I will be mum, will hold my tonge and mumchance hide all down here on my music-paper, whiles my old jester-fere[2] *in eremo,*[3] far away in the hall, travails and toils to turn the loved outlandish into the loathed mother tongue. He weens[4] that I compose, and were he to see that I write words, would but deem Beethoven did so too.

All the whole day, poor wretch, I had lien in the dark with irksome mygrym,[5] retching and spewing, as happeth with the severer seizures.

But at eventide quite suddenly came unexpected betterment. I could keep down the soup the Mother brought me / *222* / (*"Poveretto!"*);[6] with good cheer drank a glass of *rosso* (*"Bevi, bevi!"*)[7] and on a sudden felt so staunch as to allow myself a cigarette. I could even have gone out, as had been arranged the day before. Dario M. wanted to take us down to his club and introduce us to the better sort of Praenestensians, show us reading-room, billiard-room, and about the place. We had no heart to offend the good soul, but it came down to Sch.[8] going alone, I being forgiven due to my attack. From *pranzo*[9] he stalked off with a sour countenance, down the street at Dario's side to the farmers and philistines, and I stopped by myself.

I sate alone here, by my lamp, nigh to the windows with shutters closed, before me the length of the hall, and read Kirkegaard on Mozart's *Don Juan.*

Then in a clap I am stricken by a cutting cold, even as though I sat in a winter-warm room and a window had blown open towards the frost. It came not from behind me, where the windows lie; it falls on me from in front. I start up from my boke and look abroad into the hall, belike Sch. is come back for I am no more alone. There is some bodye there in the mirk,[10] sitting on the horsehair sofa that stands almost in the myddes of the room, nigher the door, with the table and chairs, where we eat our breakfasts. Sitting in the sofa-corner with legs crossed; not Sch., but another, smaller than he, in no wise so imposing and not in truth a gentilman at all. But the cold keeps percing me.

---

1. Natheles: nevertheless. **2. -fere:** companion. **3. in eremo:** in solitude. **4. weens:** supposes. **5. mygrym:** migraine.

6. Poveretto: poor fellow. **7. Bevi, bevi:** Drink, drink. **8. Sch.:** Adrian's friend, Schildknapp. **9. pranzo:** dinner. **10. mirk:** gloom.

"Chi e costà?"[11] is what I shout with some catch in my throat, propping my hands on the chair-arms, in such wise that the book falls from my knees to the floore. Answers the quiet, slow voice of the other, a voice that sounds trained, with pleasing nasal resonance:

"Speak only German! Only good old German without feignedness or dissimulation. I understand it. It happens to be just precisely my favoured language. Whiles I understand only German. But fet thee a cloak, a hat and rug. Thou art cold. And quiver and quake thou wilt, even though not taking a cold."

"Who says *thou* to me?" I ask, chafing.

"I," he says. "I, by your leave. Oh, thou meanest because thou sayest to nobody thou, not even to thy jester gentilman, but only to the trusty play-fere, he who clepes[12] thee by the first name but not thou him. No matter. There is already enough between us for us to say thou. Wel, then: wilt fet thyself some warm garment?"

I stare into the half-light, fix him angrily in mine eye. A man: rather spindling, not nearly so tall as Sch., smaller even then I. /223/ A sports cap over one ear, on the other side reddish hair standing up from the temple; reddish lashes and pink eyes, a cheesy face, a drooping nose with wry tip. Over diagonal-striped tricot shirt a chequer jacket; sleeves too short, with sausage-fingers coming too far out; breeches indecently tight, worn-down yellow shoes. An ugly customer, a bully, a *strizzi*,[13] a rough. And with an actor's voice and eloquence.

"Well?" he says again.

"First and foremost I fain would know," say I in quaking calm, "who is bold enough to force himself in to sit down here with me."

"First and foremost," he repeats. "First and foremost is not bad at all. But you are over-sensitive to any visit you hold to be unexpected and undesired. I am no flattering claw-back come to fetch you into company, to woo you that you may join the musical circle; but to talk over our affairs. Wilt fetch thy things? It is ill talking with teeth chattering."

I sat a few seconds lenger, not taking my eyes off him. And the cutting cold, coming from him, rushes at me, so that I feel bare and bald before it in my light suit. So I go. Verily I stand up and pass through the next door to the left, where my bedchamber is (the other's being further down on the same side), take my winter cloke out of the presse that I wear in Rome on tramontana days and it had to come along as I wist not where I might leave it else; put my hat on too, take my rug and so furnished go back to my place.

There he still sits in his, just as I left him.

"Ye're still there," say I, turning up my coat-collar and wrapping my plaid about my knees— "even after I've gone and come back? I marvel at it. For I've a strong suspicion y'are not there at all."

"No?" he asks in his trained voice, with nasal resonance. "For why?"

I: "Because it is nothing likely that a man should seat himself here with me on an evening, speaking German and giving out cold, with pretence to discuss with me gear whereof I wot nor would wot naught. Miche more like is it I am waxing sicke and transferring to your form the chills and fever against the which I am wrapped, sneaped by frost, and in the beholding of you see but the source of it."

He (quietly and convincingly laughing, like an actor): "Tilly-vally,[14] what learned gibber-idge[15] you talk! In good playne old German, 'tis fond and frantick. And so artificial! A clever artifice, an /224/ 'twere stolen from thine own opera! But we make no music here, at the moment. Moreover it is pure hypochondria. Don't imagine any infirmities! Have a little pride and don't lose grip of yourself! There's no sickness breaking out, after the slight attack you are in the best of youthful health. But I cry you mercy, I would not be tactless, for what is health? Thuswise, my goodly fere, your sickness does not break out. You have not a trace of fever and no occasion wherefore you should ever have any."

I: "Further, because with every third word ye utter you uncover your nothingness. You say nothing save things that are in me and come out of me but not out of you. You ape old Kumpf[16] with turns of phrase yet look not as though you ever had been in academie or higher school or ever sat next to me on the scorner's bench. You talk of the needy gentilman and of him to whom

14. tillyvally: an expression of annoyance, like "fiddle-sticks." 15. gibberidge: gibberish. 16. Kumpf: an old teacher of Adrian's.

11. Chi e costà?: Who is there? 12. clepes: calls. 13. strizzi: a tough.

I speak in the singular number,[17] and even of such as have done so and reaped but little thank. And of my opera you speak too. Whence could you know all that?"

He (laughs again his practised laugh, shaking his head as at some priceless childishness): "Yea, whence? But see, I do know it. And you will conclude therefrom to your own discredit that you do not see aright? That were truly to set all logick upsodown, as one learns at the schools. 'Twere better to conclude, not that I am not here in the flesh, but that I, here in my person, am also he for whom you have taken me all the whole time."

I: "And for whom do I take you?"

He (politely reproachful): "Tut, tut! Do not lain[18] it thus, as though you had not been long since expecting me! You wit aswel as I that our relation demands a dispicion. If I am—and that I ween you do now admit—then I can be but One. Or do you mean, what I hyght?[19] But you can still recall all the scurrile nicknames from the schoole, from your first studies, when you had not put the Good Boke out of the door and under the bench. You have them all at your fingers' ends, you may elect one—I have scant others, they are well-nigh all nicknames, with the which people, so to speke, chuck me under the chin: that comes from my good sound German popularity. A man is gratified by popularity, I trow, even when he has not sought it out and at bottom is convinced that it rests on false understanding. It is always flattering, always does a bodye good. Choose one yourself, if you would call me by name, although you commonly do not call people by name at all; for lack of interest you do not know what they hight. But choose any one you list among the pet names the peasants give me. Only one I cannot and will not abide because it /225/ is distinctly a malicious slander and fits me not a whit. Whosoever calls me *Dicis et non facis*[20] is in the wrong box. It too may even be a finger chucking my chin, but it is a calumny. I do ywisse[21] what I say, keep my promise to a tittle; that is precisely my business principle, more or less as the Jews are the most reliable dealers,

and when it comes to deceit, well, it is a common saying that it was always I, who believe in good faith and rightwiseness, who am beguiled."

I: "*Dicis et non es.*[22] Ye would forsoothe sit there against me on the sofa and speak outwardly to me in good Kumpfish, in old-German snatches? Ye would visit me deliberately here in Italy of all places, where you are entirely out of your sphere and not on the peasant tongue at all? What an absurd want of style! In Kaisersaschern I could have suffered it. At Wittenberg or on the Wartburg, even in Leipzig you would have been credible to me. But not here under this pagan and Catholic sky!"[23]

He (shaking his head and pained clucking with his tongue): "Tch, tch, tch! always this same distrust, this same lack of self-confidence! If you had the courage to say unto yourself: 'Where I am, there is Kaisersaschern'—well and good, the thing would be in frame, the Herr aestheticus[24] would needs make moan no more over lack of style. Cocksblood![25] You would have the right to speak like that, yet you just haven't the courage or you act as though you lacked it. Self-belittlement, my friend—and you underestimate me too, if you limit me thuswise and try to make a German provincial of me. I am in fact German, German to the core, yet even so in an older, better way, to wit cosmopolitan from my heart. Wouldst deny me away, wouldst refuse to consider the old German romantic wander-urge and yearning after the fair land of Italy! German I am, but that I should once in good Düreresque[26] style freeze and shiver after the sun, that Your Excellency will not grant me—not even when quite aside from the sun, I have delicate and urgent business here, with a fine, well-created human being. . . ."

Here an unspeakable disgust came over me, so that I shuddered violently. But there was no real difference between the grounds of my shudder; it might be at one and the same time for cold, too; the draught from him had got abruptly stronger, so that it went through my overcoat and pierced me to my marrow. Angrily I ask:

"Cannot you away with this nuisance, this icy draught?"

17. **needy . . . number:** acquaintances of Adrian.
18. **lain:** put.   19. **what I hyght:** what I am called.
20. **Dicis . . . facis:** say and not do.   21. **ywisse:** certainly.

22. **Dicis . . . es:** say and not be.   23. **Catholic sky:** in Italy.   24. **Herr aestheticus:** Mr. Esthetic (satirical).   25. **Cocksblood:** an oath, a corruption of "by God's blood."   26. **Düreresque:** like that of the artist Dürer.

He: "Alas, no, I regret not to be able to gratify you. But the /226/ fact is, I *am* cold. How otherwise could I hold out and find it possible to dwell where I dwell?"

I (involuntarily): "You mean in the brenning pit of fier?"

He (laughs as though tickled): "Capital! Said in the good robust and merry German way. It has indeed many other pretty names, scholarly, pathetical, the Herr Doctor ex-Theologus knows them all, as carcer, exitium, confutatio, pernicies, condemnatio,[27] and so on. But there is no remedy, the familiar German, the comic ones are still my favourites. However, let us for the nonce leave that place and the nature of it. I see by your face, you are at the point of asking about it; but that is far off, not in the least a brenning question—you will forgive me the bourd,[28] that it is not brenning! There is time for it, plenteous, boundless time—time is the actual thing, the best we give, and our gift the houre-glasse—it is so fine, the little neck, through which the red sand runs, a threadlike trickle, does not minish[29] at all to the eye in the upper cavitie, save at the very end; then it does seem to speed and to have gone fast. But that is so far away, the narrow part, it is not worth talking or thinking about. Albeit inasmuch as the glass is set and the sand has begun to run; for this reason, my good man, I would fain[30] come to an understanding with you."

I (full scornfully): "Extraordinarily Dürerish. You love it. First 'how will I shiver after the sun'; and then the houre-glasse of the *Melancolia.* Is the magic square coming too? I am prepared for everything, can get used to everything. Get used to your shamelessness, your thee-ing and thou-ing and trusty fere-ing, which soothly[31] always go particularly against the wood. After all I say 'thou' only to myself, which of likelihood explains why you do. According to you I am speaking with black Kaspar, which is one of the names, and so Kaspar and Samiel are one and the same."

He: "Off you go again!"

I: "Samiel. It giveth a man to laugh. Where then is your C-minor fortissimo of stringed tremoli,[32] wood and trombones, ingenious bug to fright children, the romantic public, coming out of the F-sharp minor of the Glen as you out of your abyss—I wonder I hear it not!"

He: "Let that be. We have many a lovelier instrument and you shall hear them. We shall play for you, when you be ripe to hear. Everything is a matter of ripeness and of dear time. Just that I would speak of with you. But Samiel—that's a folish form. I am all for that is of the folk; but Samiel, too foolish, Johann Ballhorn /227/ from Lübeck corrected it. Sammael it is. And what signifies Sammael?"

I (defiant, do not answer).

He: "What, ne'er a word but mum? I like the discreet way in which you leave me to put it in German. It means angel of death."

I (between my teeth, which will not stay properly closed): "Yes, distinctly, that is what you look like! Just like unto an angel, exactly. Do you know how you look? Common is not the word for it. Like some shameless scum, a lewd losel,[33] a make-bate, that is how you look, how you have found good to visit me—and no angel!"

He (looking down at himself, with his arms stretched out): "How then, how then? How do I look? No, it is really good that you ask me if I wot how I look, for by my troth I wot not. Or wist not, you called it to my attention. Be sure, I reck nothing at all to my outward appearance, I leave it so to say to itself. It is sheer chance how I look, or rather, it comes out like that, it happeth like that according to the circumstances, without my taking heed. Adaptation, mimicry, you know it, of course. Mummery and jugglery of mother Nature, who always has her tongue in her cheek. But you won't, my good fere, refer the adaptation, about which I know just as much and as little as the leaf butterfly, to yourself, and take it ill of me. You must admit that from the other side it has something suitable about it—on that side where you got it from, and indeed forewarned, from the side of your pretty song with the letter symbol—oh, really ingeniously done, and almost as though by inspiration:

When once thou gavest to me

---

27. carcer . . . condemnatio: Latin terms for hell: prison, exit, refutation, ruin, condemnation. 28. bourd: jest. 29. minish: diminish. 30. fain: gladly. 31. soothly: truly.

32. fortissimo . . . tremoli: very loud tremulous notes, suggestive of frightening sounds made by the devil. 33. losel: rascal.

At night the cooling draught,
With poison didst undo me

.   .   .

Then on the wound the serpent
Fastened and firmly sucked—

Really gifted. That is what we recognized betimes and why from early on we had an eye on you—we saw that your case was quite definitely worth the trouble, that it was a case of the most favourable situation, whereof with only a little of our fire lighted under it, only a little heating, elation, intoxication, something brilliant could be brought out. Did not Bismarck say something about the Germans needing half a bottle of champagne to arrive at their normal height? Meseems[34] he said something of the sort. /228/ And that of right. Gifted but halt is the German—gifted enough to be angry with his paralysis, and to overcome it by hand-over-head illumination. You, my good man, well knew what you needed, and took the right road when you made your journey and *salva venia*[35] summoned your French beloved to you."

"Hold thy tongue!"

"Hold thy tongue? We are coming on. We wax warm. At last you drop the polite plural number and say 'thou,' as it should be between people who are in league and contract for time and eternity."

"Will ye hold your tongue still?"

"Still? But we have been still for nigh five years and must after all sometime hold parley and advise over the whole and over the interesting situation wherein you find yourself. This is naturally a thing to keep wry about, but after all not at the length—when the houre-glasse is set, the red sand has begun to run through the fine-fine neck—ah, but only just begun! It is still almost nothing, what lies underneath, by comparison with all there is on top; we give time, plenteous time, abundant time by the eye, the end whereof we do not need to consider, not for a long time yet; nor need to trouble yet awhile even of the point of time where you could begin to take heed to the ending, where it might come to '*Respice finem.*'[36] Sithence it is a variable point, left to caprice and temper, and nobody knows where it should begin, and how nigh to the end one should lay it out. This is a good bourd and capital arrangement: the uncertainty and the free choice of the moment when the time is come to heed the eynde, overcasts in mist and jest the view of the appointed limit."

"Fables, fantasies!"

"Get along, one cannot please you, even against my psychology you are harsh—albeit you yourself on your Mount Zion at home called psychology a nice, neutral middle point and psychologists the most truth-loving people. I fable not a whit when I speak of the given time and the appointed end; I speak entirely to the point. Wheresoever the houre-glasse is set up and time fixed, unthinkable yet measured time and a fixed end, there we are in the field, there we are in clover. Time we sell—let us say XXIV years—can we see to the end of that? Is it a good solid amount? Therewith a man can live at rack and manger like a lord and astonish the world as a great nigromancer[37] with much divel's work; the lenger it goes on, the more forget all paralysis and in highly illuminated state rise out of himselfe, yet never transcend but remain the same, though raised to his proper stature by the half- /229/ bottle of champagne. In drunken bliss he savours all the rapture of an almost unbearable draught, till he may with more or less of right be convinced that a like infusion has not been in a thousand years and in certain abandoned moments may simply hold himself a god. How will such an one come to think about the point of time when it is become time to give heed to the end! Only, the end is ours, at the end he is ours, that has to be agreed on, and not merely silently, how silent so ever it be else, but from man to man and expressly."

I: "So you would sell me time?"

He: "Time? Simple time? No, my dear fere, that is not devyll's ware. For that we should not earn the reward, namely that the end belongs to us. What manner of time, that is the heart of the matter! Great time, mad time, quite bedivelled time, in which the fun waxes fast and furious, with heaven-high leaping and springing —and again, of course, a bit miserable, very miserable indeed, I not only admit that, I even emphasize it, with pride, for it is sitting and fit, such is artist-way and artist-nature. That, as is well known, is given at all times to excess on

---

34. **Meseems:** it seems to me.   35. **salva venia:** savior, come.   36. **Respice finem:** consider your end.

37. **nigromancer:** necromancer.

both sides and is in quite normal way a bit excessive. Alway the pendulum swings very wide to and fro between high spirits and melancholia, that is usual, is so to speak still according to moderate bourgeois Nuerremberg way, in comparison with that which we purvey. For we purvey the uttermost in this direction; we purvey towering flights and illuminations, experiences of upliftings and unfetterings, of freedom, certainty, facility, feeling of power and triumph, that our man does not trust his wits—counting in besides the colossal admiration for the made thing, which could soon bring him to renounce every outside, foreign admiration—the thrills of self-veneration, yes, of exquisite horror of himself, in which he appears to himself like an inspired mouthpiece, as a godlike monster. And correspondingly deep, honourably deep, doth he sink in between-time, not only into void and desolation and unfruitful melancholy but also into pains and sicknesse—familiar incidentally, which had alway been there, which belong to his character, yet which are only most honorably enhanced by the illumination and the well-knowen 'sack of heyre.'[38] Those are pains which a man gladly pays, with pleasure and pride, for what he has so much enjoyed, pains which he knows from the fairy-tale, the pains which the little sea-maid, as from sharp knives, had in her beautiful human legs she got herself instead of her tail. You know Andersen's Little Sea-maid? She would be a sweetheart for you! Just say the word and I will bring her to your couch." /230/

I: "If you could just keep quiet, prating jackanapes that you are!"

He: "How now! Need you always make a rude answer? Always you expect me to be still. But silence is not my motto, I do not belong to the Schweigestill family. And Mother Else, anyhow, has prattled in all proper discretion no end to you about her odd occasional guests. Neither am I come hither for the sake of silence to a pagan foreign land; but rather for express confirmation between us two and a firm contract upon payment against completion. I tell you, we have been silent more than four years—and now everything is taking the finest, most exquisite, most promising course, and the bell is now half cast. Shall I tell you how it stands and what is afoot?"

38. heyre: hair.

I: "It well appeareth I must listen."

He: "Wouldst like to besides, and art well content that thou canst hear. I trow forsooth you are on edge to hear and would grumble and growl an I kept it back, and that of right too. It is such a snug, familiar world wherein we are together, thou and I—we are right at home therein, pure Kaisersaschern, good old German air, from anno MD or thereabouts, shortly before Dr. Martinus[39] came, who stood on such stout and sturdy footing with me and threw the roll, no, I mean the ink-pot at me, long before the thirty years' frolic. Bethink thee what lively movement of the people was with you in Germany's midst, on the Rhine and all over, how full of agitation and unrest, anxiety, presentiments; what press of pilgrims to the Sacred Blood at Niklashausen in the Tauberthal, what children's crusades, bleeding of the Host, famine, Peasants' League, war, the pest at Cologne, meteors, comets, and great omens, nuns with the stigmata, miraculous crosses on men's garments, and that amazing standard of the maiden's shift with the Cross, whereunder to march against the Turk! Good time, divellishly German time! Don't you feel all warm and snug at the memory? There the right planets come together in the sign of the Scorpion, as Master Dürer has eruditely drawn in the medical broadsheet, there came the tender little ones, the swarms of animated corkscrews, the loving guests from the West Indies into the German lands, the flagellants—ah, now you listen! As though I spake of the marching guild of penitents, the Flagellants, who flailed for their own and all other sins. But I mean those flagellates, the invisible tiny ones, the kind that have scourges, like our pale Venus, the spirochaeta pallida, that is the true sort. But th'art right, it sounds so comfortingly like the depths of Middle Ages and the *flagellum haereticorum fascinariorum.*[40] Yea, verily, as fas- /231/ cinarii they may well shew themselves, our devotees, in the better cases, as in yours. They are moreover quite civilized and domesticated long since, and in old countries where they have been so many hundred years at home, they do not play such merry pranks and coarse preposterous jokes as erstwhile, with running sore

39. **Martinus:** Martin Luther, who was said to have thrown an ink-pot at the devil. 40. **flagellum . . . fascinariorum:** whip of the possessed heretics.

and plague and worm-eaten nose. Baptist Spengler the painter does not look as though he, his body wrapped up in hair, would have to shake the warning rattle withersoever he went."

I: "Is he like that—Spengler?"

He: "Why not? I suppose you think you are the only one in like case? I know thou haddest thine liefer quite by thyself and art vexed at any comparison. My dear fellow, a man always has a great many companions. Spengler, of course, is an Esmeraldus. It is not without reason that he blinks, so sly and shamefast, and not for nothing does Inez Rodde call him a sneak. So it is: Leo Zink, the *Faunus ficarius*,[41] has always heretofore escaped; but it got the clean, clever Spengler early on. Yet be calm, withhold your jealousy. It is a banal, tedious case, productive of nothing at all. He is no python, in whom we bring sensational deeds to pass. A little brighter, more given to the intellectual he may be become since the reception and would peradventure list not so much on reading the Goncourt journals or Abbé Galiani if he had not the relation with the higher world, nor had the privy memorandum. Psychology, my dear friend. Disease, indeed I mean repulsive, individual, private disease, makes a certain critical contrast to the world, to life's mean, puts a man in a mood rebellious and ironic against the bourgeois order, makes its man take refuge with the free spirit, with books, in cogitation. But more it is not with Spengler. The space that is still allotted him for reading, quoting, drinking red wine, and idling about, it isn't we who have sold it to him, it is anything rather than genialized time. A man of the world, just singed by our flame, weary, mildly interesting, no more. He rots away, liver, kidneys, stomach, heart, bowels; some day his voice will be a croak, or he will be deaf, after a few years he will ingloriously shuffle off this coyle, with a cynical quip on his lips—what then? It forceth[42] but little, there was never any illumination, enhancing or enthusiasm, for it was not of the brain, not cerebral, you understand—our little ones in that case made no force of the upper and noble, it had obviously no fascination for them, it did not come to a

metastasis into the metaphysical,[43] metavenereal,[44] meta-infectivus. . . ."

I (with venom): "How long must I needs sit and freeze and listen to your intolerable gibberish?" /232/

He: "Gibberish? Have to listen? That's a funny chord to strike. In mine opinion you listen very attentively and are but impatient to know more, yea and all. You have just asked eagerly after your friend Spengler in Munich, and if I had not cut you off, you would avidly have asked me all this whole time about hell's fiery pit. Don't, I beg of you, pretend you're put on. I also have my self-respect, and know that I am no unbidden guest. To be short, the meta-spirochaetose, that is the meningeal process, and I assure you, it is just as though certain of the little ones had a passion for the upper storey, a special preference for the head region, the meninges—the dura mater, the tentorium, and the pia—[45] which protect the tender parenchyma[46] inside and from the moment of the first general contagion swarmed passionately hither."

I: "It is with you as you say. The rampallion[47] seems to have studied *medicinam*."

He: "No more than you theology, that is in bits and as a specialist. Will you gainsay that you studied the best of the arts and sciences also only as specialist and amateur? Your interest had to do with—me. I am obliged to you. But wherefore should I, Esmeralda's friend and cohabitant, in which quality you behold me before you, not have a special interest in the medical field concerned, which borders on it, and be at home in it as a specialist? Indeed, I constantly and with the greatest attention follow the latest results of research in this field. Item, some doctores assert and swear by Peter and Paul there must be brain specialists among the little ones, amateurs in the cerebral sphere, in short a *virus nerveux*.[48] But these experts are in the afore-

---

41. **Faunus ficarius:** made like Faunus, a woodland god associated with Pan. 42. **forceth:** matters.

43. **metastasis . . . metaphysical:** a transition or transformation from the physical disease to a philosophical turn of mind. 44. **metavenereal:** developments in the brain accompanying the venereal advance of syphilis. 45. **meninges . . . pia:** the three membranes covering the brain and the spinal cord. 46. **parenchyma:** the tissue of the brain proper, as distinguished from the membranes just mentioned. The whole passage has to do with the effect of syphilis on Adrian's brain. 47. **rampallion:** rascal. 48. **virus nerveux:** a disease of the nervous system.

mentioned box. It is arsie-versie in the matter, for 'tis the brain which gapes at their visitation and looks forward expectantly, as you to mine, that it invites them to itself, draws them unto it, as though it could not bear at all to wait for them. Do you still remember? The philosopher, *De anima:* 'the acts of the person acting are performed on him the previously disposed to suffer it.' There you have it: on the disposition, the readiness, the invitation, all depends. That some men be more qualified to the practising of witch-craft, then other, and we know well how to discern them, of that already are aware the worthy authors of the *Malleus.*"[49]

I: "Slanderer, I have no connection with you. I did not invite you."

He: "La, la, sweet innocence! The far-travelled client of my little ones was I suppose not forewarned? And your doctors too you chose with sure instinct."

I: "I looked them out in the directory. Whom should I have /233/ asked? And who could have told me that they would leave me in the lash? What did you do with my two physicians?"[50]

He: "Put them away, put them away. Oh, of course we put the blunderers away in your interest. And at the right moment iwis, not too soon and not too late, when they had got the thing in train with their quackery and quicksilvery, and if we had left them they might have botched the beautiful case. We allowed them the provocation, then *basta*[51] and away with them! So soon as they with their specific treatment had properly limited the first, cutaneously emphasized general infiltration, and thus given a powerful impetus to the metastasis upwards, their business was accomplished, they had to be removed. The fools, to wit, do not know, and if they know they cannot change it, that by the general treatment the upper, the meta-venereal processes are powerfully accelerated. Indeed, by not treating the fresh stages it is often enough forwarded; in short, the way they do it is wrong. In no case could we let the provocation by quackery and quickery go on. The regression of the general penetration was to be left to itself,

that the progression up there should go on pretty slowly, in order that years, decades, of nigromantic time should be saved for you, a whole houre-glassful of divel-time, genius-time. Narrow and small and finely circumscribed it is today, four years after you got it, the place up there in you; but it is there, the hearth, the workroom of the little ones, who on the liquor way, the water way as it were, got there, the place of incipient illumination."

I: "Do I trap you, blockhead? Do you betray yourself and name to me yourself the place in my brain, the fever hearth, that makes me imagine you, and without which you were not? Betrayest to me that in excited state I see and hear you, yet you are but a bauling before my eyes!"

He: "The Great God Logick! Little fool, it is topside the other waie: I am not the product of your pia hearth up there, rather the hearth enables you to perceive me, understand, and without it, indeed, you would not see me. Is therefore my existence dependent on your incipient drunkenness? Do I belong in your subjective? I ask you! Only patience, what goes on and progresses there will give you the capacity for a great deal more, will conquer quite other impediments and make you to soar over lameness and halting. Wait till Good Friday, and 'twill soon be Easter! Wait one, ten, twelve years, until the illumination, the dazzling radiance as all lame scruples and doubts fall away and you will know for what you pay, why you make over body and /234/ soul to us. Then shall osmotic growths *sine pudore*[52] sprout out of the apothecary's sowing. . . ."

I (start up): "Hold thy foul mouth! I forbid thee to speak of my father!"

He: "Oh, thy father is not so ill placed in my mouth. He was a shrewd one, always wanting to speculate the elements. The mygrim, the point of attack for the knife-pains of the little sea-maid—after all, you have them from him. . . . Moreover, I have spoken quite correctly: osmosis, fluid diffusion, the proliferation process —the whole magic intreats of these. You have there the spinal sac with the pulsating column of fluid therein, reaching to the cerebrum, to the meninges, in whose tissues the furtive vene-

---

49. Malleus: *The Hammer of Witches,* published in the fifteenth century.   **50. two physicians:** the physicians who failed to treat Adrian's syphilis adequately in the early stages.   **51. basta:** enough.

52. sine pudore: without shame.

real meningitis is at its soundless stealthy work. But our little ones could not reach into the inside, into the parenchyma, however much they are drawn, however much they longingly draw thither—without fluid diffusion, osmosis, with the cell-fluid of the pia watering it, dissolving the tissue, and paving a way inside for the scourges. Everything comes from osmosis, my friend, in whose teasing manifestations you so early diverted yourself."

I: "Your baseness makes me to laugh. I wish Schildknapp would come back that I might laugh with him. I would tell him father-stories, I too. Of the tears in my father's eyes, when he said: 'And yet they are dead!' "

He: "Cock's body! You were right to laugh at his ruthful tears—aside from the fact that whoever has, by nature, dealings with the tempter is always at variance with the feelings of people, always tempted to laugh when they weep, and weep when they laugh. What then does 'dead' mean, when the flora grows so rankly, in such diverse colours and shapes? And when they are even heliotropic? What does 'dead' mean when the drop displays such a healthy appetite? What is sick, what well, my friend, about that we must not let the philistine have the last word. Whether he does understand life so well remains a question. What has come about by the way of death, of sickness, at that life has many a time clutched with joy and let itself be led by it higher and further. Have you forgotten what you learned in the schools, that God can bring good out of evil and that the occasion to it shall not be marred? Item, a man must have been always ill and mad in order that others no longer need be so. And where madness begins to be malady, there is nobody knows at all. If a man taken up in a rapture write in a margent note: 'Am blissful! Am beside myself! That I call new and great! Seething bliss of inspiration! My cheeks glow like molten iron! I am raging, you will /235/ all be raging, when this comes to you! Then God succour your poor sely souls!' Is that still mad healthiness, normal madness, or has he got it in the *meninges*? The bourgeois is the last to diagnose; for long in any case nothing further about it strikes him as strange, because forsooth artists are queer birds anyhow. If next day on a rebound he cry: 'Oh, flat and stale! Oh, a dog's

life, when a man can do nothing! Were there but a war, so that somewhat would happen! If I could croak in good style! May hell pity me, for I am a son of hell!' Does he really mean that? Is it the literal truth that he says there of hell, or is it only metaphor for a little normal Dürer melancolia? In summa,[53] we simply give you that for which the classic poet, the lofty and stately genius, so beautifully thanked his gods:

All do the gods give, the Eternal,
To their favourites, wholly:
All the joys, the eternal,
All the pangs, the eternal,
Wholly."

I: "Mocker and liar! *Si diabolus non esset mendax et homicida!*[54] If I must listen, at least speak to me not of sane and sound greatness and native gold! I know that gold made with fire instead of by the sun is not genuine."

He: "Who says so? Has the sun better fire then the kitchen? And sane and sound greatness! Whenever I hear of such, I laugh! Do you believe in anything like an *ingenium*[55] that has nothing to do with hell? *Non datur!*[56] The artist is the brother of the criminal and the madman. Do you ween that any important work was ever wrought except its maker learned to understand the way of the criminal and madman? Morbid and healthy! Without the morbid would life all its whole life never have survived. Genuine and false! Are we land-loping knaves? Do we draw the good things out of the nose of nothing? Where nothing is, there the Devil too has lost his right and no pallid Venus produces anything worth while! We make naught new—that is other people's matter. We only release, only set free. We let the lameness and self-consciousness, the chaste scruples and doubts go to the Devil. We physic away fatigue merely by a little charm-hyperaemia, the great and the small, of the person and of the time. That is it, you do not think of the passage of time, you do not think historically, when you complain that such and such a one could have it 'wholly,' joys and pains endlessly, without the hour-glass being set for him, the reckoning finally made. What he in his

53. **In summa:** in summary; in conclusion. **54. Si . . . homicida:** Is the devil not a liar and a murderer! **55. ingenium:** an ingenious or clever person; here, an artist. **56. Non datur:** not given; that is not right.

classical /236/ decades could have without us, certainly, that, nowadaies, we alone have to offer. And we offer better, we offer only the right and true—that is no lenger the classical, my friend, what we give to experience, it is the archaic, the primeval, that which long since has not been tried. Who knows today, who even knew in classical times, what inspiration is, what genuine, old, primeval enthusiasm, insicklied critique, unparalysed by thought or by the mortal domination of reason—who knows the divine raptus? I believe, indeed, the devil passes for a man of destructive criticism? Slander and again slander, my friend! Gog's sacrament! If there is anything he cannot abide, if there's one thing in the whole world he cannot stomach, it is destructive criticism. What he wants and gives is triumph over it, is shining, sparkling, vainglorious unreflectiveness!"

I: "Charlatan!"

He: "Yea, of a truth. When you set right the grossest false understandings about yourself, more out of love of truth than of self, then you are a cheap jack. I will not let my mouth be stopped by your shamefast ungraciousness; I know that you are but suppressing your emotions, you are listening to me with as much pleasure as the maid to the whisperer in church. . . . Let us just for an instance take the 'idea' —what you call that, what for a hundred years or so you have been calling it, sithence earlier there was no such category, as little as musical copyright and all that. The idea, then, a matter of three, four bars, no more, isn't it? All the residue is elaboration, sticking at it. Or isn't it? Good. But now we are all experts, all critics: we note that the idea is nothing new, that it all too much reminds us of something in Rimsky-Korsakov or Brahms. What is to be done? You just change it. But a changed idea, is that still an idea? Take Beethoven's notebooks. There is no thematic conception there as God gave it. He remoulds it and adds 'Meilleur.'[57] Scant confidence in God's prompting, scant respect for it is expressed in that 'Meilleur'—itself not so very enthusiastic either. A genuine inspiration, immediate, absolute, unquestioned, ravishing, where there is no choice, no tinkering, no possible improvement; where all is as a sacred mandate, a visitation received by the possessed one with fal-

57. Meilleur: better.

tering and stumbling step, with shudders of awe from head to foot, with tears of joy blinding his eyes: no, that is not possible with God, who leaves the understanding too much to do. It comes but from the divel, the true master and giver of such rapture."

Even as he spake, and easily, a change came over the fellow: as I looked straight at him meseemed he was different, sat there no /237/ longer a rowdy losel, but changed for the better, I give my word. He now had on a white collar and a bow tie, horn-rimmed spectacles on his hooked nose. Behind them the dark, rather reddened eyes gleamed moistly. A mixture of sharpness and softness was on the visage; nose sharp, lips sharp, yet soft the chin with a dimple, a dimple in the cheek too—pale and vaulted the brow, out of which the hair retreats toward the top, yet from there to the sides thick, standing up black and woolly: a member of the intelligentsia, writer on art, on music for the ordinary press, a theoretician and critic, who himself composes, so far as thinking allows him. Soft, thin hands as well, which accompany his talk with gestures of refined awkwardness, sometimes delicately stroking his thick hair at temples and back. This was now the picture of the visitor in the sofa-corner. Taller he had not grown, and above all the voice, nasal, distinct, cultivated, pleasing, had remained the same; it kept the identity in all the fluidity of appearance. Then I hear him speak and see his wide lips, pinched in at the corners under the badly shaved upper one, protrude as he articulates.

"What is art today? A pilgrimage on peas. There's more to dancing in these times then a pair of red shoon, and you are not the only one the devil depresses. Look at them, your colleagues—I know, of course, that you do not look at them, you don't look in their direction, you cherish the illusion that you are alone and want everything for yourself, all the whole curse of the time. But do look at them for your consolation, your fellow-inaugurators of the new music, I mean the honest, serious ones, who see the consequences of the situation. I speak not of the folklorists and neo-classic asylists whose modernness consists in their forbidding themselves a musical outbreak and in wearing with more or less dignity the style-garment of a pre-individualistic period. Persuade themselves and others that the tedious has become interesting, because the interesting has begun to grow tedious."

I had to laugh, for although the cold continued to pursue me, I must confess that since his alteration I felt more comfortable in his presence. He smiled as well: that is, the corners of his mouth tensed a little and he slightly narrowed his eyes.

"They are powerless too," he went on, "but I believe we, thou and I, lever prefer the decent impotence of those who scorn to cloak the general sickness under colour of a dignified mummery. But the sickness is general, and the straightforward ones shew the symptoms just as well as the producers of back-formations. Does not production threaten to come to an end? And whatever of serious stuff gets on to paper betrays effort and distaste. Extrane- /238/ ous, social grounds? Lack of demand? And as in the pre-liberal period the possibility of production depends largely on the chance of a Maecenas?[58] Right, but as explanation doesn't go far enough. Composing itself has got too hard, devilishly hard. Where work does not go any longer with sincerity how is one to work? But so it stands, my friend, the masterpiece, the self-sufficient form, belongs to traditional art, emancipated art rejects it. The thing begins with this: that the right of command over all the tone-combinations ever applied by no means belongs to you. Impossible the diminished seventh, impossible certain chromatic passing notes. Every composer of the better sort carries within himself a canon of the forbidden, the self-forbidding, which by degrees includes all the possibilities of tonality, in other words all traditional music. What has become false, worn-out cliché, the canon decides. Tonal sounds, chords in a composition with the technical horizon of today, outbid every dissonance. As such they are to be used, but cautiously and only *in extremis,* for the shock is worse than the harshest discord of old. Everything depends on the technical horizon. The diminished seventh is right and full of expression at the beginning of Op. 111. It corresponds to Beethoven's whole technical niveau, doesn't it? —the tension between consonance and the harshest dissonance known to him. The principle of tonality and its dynamics lend to the chord its

58. **Maecenas:** a wealthy Roman patron of the arts; hence, any such person.

specific weight. It has lost it—by a historical process which nobody reverses. Listen to the obsolete chord; even by itself alone it stands for a technical general position which contradicts the actual. Every sound carries the whole, carries the whole story in itself. But therefore the judgment of the ear, what is right and what wrong, is indisputably and directly related to it, to this one chord, in itself not false, entirely without abstract reference to the general technical niveau: we have there a claim on rightness which the sound image makes upon the artist—a little severe, don't you think? Then does not his activity exhaust itself in the execution of the thing contained within the objective conditions of production? In every bar that one dares to think, the situation as regards technique presents itself to him as a problem. Technique in all its aspects demands of him every moment that he do justice to it, and give the only right answer which it at any moment permits. It comes down to this, that his compositions are nothing more than solutions of that kind; nothing but the solving of technical puzzles. Art becomes critique. That is something quite honourable, who denies it? Much rebellion in strict obedience is needed, much independence, much courage. But the danger of /239/ being uncreative—what do you think? Is it perhaps still only a danger, or is it already a fixed and settled fact?"

He paused. He looked at me through his glasses with his humid reddened eyes, raised his hand in a fastidious gesture, and stroked his hair with his two middle fingers. I said:

"What are you waiting for? Should I admire your mockery? I have never doubted ye would know how to say to me what I know. Your way of producing it is very purposeful. What you mean by it all is to shew me that I could avail myself of, nor have, no one otherwise then the divel to kindle me to my work. And ye could at the same time not exclude the theoretic possibility of spontaneous harmony between a man's own needs and the moment, the possibility of 'rightness,' of a natural harmony, out of which one might create without a thought or any compulsion."

He (laughing): "A very theoretic possibility, in fact. My dear fellow, the situation is too critical to be dealt with without critique. Moreover I reject the reproach of a tendentious illumination of things. We do not need to involve ourselves further in dialectic extravagances on your account. What I do not deny is a certain general satisfaction which the state of the 'work' generally vouchsafes me. I am against 'works,' by and large. Why should I not find some pleasure in the sickness which has attacked the idea of the musical work? Don't blame it on social conditions. I am aware you tend to do so, and are in the habit of saying that these conditions produce nothing fixed and stable enough to guarantee the harmony of the self-sufficient work. True, but unimportant. The prohibitive difficulties of the work lie deep in the work itself. The historical movement of the musical material has turned against the self-contained work. It shrinks in time, it scorns extension in time, which is the dimensions of a musical work, and lets it stand empty. Not out of impotence, not out of incapacity to give form. Rather from a ruthless demand for compression, which taboos the superfluous, negates the phrase, shatters the ornament, stands opposed to any extension of time, which is the life-form of the work. Work, time, and pretence, they are one, and together they fall victim to critique. It no longer tolerates pretence and play, the fiction, the self-glorification of form, which censors the passions and human suffering, divides out the parts, translates into pictures. Only the non-fictional is still permissible, the unplayed, the undisguised and untransfigured expression of suffering in its actual moment. Its impotence and extremity are so ingrained that no seeming play with them is any lenger allowed." /240/

I (very ironically): "Touching, touching! The devil waxes pathetic. The poor devil moralizes. Human suffering goes to his heart. How high-mindedly he shits on art! You would have done better not to mention your antipathy to the work if you did not want me to realize that your animadversions are naught but divel-farting."

He (unperturbed): "So far, so good. But at bottom you do agree that to face the facts of the time is neither sentimental nor malicious. Certain things are no longer possible. The pretence of feeling as a compositional work of art, the self-satisfied pretence of music itself, has become impossible and no longer to be preserved —I mean the perennial notion that prescribed

and formalized elements shall be introduced as though they were the inviolable necessity of the single case. Or put it the other way round: the special case behaving as though it were identical with the prescribed and familiar formula. For four hundred years all great music has found its satisfaction in pretending that this unity has been accomplished without a break—it has pleased itself with confusing the conventional universal law to which it is subject with its own peculiar concern. My friend, it cannot go on. The criticism of ornament, convention, and the abstract generality are all the same one. What it demolishes is the pretence in the bourgeois work of art; music, although she makes no picture, is also subject to it. Certainly, this 'not making a picture' gives her an advantage over the other arts. But music too by untiringly conforming her specific concerns to the ruling conventions has as far as she could played a role in the highbrow swindle. The inclusion of expression in the general appeasement is the innermost principle of musical pretence. It is all up with it. The claim to consider the general harmonically contained in the particular contradicts itself. It is all up with the once bindingly valid conventions, which guaranteed the freedom of play."

I: "A man could know that and recognize freedom above and beyond all critique. He could heighten the play, by playing with forms out of which, as he well knew, life has disappeared."

He: "I know, I know. Parody. It might be fun, if it were not so melancholy in its aristocratic nihilism. Would you promise yourself much pleasure and profit from such tricks?"

I (retort angrily): "No."

He: "Terse and testy. But why so testy? Because I put to you friendly questions of conscience, just between ourselves? Because I shewed you your despairing heart and set before your eyes with the expert's insight the difficulties absolutely inseparable from /241/ composition today? You might even so value me as an expert. The Devil ought to know something about music. If I mistake not, you were reading just now in a book by the Christian in love with aesthetics. He knew and understood my particular relation to this beautiful art—the most Christian of all arts, he finds—but Christian in reverse, as it were: introduced and developed by Christianity indeed, but then rejected and banned as the Divel's Kingdom—so there you are. A highly theological business, music—the way sin is, the way I am. The passion of that Christian for music is true passion, and as such knowledge and corruption in one. For there is true passion only in the ambiguous and ironic. The highest passion concerns the absolutely questionable. . . . No, musical I am indeed, don't worry about that. I have sung you the role of poor Judas because of the difficulties into which music like everything else has got today. Should I not have done so? But I did it only to point out to you that you should break through them, that you should lift yourself above them to giddy heights of self-admiration, and do such things that you will behold them only with shudders of awe."

I: "An annunciation, in fact. I am to grow osmotic growths."

He: "It comes to the same thing. Ice crystals, or the same made of starch, sugar, and cellulose, both are nature; we ask, for which shall we praise Nature more. Your tendency, my friend, to inquire after the objective, the so-called truth, to question as worthless the subjective, pure experience: that is truly petty bourgeois, you ought to overcome it. As you see me, so I exist to you. What serves it to ask whether I really am? Is not 'really' what works, is not truth experience and feeling? What uplifts you, what increases your feeling of power and might and domination, damn it, that is the truth—and whether ten times a lie when looked at from the moral angle. This is what I think: that an untruth of a kind that enhances power holds its own against any ineffectively virtuous truth. And I mean too that creative, genius-giving disease, disease that rides on high horse over all hindrances, and springs with drunken daring from peak to peak, is a thousand times dearer to life than plodding healthiness. I have never heard anything stupider then that from disease only disease can come. Life is not scrupulous—by morals it sets not a fart. It takes the reckless product of disease, feeds on and digests it, and as soon as it takes it to itself it is health. Before the fact of fitness for life, my good man, all distinction of disease and health falls away. A whole host and generation of youth, receptive, sound to the core, flings itself on the work of the morbid genius, made genius by disease: /242/ admires it, praises it, exalts it, carries it away, assimilates it unto itself and makes it over to culture, which lives not on home-made bread alone, but as well on provender and poison from the apothecary's shop at the sign of the Blessed Messengers. Thus saith to you the unbowdlerized Sammael. He guarantees not only that toward the end of your houre-glasse years your sense of your power and splendour will more and more outweigh the pangs of the little sea-maid and finally mount to most triumphant well-being, to a sense of bursting health, to the walk and way of a god. That is only the subjective side of the thing, I know; it would not suffice, it would seem to you unsubstantial. Know, then, we pledge you the success of that which with our help you will accomplish. You will lead the way, you will strike up the march of the future, the lads will swear by your name, who thanks to your madness will no longer need to be mad. On your madness they will feed in health, and in them you will become healthy. Do you understand? Not only will you break through the paralysing difficulties of the time—you will break through time itself, by which I mean the cultural epoch and its cult, and dare to be barbaric, twice barbaric indeed, because of coming after the humane, after all possible root-treatment and bourgeois raffinement. Believe me, barbarism even has more grasp of theology then has a culture fallen away from cult, which even in the religious has seen only culture, only the humane, never excess, paradox, the mystic passion, the utterly unbourgeois ordeal. But I hope you do not marvel that 'the Great Adversary' speaks to you of religion. Gog's nails! Who else, I should like to know, is to speak of it today? Surely not the liberal theologian! After all I am by now its sole custodian! In whom will you recognize theological existence if not in me? And who can lead a theological existence without me? The religious is certainly my line: as certainly as it is not the line of bourgeois culture. Since culture fell away from the cult and made a cult of itself, it has become nothing else then a falling away; and all the world after a mere five hundred years is as sick and tired of it as though, *salva venia,* they had ladled it in with cooking-spoons."

It was now, it was even a little before this,

when he was uttering his taunts and mockage about the theological existence of the Devil and being the guardian of the religious life, speaking in flowing language like a lectour, that I noticed the merchaunte before me on the sofa had changed again; he seemed no longer to be the spectacled intellectual and amateur of music who had awhile been speaking. And he was no lenger just sitting in his /243/ corner, he was riding légèrement, half-sitting, on the curved arm of the sofa, his fingertips crossed in his lap and both thumbs spread out. A little parted beard on his chin wagged up and down as he talked, and above his open lips with the sharp teeth behind them was the little moustache with stiff twisted points. I had to laugh, in all my frozenness, at his metamorphosis into the old familiar.

"Obedient servant," I say. "I ought to know you; and I find it most civil of you to give me a privatissimum here in our hall. As ye now are, my Protean friend, I look to find you ready to quench my thirst for knowledge and conclusively demonstrate your independent presence by telling me not only things I know but also of some I would like to know. You have lectured me a good deal about the houre-glasse time you purvey; also about the payment in pains to be made now and again for the higher life; but not about the end, about what comes afterwards, the eternal obliteration. That is what excites curiosity, and you have not, long as you have been squatting there, given space to the question in all your talk. Shall I not know the price in cross and kreuzer? Answer me: what is life like in the Dragon's Den? What have they to expect, who have listened to you, in the *spelunca?*"[59]

He (laughs a falsetto laugh): "Of the *pernicies,* the *confutatio*[60] you want to have knowledge? Call that prying, I do, the exuberance of the youthful scholar. There is time enough, so much that you can't see to the end of it, and so much excitement coming first—you will have a plenty to do besides taking heed to the end, or even noticing the moment when it might be time to take heed to the ending. But I'll not deny you the information and do not need to palliate, for what can seriously trouble you, that is so far off? Only it is not easy actually to speak

59. **spelunca:** cave, here the pit of hell. 60. **pernicies . . . confutatio:** other Latin terms for hell.

thereof—that is, one can really not speak of it at all, because the actual is beyond what by word can be declared; many words may be used and fashioned, but all together they are but tokens, standing for names which do not and cannot make claim to describe what is never to be described and denounced in words. That is the secret delight and security of hell, that it is not to be informed on, that it is protected from speech, that it just is, but cannot be public in the newspaper, be brought by any word to critical knowledge, wherefor precisely the words 'subterranean,' 'cellar,' 'thick walls,' 'soundlessness,' 'forgottenness,' 'hopelessness,' are the poor, weak symbols. One must just be satisfied with symbolism, my good man, when one is speaking of hell, for there everything ends—not only the word that describes, but everything altogether. This /244/ is indeed the chiefest characteristic and what in most general terms is to be uttered about it: both that which the newcomer thither first experiences, and what at first with his as it were sound senses he cannot grasp, and will not understand, because his reason or what limitation soever of his understanding prevents him, in short because it is quite unbelievable enough to make him turn white as a sheet, although it is opened to him at once on greeting, in the most emphatic and concise words, that *'here everything leaves off.'* Every compassion, every grace, every sparing, every last trace of consideration for the incredulous, imploring objection 'that you verily cannot do so unto a soul': it is done, it happens, and indeed without being called to any reckoning in words; in soundless cellar, far down beneath God's hearing, and happens to all eternity. No, it is bad to speak of it, it lies aside from and outside of speech, language has naught to do with and no connection with it, wherefore she knows not rightly what time-form to apply to it and helps herself perforce with the future tense, even as it is written: 'There shall be wailing and gnashing of teeth.' Good; these are a few word-sounds, chosen out of a rather extreme sphere of language, yet but weak symbols and without proper reference to what 'shall be' there, unrecorded, unreckoned, between thick walls. True it is that inside these echoless walls it gets right loud, measureless loud, and by much overfilling the ear with screeching and beseeching, gurgling and groaning, with yauling and bauling and caterwauling, with horrid winding and grinding and racking ecstasies of anguish no man can hear his own tune, for that it smothers in the general, in the thick-clotted diapason of trills and chirps lured from this everlasting dispensasion of the unbelievable combined with the irresponsible. Nothing forgetting the dismal groans of lust mixed therewith; since endless torment, with no possible collapse, no swoon to put a period thereto, degenerates into shameful pleasure, wherefore such as have some intuitive knowledge speak indeed of the 'lusts of hell.' And therewith mockage and the extreme of ignominy such as belongs with martyrdom; for this bliss of hell is like a deep-voiced pitifull jeering and scorne of all the immeasureable anguish; it is accompanied by whinnying laughter and the pointing finger; whence the doctrine that the damned have not only torment but also mockery and shame to bear; yea, that hell is to be defined as a monstrous combination of suffering and derision, unendurable yet to be endured world without end. There will they devour their proper tongues for greatness of the agony, yet make no common cause on that account, for rather they are full of ha- /245/ tred and scorn against each other, and in the midst of their trills and quavers hurl at one another the foulest oaths. Yea, the finest and proudest, who never let a lewd word pass their lips, are forced to use the filthiest of all. A part of their torment and lust of shame standeth therein that they must cogitate the extremity of filthiness."

I: "Allow me, this is the first word you have said to me about what manner of suffering the damned have to bear. Pray note that you have only lectured to me on the affects of hell, but not about what objectively and in fact must await the damned."

He: "Your curiosity is childish and indiscreet. I put that in the foreground; but I am very well aware indeed, my good soul, what hides behind it. You assaye to question me in order to be feared, to be afraid of the pangs of hell. For the thought of backward turning and rescue, of your so-called soul-heal, of withdrawing from the promise lurks in the back of your mind and you are acting to summon up the *attritio cordis,* the heartfelt anguish and dread of what is to come, of which you may well have

heard, that by it man can arrive at the so-called blessedness. Let me tell you, that is an entirely exploded theology. The attrition-theory has been scientifically superseded. It is shown that *contritio* is necessary, the real and true protestant remorse for sin, which means not merely fear repentance by churchly regulation but inner, religious conversion; ask yourself whether you are capable of that; ask yourself, your pride will not fail of an answer. The longer the less will you be able and willing to let yourself in for *contritio,* sithence the extravagant life you will lead is a great indulgence, out of the which a man does not so simply find the way back into the good safe average. Therefore, to your reassurance be it said, even hell will not afford you aught essentially new, only the more or less accustomed, and proudly so. It is at bottom only a continuation of the extravagant existence. To knit up in two words its quintessence, or if you like its chief matter, is that it leaves its denizens only the choice between extreme cold and an extreme heat which can melt granite. Between these two states they flee roaring to and fro, for in the one the other always seems heavenly refreshment but is at once and in the most hellish meaning of the word intolerable. The extreme in this must please you."

I: "It liketh me. Meanwhile I would warn you lest you feel all too certain of me. A certain shallowness in your theology might tempt you thereto. You rely on my pride preventing me from the *contritio* necessary to salvacion, and do not bethink yourself that /246/ there is a prideful *contritio.* The remorse of Cain, for instance, who was of the firm persuasion that his sin was greater than could ever be forgiven him. The *contritio* without hope, as complete disbelief in the possibility of mercy and forgiveness, the rocklike firm conviction of the sinner that he has done too grossly for even the Everlasting Goodness to be able to forgive his sin—only that is the true *contritio.* I call your attention to the fact that it is the nighest to redemption, for Goodness the most irresistible of all. You will admit that the everyday sinner can be but very moderately interesting to Mercy. In his case the act of grace has but little impetus, it is but a feeble motion. Mediocrity, in fact, has no theological status. A capacity for sin so healless that it makes its man despair from his heart of redemption—that is the true theological way to salvation."

He: "You are a sly dog! And where will the likes of you get the single-mindedness, the naïve recklessness of despair, which would be the premise for this sinfull waye to salvacion? Is it not playne to you that the conscious speculation on the charm which great guilt exercises on Goodness makes the act of mercy to the uttermost unpossible to it?"

I: "And yet only through this *non plus ultra*[61] can the high prick of the dramatic-theological existence be arrived at; I mean the most abandoned guilt and the last and most irresistible challenge to the Everlasting Goodness."

He: "Not bad. Of a truth ingenious. And now I will tell you that precisely heads of your sort comprise the population of hell. It is not so easy to get into hell, we should long have been suffering for lack of space if we let Philip and Cheyney[62] in. But your theologian in grain, your arrant wily-pie who speculates on speculation because he has speculation in his blood already from the father's side—there must be foul work an he did not belong to the divel."

As he said that, or even somewhat afore, the fellow changed again, the way clouds do, without knowing it, apparently; is no longer sitting on the arm of the couch before me in the room; there back in the sofa-corner is the unspeakable losel, the cheesy rapscallion in the cap, with the red eyes. And says to me in his slow, nasal, actor's voice:

"To make an end and a conclusion will be agreeable to you. I have devoted much time and tarried long to entreat of this matter with you—I hope and trust you realize. But also you are an attractive case, that I freely admit. From early on we had an eye on you, on your quick, arrogant head, your mighty *ingenium* and /247/ *memoriam.* They have made you study theology, as your conceit devised it, but you would soon name yourself no lenger of theologians, but put the Good Boke under the bench and from then on stuck to the figures, characters, and incantations of music, which pleased us not a little. For your vaine glory aspired to the elemental, and you thought to gain it in the form most

mete for you, where algebraic magic is married with corresponding cleverness and calculation and yet at the same time it always boldly warres against reason and sobriety. But did we then not know that you were too clever and cold and chaste for the element; and did we not know that you were sore vexed thereat and piteously bored with your shamefast cleverness? Thus it was our busily prepensed plan that you should run into our arms, that is, of my little one, Esmeralda, and that you got it, the illumination, the aphrodisiacum of the brain, after which with body and soul and mind you so desperately longed. To be short, between us there needs no crosse way in the Spesser's Wood[63] and no cercles. We are in league and business—with your blood you have affirmed it and promised yourself to us, and are baptized ours. This my visit concerns only the confirmation thereof. Time you have taken from us, a genius's time, highflying time, full XXIV years *ab dato recessi,* which we set to you as the limit. When they are finished and fully expired, which is not to be foreseen, and such a time is also an eternity— then you shalbe fetched. Against this meanwhile shall we be in all things subject and obedient, and hell shall profit you, if you renay all living creature, all the Heavenly Host and all men, for that must be."

I (in an exceeding cold draught): "What? That is new. What signifies the *clausula?*"

He: "Renounce, it means. What otherwise? Do you think that jealousy dwells in the height and not also in the depths? To us you are, fine, well-create creature, promised and espoused. Thou maist not love."

I (really have to laugh): "Not love! Poor divel! Will you substantiate the report of your stupidity and wear a bell even as a cat, that you will base business and promise on so elastic, so ensnaring a concept as love? Will the Devil prohibit lust? If it be not so, then he must endure sympathy, yea, even *caritas,* else he is betrayed just as it is written in the books. What I have invited, and wherefore you allege that I have promised you—what is then the source of it, prithee, but love, even if that poisoned by you

<hr>

61. **non plus ultra:** nothing further than this.   62. **Philip and Cheyney:** Tom, Dick, and Harry.

63. **Spesser's Wood:** a wood, mentioned in early versions of the Faust story, where devils appeared to Faust.

with God's sanction? The bond in which you assert we stand has itself to do with love, you doating fool. You allege that I /248/ wanted it and repaired to the wood, the crosse-waye, for the sake of the work. But they say that work itself has to do with love."

He (laughing through his nose): "Do, re, mi! Be assured that thy psychological feints do not trap me, any better then do the theological. Psychology—God warrant us, do you still hold with it? That is bad, bourgeois nineteenth century. The epoch is heartily sick of it, it will soon be a red rag to her, and he will simply get a crack on the pate, who disturbs life by psychology. We are entering into times, my friend, which will not be hoodwinked by psychology. . . . This *en passant*. My condition was clear and direct, determined by the legitimate jealousy of hell. Love is forbidden you, in so far as it warms. Thy life shall be cold, therefore thou shalt love no human being. What are you thinking, then? The illumination leaves your mental powers to the last unimpaired, yes, heightens them to an ecstasie of delirium—what shall it then go short of save the dear soul and the priceless life of feeling? A general chilling of your life and your relations to men lies in the nature of things—rather it lies already in your nature; in feith we lay upon you nothing new, the little ones make nothing new and strange out of you, they only ingeniously strengthen and exaggerate all that you already are. The coldness in you is perhaps not prefigured, as well as the paternal head paynes out of which the pangs of the little sea-maid are to come? Cold we want you to be, that the fires of creation shall be hot enough to warm yourself in. Into them you will flee out of the cold of your life. . . ."

I: "And from the burning back to the ice. It seems to be hell in advance, which is already offered me on earth."

He: "It is that extravagant living, the only one that suffices a proud soul. Your arrogance will probably never want to exchange with a lukewarm one. Do you strike with me? A work-filled eternity of human life shall you enjoy. When the houre-glasse runs out, then I shall have good power to deal and dole with, to move and manage the fine-created Creature after my way and my pleasure, be it in life, soul, flesh, blood or goods—to all eternity!"

There it was again, the uncontrollable disgust that had already seized me once before and shaken me, together with the glacial wave of cold which came over me again from the tight-trousered *strizzi* there. I forgot myself in a fury of disgust, it was like a fainting-fit. And then I heard Schildknapp's easy, everyday voice, he sat there in the sofa-corner, saying to me:

"Of course you didn't miss anything. Newspapers and two /249/ games of billiards, a round of Marsala and the good souls calling the *governo* over the coals."

I was sitting in my summer suit, by my lamp, the Christian's book on my knee. Can't be anything else: in my excitement I must have chased the losel out and carried my coat and rug back before Schildknapp returned. /250/

KARL SHAPIRO

The Progress of Faust

He was born in Deutschland, as you would sus-
    pect,
And graduated in magic from Cracow
In Fifteen Five. His portraits show a brow
Heightened by science. The eye is indirect,
As of bent light upon a crooked soul,
And that he bargained with the Prince of Shame
For pleasures intellectually foul
Is known by every court that lists his name.

His frequent disappearances are put down
To visits in the regions of the damned   10
And to the periodic deaths he shammed,
But, unregenerate and in Doctor's gown,
He would turn up to lecture at the fair
And do a minor miracle for a fee.
Many a life he whispered up the stair
To teach the black art of anatomy.

He was as deaf to angels as an oak
When, in the fall of Fifteen Ninety-four,
He went to London and crashed through the
    floor
In mock damnation of the playgoing folk.   20
Weekending with the scientific crowd,
He met Sir Francis Bacon and helped draft
"Colours of Good and Evil" and read aloud
An obscene sermon at which no one laughed.

He toured the Continent for a hundred years
And subsidized among the peasantry
The puppet play, his tragic history;
With a white glove he boxed the devil's ears

And with a black his own. Tired of this,
He published penny poems about his sins,   30
In which he placed the heavy emphasis
On the white glove which, for a penny, wins.

Some time before the hemorrhage of the Kings
Of France, he turned respectable and taught;
Quite suddenly everything that he had thought
Seemed to grow scholars' beards and angels'
    wings.
It was the Overthrow. On Reason's throne
He sat with the fair Phrygian on his knees
And called all universities his own,
As plausible a figure as you please.   40

Then back to Germany as the sages' sage
To preach comparative science to the young
Who came from every land in a great throng
And knew they heard the master of the age.
When for a secret formula he paid
The devil another fragment of his soul,
The scholars wept, and several even prayed
That Satan would restore him to them whole.

Backwardly tolerant, Faustus was expelled   50
From the Third Reich in Nineteen Thirty-nine.
His exit caused the breaching of the Rhine,
Except for which the frontier might have held.
Five years unknown to enemy and friend
He hid, appearing on the sixth to pose
In an American desert at war's end
Where, at his back, a dome of atoms rose.

3. Criticism

The essays on Christopher Marlowe's *Doctor Faustus,* by Robert Ornstein, Wolfgang Clemen, and C. L. Barber, introduce some of the critical controversy surrounding the play: What was the extent of Marlowe's authorship, especially of the comic scenes? Was Marlowe a Christian or an atheist and, consequently, what is the meaning, Christian or otherwise, of his version of the Faust story? Ornstein's "The Comic Synthesis in *Doctor Faustus"* was published in *ELH: A Journal of English Literary History,* Vol. XXII (September 1955), pp. 165-72. Professor Ornstein, an author of numerous books and articles, is chairman of the Department of English at Western Reserve University in Cleveland, Ohio. The selection by Clemen appeared in his *English Tragedy Before Shakespeare,* translated by T. S. Dorsch (New York: Barnes and Noble, 1961), pp. 147-54. Clemen, a noted German Shakespearian scholar, has also written a number of books and articles, including *The Development of Shakespeare's Imagery.* C. L. Barber's article was first printed in the *Tulane Drama Review,* Vol. VIII (1964), pp. 92-119. Professor Barber is chairman of the Department of English at Indiana University at Bloomington.

The pieces by Victor Lange and Erich Heller are valuable aids to understanding Goethe's *Faust.* In addition, Heller's essay includes an excellent summation of the Faust tradition from its beginning to Thomas Mann. It contains a discussion of the differences between the Spies *Faustbuch* and the English translation, an analysis of the reasons for the changing points of view toward Dr. Faustus in the various periods under consideration, incisive statements about the meaning of Goethe's *Faust* and Mann's novel, and some suggestions about the significance of the Faust theme in the period of weapons of mass destruction. Victor Lange, scholar and author, is the founder of Goethe House in New York City. Professor Lange is chairman of the Department of Germanic Languages at Princeton University. The piece I have called "Goethe and *Faust"* was originally Lange's introduction to the Modern Library translation of Goethe's *Faust* by Bayard Taylor (New York: Random House, 1950), pp. v–xxi. Erich Heller, a noted scholar of Czechoslovakian origin, is professor of German at Northwestern University. His "Faust's Damnation, the Morality of Knowledge" is from *The Artist's Journey into the Interior* (New York: Random House, 1965), pp. 3–44.

The last three articles deal with Thomas Mann's novel *Doctor Faustus.* Hans E. Holthusen is a German author and critic. His "World Without Transcendence," translated by Henry Hatfield, is reprinted from Hatfield's *Thomas Mann: A Collection of Critical Essays* (Englewood Cliffs, N.J.: Prentice-Hall, 1964), pp. 123–32. Although Holthusen has stated that he now has reservations about certain of the views expressed in his article, the piece is of considerable interest and raises issues that Bernhard Blume discusses in his essay. Erich Kahler, born in Prague, now teaches at Cornell University and is a member of the Institute for Advanced Studies at Princeton. His *"Doctor Faustus:* 'Terminal Work' of an Art Form and an Era," translated by Francis C. Golffing, was first published in *Commentary* (April 1949), pp. 348–57. Bernhard Blume is professor of German at the University of California at San Diego. The selection from his "Aspects of Contradictions," translated by Henry Hatfield, is also reprinted from Hatfield's *Thomas Mann.*

Footnotes in each article are by the authors, except for the bracketed footnotes in Erich Heller's article, added by the editor of this volume, and similar footnotes in the articles by Holthusen and Blume, added by Henry Hatfield.

Robert Ornstein

The Comic Synthesis in Doctor Faustus

I do not propose in this article to argue Marlowe's authorship of the prose comedy in *Doctor Faustus,* though for convenience I will follow tradition in attributing to him those scenes under discussion. Actually, the problem of authorship is irrelevant here, for my concern is with the integrity of the play as a work of dramatic art, not with the integrity of the text as a literary document. I use the traditional version of *Doctor Faustus* because it is the one known to the vast majority of readers.[1] But my discussion would, in general, apply as well to Dr. Greg's conjectural reconstruction of the B-Text.[2] I intend no apology for the crude buffoonery in *Doctor Faustus.* I would suggest, however, that there is more than one level of comedy in the play—that the slapstick scenes which tickled groundling fancies unite with the seemingly fragmented main action to form a subtly ironic tragic design.

To begin with, let us admit that Sir Philip Sidney's criticism of the Elizabethan stage was well taken though somewhat aca- /165/ demic. Marlowe's contemporaries did mingle kings and clowns "not because the matter so carrieth," but because an Elizabethan audience expected variety and comedy. After all, high seriousness and buffoonery had long before joined hands in the Miracles and Moralities, and popular taste weighed more heavily than critical theory in the public theatres. But the custom of mingling kings and clowns could not remain a naive literary practice as Elizabethan drama matured. Like all literary practices, it was sophisticated

for better and for worse. When imagination faltered, clowns—the musicians in *Romeo and Juliet,* for instance—made purely routine appearances in tragedy. But when inspiration mounted, the Elizabethan comedians found themselves in more significant roles: as the grave diggers in *Hamlet* or as the drunken Porter in *Macbeth* (a character rejected by Coleridge, ironically enough, as a "disgusting" interpolation by the actors).

It was inevitable too that incongruous mixtures of kings and clowns should have developed into formalized contrasts used to enhance the beauty and substance of a main dramatic action. The highly stylized device of the antimasque merely refined the once indiscriminate jostle of coarse and courtly elements in the masque. The popular drama produced less formalized, more satiric "antimasques" of clownish servants who aped the manners and pretensions of their betters. In Shakespeare's romantic comedies a pair of rustic sweethearts stumble through the arabesques of courtship, naturalizing by their improbable amour the artificial languors and melancholies of courtly heroes and heroines. In Ford's tragedies we find comic foils remarkably similar in one respect to the clowns in *Doctor Faustus.* Like Rafe [Dick] and Robin, they are not very amusing. The best are innocuous, the majority unattractive, and the rest simply offensive. Ford, lacking a sense of humor, and at times a sense of decency, tried to use comic lewdness to set off more delicate and consuming passions.[3] His was the last and least successful attempt to subtilize the comic contrasts of Elizabethan drama. Marlowe's was an imperfect but brilliant innovation.

Comparing Marlowe's clowns to those in Ford's tragedies, however, merely underlines the

---

[1]My text of *Faustus* will be that edited by C. F. T. Brooke and N. B. Paradise, *English Drama 1508–1642* (New York, 1933).

[2]W. W. Greg, *Doctor Faustus: A Conjectural Reconstruction* (Oxford, 1950). Dr. Greg has argued convincingly for the superiority of the B-Text over the "A," traditionally used as the basis for editions of *Faustus.* See *Doctor Faustus: Parallel Texts* (Oxford, 1950), Introduction.

[3]See, for instance, *Love's Sacrifice,* in which the witty lecheries of Ferentes contrast with the nobler passions of Fernando and Bianca.

unique function of the comic /*166*/ contrasts in *Doctor Faustus*. Obviously Marlowe does not enhance the main action of his tragedy by reducing it to absurdity scene by scene. He does not magnify Faustus' achievements by having clowns parody them immediately afterwards. (By analogy, no Elizabethan would try to heighten the beauty of a masque by closing it with grotesque dances. The antimasque must come first; it must prepare the audience for the familiar contrast, for the metamorphosis of antic into courtly elegance.) Yet the pattern of *Doctor Faustus* is consistently "wrong." In the first scene Faustus announces his intellectual supremacy and his decision to gain a deity through magic. In the second scene Wagner apes his master's display of learning by chopping logic with two scholars. In the third scene Faustus agrees to sell his soul for power and voluptuousness. Immediately afterwards the Clown considers bartering his soul for a shoulder of mutton and a taste of wenching. In the following scenes Faustus makes his compact with the Devil, discusses astronomy with Mephistophilis, and is entertained by the Seven Deadly Sins. He then launches his career as a magician by snatching away the Pope's food and drink. Next Rafe and Robin burlesque Faustus' conjurations and try to steal a goblet from a Vintner.

Judging by their enthusiasm for the play, however, Marlowe's contemporaries did not find the pattern of *Doctor Faustus* "wrong." Perhaps because parody is its own excuse for being when its target is the heroic stance. Is there not something infinitely reassuring in the clown who apes the manner and the mannerism of the superman? And the ironic comedy in *Doctor Faustus* is more than reassuring. Its intention, I think, is both didactic and comic. Simultaneously nonsensical and profound, it clarifies our perception of moral values.

We see the world through the lenses of custom: when false values pass current, even elemental truths appear distorted, naive, or absurd. The ironist often deals in elemental absurdities —the absurdity of eating children to cure poverty or of mortgaging one's immortal soul for a piece of mutton (if it be well roasted). We smile at such absurdities because we have a more sensible and realistic appraisal of the world. We know that society does not and

would not eat children. We know that no man, however foolish, would damn his soul to satisfy /*167*/ his belly—to gain infinite power, yes, but we consider such aspiration heroic. We smile, however, only until we discover beneath the surface of our sensible view of life the grim absurdity depicted by the ironist—only until sensible or grandiose appearance and absurd reality melt into one. Because the ironist (like the Shakespearean Fool) is licensed to reveal "absurd" truths only when he amuses his audience, Marlowe entertains us with Clowns and with the ancient but eternally successful comedy of futility. It is hardly accidental that in the crucial scene when Faustus first repents Lucifer appears, impresario-like, with the Seven Deadly Sins. Faustus "feeds" on the spectacle and jests with these harmless bogies of the superstitious mind. Entranced by Lucifer's vaudeville show he forgets salvation. Lucifer is also entertained but on a more intellectual plane. The consummate cynic, he diverts his victim with a picture gallery that suggests Faustus' own futility.

Professor Harry Levin describes Marlowe's Deadly Sins as a "quaint procession of gargoyles" and interprets Faustus' unalloyed amusement as a sign of moral decay.[4] I would agree but also add that the Deadly Sins are supposed to be amusing in *Doctor Faustus* as they are in much of medieval literature. The fourteenth century artist took sin seriously enough and yet caricatured it even as he caricatured Satan, archenemy of God, who appears in the Miracles and Moralities as a comic villain beaten off the stage to the accompaniment of divine and human laughter. The medieval playwright gave the Devil his due; he showed the human soul caught in a satanic web of pleasure and deceit. But he showed also the inevitable triumph of God's love which made the efforts of satanic evil vain and risible. In short, the medieval mind understood the ludicrousness of insatiable desire. It knew that vice (to use Santayana's definition) is "human nature strangled by the suicide of attempting the impossible."[5] /*168*/

[4]Harry Levin, *The Overreacher: A Study of Christopher Marlowe* (Cambridge, Mass., 1952), p. 119.
[5]In his essay on Dickens (from *Soliloquies in England and Later Soliloquies*), Santayana argues that we do not connect Dickens' caricatures with real personalities because we cannot face the honesty of his

Of course Faustus is never ludicrous; he is no fustian villain ranting of his powers. But from the beginning there is casuistic self-deception in his speeches. Blind to the ever-present possibility of grace, he facilely reduces theology to the dogma of pitiless damnation. Misunderstanding his relationship with God, he completely mistakes his rapport with the Devil. He thinks that through magic he has gained control of the spirit world and of Mephistophilis, who appears at his command and changes shape to please him. Faustus finds Mephistophilis "pliant . . . full of obedience and humility." Mephistophilis, a scrupulous corrupter, insists that he has only one master—Lucifer—but Faustus will not believe him. When Mephistophilis shudders at the terrors of damnation, Faustus sets himself up as an example of fortitude to the angel who openly warred against God. Later he argues with Mephistophilis about the reality of hell even though indisputable evidence of its reality stands before him.

Fleeing his own Master, Faustus contracts with the Devil for the services of Mephistophilis, who, like the cunning slave of Roman comedy, quickly gains the upper hand. Frightening and distracting Faustus from salvation, he caters to his sensuality and diverts his creative energies into court performances and practical jokes. Though at times compassionate, Mephistophilis has his joke with Faustus on the subject of lechery. Lucifer toys with his dupe on a grander scale. He assures Faustus that "in hell is all manner of delight" and promises an excursion through it:

. . . I will send for thee at midnight.
In meantime take this book; peruse it thoroughly
and thou shalt turn thyself into what shape thou wilt.
(vi. 199–201)

The Devil is as good as his word. He does send for Faustus at midnight. And he does help Faustus to change his shape. But the transformation is from aspiring hero to despairing libertine.

At the beginning of the play Faustus' plans, though egocentric and grandiose, are constructive. He wants pleasure, riches, and power, but he also intends to make all learning his province, better the lot of students, improve geography, and defeat tyranny. Faustus' dreams of creativity, however, are /169/ only dreams; indeed, the measure of his tragic fall is the increasing disparity between his aspirations and his achievements. He travels at first, takes in the wonders of the world, and wins fame as a magician. But on the stage itself Faustus' accomplishments grow increasingly petty: he discomforts the Pope, horns a Knight, entertains an Emperor, cheats a Horse-Courser, and delights a Duchess with grapes out of season. Here is travesty of a high order! In the latter half of the play, the mighty Faustus parodies his own high-vaulting thoughts and ambitions even as Wagner and the Clown had parodied them earlier. Or more correctly, as Faustus changes shape the tragic-comic contrast begins to coalesce. Scene by scene the apposing images approach one another until at last we discover beneath the exalted appearance of the fearless rebel the figure of the fool. When Faustus steals the Pope's cup and Robin steals the Vintner's goblet the tragic and comic images nearly merge. The difference between hero and clown is one of degree, not of kind.

We need no acquaintance with Elizabethan ethical psychology to appreciate the ironic fate of a hero who in striving to be a god becomes less than a man. Only a dimwitted Clown would sell his soul for a mutton roast and a bit of lechery. Yet Faustus ends his days in "belly cheer," carousing and swilling with the students. The scholar who pursued knowledge beyond the utmost bound of human thought finally takes Helen for his paramour to drown vexatious thought in wantonness.[6] Actually it does not matter whether one sells one's soul for infinite power or for belly cheer. Both transactions are ridiculous, the first even more than the second because it is far less realistic. Faustus, who

---

comic realism. Our failure to connect Marlowe's clowns, caricatures of the tragic hero, with Faustus is perhaps due to a comparable failure to recognize that Marlowe was also, in a sense, a comic and moral realist.

[6]The ecstatic poetry of Faustus' apostrophe to Helen (xiii. 112–31) does not mask the corruption of his genius. Once before in despair he had summoned Homer, the "maker," who sang of Troy. In the lines to Helen, however, he identifies himself with an effeminate Paris, whose sensuality destroyed the topless towers of Ilium. As the comparison to Jupiter and Semele suggests, Faustus does not take Helen—he abandons himself to her.

dreamed of commanding the powers of heaven and earth, finds that he cannot check the movement of the stars when death threatens. In his vain rebellion there is comedy; in his fall from grace irrevocable tragedy.[7] /*170*/

I do not mean to suggest any ambiguity or ambivalence in Marlowe's attitude towards his tragic hero. Despite persistent arguments,[8] it is difficult to believe that Marlowe secretly identified himself with Faustus and that Faustus' catastrophe is a sop to Nemesis or to conventional morality. For Marlowe gives an almost Dostoievskian sense of damnation as an earthly as well as spiritual fact; he depicts the corruption of the mind that destroys the soul. Like Mephistophilis (and like Ivan Karamazov)[9] Faustus makes his own personal hell of negation, a hell that "hath no limits, nor is circumscrib'd/In one self place." But he attempts to escape it in death by losing himself in the natural forces that were to have been his agents of creation:

> Mountains and hills, come, come and fall on me,
> And hide me from the heavy wrath of God!
> That when you vomit forth into the air,

My limbs may issue from your smoky mouths.
No! no!
Then will I headlong run into the earth;

. . .

O, it strikes, it strikes! Now, body, turn to air,
Or Lucifer will bear thee quick to hell.

> *Thunder and lightning*

O soul, be chang'd into little water-drops,
And fall into the ocean—ne'er be found.

(xiv. 143–78) /*171*/

Here is the ultimate irony; Faustus would escape the negation of hell by annihilating body and soul. The diseased creative will succumbs at last to frenzied desire for self-destruction—for nothingness. *Consummatum est!*

To say that *Doctor Faustus* can be read as the tragedy of a creative mind destroying itself in fascination with the esoteric is not to make of the play a secularized Christian allegory. Marlowe adds new dimension to the Morality framework; he does not use it as a literary, "mythical" apparatus. Hell is a reality in *Doctor Faustus* whether experienced in an earthly nihilistic despair or in the horror of an eternal void. Marlowe's religious thought may be heterodox in some respects, but his ethics are sound. We are always aware that Faustus the aspiring titan is also the self-deluded fool of Lucifer. The emancipated intellectual who confounds hell in Elysium spends his last hours as a lonely, terrified penitent.

Doctor Faustus, then, is not the tragical history of a glorious rebellion. For Marlowe shared with his admiring contemporary, George Chapman, the disenchanted vision of the aspiring mind—the knowledge that the Comic Spirit hovers over the Icarian flight of the self-announced superman. /*172*/

---

[7] The balance of tragic and comic elements in *Faustus* is somewhat comparable to that in *Paradise Lost*. C. S. Lewis has suggested that Satan might have been a comic figure had Milton chosen to emphasize, more than he does, the absurdity of diabolical ambition (*A Preface to Paradise Lost* [Oxford, 1952], pp. 92–93). Like Faustus, Satan changes his shape; the brightest of angels becomes the scarred fallen leader who, reaching toward heaven, transforms himself into cormorant, toad, and "monstrous Serpent." Satan, however, is the unwitting fool of God, the brilliant schemer whose victory turns to ashes and whose evil will produces good, the "fortunate" fall of man. Faustus' destiny is more obscure and pathetic; he is Lucifer's fool, not God's.

[8] See, for example, Paul H. Kocher, *Christopher Marlowe: A Study of His Thought, Learning, and Character* (Chapel Hill, 1946), pp. 118–19.

[9] Compare the two intellectuals, Faustus and Ivan Karamazov. Both rebel against God because they cannot believe in His redeeming love; and they cannot believe because they are detached, superior beings incapable of ordinary human sympathies. Both reject intellectually what they cannot emotionally "conceive of" and accept. Spiritually isolated, trapped by their own dialectical subtleties, they dissipate their creative gifts. They escape the restrictive bonds of morality only to discover too late that they have cut themselves off from the humanity of those who would save them.

Wolfgang Clemen

Doctor Faustus

Marlowe's *Doctor Faustus*[3] signalizes a new stage in the history of English drama in so far as here for the first time a playwright embodied in dramatic form a symbolic representation of his own spiritual wrestlings. A spiritual conflict had, it is true, been dramatized in the Morality Plays—in *Everyman,* for example. There, however, it had been the universal human conflict between good and evil, entirely divorced from the individual standpoint of the playwright. In contrast to this, although to some extent he employs the same technique as the Moralities, Marlowe endows Faustus with his own personal problems, and dramatizes his own conflicting /*147*/ ideas about the fundamental issues of human life.[1] Thus *Doctor Faustus* develops into a spiritual tragedy, in the sense that the external circumstances and events of the play no longer have any intrinsic value, but are significant only in so far as they enable us to understand Faustus's spiritual state and to see what goes on inside his mind. In this context we may disregard the interpolated episodes, which were provided partly as comic relief and partly to pander to the audience's fondness for spectacle; Marlowe's authorship of these episodes is very questionable, and in any case they do not represent the core of the play.[2] *Doctor Faustus* is, like *Tamburlaine,* a single-character play, in that the action proceeds entirely from the central figure and is entirely dependent on him; with the difference, however, that this action is not kept in motion, as in *Tamburlaine,* by the "acting" and willing of the hero, but represents, as in *Everyman,* the temptations, conflicts, and inner struggles by which Faustus himself is beset. The other characters have therefore very little existence of their own; Faustus's antagonists are not human beings, but ultimately supernatural powers which ally themselves with the forces in his own soul.[3]

This specific pattern is responsible for some of the essential qualities in Faustus's speeches. Although his soliloquies and longer speeches do not by any means take up the greatest amount of space in the play, for it abounds in dialogue, they are nevertheless its lifeblood, and the most important part of what it has to say.

These speeches are the natural vehicle for the expression of the spiritual warfare and the conflicts of ideas that take place in Faustus himself, the successive stages of which also determine the external structure of the play. This no longer takes the form of parallel /*148*/ scenes presenting contrasts or variations on a theme,[1] but is a true sequence of scenes which have their basis entirely in Faustus's own development. Thus Marlowe in this play advances a further step towards dramatic unity, towards a full internal coherence in the dramatic structure.[2] Not only is Faustus himself on the stage during the greater part of the play, not only does he sustain its spirit from beginning to end, but his speeches

Page 147: 3. Greg is followed in placing *Faustus* late in Marlowe's development, though not later than *Edward II.*

Page 148: 1. Here and later, cf. Ellis-Fermor, *op. cit.,* Chap. V.

2. Even in the other parts the state of the text makes judgement of the play difficult; however, as far as the thesis of this book is concerned, the comments made above can be justified in the face of all textual uncertainties. Cf. Greg, *The Tragical History of the Life and Death of Dr. Faustus: A Conjectural Reconstruction,* Oxford, 1950; *Marlowe's Doctor Faustus, 1604–1616* (esp. pp. 97 ff. for detailed discussion of the problem); Wilson, *Marlowe and the Early Shakespeare.*

3. Cf. Poirier, *op. cit.,* p. 114. Fischer, *op. cit.,* p. 134, adopts a different standpoint.

Page 149: 1. Cf. Schirmer, *Geschichte der englischen Literatur,* Vol. I, 1954, p. 251.

2. With the reservations applied to the text, however; see p. 148, note 2. Cf. also Wilson, *op. cit.,* pp. 70 ff.

and soliloquies open before us a path of spiritual experience the different stages of which are organically related to one another. This was not the case in *Tamburlaine*. There the longer speeches merely represented variously stated expressions of the same mental attitude and of the same determination on the protagonist's part to impose his will on others; they cannot be said to give us any feeling of development in him.

The internal conflict which we see going on through all of Faustus's speeches and soliloquies may affect their structure and diction. This is to be seen happening already in the opening soliloquy, with which Goethe's presentation of Faust has so often been compared. Here is a short excerpt:

"Stipendium peccati mors est." Ha! *"Stipendium,"* etc.
The reward of sin is death: that's hard.

Reads.

*"Si pecasse negamus, fallimur
Et nulla est in nobis veritas."*
If we say that we have no sin,
We deceive ourselves, and there is no truth in us.
Why, then, belike we must sin,
And so consequently die;
Ay, we must die an everlasting death.

(I. i. 39–47)[3]

In this, as in many other passages, Latin or English sayings in the form of moral maxims and *dicta* are introduced, and at first sight it might seem that the same thing is being done here as was done by Seneca and his direct imitators in England, namely, that epigrams /*149*/ and sententious maxims are being dragged in at every conceivable opportunity. But in *Faustus* these sayings have an entirely different function, both in the text of the play and in the train of thought. They are not just rhetorical adornments imposed on the speeches; they are judgements that Faustus arrives at for himself, truths that he lays out before himself for examination, and which call out in him new questions or contradictions. There is serious meaning in these maxims of his; they represent for him the heads round which his thoughts revolve.

Analysis of this soliloquy as a whole, as of the

majority of Faustus's speeches and soliloquies, shows that in this play we have got away from the form of set speech which deals successively, according to a plan prescribed in advance, with stereotyped themes and motifs; in its place we have self-communion, which evolves according to the promptings of the moment. Up till this time the practice of systematizing the set speech and tricking it out with rhetorical devices had stifled and deadened the processes of real thought and feeling. Here, however, Faustus is actually thinking at the same time as he is speaking; the speech grows step by step, keeping pace with the progress of his thoughts, and this is a very significant fact for the future development of dramatic speech. The voicing of genuine doubt and irresolution has taken the place here of the old see-saw of argument and counter-argument, and instead of a character talking to himself, using his speech as a means of self-revelation for the benefit of the audience, we have true soliloquy; instead of quotations and maxims with a purely decorative function, we have personal judgements which the speaker has painfully arrived at by puzzling them out for himself.

There are some exceptions, of course. A few of Faustus's speeches follow the earlier method of providing internal directions for stage-business (*e.g.,* I. iii. 1–15) or merely reporting action (*e.g.,* III. i. 1–24). Others again are reminiscent of the wishful thinking that was so characteristic of Tamburlaine's speeches, for Faustus shares with Tamburlaine his aspirations towards the remote, the fabulous, and the unattainable.[1] In a good many passages, however, it is evident that a new language has been created to express hesitation /*150*/ and irresolution and the fluctuations of a mind torn by changing moods—for the expression, in short, of spiritual conflict. Thus the handling of the soliloquy in such a way that for the first time in English drama it reproduces the actual inner experience of a soliloquy has led in this play to the development of a new type of speech, and one that is unmistakably different from anything that had been heard before. This is illustrated in the following two short soliloquies, neither of which expresses any particular "point of view," any "plan," any *ad hoc* form of self-revelation; on the other hand,

3. This speech should probably be printed as prose; cf. Greg's *Conjectural Reconstruction*, p. 3.

Page 150: 1. Cf. I. i. 79–97; I. iii. 104–16.

they both mirror exactly what goes on in Faustus's mind in those moments when he is alone:

Now, Faustus, must
Thou needs be damn'd, and canst thou not be sav'd.
What boots it, then, to think on God or heaven?
Away with such vain fancies, and despair;
Despair in God, and trust in Belzebub:
Now go not backward; Faustus, be resolute:
Why waver'st thou? O, something soundeth in mine
 ear,
"Abjure this magic, turn to God again!"
Ay, and Faustus will turn to God again.
To God? he loves thee not;
The God thou serv'st is thine own appetite,
Wherein is fix'd the love of Belzebub:
To him I'll build an altar and a church,
And offer lukewarm blood of new-born babes.
         (II. i. 1-14)

What might the staying of my blood portend?
Is it unwilling I should write this bill?
Why streams it not, that I may write afresh?
Faustus gives to thee his soul: oh, there it stay'd!
Why shouldst thou not? is not thy soul thine own?
Then write again, *Faustus gives to thee his soul.*
         (II. i. 64-9)

It is not only in the soliloquies that we are made aware of these fluctuations and conflicts in Faustus's mind; this also happens in some of the speeches that he utters in the presence of others. These /151/ often have a passionate intensity which must suggest that Marlowe was translating into dramatic speech his own personal and most deeply experienced spiritual struggles (cf. II. ii. 18–32).[1] And this is a very remarkable, indeed astonishing, thing to find in the drama of this period, not excluding Shakespeare's.

Faustus's famous last soliloquy shows how these processes of thought and feeling may be given a setting in time, and here too the irrevocability of the fleeting time is emphasized by the stage-device of the clock that strikes the half-hours from eleven o'clock to midnight. This is one of the outstanding passages of pre-Shake-

spearian drama; W. W. Greg describes it as "spiritual drama keyed to its highest pitch."[2] Here are the first twenty lines or so:

    The clock strikes eleven.
Ah, Faustus,
Now hast thou but one bare hour to live,
And then thou must be damn'd perpetually.
Stand still, you ever moving spheres of heaven,
That time may cease, and midnight never come;
Fair Nature's eye, rise, rise again, and make
Perpetual day; or let this hour be but
A year, a month, a week, a natural day,
That Faustus may repent and save his soul!
O lente, lente currite, noctis equi!
The stars move still, time runs, the clock will strike,
The devil will come, and Faustus must be damn'd.
O, I'll leap up to my God!—Who pulls me down?—
See, see, where Christ's blood streams in the firmament!
One drop would save my soul, half a drop: ah, my Christ!—
Ah, rend not my heart from naming of my Christ!
           /152/
Yet will I call on him: O, spare me, Lucifer!—
Where is it now? 'tis gone: and see, where God
Stretcheth out his arm, and bends his ireful brows!
Mountains and hills, come, come, and fall on me,
And hide me from the heavy wrath of God!
No, no!
Then will I headlong run into the earth:
Earth, gape! O, no, it will not harbour me!
         (V. ii. 136-60)

It is a very long way from this to the rhetorical rant of the common run of pre-Shakespearian tragic heroes when they are at the point of death. Here it is deep spiritual experience that is being transmuted into drama, reproduced with unexampled immediacy and verisimilitude in the diction and imagery, and, too, in the exclamatory character of the soliloquy.[1] This is a true soliloquy, the utterance of a tragic hero who is overcome by a sense of desertion in the agony of his returning self-knowledge and his realization that he must carry on his struggle completely unaided. The tendency towards abstract thinking which elsewhere marks Faustus's speeches has been replaced here by the capacity to see spiritual abstractions in concrete terms as visible figures and actions, so that the spiritual

---

Page 152: 1. In the same way Tamburlaine's self-obsessed monologues might be regarded as a reflection of Marlowe's own personal preoccupations. However, the consciousness of two souls within his breast, the need to grapple with two alternatives, makes Faustus's speeches a species of dialogue with himself, a theatre of conflict.

2. *Marlowe's Doctor Faustus, 1604–1616,* p. 10.
Page 153: 1. Cf. Ellis-Fermor, *op. cit.,* p. 68.

conflict is transformed into something that happens before our eyes. It impresses itself on us so strongly as "happening" for the further reason that here, probably for the first time in pre-Shakespearian drama, time is made a part of the very substance of the speech; the swift and irresistible passing of that final hour before midnight is conveyed by the unrealistic but in the dramatic sense unusually effective compression of this period of time into a speech of fifty-eight lines.[2] It is true that the soliloquy opens with the conventional apostrophe to the heavenly spheres to stand still and the appeal to the sun to go on shining through the night. However, in this instance both appeals have their rise in Faustus's horror at the unstayable passing of time. They are not just dragged in from outside, and then immediately forgotten; the image is kept alive, so that a few lines later we read, "The stars move still . . ." The same is /153/ true of the later invocation to the stars (ll. 160 ff.) and the images of heaven and the clouds, which are instinct with the agonized impotence of the soul that is shut off from all hope of salvation and

2. Cf. Levin, *op. cit.,* p. 128.

is "damn'd perpetually." Desire and the frustration of desire, aspiration and its violent disappointment, here affect the character of the language itself, down to the very movement of the sentence and the choice of diction. The thrusting together within a single line of two short statements, the second of which negatives the first and despairingly acknowledges it as something impossible of fulfilment, may be classed as a form of antithesis, but it is antithesis which has ceased to be a mere rhetorical trick, because in this case it has been overlaid with reality. The tendency in the language towards a lapidary conciseness and direct simplicity, already apparent in a few of the dialogue-passages, but also to the fore in the present speech, suggests that a new type of subject-matter and a remarkable intensification of experience have forced the playwright to seek out new forms of expression and style. In passages like this we find Marlowe's most mature dramatic writing, and the power with which Faustus's spiritual experience is conveyed in certain scenes of the play places *Doctor Faustus,* for all its deficiencies, at the very summit of Marlowe's achievement. /154/

C. L. Barber

"The Form of Faustus' Fortunes Good or Bad"

Doctor Faustus tends to come apart in paraphrase. It can be turned into a fable about a Modern Man who seeks to break out of Medieval limitations. On the other hand, when one retells the story in religious terms, it tends to come out as though it were Marlowe's source, *The History of the Damnable Life and Deserved Death of Doctor John Faustus.* The truth is that the play is irreducibly dramatic. Marlowe dramatizes blasphemy, but not with the single perspective of a religious point of view: he dramatizes blasphemy as heroic endeavor. The play is an expression of the Reformation; it is profoundly shaped by sixteenth-century religious thought and ritual. But in presenting a search

for magical dominion, Marlowe makes blasphemy a Promethean enterprise, heroic and tragic, an expression of the Renaissance.[1]

The emergence of a new art form puts man in a new relation to his experience. Marlowe could present blasphemy as heroic endeavor, and the tragic ironies of such endeavor, because he had the new poetic drama, which put poetry in dynamic relation to action—indeed he himself had been the most important single pioneer in creating this form, in *Tamburlaine.* This creation, in turn, depended on the new professional

[1]This essay is adapted from a study centering on *Tamburlaine* and *Doctor Faustus,* to be entitled *Marlowe and the Creation of Elizabethan Tragedy.*

repertory theatre to which, when he came down from Cambridge in 1587, he brought his talents, and his need to project possibilities of human omnipotence. The London theatre was a "place apart" of a new kind, where drama was not presented as part of a seasonal or other social occasion but in its own right. Its stage gave a special vantage on experience: /92/

> Only this (Gentlemen) we must perform
> The form of Faustus' fortunes good or bad.
> To patient judgements we appeal our plaud . . .
>
> (7-9)[2]

Marlowe, with characteristic modernity, calls his play just what we call it—a form. He has an audience which includes gentlemen, to whose patient judgments he appeals. In this new situation, blasphemy can be "good or bad."

Professor Lily B. Campbell has related *Doctor Faustus* to fundamental tensions in Reformation religious experience in an essay which considers Marlowe's hero, against the background of Protestant casuistry, as "a case of Conscience."[3] She focuses on Faustus' sin of despair, his inability to believe in his own salvation, a sin to which Protestants, and particularly Calvinistic Protestants, were especially subject. They had to cope with the immense distance of Calvin's God from the worshipper, and with God's terrifying, inclusive justice, just alike to the predestined elect and the predestined reprobate. And they had to do without much of the intercession

---

[2]Line references for Marlowe's plays are to *The Works of Christopher Marlowe,* edited by C. F. Tucker Brooke, 1946 (first edition, 1910). I have modernized the spelling. The punctuation has been modernized with one exception, the use of the colon to indicate a pause; this feature of Marlowe's punctuation is so effectively and consistently used that to substitute full stop or comma often involves losing part of the sense. Almost everything I find occasion to use is in the 1604 Quarto; and I find its readings almost always superior to those of 1616. This experience inclines me to regard most of the 1604 text (with some obvious interpolations) as Marlowe's, or close to Marlowe's, whereas most of the additional matter in the 1616 version seems to me to lack imaginative and stylistic relation to the core of the play. Thus my experience as a reader runs counter to the conclusions in favor of the 1616 Quarto which W. W. Greg arrives at from textual study and hypothesis.

[3]"*Doctor Faustus:* A Case of Conscience," PMLA, Vol. LXVII, No. 2 (March 1952), pp. 219-39; for Spira, pp. 225-32.

provided by the Roman church, its Holy Mother, its Saints, its Masses and other works of salvation. Faustus' entrance into magic is grounded in despair. He quotes crucial texts, regularly heard as part of the Anglican service: /93/

Jerome's Bible, Faustus, view it well.
Stipendium peccati mors est: ha, *Stipendium peccati mors est.*
The reward of sin is death: that's hard.
Si peccasse negamus, fallimur, et nulla est in nobis veritas.
If we say that we have no sin,
We deceive ourselves, and there's no truth in us.
Why then belike
We must sin, and so consequently die.
Ay, we must die an everlasting death:
What doctrine call you this, *che sera, sera,*
What will be, shall be? Divinity, adieu,
These metaphysics of magicians
And necromantic books are heavenly: . . .

(65-78)

Faustus leaves out the promises of divine grace which in the service go with "the reward of sin is death"; here, as always, he is unable to believe in God's love for him. But he does believe, throughout, in God's justice.

Miss Campbell observes that it was peculiarly the God-fearing man who was vulnerable to despair, dragged down, like Spenser's Red Cross Knight in the Cave of Despair, by a sense of his sins. What Despair in his cave makes Spenser's knight forget, by insisting on his sinfulness, is God's love; as Una tells him in snatching away the dagger: "Where Justice grows, there grows eke greater Grace." Faustus forgets this too: vivid as is his sense of the lost joys of heaven, he never once expresses any sense that God could love him in spite of his sins. ". . . Faustus will turn to God again. / To God? he loves thee not" (440-41). Lucifer himself points to divine justice: "Christ cannot save thy soul, for he is just" (697).

Miss Campbell parallels Faustus as Marlowe presents him with the experience of Francis Spira, a historical case of conscience which became an exemplar of despair for Protestants. This Italian lawyer, who in 1548 died of no outward cause, surrounded by counseling Catholic doctors but miserably certain of his own damnation, had recanted Protestant views under Catholic pressure. Earlier he had been enthusiastic in his conviction of the truth of justification by faith. In his last weeks, Spira was tormented by a burning physical sensation of thirst which no drink could assuage.

Spira, dying in terror, could no longer believe in the efficacy of the Roman rites. Faustus embraces magical rituals; they are some- /94/ thing he can *do*. It can help in understanding his turning to magic—and, indirectly, Marlowe's turning to poetic drama—if we consider the tensions which were involved, for the Elizabethan church, in the use and understanding of Holy Communion. Faustus near the end expresses his longing for communion in imagery which reflects these tensions:

O I'll leap up to my God: who pulls me down?
See, see, where Christ's blood streams in the firmament.
One drop would have my soul, half a drop, ah, my Christ.
Ah, rend not my heart for naming of my Christ,
Yet will I call on him: O, spare me, Lucifer!
Where is it now? 'tis gone: and see, where God
Stretcheth out his arm, and bends his ireful brows.

(1431–38)

The immense distance away that the blood is, streaming in the sky like the Milky Way, embodies the helplessness of the Protestant who lacks faith in his own salvation. Calvin taught that communion could come by the lifting up of the soul to heaven, that it was not necessary that the essence of the flesh descend from heaven. But Faustus must try to leap up by himself, without the aid of Grace. His focus on the one drop, half a drop, that he feels would save his soul, expresses the Reformation's tendency to isolate the individual in his act of communion, and to conceive of it, as Dom Gregory Dix underscores in his great history, *The Shape of the Liturgy*, "as something passive, as a reception."[4] At the same time, the cosmological immensity of the imagery embodies Marlowe's characteristic sense of the vastness of the universe and, here, of the tremendousness of the God who rules it and yet concerns himself with every life, stretching out his arm and bending his ireful brows.

The piety of the late Middle Ages had dwelt on miracles where a host dripped actual blood,

and had depicted scenes where blood streamed down directly from Christ's wounds into the chalice on the altar. The Counter-Reformation, in its own way, pursued such physical imagery and literal conceptions, which remained viable for the Roman Catholic world as embodiments of Grace. A hunger for this kind of physical resource appears in the way that Faustus /95/ envisages Christ's blood, visibly streaming, in drops to be drunk. But for the Elizabethan church, such thinking about Communion was "but to dream of a gross carnal feeding," in the words of the homily "Of the worthy taking of the Sacraments."[5] We have good reason to think that Marlowe had encountered Catholic ceremony during his absences from Cambridge, when the reasonable assumption is that he was working at intervals as a secret agent among Catholic English exiles and students on the Continent. The letter from the Privy Council which secured him his degree is best explained on that hypothesis, since it denies a rumor that he is "determined to have gone beyond the seas to Reims and there to remain" (as secret Catholics were doing after graduation) and speaks of his having been employed "in matters touching the benefit of his country."[6] To have acted the part of a possible student convert would have involved understanding the Catholic point of view. And we have Marlowe the Scorner's talk, filtered through Baines, "That if there be any god or any good religion, then it is in the Papists' because the service of god is performed with more ceremonies, as elevation of the mass, organs, singing men, shaven crowns, *etc.* . . . That all protestants are hypocritical asses. . . ."[7]

What concerns us here is the way *Doctor Faustus* reflects the tension involved in the

[4]Dom Gregory Dix, *The Shape of the Liturgy* (Westminster: 1945), p. 635.

[5]The homily was issued in the *Seconde Tome of Homilies,* sanctioned by the Convocation of Canterbury in 1563 and "appointed to be read in all churches." It is quoted by C. W. Dugmore in *The Mass and the English Reformers* (London: 1958), p. 233. I am greatly indebted to Professor Dugmore's book, and to Dom Gregory Dix's *The Shape of the Liturgy,* throughout this discussion. Professor Dugmore, in exploring in detail Tudor views of the real presence in the elements of the Lord's Supper, and their background, brings into focus exactly the tensions that are relevant to *Doctor Faustus.*

[6]John Bakeless, *The Tragical History of Christopher Marlowe,* Vol. I, p. 77.

[7]Bakeless, *op. cit.,* Vol. I, p. 111.

Protestant world's denying itself miracle in a central area of experience. Things that had seemed supernatural events and were still felt as such in Reims, were superstition or magic from the standpoint of the new Protestant focus on individual experience. Thus the abusive Bishop Bale calls the Roman priests' consecration of the elements "such a charm of /96/ enchantment as may not be done but by an oiled officer of the pope's generation."[8] Yet the Anglican church kept the basic physical gestures of the Mass, with a service and words of administration which leave open the question of how Christ's body and blood are consumed. And Anglican divines, while occasionally going all the way to the Zwinglian view of the service as simply a memorial, characteristically maintained a real presence, insisting, in Bishop Jewell's words, that "We feed not the people of God with bare signs and figures."[9] Semantic tensions were involved in this position; the whole great controversy centered on fundamental issues about the nature of signs and acts, through which the age pursued its new sense of reality.

In the church of the Elizabethan settlement, there was still, along with the Reformation's insistence that "Christ's Gospel is not a ceremonial law . . . but it is a religion to serve God, not in bondage to the figure and shadow,"[10] an ingrained assumption that the crucial physical acts of worship had, or should have, independent meaning. This was supported by the doctrine of a real though not physical presence of Christ. But for many worshippers the physical elements themselves tended to keep a sacred or taboo quality in line with the old need for physical embodiment. We can, I think, connect the restriction of the impulse for physical embodiment in the new Protestant worship with a compensatory fascination in the drama with magical possibilities and the incarnation of meaning in physical gesture and ceremony: the drama carries on, for the most part in secular terms, the preoccu-

pation with a kind of realization of meaning which had been curtailed but not eliminated in religion. In secular life, the cult of royalty, as for example Elizabeth's magical virginity, carried it on also—bulking of course far larger than the drama for the age itself if not for posterity. /97/

In *Doctor Faustus* we have the special case where religious ritual, and blasphemous substitutes for ritual, are central in a drama. The Prayer Book's admonition about the abuse of Holy Communion strikingly illuminates Marlowe's dramatization of blasphemy:

> Dearly beloved in the Lord: ye that mind to come to the holy Communion of the body and blood of our Saviour Christ, must consider what S. Paul writeth to the Corinthians, how he exhorteth all persons diligently to try and examine themselves, before they presume to eat of that bread, and drink of that cup: for as the benefit is great, if with a truly penitent heart and lively faith we receive that holy sacrament (for then we spiritually eat the flesh of Christ, and drink his blood, then we dwell in Christ and Christ in us, we be one with Christ, and Christ with us:) so is the danger great, if we receive the same unworthily. For then we be guilty of the body and blood of Christ our Saviour. We eat and drink our own damnation, not considering the Lord's body.[11]

To eat and drink damnation describes not only Faustus' attitude but the physical embodiment of it, as we shall see in considering the ramifications of gluttony in the play.

Blasphemy implies belief of some sort, as T. S. Eliot observed in pointing, in his seminal 1918 essay, to blasphemy as crucial in Marlowe's work; blasphemy involves also, consciously or unconsciously, the magical assumption that signs can be identified with what they signify. Ministers were warned by several rubrics in the Tudor Prayer Books against allowing parishioners to convey the bread of the sacrament secretly away, lest they "abuse it to superstition and wickedness."[12] Such abuse depends on believing,

---

[8]Dugmore, *op. cit.,* p. 234, from *Selected Works,* P. S., 197. An Order of Council under Warwick in 1549 characteristically refers to "their Latin service, their conjured bread and water, with such like vain and superstitious ceremonies." *Ibid.,* 142.

[9]Dugmore, *op. cit.,* p. 229.

[10]*The First and Second Prayer Books of Edward VI* (London: 1949 [Everyman's Library, No. 448]), p. 3.

[11]*Liturgical Services . . . in the Reign of Queen Elizabeth,* Parker Society, Vol. XXX, ed. William K. Clay (Cambridge: 1847), p. 189.

[12]From a rubric of the first Prayer Book of Edward VI, where the danger of such theft is made an argument against allowing the communicants to take the bread in their own hands. (*The Two Liturgies,* A.D. 1549, and A.D. 1552: etc., Parker Society, Vol. XXIX,

or feeling, that, regardless of its context, the bread is God, so that /98/ by appropriating it one can magically take advantage of God. Spelled out in this way, the magical thinking which identifies sign and significance seems so implausible as to be trivial. But for the sort of experience expressed in *Doctor Faustus,* the identifications and displacements that matter take place at the levels where everyone is ignorant, the regions where desire seeks blindly to discover or recover its objects. Faustus repeatedly moves through a circular pattern, from thinking of the joys of heaven, through despairing of ever possessing them, to embracing magical dominion as a blasphemous substitute. The blasphemous pleasures lead back, by an involuntary logic, to a renewed sense of the lost heavenly joys for which blasphemy comes to seem a hollow substitute—like a stolen Host found to be only bread after all. And so the unsatisfied need starts his Ixion's wheel on another cycle.

The irony which attends Faustus' use of religious language to describe magic enforces an awareness of this circular dramatic movement. "Divinity, adieu! / These . . . necromantic books are heavenly" (76–77). What seems to be a departure is betrayed by "heavenly" to be also an effort to return. "Come," Faustus says to Valdes and Cornelius, "make me blest by your sage conference" (126–27). And Valdes answers that their combined skill in magic will "make all nations to canonize us" (149). In repeatedly using such expressions, which often "come naturally" in the colloquial language of a Christian society, the rebels seem to stumble uncannily upon words which condemn them by the logic of a situation larger than they are. So Mephistophilis, when he wants to praise the beauty of the courtesans whom he can give to Faustus, falls into saying:

> As wise as Saba, or as beautiful
> As was bright Lucifer before his fall.
>
> (589–90)

ed. Joseph Ketley [Cambridge: 1844], p. 97.) The Second Prayer Book of Edward and the Prayer Book of Elizabeth provided that "to take away the superstition which any person hath, or might have in the bread and wine, it shall suffice that the bread be such, as is usual to be eaten at the table . . ." and that "if any of the bread or wine remain, the Curate shall have it to his own use." (*Ibid.,* pp. 282–83, and Clay, *op. cit.,* p. 198.)

The auditor experiences a qualm of awe in recognizing how Mephistophilis has undercut himself by this allusion to Lucifer when he was still the star of the morning, bright with an altitude and innocence now lost.

The last and largest of these revolutions is the one that begins with showing Helen to the students, moves through the Old Man's effort to guide Faustus' steps "unto the way of life," (1274) and /99/ ends with Helen. In urging the reality of Grace, the Old Man performs the role of Spenser's Una in the Cave of Despair, but Faustus can only think "Hell calls for right" (1287). Mephistophilis, like Spenser's Despair, is ready with a dagger for suicide; Marlowe at this point is almost dramatizing Spenser. Faustus asks for "heavenly Helen," "To glut the longing of my heart's desire" and "extinguish clean / Those thoughts that do dissuade me from my vow" (1320–24). The speech to Helen is a wonderful poetic fusion of many elements, combining chivalric worship of a mistress with humanist intoxication over the project of recovering antiquity. In characteristic Renaissance fashion, Faustus proposes to relive classical myth in a Medieval way: "I will be Paris . . . wear thy colors" (1335, 1338). But these secular elements do not account for the peculiar power of the speech; the full awe and beauty of it depend on hoping to find the holy in the profane. The prose source can provide a useful contrast here; Helen is described there so as to emphasize a forthright sexual appeal:

> her hair hanged down as fair as the beaten gold, and of such length that it reached down to her hams, with amorous coal-black eyes, a sweet and pleasant face, her lips red as a cherry, her cheeks of rose all colour, her mouth small, her neck white as the swan, tall and slender of personage . . . she looked round about her with a rolling hawk's eye, a smiling and wanton countenance . . .

On the stage, of course, a full description was not necessary; but Marlowe in any case was after a different kind of meaning. He gives us nothing of the sort of enjoyment that the Faust book describes in saying that Helen was "so beautiful and delightful a piece" that Faustus "made her his common concubine and bedfellow" and "could not be one hour from her . . . and to

his seeming, in time she was with child."[13] There
is nothing sublime about this account, but it has
its own kind of strength—an easy, open-eyed
relishing which implies that sensual fulfillment
is possible and satisfying in its place within a
larger whole. The writer of the Faust book
looked at Helen with his own eyes and his own
assumption that the profane and the holy are
separate. But for Marlowe—it was his great,
transforming contribution to /100/ the Faust
myth—the magical dominion and pleasures of
Dr. Faustus ambiguously mingle the divine and
the human, giving to the temporal world a wonder and excitement which is appropriated, dar-
ingly and precariously, from the supernatural.

The famous lines are so familiar, out of context, as an apotheosis of love, that one needs to
blink to see them as they fit into the play's motion, with the play's ironies. (Eartha Kitt, telling
Life magazine about playing Helen opposite
Orson Welles, ignored all irony, saying simply
"I made him immortal with a kiss.") By contrast
with the Helen of the source, who has legs, Marlowe's Helen is described only in terms of her
face and lips; and her beauty is *power:*

> Was this the face that launch'd a thousand ships,
> And burnt the topless towers of Ilium?
>
> (1328–29)

The kiss which follows is a way of reaching this
source of power; it goes with a prayer, "Make
me immortal with a kiss," and the action is like
taking communion, promising, like communion,
a way to immortality. It leads immediately to
an ecstasy in which the soul seems to leave the
body: "Her lips suck forth my soul: see where
it flies!" The speech ends with a series of wor-
shipping gestures expressing wonder, awe, and a
yearning towards encountering a fatal power. It
is striking that Helen comes to be compared to
Jupiter, god of power, rather than to a goddess:

> O thou art fairer than the evening air
> Clad in the beauty of a thousand stars;
> Brighter art thou than flaming Jupiter
> When he appeared to hapless Semele;
> More lovely than the monarch of the sky
> In wanton Arethusa's azured arms;
> And none but thou shall be my paramour.
>
> (1341–48)

[13]*The History of the Damnable Life and Deserved
Death of Dr. John Faustus* (1592), ed. by William
Rose, London, n.d., p. 179 and pp. 193–94.

Upward gestures are suggested by "the evening
air" and "the monarch of the sky"; Faustus' attitude towards Helen is linked to that of hapless
Semele when Jupiter descended as a flame, and
to that of the fountain nymph Arethusa when
she embraced Jupiter in her spraylike, watery,
and sky-reflecting arms. Consummation with the
power first described in Helen's face is envisaged
as dissolution in fire or water. /101/

I can imagine a common-sense objection at
this point to the effect that after all Faustus'
encounter with Helen is a sexual rhapsody, and
that all this talk about it does not alter the fact,
since after all a kiss is a kiss. Mistresses, it could
be added, are constantly compared to heaven
and to gods, and lovers often feel, without being
blasphemers, that a kiss makes mortality cease
to matter. But it is just here that, at the risk of
laboring the obvious, I want to insist that Marlowe's art gives the encounter meaning both as
a particular kind of sexual experience *and* as
blasphemy.

The stage directions of the 1604 text bring
the Old Man back just at the moment when
Faustus in so many words is making Helen into
heaven:

> Here will I dwell, for heaven be in these lips
> And all is dross that is not Helena:
>
> *Enter old man.*
>
> (1333–34)

This figure of piety is a presence during the rest
of the speech; his perspective is summarized
after its close: "Accursed Faustus, miserable
man, / That from thy soul exclud'st the grace of
Heaven."

Another perspective comes from the earlier
scenes in the play where the nature of heaven
and the relation to it of man and devil is established in conversations between Mephistophilis
and Faustus. For example, the large and final
line in the later scene, "And all is dross that is
not Helena," has almost exactly the same movement as an earlier line of Mephistophilis' which
ends in "heaven."

> And, to be short, when all the world dissolves,
> And every creature shall be purified,
> All place shall be hell that is not heaven.
>
> (556–59)

One does not need to assume a conscious recognition by the audience of this parallel, wonderfully ironic as it is when we come to hear it as an echo.[14] What matters is the recurrence of similar gestures in language about heaven and its substitutes, so that a meaning of heaven, and postures towards it, are established. /*102*/

The most striking element in this poetic complex is a series of passages involving a face:

> Why, this is hell, nor am I out of it:
> Think'st thou that I, that saw the face of God,
> And tasted the eternal joys of heaven,
> Am not tormented with ten thousand hells,
> In being depriv'd of everlasting bliss?
>
> (312–16)

Just as Faustus' rapt look at Helen's face is followed by his kiss, so in the lines of Mephistophilis, "saw the face of God" is followed by "tasted the eternal joys of heaven."

Both face and taste are of course traditional religious imagery, as is motion upward and downward. Marlowe's shaping power composes traditional elements into a single complex gesture and imaginative situation which appears repeatedly. The face is always high, something above to look up to, reach or leap up to, or to be thrown down from:

> FAUST. Was not that Lucifer an angel once?
> MEPH. Yes, Faustus, and most dearly lov'd of God.
> FAUST. How comes it then that he is prince of devils?
> MEPH. Oh, by aspiring pride and insolence;
> For which God threw him from the face of heaven.
>
> (300–04)

A leaping-up complementary to this throwing-down, with a related sense of guilt, is expressed in Faustus' lines as he enters at midnight, about to conjure and eagerly hoping to have "these joys in full possession":

> Now that the gloomy shadow of the night,
> Longing to view Orion's drizzling look,
> Leaps from th' antarctic world unto the sky,
> And dims the welkin with her pitchy breath,
> Faustus, begin thine incantations . . .
>
> (235–39)

[14]The echo was first pointed out to me by Professor James Alfred Martin, Jr. of Union Theological Seminary.

Here the reaching upward in *leaps* is dramatized by the word's position as a heavy stress at the opening of the line. There is a guilty suggestion in *gloomy*—both discontented and dark—linked with *longing to view*. An open-mouthed panting is suggested by *pitchy breath,* again with dark associations of guilt which carry /*103*/ through to Faustus' own breath as he says his *incantations* (itself an open-throated word). The whole passage has a grotesque, contorted quality appropriate to the expression of an almost unutterable desire, at the same time that it magnificently affirms this desire by throwing its shadow up across the heavens.

A more benign vision appears in the preceding scene, where the magician Valdes promises Faustus that "serviceable spirits" will attend:

> Sometimes like women, or unwedded maids,
> Shadowing more beauty in their airy brows
> Than has the white breasts of the queen of love.
>
> (156–58)

Here we get an association of the breast with the face corresponding to the linkage elsewhere of tasting power and joy with seeing a face. The lines suggest by "airy brows" that the faces are high (as well as that the women are unsubstantial spirits).

The complex we have been following gets its fullest and most intense expression in a passage of Faustus' final speech, where the imagery of communion with which we began is one element. To present it in this fuller context, I quote again:

> The stars move still, time runs, the clock will strike,
> The devil will come, and Faustus must be damn'd.
> O I'll leap up to my God: who pulls me down?
> See, see, where Christ's blood streams in the firmament.
> One drop would save my soul, half a drop, ah, my Christ.
> Ah, rend not my heart for naming of my Christ,
> Yet will I call on him: O, spare me, Lucifer!
> Where is it now? 'tis gone: and see, where God
> Stretcheth out his arm, and bends his ireful brows:
>
> (1429–37)

Here the leap is discovered to be unrealizable. Faustus' blasphemous vision of his own soul with Helen—"See, where it flies"—is matched now by "See, see, where Christ's blood streams." It is "in the firmament," as was Orion's drizzling look. A paroxysm of choking tension at once overtakes Faustus when he actually envisages drinking Christ's blood. And yet—"one drop would save my soul." Such communion is denied by the companion vision of the face, now dreadful, "ireful brows" instead of "airy brows," above and bending down in overwhelming anger. /104/

When we turn to consider the presentation of the underside of Faustus' motive, complementary to his exalted longings, the Prayer Book, again, can help us understand Marlowe. The Seventeenth of the Thirty-Nine Articles contains a warning remarkably applicable to Faustus:

> As the godly consideration of Predestination, and our election in Christ, is full of sweet, pleasant, and unspeakable comfort to godly persons. . . . So, for curious and carnal persons, lacking the spirit of Christ, to have continually before their eyes the sentence of God's Predestination, is a most dangerous downfall, whereby the Devil doth thrust them either into desperation, or into wretchlessness of most unclean living, no less perilous than desperation.[15]

Faustus is certainly a "curious and carnal person," and he has "the sentence of God's Predestination" continually before his eyes, without "the spirit of Christ." The Article relates this characteristically Calvinist predicament to the effort to use the body to escape despair: "wretchlessness" (for which the New English Dictionary cites only this instance) seems to combine wretchedness and recklessness. The phrase "most unclean living" suggests that the appetites become both inordinate and perverse.

The psychoanalytic understanding of the genesis of perversions can help us to understand how, as the Article says, such unclean living is spiritually motivated—like blasphemy, with which it is closely associated. We have noticed how blasphemy involves a magical identification of action with meaning, of sign with significance. A similar identification appears in perversion as Freud has described it. Freud sees in perversions a continuation of the secondary sexual satisfactions dominant in childhood. The pervert, in this view, is attempting, by repeating a way of using the body in relation to a certain limited sexual object, to recover or continue in adult life the meaning of a relationship fixed on this action and object in childhood. So, for example,

the sucking perversions may seek to establish a relationship of dependence by eating someone more powerful. Faustus lives for twenty-four years "in all voluptuousness," in "wretchlessness of most unclean living": it is the meanings that he seeks in sensation that make his pleasures unclean, violations of taboo. We have seen how what /105/ he seeks from Orion or from Helen is an equivalent for Christ's blood, how the voluptuousness which is born of his despair is an effort to find in carnal satisfactions an incarnation. Perversion can thus be equivalent to a striving for a blasphemous communion. In the same period that T. S. Eliot wrote the essay in which he pointed to the importance of Marlowe's blasphemy, his poem *Gerontion* expressed a vision of people in the modern world reduced to seeking spiritual experience in perverse sensuality and aestheticism:

> In the juvescence of the year
> Came Christ the tiger
> In depraved May, dogwood and chestnut, flowering judas,
> To be eaten, to be divided, to be drunk
> Among whispers; by Mr. Silvero,
> With caressing hands, at Limoges
> Who walked all night in the next room;
> By Hakagawa, bowing among the Titians;
> Madame de Tornquist, in the dark room,
> Shifting the candles; Fräulein von Kulpe,
> Who turned in the hall, one hand on the door.

As I read the elusive chronology of Eliot's poem, Marlowe would have envisaged Helen in the luxuriance of a "depraved May" associated with the Renaissance, from which we come down, through a characteristically telescoped syntax, to the meaner modern versions of a black mass. What immediately concerns us here is the seeking of incarnation in carnal and aesthetic satisfactions. The perverse has an element of worship in it.

When we consider the imagery in *Doctor Faustus* in psychoanalytic terms, an oral emphasis is very marked, both in the expression of longings that reach towards the sublime and in the gluttony which pervades the play and tends towards the comic, the grotesque, and the terrible. It is perhaps not fanciful to link the recurrent need to leap up which we have seen with an infant's reaching upward to mother or breast,

[15]Clay, *op. cit.*, p. 189.

as this becomes fused in later life with desire for women as sources of intoxicating strength: the face as a source of power, to be obliviously kissed, "airy brows" linked to "the white breasts of the queen of love." The two parents seem to be confused or identified so that the need appears in fantasies of somehow eating the father, panting for Orion's /106/ drizzling look. This imagery neighbors directly religious images, Christ's streaming blood, the taste of heavenly joys.

It is because Faustus has the same fundamentally acquisitive attitude towards both secular and religious objects that the religious joys are unreachable. The ground of the attitude that sustenance must be gained by special knowledge or an illicit bargain with an ultimately hostile power is the deep conviction that sustenance will not be given freely, that life and power must come from a being who condemns and rejects Faustus. We can see his blasphemous need, in psychoanalytic terms, as fixation or regression to infantile objects and attitudes, verging towards perverse developments of the infantile pursued and avoided in obscure images of sexual degradation. But to keep the experience in the perspective with which Marlowe's culture saw it, we must recognize that Faustus' despair and obsessive hunger go with his inability to take part in Holy Communion. In Holy Communion, he would, in the words of the Prayer Book, "spiritually eat the flesh of Christ, and drink his blood . . . dwell in Christ . . . be one with Christ." In the Lord's Supper the very actions towards which the infantile, potentially disruptive motive tends are transformed, for the successful communicant, into a way of reconciliation with society and the ultimate source and sanction of society. But communion can only be reached by "a truly contrite heart" which recognizes human finitude, and with "a lively faith" in the possibility of God's love. Psychoanalytic interpretation can easily lead to the misconception that when we encounter infantile or potentially perverse imagery in a traditional culture it indicates, *a priori,* neurosis or degradation. Frequently, on the contrary, such imagery is enacted in ritual and used in art as a way of controlling what is potentially disruptive.[16] We are led by these con-

siderations to difficult issues about the status and limits of psychoanalytic interpretation beyond the scope of this essay, and to ultimate issues about whether worship is necessary which each of us must settle as we can. /107/

But for our purposes here, the necessary point is the perspective which the possibility of Holy Communion gives within Marlowe's play. Tragedy involves a social perspective on individual experience; frequently this perspective is expressed by reference to ritual or ceremonial acts, acts whose social and moral meaning is felt immediately and spontaneously. The hero one way or another abuses the ritual because he is swept away by the currents of deep aberrant motives associated with it, motives which it ordinarily serves to control. In *Doctor Faustus* this public, social ritual is Holy Communion. How deeply it is built into sensibility appears, for example, when Faustus stabs his arm:

My blood congeals, and I can write no more.
. . .
Faustus gives thee his soul. Ah, there it stayed.
Why shouldst thou not? Is not thy soul thy own?

(494, 499–500)

This is the crucial moment of the black mass, for Faustus is imitating Christ in sacrificing himself—but to Satan instead of to God. A moment later he will repeat Christ's last words, "Consummatus est." His flesh cringes to close the self-inflicted wound, so deeply is its meaning understood by his body.

The deep assumption that all strength must come from consuming another accounts not only for the desperate need to leap up again to the source of life, but also for the moments of reckless elation in fantasy. Faustus uses the word "fantasy" in exactly its modern psychological sense:

. . . your words have won me at the last,
To practice magic and concealed arts:
Yet not your words only, but mine own fantasy,
Which will receive no object, for my head
But ruminates on necromantic skill.

(129–33)

---

[16]In an essay on "Magical Hair" (*Journal of the* *Royal Anthropological Institute,* V. 88, Pt. II, pp. 147–69) the anthropologist Edmund Leach has made this point in a most telling way in evaluating the psychoanalytic assumptions of the late Dr. Charles Berg in his book *The Unconscious Significance of Hair.*

Here "ruminates" carries on the imagery of gluttony. Moving restlessly round the circle of his
desires, Faustus wants more from nature than
nature can give, and gluttony is the form his
"unclean living" characteristically takes. The
verb "glut" recurs: "How am I glutted with
conceit of this!" "That heavenly Helen . . . to
glut the longing. . . ." The Prologue summarizes his career in the /108/ same terms,[17] introducing like an overture the theme of rising up
by linking gluttony with a flight of Icarus:

Till swoll'n with cunning, of a self conceit,
His waxen wings did mount above his reach,
And melting heavens conspir'd his overthrow.
For falling to a devilish exercise,
And glutted now with learnings golden gifts,
He surfeits upon cursed Negromancy.

(20–25)

On the final night, when his fellow scholars try
to cheer Faustus, one of them says, " 'Tis but a
surfeit, never fear, man." He answers, "A surfeit
of deadly sin, that hath damn'd both body and
soul" (1364–67). How accurately this exchange
defines the spiritual, blasphemous motivation of
his hunger!

Grotesque and perverse versions of hunger appear in the comedy. Like much of Shakespeare's
low comedy, the best clowning in *Doctor Faustus*
spells out literally what is metaphorical in the
poetry. No doubt some of the prose comedy,
even in the 1604 Quarto, is not by Marlowe; but
when the comic action is a burlesque that uses
imaginative associations present in the poetry, its
authenticity is hard to doubt. Commentators are
often very patronizing about the scene with the
Pope, for example; but it carries out the motive
of gluttony in a delightful and appropriate way
by presenting a Pope "whose *summum bonum*
is in belly cheer" (855), and by having Faustus

[17] I first became aware of this pattern of gluttonous
imagery in teaching a cooperative course at Amherst
College in 1947—before I was conscious of the blasphemous complex of taste, face, *etc.* Professor R. A.
Brower pointed to the prologue's talk of glut and surfeit as a key to the way Faustus' career is presented
by imagery of eating. His remark proved an Open
Sesame to the exploration of an "imaginative design"
comparable to those he exhibits so delicately and effectively in his book, *The Fields of Light* (Oxford:
1951). This pattern later fell into place for me in relation to the play's expression of the blasphemous motives which I am analyzing.

snatch his meat and wine away and render his
exorcism ludicrous, baffling magic with magic.
Later Wagner tells of Faustus himself carousing
and swilling amongst the students with "such
belly-cheer / As Wagner in his life ne'er saw the
like" (1343–44). The presentation of the Seven
Deadly Sins, though of course traditional, comes
back to hunger /109/ again and again, in gross
and obscene forms; after the show is over, Faustus exclaims "O, this feeds my soul!" One could
go on and on.

Complementary to the active imagery of eating is imagery of being devoured. Such imagery
was of course traditional, as for example in cathedral carvings of the Last Judgment and in
the Hell's mouth of the stage. With being devoured goes the idea of giving blood, also traditional but handled, like all the imagery, in a
way to bring together deep implications. To
give blood is for Faustus a propitiatory substitute
for being devoured or torn in pieces. The relation is made explicit when, near the end, Mephistophilis threatens that if he repents, "I'll in
piece-meal tear thy flesh." Faustus collapses at
once into propitiation, signalled poignantly by
the epithet "sweet" which is always on his hungry lips:

Sweet Mephistophilis, intreat thy Lord
To pardon my unjust presumption,
And with my blood again I will confirm
My former vow I made to Lucifer.

(1307–10)

By his pact Faustus agrees to be devoured later
provided that he can do the devouring in the
meantime. Before the signing, he speaks of pay-
ing by using other people's blood:

The god thou servest is thine own appetite,
Wherein is fix'd the love of Belsabub.
To him I'll build an altar and a church,
And offer luke warm blood of new born babes.

(443–46)

But it has to be his own blood. The identification of his blood with his soul (a very common
traditional idea) is underscored by the fact that
his blood congeals just as he writes "gives thee
his soul," and by Mephistophilis' vampire-like
exclamation, as the blood clears again under the
influence of his ominous fire: "O what will I
not do to obtain his soul."

Faustus' relation to the Devil here is expressed in a way that was characteristic of witchcraft—or perhaps one should say, of the fantasies of witchhunters about witchcraft. Witch lore often embodies the assumption that power can be conveyed by giving and taking the contents of the body, with which the soul is identified, /110/ especially the blood. To give blood to the devil —and to various animal familiars—was the ritual expression of submission, for which in return one got special powers. Witches could be detected by the "devil's mark" from which the blood was drawn. In stabbing his arm, Faustus is making a "devil's mark" or "witch's mark" on himself.[18]

The clown contributes to this theme in his role as a commonsense prose foil to the heroic, poetic action of the protagonist. Between the scene where Faustus proposes a pact to buy Mephistophilis' service and the scene of the signing, Wagner buys a ragged but shrewd old "clown" into his service. He counts on hunger:

> . . . the villain is bare, and out of service, and so hungry that I know he would give his soul to the Devil for a shoulder of mutton, though it were blood raw.
>
> (358–61)

We have just heard Faustus exclaim:

> Had I as many souls as there be stars,
> I'd give them all for Mephistophilis.
>
> (338–39)

But the clown is not so gullibly willing to pay all:

> How, my soul to the Devil for a shoulder of mutton, though 'twere blood raw? Not so, good friend, by 'rlady I had need to have it well roasted, and good sauce to it, if I pay so dear.
>
> (362–65)

After making game of the sturdy old beggar's ignorance of Latin tags, Wagner assumes the role of the all-powerful magician:

[18]These notions, which are summarized in most accounts of witchcraft, are spelled out at length in M. A. Murray, *The Witch-Cult in Western Europe* (Oxford: 1921), pp. 86–96 and *passim*. One may have reservations as to how far what Miss Murray describes was acted out and how far it was fantasy; but the pattern is clear.

Bind yourself presently unto me for seven years, or I'll turn all the lice about thee into familiars, and they shall tear thee in pieces.

> (377–80)

But again the clown's feet are on the ground:

> Do you hear sir? you may save that labour, they are too familiar with me already. Swounds, they are as bold with my flesh, as if they paid for me meat and drink. /111/

This scene has been referred to as irrelevant padding put in by other hands to please the groundlings! Clearly the clown's independence, and the *detente* of his common man's wit which brings things down to the physical, is designed to set off the folly of Faustus' elation in his bargain. Mephistophilis, who is to become the hero's "familiar spirit" (as the Emperor calls him later at line 1011), "pays for" his meat and drink, and in due course will "make bold" with his flesh. The old fellow understands such consequences, after his fashion, as the high-flown hero does not.

One final, extraordinarily complex image of surfeit appears in the last soliloquy, when Faustus, frantic to escape from his own greedy identity, conceives of his whole body being swallowed up by a cloud and then vomited away:

> Then will I headlong run into the earth:
> Earth gape. O no, it will not harbour me:
> You stars that reign'd at my nativity,
> Whose influence hath allotted death and hell,
> Now draw up Faustus like a foggy mist
> Into the entrails of yon labouring cloud,
> That when you vomit forth into the air,
> My limbs may issue from your smoky mouths,
> So that my soul may but ascend to heaven:
>
> (1441–49)

Taken by themselves, these lines might seem to present a very far-fetched imagery. In relation to the imaginative design we have been tracing they express self-disgust in terms exactly appropriate to Faustus' earlier efforts at self-aggrandizement. The hero asks to be swallowed and disgorged, anticipating the fate his sin expects and attempting to elude damnation by separating body and soul. Yet the dreadful fact is that these lines envisage death in a way which makes it a consummation of desires expressed earlier. Thus in calling up to the "stars which reigned

at my nativity," Faustus is still adopting a pos-
ture of helpless entreaty towards powers above.
He assumes their influence to be hostile but
nevertheless inescapable; he is still unable to believe in love. And he asks to be "drawn up,"
"like a foggy mist," as earlier the "gloomy
shadow," with its "pitchy breath," sought to
leap up. The whole plea is couched as an eat-
or-be-eaten bargain: you may eat my body if
you will save my soul. /112/

In the second half of the soliloquy Faustus
keeps returning to this effort to distinguish body
and soul. As the clock finally strikes, he asks for
escape in physical dissolution:

> Now, body, turn to air,
> Or Lucifer will bear thee quick to hell:
> *Thunder and lightning.*
> Oh soul, be chang'd into little water-drops,
> And fall into the ocean, ne'er be found:
>
> (1470–73)

It is striking that death here is envisaged in a
way closely similar to the visions of sexual consummation in the Helen speech. The "body,
turn to air," with the thunder and lightning, can
be related to the consummation of hapless
Semele with flaming Jupiter; the soul becoming
little water-drops recalls the showery consummation of Arethusa. Of course the auditor need not
notice these relations, which in part spring naturally from a pervasive human tendency to
equate sexual release with death. The auditor
does feel, however, in these sublime and terrible
entreaties, that Faustus is still Faustus. Analysis
brings out what we all feel—that Faustus cannot
repent. Despite the fact that his attitude towards
his motive has changed from exaltation to horror, he is still dominated by the same motive—
body and soul are one, as he himself said in the
previous scene: "hath damned both body and
soul." The final pleas themselves confirm his
despair, shaped as they are by the body's desires
and the assumptions those desires carry.

I said at the outset that because Marlowe
dramatizes blasphemy as heroic endeavor, his
play is irreducibly dramatic. But in the analytical process of following out the themes of blasphemy and gluttony, I have been largely ignor-
ing the heroic side of the protagonist, the
"Renaissance" side of the play. It is high time
to emphasize that Marlowe was able to present

blasphemy as he did, and gluttony as he did,
only because he was able to envisage them as
something more or something else: "his dominion that exceeds in this / Stretcheth as far as
doth the mind of man." We have been considering how the play presents a shape of longing
and fear /113/ which might have lost itself in
the fulfillment of the Lord's Supper or become
obscene and hateful in the perversions of a
witches' sabbath. But in fact Faustus is neither
a saint nor a witch—he is Faustus, a particular
man whose particular fortunes are defined not
by ritual but by drama.

When the Good Angel tells Faustus to "lay
that damned book aside . . . that is blasphemy,"
the Evil Angel can answer in terms that are not
moral but heroic:

> Go forward, Faustus, in that famous art
> Wherein all nature's treasury is contain'd:
> Be thou on earth as Jove is in the sky,
> Lord and commander of these elements.
>
> (102–05)

It is because the alternatives are not simply
good or evil that Marlowe has not written a
morality play but a tragedy: there is the further,
heroic alternative. In dealing with the blasphemy, I have emphasized how the vision of
magic joys invests earthly things with divine at-
tributes; but the heroic quality of the magic depends on fusing these divine suggestions with
tangible values and resources of the secular
world.

This ennobling fusion depends, of course, on
the poetry, which brings into play an extraordinary range of contemporary life:

> From Venice shall they drag huge argosies
> And from America the golden fleece
> That yearly stuffs old Philip's treasury.
>
> (159–61)

Here three lines draw in sixteenth-century classical studies, exploration and commercial adventure, national rivalries, and the stimulating
disruptive influence of the new supply of gold
bullion. Marlowe's poetry is sublime because it
extends desire so as to envisage as objects of
passion the larger life of society and nature:
"Was this the face that . . ."—that did what?
". . . launched a thousand ships." "Clad in the
beauty of . . ."—of what? ". . . a thousand

stars." *Doctor Faustus* is a sublime play because Marlowe was able to occupy so much actual thought and life by following the form of Faustus' desire. At the same time, it is a remorselessly objective, ironic play, because it dramatizes the ground of the desire which /114/ needs to ransack the world for objects; and so it expresses the precariousness of the whole enterprise along with its magnificence.

Thus Faustus' gluttonous preoccupation with satisfactions of the mouth and throat is also a delight in the power and beauty of language: "I see there's virtue in my heavenly words." Physical hunger is also hunger for knowledge; his need to depend on others, and to show power by compelling others to depend on him, is also a passion for learning and teaching. Academic vices and weaknesses shadow luminous academic virtues: there is a fine, lonely, generous mastery about Faustus when he is with his colleagues and the students; and Mephistophilis too has a moving dignity in expounding unflinchingly the dreadful logic of damnation to Faustus as to a disciple. The inordinate fascination with secrets, with what cannot be named, as Mephistophilis cannot name God, includes the exploring, inquiring attitude of "Tell me, are there many heavens above the moon?" The need to leap up becomes such aspirations as the plan to "make a bridge through the moving air / To pass the ocean with a band of men." Here we have in germ that sense of man's destiny as a vector moving through open space which Spengler described as the Faustian soul form. Faustus' alienation, which we have discussed chiefly as it produces a need for blasphemy, also motivates the rejection of limitations, the readiness to alter and appropriate the created universe—make the moon drop or ocean rise—appropriating them for *man* instead of for the greater glory of God, because the heavens are "the book of Jove's high firmament," and one can hope for nothing from Jove. Perhaps most fundamental of all is the assumption that power is something outside oneself, something one does not become (as a child becomes a man); something beyond and stronger than oneself (as God remains stronger than man); *and yet* something one can capture and ride—by manipulating symbols.

Marlowe of course does not anticipate the kind of manipulation of symbols which actually has, in natural science, produced this sort of power; Mephistophilis answers Faustus with Ptolemy, not Copernicus—let alone the calculus. But Marlowe was able to exemplify the creative function of controlling symbols by the way the form of poetic drama which he developed uses poetry. He made poetic speech an integral part of drama by exhibiting it as a mode of action: Faustus can assert about himself, "This word /115/ damnation terrifies not him, / For he confounds hell in Elysium." The extraordinary pun in "confounds hell in Elysium" suggests that Faustus is able to change the world by the way he names it, to *destroy* or *baffle* hell by *equating* or *mixing* it with Elysium.[19]

Professor Scott Buchanan, in his discussion of tragedy in *Poetry and Mathematics,* suggested that we can see tragedy as an experiment where the protagonist tests reality by trying to live a hypothesis. Elizabethan tragedy, seen in this way, can be set beside the tentatively emerging science of the period. The ritualistic assumptions of alchemy were beginning to be replaced by ideas of observation; a clear-cut conception of the experimental testing of hypothesis had not developed, but Bacon was soon to speak of putting nature on the rack to make her yield up her secrets. Marlowe knew Thomas Harriot: Baines reports his saying "That Moses was but a juggler, and that one Heriots being Sir W. Raleigh's man can do more than he." Faustus' scientific questions and Mephistophilis' answers are disappointing; but the hero's whole enterprise is an experiment, or "experience" as the Elizabethans would have termed it. We watch as the author puts him on the rack.

FAUST. Come, I think hell's a fable.
MEPH. Ay, think so still, 'till experience change thy mind.

(559–60)

In *Tamburlaine,* Marlowe had invented a hero who creates himself out of nothing by naming himself a demigod. By contrast with the universe assumed in a play like *Everyman,* where everything has its right name, *Tamburlaine* assumes an open situation where new right

[19]In a commentary on the Virgilian and Averroist precedents for this line, in *English Studies,* XLI, No. 6 (December 1960), pp. 365–68, Bernard Fabian argues for a sense of it consistent with my reading here.

names are created by the hero's combination of powers: he conceives a God-like identity for himself, persuades others to accept his name by the "strong enchantments" of an Orphic speech, and imposes his name on stubborn enemies by the physical action of "his conquering sword." This self-creating process is dramatized by tensions between what is expressed in words and what is conveyed by physical action on the stage: the hero declares /116/ what is to happen, and we watch to see whether words will become deeds—whether, in the case of Tamburlaine, man will become demigod.

The high poetry, the bombast, of Marlowe and kindred Elizabethans is not shaped to express what is, whether a passion or a fact, but to make something happen or become—it is incantation, a willful, self-made sort of liturgy. The verbs are typically future and imperative, not present indicative. And the hero constantly talks about himself as though from the outside, using his own name so as to develop a self-consciousness which aggrandizes his identity, or cherishes it, or grieves for it: "Settle thy studies, Faustus, and begin . . ." (29); "What shall become of Faustus, being in hell forever?" (1382–83). In the opening speech, Faustus uses his own name seven times in trying on the selves provided by the various arts. In each unit of the speech, the words are in tension with physical gestures. As Faustus "levels at the end of every art," he reaches for successive volumes; he is looking in books for a miracle. But the tension breaks as he puts each book aside because "Yet art thou still but Faustus and a man." When finally he takes up the necromantic works, there is a temporary consummation, a present-indicative simultaneity of words and gestures: "Ay, these are those that Faustus most desires." At this point, the actor can use gesture to express the new being which has been seized, standing up and spreading his arms as he speaks the tremendous future-tense affirmation: "All things that move between the quiet poles / Shall be at my command. . . ." At the very end of the play Faustus' language is still demanding miracles, while the *absence* of corroborating physical actions make clear that the universe cannot be equated with his self: "Stand still, you ever-moving spheres of heaven. . . ." King Lear in the storm, at the summit of Elizabethan

tragedy, is similarly trying (and failing) to realize a magical omnipotence of mind: ". . . all-shaking thunder, / Smite flat the thick rotundity of the world. . . ."

The double medium of poetic drama was peculiarly effective to express this sort of struggle for omnipotence and transcendent incarnation along with its tragic and comic failure. The dramatist of genius can do two things at once: Marlowe can "vaunt his heavenly verse," animating the reach of Faustus' motive—and putting into /117/ his hero much that, on the evidence of his other plays and of his life (beyond our scope here), was in himself. At the same time he is judge and executioner, bringing his hero remorselessly to his terrible conclusion. At the end of the text of *Doctor Faustus*, Marlowe wrote *"Terminat hora diem, Terminat Author opus."* As my friend Professor John Moore has remarked, it is as though he finished the play at midnight! The final hour ends Faustus' day; but Marlowe is still alive. As the author, he has been in control: *he* has terminated the work and its hero. This is another kind of power from that of magical dominion, a power that depends on the resources of art, realized in alliance with the "patient judgements" in an audience. It has not been a drumhead trial and execution, moreover, based on arbitrary, public-safety law. Though the final Chorus pulls back, in relief, to such a position, we have seen in detail, notably in the final soliloquy, how the fate of the hero is integral with his motive. In *Tamburlaine*, it was the hero who said "I thus conceiving and subduing both. . . . Shall give the world to note for all my birth, / That Vertue solely is the sum of glorie." Fundamental artistic limitations resulted from the identification of Marlowe with his protagonist in that play. But now, at the end of *Doctor Faustus*, Marlowe has earned an identity apart from his hero's—he is the author. He has done so by at once conceiving and subduing the protagonist.

The analogy between tragedy and a scapegoat ritual is very clear here: Faustus the hero has carried off into death the evil of the motive he embodied, freeing from its sin, for the moment, the author-executioner and the participating audience. The crop of stories which grew up about one devil too many, a real one, among the actors shows how popular tendencies to project evil in demons were put to work (and controlled, so far as "patient judgements" were concerned) by Marlowe. Popular experience of public executions provided, as Mr. John Holloway has recently pointed out (and Wyndham Lewis before him),[20] another paradigm for tragedy. We can add that, in Marlowe's case at least, some of the taboo quality which tends to stick to an executioner attached to the tragedian, a sense of his contamination by the sin of the /*118*/ victim. He proudly claims, in classical terms, the prerogative of the author who termi-

[20]*The Story of the Night* (London: 1961); *The Lion and the Fox* (London: 1927).

nates the work, has done with it. But in his own life what was working in the work caught up with him by the summons to appear before the Privy Council, and the subsequent death at Deptford—whether it was a consequence of his own tendency to give way to "sudden cruelty," or a successfully camouflaged murder to get rid of a scandalous client of Thomas Walsingham. Art, even such austere art as *Doctor Faustus,* did not save the man in the author. But the author did save, within the limits of art, and with art's permanence, much that was in the man, to become part of the evolving culture in which his own place was so precarious. /*119*/

Victor Lange

Goethe and Faust

I

Like Dante and Milton, Goethe is often identified with one central achievement. His *Faust* crowns and symbolizes a long life of incomparable scope and variety which encompasses the space of nearly a century, from 1749 to 1832, and which illuminates with extraordinary brilliance the features of an age that was decisive in the making of the modern mind. In every one of his works, from *The Sorrows of Young Werther* to the serenely elegiac poems of his old age, Goethe is concerned with the nature of modern man and the special moral and intellectual challenges with which he finds himself confronted. And it is characteristic of Goethe's sense of the relevance of poetic symbols that, prompted by his experiences as man of letters, scientist and social philosopher, he should again and again have turned to the figure of the great magus of the Renaissance.

Even as a child in Frankfurt he must have come upon representations in prose or crudely dramatic form of the history of Doctor Georg Faust, a contemporary of Luther's and a figure of remarkable independence of thought and belief, typical of the revolutionary spiritual climate

of the sixteenth century. Faust's classical and alchemistic learning, his defiance of the then current modes of salvation and, even more important, his hypnotic personality made him, soon after his death in 1540, the subject of popular imagination. In the Frankfurt *Faust-Book* of 1587 and in Marlowe's *Tragical History of /v/ Doctor Faustus,* written only a few years later, he emerged as a definite poetic character: the magician and necromancer who sold his soul to the Devil became the symbol of an all-consuming greed for power and a ruthless, superhuman desire to be the "great emperor of the world." But by the early eighteenth century the Christian theme of the sufferings of the heretic which had sustained the earlier treatments of the Faust saga had lost much of its compelling appeal. When Goethe first saw a melodramatic version of it on the puppet stage, he can no longer have been struck by the specifically Christian implications of the story. In the rationalistic climate of that enlightened century, the problem of Faust, his rejection of orthodoxy, had become, if not wholly secularized, at least subject to the scrutiny of worldly skepticism.

Goethe's years of study at the Universities of

Leipzig and Strasbourg may have reinforced in his mind the contemporary view of Faust as a rebel not against Christian dogma only, but against any sort of categorical system of values. His interest in the great representatives of the nature philosophy of the Renaissance, in Paracelsus, Campanella, and Giordano Bruno became increasingly alive and, moved by a new enthusiasm for the Shakespearean tragic hero, he planned a number of dramatic portraits of the "titanic" man, of Caesar, Mohammed, Prometheus, Goetz von Berlichingen. It may have been at that time, shortly after 1770, that the figure of Faust offered itself to Goethe as a representative symbol not only of greed for power, or of superhuman intelligence, but of a type of perception which, indicative of the modern mind, sought to penetrate the paradoxes of knowledge and life. Even before 1775 when he went to Weimar to accept a court position that was to grow more demanding and more responsible as the years went by, he appears to have completed the *Urfaust,* a dramatic /vi/ sketch, unpublished at the time, in which the core of Faust's story, his association (not his pact) with Mephistopheles, his love for Margaret, and his eventual doom are represented in a rapid sequence of picturesque scenes, some in verse, some in prose.

Goethe's first ten years in Weimar were years of adjustment; his interests were divided between public service, an increasing devotion to science, and philosophical and poetic exercises that indicate his growing desire for inner stability. His journey to Italy in 1786–88 represents a decisive turn in his development. In the light of his deepened attachment to the world of forms and to a sense of personal discipline, he could now complete some of his best poetic projects that had for long remained fragmentary. The so-called *Faust-Fragment* of 1790 shows the result of this self-scrutiny: Goethe recast several of the familiar scenes, and added a number of significant passages that give further reality to Faust's moral situation. During the years between 1794 and 1805, Schiller's friendship and encouragement were of inestimable importance to Goethe; it was he who suggested a reconsideration of the whole Faust scheme, and in June, 1797, Goethe once again turned his full attention to *Faust,* composed the "Dedication,"

the "Prelude on the Stage" and the "Prologue in Heaven," and thus placed the familiar incidents of Faust's life in a larger ethical context— the tension between the creative energies of the Lord and the destructive forces of Mephistopheles. *Faust,* in the form in which we know it, did not appear until 1808.

Goethe was then nearly sixty years old, at the height of a distinguished life and in full mastery of his poetic powers. In a rich philosophical novel, *Wilhelm Meister's Apprenticeship,* he had set forth his idea of a fruitful life, and in *Hermann and Dorothea* he had elaborated his /vii/ central theme of the interplay of chaos and order. No less revealing of the diversity of his interests were the published results of his studies in optics and botany. Indeed, his scientific and historical knowledge provided essential elements for the First Part of *Faust,* and when he contemplated a continuation of it, he did so because he hoped that an imaginative treatment of Faust's later career might offer a poetic vehicle for an even more impressive representation of modern philosophical ideas.

As early as 1800 he had begun the "Helen" episode, which was later to evolve into the third act of the Second Part, but for some time work on *Faust* was again suspended. Two novels, *Elective Affinities* (1809) and *Wilhelm Meister's Travels* (1821), another major scientific work, *The Science of Color* (1810), his autobiography, *Poetry and Truth,* and the splendid series of *Divan* poems give to the years between 1808 and 1825 their unmistakable character: all these works are the products of a circumspect and skeptical mind, who with all his deliberate detachment from the literary fashions of his romantic contemporaries and from the political demands of the day, remains the dominant figure of his time. In 1825, seventy-six years of age, he resumed *Faust* and the poem remained his "Hauptgeschaeft," his main business, until it was completed in July, 1831, eight months before his death.

2

It is not surprising that a work of such slow and irregular growth as *Faust* should not easily reveal its unity, indeed that it should prove most rewarding when tested with a variety of critical tools. We must, first of all, remember that it is a product of imagination and that before inquiring into its philosophical meaning we should recognize the power of its poetic effects. Even in the English translation, we can feel that each scene is filled with a /*viii*/ special atmosphere and that each uses the sort of language, imagery, and rhythm appropriate to it: the sweeping lines of the "Prologue in Heaven" are followed by the tense and throbbing verse of the study scenes. The "Easter Walk" with its solid figures and its bright colors offers a beautiful combination of promise and recollection; the Gretchen eposides develop swiftly in purely lyrical terms; and for the incidents of nature magic in the "Witches' Kitchen" and at the "Walpurgisnight" revels, Goethe uses a curiously suggestive kind of speech by which he anticipates the unrealistic devices of the Second Part. There the symbolic and metaphorical intentions are far more deliberate but they are also, we must admit, not always fully realized. In the company of the earlier Faust, of Gretchen, Mephistopheles, and perhaps especially of the minor figures such as the students, neighbor Martha, and Valentine, we are touched, moved, elevated or shocked. The Second Part stirs our feelings less immediately; it challenges our intellectual perception in a more oblique and demanding manner. But by the continued presence of his whole poetic personality Goethe sustains throughout the play a remarkably powerful imaginative energy.

This is not, of course, to say that the full force of the poem can be felt on its surface; it is a calculated work of art and the organizing mind behind it has made use of many resources. We should recognize the suitability of the free arrangement of the scenes in the First Part and of the more spacious architecture of the five acts of the Second. We must be aware of the associations of symbols such as the Earth Spirit or the setting of "Forest and Cavern" and relate them to particular philosophical impulses. We must bring knowledge as well as feeling to the play, especially to the Second Part, which is, in a comprehensive sense, concerned with knowledge itself. /*ix*/

But while the reader of *Faust* cannot miss the beauty or profundity of detail, he may find himself puzzled by the problem of the unity, of the central meaning, that holds this enormously suggestive poem together. The simple moral of the old Faust plot is here no longer adequate. If it had been Goethe's intention merely to retell the case history of a man who loses his soul, he would not have needed the intricate machinery of human involvement and superhuman guidance, he would not have given Faust the extraordinary dimensions of thought and passion, nor matched him against the brilliantly cynical intelligence of Mephistopheles. He could have made certain that any doubt as to the purpose of this spectacle should be resolved in the mind of the reader. Instead, Goethe himself was careful not to prejudice the interpretation of the work. In one of the many revealing conversations with Eckermann, he said, on May 6, 1827: "They come and ask what idea I meant to embody in my *Faust;* as if I knew myself, and could inform them. From heaven, through the world, to hell, would indeed be something; but this is no idea, only a course of action. And further: that the devil loses the wager, and that a man continually struggling from difficult errors towards something better, should be redeemed, is an effective—and, to many, a good enlightening—thought; but it is no idea at the foundation of the whole, or of every individual scene. It would have been a fine thing indeed if I had strung so rich, varied, and highly diversified a life as I have brought to view in *Faust* upon the slender string of one pervading idea." We may perhaps reach a more certain conclusion as to Goethe's purpose if we summarize briefly the successive phases of the plot.

3

Neither the "Dedication" nor the "Prelude on the /*x*/ Stage" contains anything that is related to the action of the play: the first states the poet's attitude toward the material he is about to present, the second indicates the special nature of the spectacle to be produced. But the bearing of the "Prologue in Heaven" upon the subsequent plot cannot be overemphasized—it is the key to everything that is to come. Among the angelic host praising the Lord and His Creation, there appears Mephistopheles, one of the Lord's servants, whose function it is, like that of Satan in *Job,* to question and, where he can, to undermine all evidences of creative life. He cannot praise nor be wholly indifferent; his detachment makes him the supremely ironic spirit, for whom all efforts, especially those of man, seem ludicrous, pointless and absurd. The Lord insists that the sense of discrimination between good and evil, even though it may not easily be realized in a life of positive action, represents the true character of the human being. As long as this perception of values is active, it should entitle man to eventual salvation. This is the meaning of the term "striving" which the Lord recognizes as the essence of man's character and which, not in the sense of aggressive and amoral ruthlessness, but of a persistent power of moral judgment, Goethe offers as the central concept of Faust's career. Mephistopheles dares to test this divine assumption and hopes to disprove the validity of the Lord's thesis by destroying the sense of good and evil in one conspicuous specimen, Faust. The Lord agrees; he knows that as long as man lives, he is in any case immersed in the destructive element, but that his unceasing awareness of the great moral issues will preserve his human integrity.

When we first meet Faust he is a man of incomparable learning who has mastered every field of knowledge without, however, having found anywhere the reassurance of insight into ultimate meanings. As he speculates upon /xi/ the symbols of cosmic significance, he must admit his human limitations; he can only hope, through the Earth Spirit, to reach an understanding at least of all earthly experience. But that, too, is shown to be impossible. His despair is profound—the scene with his obtuse, rationalistic assistant Wagner gives to it dramatic emphasis—and he contemplates suicide. At the moment of surrender he is held back by a sudden welling-up of childhood memories, which now, at the sound of the Easter bells, restore his determination to live. Before the city gates in the company of the townspeople he longs again for a rich and meaningful life: no matter what aid may offer itself, natural or supernatural, he will not reject it. When Mephistopheles emerges from his disguise, ironically present at Faust's attempt to translate the beginning of the Gospel of St. John, he finds Faust ready to come to terms. He can give him satisfaction and hopes that by extinguishing Faust's "striving," he may demonstrate not only Faust's but God's failure.

Faust is not easily deceived. He insists that his

desires are not the obvious ones; they are superhuman in kind, and above all, in intensity; they may baffle and perhaps even defeat Mephistopheles. But the tempter can only smile at Faust's peculiarities; they seem to him no more than human; he knows that the weakness of reason which they seem to imply will only serve his own ends. This theme, the paradoxical nature of reason, is the subject matter of many of Mephistopheles' speculations, and especially of the interview with the naïve student.

What Mephistopheles now has to offer Faust is not sufficiently seductive: the banal amusements of the drinking students leave the mature man indifferent and the tricks and gestures by which his youth is to be restored in the Witches' Kitchen strike Faust as childish and repulsive. Before Mephistopheles can provide an /xii/ experience of still cruder physical satisfaction, Faust, himself, without assistance or prompting, meets Margaret. Their love, maudlin and commonplace to Mephistopheles, draws them together in a genuine but incongruous attachment. Margaret's simple, circumscribed world cannot survive under the torrential force of Faust's passion. As soon as Mephistopheles recognizes the evolving tragedy, he seizes upon it as a further test of Faust's moral energies. Through him, Faust becomes the cause of Valentine's death. They must flee, and in the satanic frenzy of the Walpurgis-night, Faust seems for a brief moment close to a total suspension of moral perception. But the most powerful means of seduction cannot destroy Faust's memory of Margaret; as he comes to rescue her, he is overwhelmed by the spectacle of a moral decision in Margaret that is clearer and, in spite of her madness, more resolute than he himself can achieve. She refuses to be freed by Mephistophelian devices and submits to the judgment of God. Faust, most deeply stirred and here, perhaps, farthest from the kind of amorality that Mephistopheles hopes to achieve, is forcibly reminded of his attachment to his servant; as a voice from above promises Margaret forgiveness, Mephistopheles disappears with Faust.

Impressive in its dramatic sweep though the First Part may be, readers have always felt that the fate of Faust, undoubtedly the main unifying element in this phase of the poem, is at the end left in abeyance. If Goethe wished to continue the story of Faust's life and death, to complete it along the lines of the old *Faust-Book,* he had much episodic material that was as yet unused—Faust's appearance at the emperor's court and his evocation of Helen of Troy were certainly promising dramatic episodes. And that, in continuing his work on *Faust* (even before the First Part was published) he turned /xiii/ first of all to the Helen episode, seems to suggest that he hoped to find there a logical extension and perhaps even the conclusion of Faust's history.

But when, twenty-five years later, he resumed work on *Faust,* his perspectives, poetic as well as philosophical, had changed, and the Second Part was to derive its coherence not from the figure of Faust but from the unity of Goethe's own view of life, and especially of civilization, attached to Faust's experience but frequently enough independent of it.

"The first part is almost entirely subjective," Goethe remarked to Eckermann in February, 1831. "It all issues from a more confused, more passionate individual, and this twilight may well explain its great appeal. But in the Second Part there is scarcely anything subjective, here there appears a higher, broader, brighter, less passionate world, and those who have not knocked about a bit and gathered experience will not be able to make much of it."

The five acts of the Second Part contain Goethe's most moving comments on the culture of his time. We find Faust, in a magnificent opening scene, restored (though not morally exonerated) by the impartial forces of nature. With an unexpectedly clear realization of the limits of experience, but still devoted to the pursuit of the "highest form of life," he decides to live resolutely within this world. He appears at court, where Mephistopheles, disguised as the jester, has promised relief to the pleasure-loving but bankrupt emperor. As a frivolous stunt Faust undertakes to produce the apparition of Helen, and he must venture alone to the timeless and spaceless realm of the "Mothers," where Helen dwells—a descent into the area of purest beauty, which to Mephistopheles is no more than a journey into nothing. Faust appears at court with the image which is not the true Helen but only an idol; and when in a /xiv/ moment of blinding desire he reaches for her, she disappears, striking him to the ground.

In the second act Mephistopheles has carried the unconscious Faust back to his old study where Wagner has meanwhile come close to the successful production of an artificial "homunculus." This wraithlike creature has extraordinary powers of perception; he recognizes Faust's longing for Helen and offers to guide him from the murky North to Greece where in that night the spirits of classical demons are about to assemble. Mephistopheles, eager to be present at this "Classical Walpurgis-night," hides his devilish—northern—features, which would have no place in that world of beauty, behind the mask of Phorcyas, one of the ugliest creatures of Greek mythology. While Faust searches for Helen, Homunculus, a mere bodiless abstraction, attempts to achieve reality, but during the orgies of the nature elements he destroys himself.

The scene in which Faust was to find Helen and plead for her release was never written. At the beginning of the third act we find Helen returned to the palace at Sparta, terrified and insulted by Phorcyas-Mephistopheles and eventually persuaded to accept the protection of Faust, now the powerful lord of a neighboring castle. In a scene of superb poetry the wedding between Helen and Faust, between the classical and romantic sensibilities, takes place. Their child, Euphorion, cannot live: like Icarus he attempts to fly and crashes at the feet of his parents. "We imagine," say the stage directions, "that in the dead body we perceive a well-known form; yet the corporeal part vanishes at once, and the aureole rises like a comet toward heaven. The garment, mantle and lyre remain upon the ground." With this image, and the splendid dirge that follows, Goethe paid his tribute to Byron. Helen must follow Euphorion; only her garment and veil remain in Faust's arms. /xv/

What this enormously ramified search for Helen and her eventual loss mean for Faust can hardly be defined by one single set of criteria: it is a spiritual crisis that rests upon religious as well as aesthetic experiences and that reflects Goethe's own maturest view of the classical ideal. The union with Helen reminds Faust of the precarious meaning of all existence: early in the fourth act, he recalls "the grand significance of fleeting days," *fluechtger Tage grossen Sinn.* But he recognizes the vision of Helen as a deceptive dream in which he cannot acquiesce. Another vision points to what seems a more substantial form of spiritual beauty crystallizing the memory of Margaret.

Mephistopheles once again offers Faust the satisfactions of lust and passion. But Faust brushes these suggestions aside. Even fame seems insubstantial to him: "the Deed is everything, the Glory naught." The encounter with Helen has made him impatient for heroic action; he will now conquer "the aimless force of elements unruly" and compel the useless ocean to yield fertile soil. The true motive for this titanic project has been variously interpreted. It is certainly, in contrast to Mephistopheles' temptation, an affirmation of a creative desire and his determination to assume social responsibilities; but it is a decision that is not yet free of selfish will to power. Aided by Mephistopheles' magic he wins a crucial war for the emperor and is given as a reward the right to reclaim a barren stretch of swamp. He is now a hundred years old. Early in the fifth act, he surveys from the terrace of his palace the lands that he has claimed from the sea. Only one small settlement within his property is not yet in his control. With the same ruthless impatience that has so often jeopardized his actions, he orders Mephistopheles to remove the old couple living there. Mephistopheles soon returns to report, not their resettlement, but their destruction, and Faust, horrified /xvi/ at his own dependence upon Mephistopheles' demonic cynicism, turns away from him. As he faces his death he has come to realize the futility of his association with "magic."

> Not yet have I my liberty made good:
> If I could banish Magic's fell creations,
> And totally unlearn the incantation,—
> Stood I, O Nature! Man alone in thee,
> Then were it worth one's while a man to be!
> Ere in the Obscure I sought it, such was I,—
> Ere I had cursed the world so wickedly.

In a superb scene in which Anguish, *die Sorge,* nearly overwhelms him, he remembers his resolve to free himself of supernatural help and, although Anguish blinds him, it cannot destroy him. Mistaking the chatter of lemures digging his grave for the noise of workmen, he envisages his community of free people on free soil. But "the highest moment" which was to be his last

is not an achievement, it is a mere anticipatory vision.

> Then dared I hail the Moment fleeing:
> Ah, still delay, thou art so fair!

With these last words "Faust sinks back: the lemures take him and lay him upon the ground." The sepulcher scene which follows is no more than a dramatic concession. Mephistopheles has, in effect, long ago lost all chance of winning the wager and his last, theatrical attempt to snatch Faust's body from the angels cannot succeed.

4

It is sometimes asked whether Faust's end is not curiously incongruous, whether a life so violent and so little exemplary ought not by rights to have fallen to Mephistopheles, whether it is not merely a poetic or perhaps we may even say a divine trick that Faust should be saved. This is a crucial test of interpretation and it must be faced most seriously. /xvii/

The critics of the nineteenth century were agreed that Faust's pursuit of meaning was fraught with error and hubris, but they felt justified to read into Faust's later life—beginning at the emperor's court—a clearer recognition of human obligations, culminating in the attainment of the highest form of social responsibility. Faust's salvation represented from this point of view a deserved reward for his persistent striving from darkness to clarity.

But this optimistic and liberal reading of the poem offers countless difficulties and it was bound to disturb those in our own day who remembered Goethe's use of the word "tragedy" in the title of both parts, a term which otherwise he seldom used, and never in a casual sense. Faust's active life, his commendable if intermittent striving for any sort of security of action or knowledge, cannot serve as a key to the play. It is charged with error and confusion. Indeed, Faust's problem is insoluble in the course of life itself: he is forever torn between faith and despair and whenever he seems to be close to the attainment of spiritual patience, he is plunged again into the element of insecurity. His own extravagant passion and—almost as another aspect of his own self—Mephistopheles' cynicism, never cease to threaten his chances, not of a just compensation but of redemption and forgiveness. It is not until his end that he succeeds in freeing himself of the deceptive magic which tends to obscure the infinite magnitude of man's task to maintain himself between cosmos and chaos. His titanic wavering between superhuman longing and radical self-debasement, between his will to transcend and his suicidal paralysis, between his curse of all faith, hope, love and patience at one time and his ecstatic praise of a pantheistic Godhead at another—these are the extremes of experience between which Faust must go his way. /xviii/

We should, for instance, remember Faust's attitude, throughout the play, toward the "word." It is to him the metaphor of all life, the unfathomable vehicle of an inexpressible substance. And we must in comparison listen to the cynical ease with which Mephistopheles—not only in his interview with the student—offers the word as the ready and effective device of confusion and deceit. What is tragically ambivalent to Faust is to Mephistopheles a sardonic comedy of errors. Ambiguity is for Faust—and in the opposite sense for Mephistopheles—the essence of all experience. His concern once he is associated with Mephistopheles is not merely with finding satisfaction, but with transcending, in finding it, the ever-present conflict between elation and dejection, between hope and despair. The Lord's confident assumption is that Faust has the power, if not to eliminate this conflict, at least to subordinate it to a compelling vision of man's moral responsibilities. That he may be tricked into forgetting the elemental force of this conflict and that trivial satisfactions may dull his moral sense and lead Faust to spiritual stagnation, that is Mephistopheles' hope.

The pivot upon which the meaning of the poem turns is the wager between the Lord and Mephistopheles. If this is fully realized, the pact between Faust and Mephistopheles assumes its proper—and secondary—function. It amounts to little more than the joining of the two partners in an enterprise in which Faust will dramatically demonstrate his powers of spiritual judgment and Mephistopheles his ingenuity as a provider of physical and intellectual distractions.

Still, we may find it disquieting, and perhaps incompatible with our more realistic predilections, that Faust's sense of discrimination should remain so speculative, that it is never translated into the practical evidence of beneficial action. Faust does little if any good; he be- /xix/ comes, on the contrary, increasingly involved in guilt and violence. What are we to think, for instance, of his love for Margaret? However touching its poetic rendering may be, is it not for Faust essentially a means of self-expansion? His divided nature makes it impossible for him to establish an ordered and satisfying relationship and his complexity is not relieved but only made more terrifying by contrast with the simple and clearly-defined feelings of Margaret, her orthodox belief and her eventual surrender to the judgment of God. We may be moved by the pathos of Margaret's fate, but it is Faust, not she, who is the truly tragic figure. No matter how much Mephistopheles may wish to trivialize this love, to exploit its elements of sensuality and crime, Faust remains aware of the deep and irreconcilable conflicts which are inherent in his passion. The scene "Forest and Cavern" is the most telling instance of Faust's inner rallying, but the introspection of that moment forces him again into despair and nihilism. His fall is deepest during the sexual orgies of the Walpurgis-night; yet even there, his conscience, his powers of distinction between sense and madness awaken, and the spectacle of Margaret's agony in the dungeon and her acceptance, enviable enough from Faust's point of view, of the categorical verdict of the Church move him most deeply. His departure with Mephistopheles suggests not his surrender to the element of evil, but an awareness of his continued tragic involvement in it. Throughout the five acts of the Second Part, the integrity of Faust's actions can often be questioned. He is still, and perhaps even more recklessly so, the romantic striver after the certainty that only fatal self-delusion could ever hope to achieve.

To his very end Faust is not a "good man." What Goethe has represented in the person of Faust and in the poem as a whole is not, after all, a model either of excellence or of depravity. It is rather an account, ren- /xx/ dered with compassion as well as critical intelligence, of modern man. Faust's "two souls," his extremes of effusion and action, are the source of his highest as well as his lowest aspirations. But between ultimate knowledge of good and evil and unexceptionable, virtuous deeds, there lies, for

Faust, a gulf which is, in the pursuit of our earthly life, unbridgeable. His last speeches acknowledge the tragic, the ultimately ambiguous nature of all human effort. There can be no other reason for the final scene which resumes and completes the religious theme of the "Prologue in Heaven." Faust's quest on earth is given its true meaning only within the frame of "divine reconciliation": the forgiveness that is commensurate with his striving must come from above; it can be shown only poetically in symbols of extremely rarefied spirituality. "You must admit," Goethe said in 1831, "that the conclusion where the redeemed soul is carried up, was difficult to manage; and that, amid such supersensual, scarcely conceivable matters, I might easily have lost myself in the void—if I had not, by means of sharply-defined figures, and images

from the Christian Church, given my poetical design a desirable form and substance." Classical mythology would hardly have conveyed the full meaning of the essentially modern, Christian transfiguration of Faust—the radical experience of inadequacy that must remain insubstantial without the constant "striving" for an awareness of good and evil and that can be resolved, not in secular justice, but only in divine grace. In stages of extraordinarily rich meaning and poetic power Faust's earthly remains are at last transformed into pure perception, and Margaret, Mephistopheles' great metaphysical antagonist, can now lead Faust to clarity. Her unselfish love merges with that of the Blessed Virgin to elevate him to forgiveness.

> Earth's insufficiency—Here grows to Event;
> The Indescribable—Here it is done./xxi/

Erich Heller

Faust's Damnation: The Morality of Knowledge

I

A few years ago one of the Cambridge colleges had a very conservative Master. He regarded the newfangled Cambridge Ph.D. degree as a vulgar concession to transatlantic academic pilgrims, and the publishing of papers as one of the more degrading forms of self-advertisement. "In my time," he used to say, "it was of the essence of a gentleman that his name should never appear in print." It so happened that the College had just elected into a Fellowship a young man who not only had a few papers to his name but also the temerity to propose, at the first Fellows' meeting in which he took part, a number of measures concerning College policy. The Master listened frowningly, and when the novice had finished, he said: "Interesting, interesting" —and "interesting" meant that he was both alarmed and bored, two states of mind that he was expert at blending—"interesting; but it would seem to me that your suggestions are a little contradictory to the tradition of the Col-

lege." "Not at all, Master," replied the aspiring reformer, "I have studied the history of the College and I can assure you that my proposals are perfectly in keeping with the ways of the College over the last three hundred years." "This may well be," said the Master, "but wouldn't you agree that the last three hundred years have been, to say the least of them, rather exceptional?"

Of course, he was right; and speaking of Dr. Faustus means to speak of the "exceptionalness," in at least one /3/ respect, of the last three hundred, or even four hundred, years. For what is exceptional and even extravagant about those centuries is shown, in the most timely manner imaginable, by the transformations of meaning which the story of Dr. Faustus has undergone since this "insatiable speculator" and experimenter made his first appearance in literature —in the year 1587, in Germany, when the religious life of the country was dominated by Martin Luther. It was then that a certain Johann Spies printed and published in Frankfurt am Main the catastrophic record of the learned man Faustus who was, as we read, "fain to love forbidden things after which he hankered day and night, taking unto himself the wings of an eagle in order to search out the uttermost parts of heaven and earth," until he decided to "try out and put into action certain magic words, figures, characters and conjurations, in order to summon up the Devil before him,"[1] and whose "apostasy was nothing more nor less than his pride and arrogance, despair, audacity and insolence, like unto those giants of whom the poets sing . . . that they made war on God, yea, like unto that evil angel who opposed God, and was cast off by God on account of his arrogance and presumption."[2] With his magic words, figures, characters, and conjurations, Faustus gathered sufficient intelligence of the Devil to know how to bargain with him. He must have owned a particularly precious soul, for he sold it at an exquisite price: before going to Hell, he was to enjoy twenty-four years of researcher's bliss, a period of time during which Hell was to profit him greatly if he but /4/ renounced "all living creatures, and the whole heavenly host, and all human beings, for so it must be."[3]

The text of the covenant, signed by Dr. Faustus with his blood, was as follows:

I, John Faustus, Doctor, do openly acknowledge with my own hand . . . that since I began to study and speculate the elements, and since I have not found through the gifts that have been graciously bestowed upon me from above, enough skills; and for that I find that I cannot learn them from human beings, now have I surrendered unto this spirit Mephistopheles, ambassador of the hellish Prince of Orient, upon such condition that he shall teach me, and fulfil my desire in all things, as he has promised and vowed unto me . . .[4]

This grimly didactic and ruthlessly pious tale captured the popular imagination as no other piece of German writing had done—with the exception of Luther's Bible; and like Luther's German Bible it played upon the instrument of the age with that sureness of touch attainable only through the collaboration between a player of some genius and a score inspired by the *Zeitgeist*. Indeed, the story of Dr. Faustus was a great invention, and it was to be treated again and again on many levels of seriousness and macabre jocularity: two students in Tübingen cast it into verse, pictorial artists seized hold of it, and soon it set out upon its career as the puppet-players' enduring success. It made its way into England in a version which even claimed to be an improvement on the original. The translator introduced himself as P. F., *Gent.*, on the title page of *The Historie of the Damnable Life and Deserved Death of /5/ Doctor John Faustus, newly imprinted and in convenient places imperfect matter amended: according to the true Copie printed in Franckfort*. Its chronology is uncertain; but the translation must have followed the "true Copie" with remarkable speed. For it was this English text which was read by Marlowe; and instantly the provincial German tale was received into the poetic order of the Elizabethan stage: in the nick of time—for in 1593 Marlowe was killed in a tavern brawl.

Clearly, that Johann Spies in Frankfurt am Main was either a very lucky or a very brilliant publisher: he had put into circulation a modest little volume by a modestly anonymous author and it proved to be the book of the epoch—and of many epochs. If ever a work made literary history, this one did. Marlowe, Lessing, Goethe, Heine, Grabbe, Lenau, Valéry, Thomas Mann —this is a register of only its more notorious debtors. But its fascination was, and has remained, not only literary. Spies's publication was a tract for the times, bidding farewell to its readers with the admonition of Peter: "Be sober, be vigilant, because your adversary, the Devil, as a roaring lion, walketh about seeking whom he may devour,"[5] and leaving them in no doubt where, at that hour, the lion roared most greedily: in the minds of men, all of a sudden curiously suspicious of the instructions their Church

[1] J. Scheible: *Das Kloster* (Stuttgart, 1846), II, 943. The translations are partly E. M. Butler's, from her book *The Fortunes of Faust* (Cambridge, 1952), to which I am indebted for many suggestions, partly the first English translator's, P. F., *Gent.*, in the modernized version rendered by William Rose in his edition of *The History of the Damnable Life and Deserved Death of Doctor John Faustus* (London, 1925), and partly my own.
[2] *Ibid.* 950.
[3] *Ibid.* 951.
[4] *Ibid.* 950 f.

[5] *Ibid.* 1069.

had given them about their world and their place in it, and restlessly determined to probe forbidden depths. That time has passed, the mind has won its freedom, and the beast has not yet devoured us. Yet after centuries of free thought, /6/ free science, free testing, and free daredevilry, there stood a doctor of nuclear physics in an American desert, watching the first experimental explosion of the atomic bomb, and saying that for the first time in his life he knew what sin was. The story published by Johann Spies of Frankfurt am Main in 1587 has certainly proved its power to stay, indeed far beyond the moment at which Marlowe's Faustus, at the end of his second monologue, announced:

> Yea, stranger engines for the brunt of war,
> Than was the fiery keel at Antwerp's bridge,
> I'll make my servile spirits to invent.

Which were the passages in the original German text that were found wanting by the English translator P. F., *Gent.?* What was the "imperfect matter" that he chose to amend in "convenient places"? Was he, the Elizabethan, a man of such literary sophistication that he could not abide any native Lutheran crudities? No. It surely was not upon the prompting of sheer aesthetic refinement that he replaced the original's very condemnatory diagnosis of Faust's motives, ". . . for his frowardness, lawlessness, and wantonness goaded him on," by the simple and surely less condemnatory statement, ". . . for his Speculation was so wonderful";[6] or that the remorseful exclamation of the German Faustus, ". . . had I but had godly thoughts!" was changed in English to the far less contrite ". . . had not I desired to know so much."[7] From such comparisons it would emerge that the amendments were not at all a matter of literary elegance. True, they were a matter of style: but of a comprehensive style of thought, feeling, and /7/ belief. A revolution of sensibility was astir between the wanton, lewd, disreputable, and godless enterprises of the German magician and the "wonderful Speculation" of P. F.'s audacious scholar. The textual changes he made may have been slight, but their specific gravity was considerable: P. F., *Gent.*, was driven—more by historical compulsion than literary design—to raise the moral stature of Dr. Faustus. For such were the calendar and geography of the times that yesterday's wicked wizard would cross the frontier as tomorrow's candidate for historic grandeur. It was in the Englishman's, not the German's, text that the villainous scholar registered at the University of Padua as "Dr. Faustus, the insatiable Speculator."[8]

No textual exegesis would be required to show the dramatic metamorphosis that took place in the estimate of Faust's soul when Marlowe seized hold of the story; for at this point it would be enough to set the title of the original Faust-book, *The Historie of the Damnable Life and Deserved Death of Doctor John Faustus,* against the title of Marlowe's drama: *The Tragical History of Doctor Faustus.* Exit—and exit for good —the despicable, damnable blackguard, and enter *the tragic hero.* To be sure, there still is damnation. But it is the downfall of a Prometheus and not the homecoming to Hell of a depraved creature. At least this is so in the fullness of Marlowe's poetic conception, notwithstanding the frequent vacuities of a dramatic execution for which, very probably, the poet himself is not entirely responsible. Even if no plausible rumors had reached us of Marlowe's unorthodox tempera- /8/ ment, blasphemous tongue, and dissolute living; even if we did not know that the man who taught him at Corpus Christi, Cambridge, was burned for heresy, we yet would be struck by the running battle fought in his *Doctor Faustus* between poetry and story: the sensibility of the writer is in a state of flagrant insurrection against the opinions of his fable. Again and again, the truth of the poetic imagination gives the lie to the religious assertiveness of the plot, and moments of exquisite poetry punish Hell for its insistence upon the theologically proper outcome. Let the groundlings be righteously entertained by the farcical paraphernalia of Faustus's "frowardness, lawlessness, and wantonness"; in the upper ranks it is known that his "Speculation" is "so wonderful"—or in Marlowe's words: "Here, Faustus, tire thy brain, to gain a deity!"[9] This could not be otherwise with a poet who shortly before, in *Tamburlaine,* had wished his

[6]*Ibid.* 943, and Rose, 68.
[7]Scheible, II, 964, and Rose, 92.

[8]Rose, 125.
[9]Christopher Marlowe: *The Tragical History of Doctor Faustus,* I, i, l. 64.

birthday blessings on the new aeon—the Faustian Age, as it was called by a much later historian—and wished them in the name of Nature that teaches us "to have aspiring minds" and in

> Our souls, whose faculties can comprehend
> The wondrous architecture of the world,
> And measure every wand'ring planet's course,
> Still climbing after knowledge infinite,
> And always moving as the restless spheres,
> Wills us to wear ourselves, and never rest . . .[10]

Such a soul, created by a God who is not "in one place circumscriptable,"

> But everywhere fills every continent
> With strange infusion of his sacred vigour[11]—,/9/

such a soul, created by such a godhead, would surely have to commit an offense much more abominable than Dr. Faustus ever did to deserve the divine wrath that, against the very testimony of the poetry, settles even with Marlowe the ultimate fate of the profound Speculator. Spiritual perdition for having wrestled with the problem of a world

> Whose deepness doth inspire such forward wits
> To practice more than heavenly power permits[12]—?

Yes—damned despite the very testimony of the poetry: for these last lines, upholding the belief in a deity who is outraged by the depths with which He himself has equipped world and man alike, are flat and stale, certainly flatter than those which sense the "strange infusion of his sacred vigour," and are, with all their verse and rhyme, much more prosaic than the words in prose with which the Faustus of the first German Faust-book stands condemned: "Thou hast abused the glorious gift of thine understanding!"[13]

The condemned hero emerges from Marlowe's drama, by the verdict of its poetry, as incomparably more divine than the avenging divinity who, far from filling every continent with a "strange infusion of his sacred vigour," appears to be a theological pedant who employs petty demons peddling silly provocations—and so they

fly, inglorious *agents provocateurs*, "in hope to get his glorious soul,"[14] as Mephistopheles announces to Faustus. In this incongruity between the mind of its language and the mind of its action lies, as literary criticism would have to insist, the dramatic failure of Marlowe's *Doctor Faustus*. /10/ But literary criticism—the contemporary poor substitute for indisposed theology—would thus rightly imply that Marlowe's sensibility was unable to do poetic justice to the doctrine of the Fall. For Marlowe would have had to do precisely this in order to make a perfect dramatic success of *Doctor Faustus;* and in his incompetence to do so he was fortified by the sensibility of his age. The author of *Hamlet,* whose genius not only registered but opposed the current of the times, might have succeeded with the subject of Dr. Faustus; but not Marlowe. His intellectual mood was more like Francis Bacon's; and Bacon even believed that mankind would regain Paradise by climbing with empirical resolution to the top of the Tree of Knowledge, of the very tree which the author of the German Faust-book had planted in the center of his story, with Faustus as a second Adam, Mephisto in his old serpentine role, and Helen of Troy as a somewhat shadowy Eve. With Marlowe's poetry, spring has come to the tree which once, in its mythological robustness, would have seemed immune from the seasonal changes. Suddenly it stands in full blossom, and in the absence of ripe apples, Eve launches a thousand ships manned with explorers to explore the enticingly uncharted seas. Who speaks of Faust's sin? The plot, but not the poetry.* /11/

---

[10]Christopher Marlowe: *The First Part of Tamburlaine the Great,* II, vii.

[11]Christopher Marlowe: *The Second Part of Tamburlaine the Great,* II, ii.

[12]*Doctor Faustus,* I, xx, ll. 27–28.

[13]Scheible, II, 973.

[14]*Doctor Faustus,* I, iii, l. 52.

*"But this simply is not true," says, in reply to this remark, Mr. J. B. Steane in his recent book *Marlowe, A Critical Study* (Cambridge, 1964, p. 366)—and an admirably learned, sound, and thoughtful book it is! He had read the above paragraphs about Marlowe's *Doctor Faustus* when they first appeared (*The Listener,* London, January 11, 1962) and decided to add to his work an Appendix in which he takes issue with my interpretation. Had he responded to the somewhat aphoristic utterance above by saying "This is not simply true," I should certainly not have objected. Simple and literal truths are not the domain of the aphoristic, and in the case of my observation it is indeed self-evident that it cannot be literally true. For a poetic drama with a "sinful" plot cannot but speak "poetically" about sin; and Marlowe's tragedy does so, as Mr. Steane reminds us, right at the beginning when

"Would you not agree that the last three or four hundred years have been rather exceptional?" Yes; for in the course of those centuries the poetic truth of *Doctor Faustus* was rendered into the prose of science; and in the process /12/ it shed all the theological inhibitions fostered by the morality of the old Faustian plot—the morality of the Tree of Knowledge. The serpent was chased off its branches, and the tree, bearing sinful fruit no more, received, on the /13/ contrary, its glorification at the hands of the new age. The searching mind and the restless imagination were declared sacrosanct. It was a stupendous revolution, glorious and absurd. Its glories need no recalling. They still lie in state /14/ in our universities, our theaters, and our museums of art and science. But its absurd consequences pursue us with keener vivacity. For we make a living, and shall make a dying, on the once triumphant Faustian spirit, now at the stage of its degeneracy. Piccolo Faustus has taken over the world of the mind. Wherever he sees an avenue, he will explore it—regardless of the triviality or the disaster to which it leads; wherever he sees the chance of a new departure, he will take it—regardless of the desolation left behind. He is so unsure of what *ought* to be known that he has come to embrace a preposterous superstition: everything that *can* be known is also *worth* knowing—including the manifestly worthless. Already we are unable to see the wood for the trees of knowledge; or the jungle either. Galley-slaves of the free mind's aimless voyaging, we mistake our unrestrainable curiosity, the alarming symptom of spiritual tedium, for scientific passion. Most of that which flourishes in these days as "science," said Kierkegaard, is not science but indiscretion; and he and Nietzsche /15/ said that the natural sciences will engineer our destruction.

---

the Chorus introduces the plot and the protagonist. The question is only whether the poetry can be felt to be in profound accord with the opinion it utters:

> And glutted now with learning's golden gifts,
> He surfeits upon cursèd necromancy;
> Nothing so sweet as magic is to him,
> Which he prefers before his chiefest bliss:
> And this the man that in his study sits.

To be sure, Mr. Steane is too intelligent a critic to leave the refutation of my "aphorism" entirely to the obvious *opinion* of the Prologue. The "poetry" has to "enforce" his point; and therefore Mr. Steane contrasts "the harshness of the second line" (in the harshness of which he sees, I take it, a superior or at least a very suggestive poetic quality) to "the easy, oily smoothness of the first": "In the first we slither down the well-oiled road to damnation and in the second can already hear hell call with a roaring for its victim" (pp. 366–67). Is it, I wonder, a confession of deafness when I say that no great poetic noise whatever reaches my ear from that second line of the Chorus? What I do hear with a readier ear comes from Mr. Steane's sentences. It is the small voice of "modern criticism" as it slithers down its well-oiled road to special pleading. Surely, what Mr. Steane does with that, in my judgment, conventionally versified Prologue, is making too much of it. Those verses do their job effectively enough but have not sufficient poetic strength to support the heavy burden of so subtle an interpretation. For would it not be equally convincing—that is, equally unconvincing—if I, in order to "enforce" *my* point, said of those lines that the (not all *that* oily) lyricism of "learning's golden gifts" betrays the poet's spontaneous sympathies, while the "cursèd necromancy" is a poetically uninspired concession to the orthodoxy of the plot? (I am not saying it. But what I am inclined to say is that the only line carrying indisputable conviction, and therefore the only indisputably successful line, is the last: "And this the man that in his study sits.") Mr. Steane thinks I am wrong in assuming that Marlowe's mind, when he wrote *Doctor Faustus*, was "in very much the same state" as it was when he wrote *Tamburlaine* (p. 367), namely in a passionately rebellious one. Yet in discussing the uncertain chronology of Marlowe's works, Mr. Steane himself believes that *Doctor Faustus* follows immediately upon *Tamburlaine*, and believes this because of "the Tamburlaine-like relish of Faustus' early speeches." Moreover, he quotes twice, and twice approvingly, the dating of another scholar who also sees in *Faustus* the successor to *Tamburlaine* because of "the natural kinship between the two states of mind . . ." (p. 119 and p. 355). I do agree with him and therefore must, fortunately, disagree with him when in the Appendix he disagrees with my agreement. But joking apart: the serious problem of interpretation raised by Mr. Steane's valuable book cannot be settled by even the longest footnote. What Mr. Steane perceptively calls "the debate" poetically conducted within Marlowe's mind, the tragic debate between the human mind's claim to autonomous sovereignty and the universe's maneuvers to frustrate the mind's heroic experiments in absolute freedom—this debate, noticeable already in *Tamburlaine*, has certainly acquired a deeper and darker color in *Doctor Faustus*. And Marlowe would not be the remarkable poet he is if it were only the plot of *Doctor Faustus*, and not also its poetry, that showed the deepening and darkening of the soul's anxieties. But this does not, and cannot, mean that the *poetry* of *Doctor Faustus*, insofar as it is Marlowe's own poetry, simply speaks of sin in the manner in which the original Faust-book does speak of it. The prose of the Faust-

Yet even at its splendid beginning, there was something absurdly reckless in the Faustian worship of the human mind and in the mind's absolute emancipation from the vigilance of moral judgment, something hysterically abandoned in thus hallowing of all human faculties just the one which Adam had been taught to fear above all others. The very child of sin was now brought up in the belief that he could do no wrong, and before long Faust's soul was to be kidnaped from Hell and taken to Heaven by the poets as a reward for his mind's insatiability.

Dr. Faustus—is he damned or is he saved? Who would not suspect that the question has been emptied of meaning? Can we, from within our secular sensibilities, make sense of these words at all? Are they more than sonorous echoes from outlived theological solemnities, vibrating with a vague promise or a not so vague intimidation? Where there is now talk of hellfire, what comes to mind with banal inevitability

—for the gods strike those whom they wish to destroy with the sense of the occasion's banality—is, of course, not an eternity of the soul's torment but that thing to end all things, the stale, murderous, unthinkable, unspeakable, banal thing, the Bomb, which, whether or not it will do its work, has done its work already: its very existence frustrates the spirit, its very contemplation corrupts the mind. Indeed, the Bomb does readily come to mind—yet, alas, not quite so readily that which has made it possible: the wings of the eagle that Dr. Faustus took upon himself in order to search out the uttermost parts of heaven and earth, and the in- /16/ nermost parts of life and matter, and to bring them within the reach of man's ever-blundering power, untutored helplessness, and mortal folly. Man, a creature that, upon the irrefutable evidence of his history, cannot control himself, in control of all life on earth: the Faustian Leonardo da Vinci had an inkling of this scientific

---

book knows of no *glorious* Faustus; Marlowe's poetry does. Therefore it is possible to say that it knows of no sin at all. What it does know, sometimes, is the tragic splendor of its hero's *hubris*. Thus, while the original Faust-book achieves, within the limits of its limited art, perfect harmony between the Christian sensibility embodied in its plot and the Christian sensibility embodied in its language, Marlowe's *Doctor Faustus* realizes, insofar as it is poetically successful, the unresolvable tension between what I have called the mind of its language and the mind of its action. It is precisely this tension that makes Marlowe's work—for me as much as for Mr. Steane—incomparably more "exciting" than is the book that Johann Spies published in Frankfurt am Main. For Spies' publication is a *morality,* and Marlowe's drama a *tragedy;* and this has been the focal point of my argument. In saying that much in this essay, I certainly had in mind what is for me the most moving and poetically most accomplished passage in *Doctor Faustus:*

FAUST.   Where are you damn'd?
FAUST.   How comes it then that thou art out of hell?
MEPH.   In hell.
MEPH.   Why this is hell, nor am I out of it:
Think'st thou that I, who saw the face of God,
And tasted the eternal joys of heaven,
Am not tormented, with ten thousand hells,
In being depriv'd of everlasting bliss?

. . .

FAUST.   What, is great Mephistophelis so passionate
For being deprivèd of the joys of heaven?
Learn thou of Faustus manly fortitude,
And scorn those joys thou never shalt possess.
(Scene III, ll. 77–90)

I am quite sure that Mr. Steane is wrong in using these lines as an argument against my argument. Quoting them, he says that "religion asserts itself in many deeply impressive lines of poetry" (p. 366), intending thus to refute my saying that "the truth of the poetic imagination" of *Doctor Faustus* "gives the lie to the religious assertiveness of the plot." When I said what I said, I thought of exactly those lines. For the divine countenance blissfully invoked and agonizingly lost in these verses is not the godhead's face that such Christian painters as Giotto or Fra Angelico painted. It is of Botticelli's making, from a time when he was unable to distinguish between the Blessed Virgin and Aphrodite. "Why this is hell, nor am I out of it"—"this" being "a grove," one has to assume, near Wittenberg—is certainly one of the more unorthodox geographical definitions of Hell. For it is, Wittenberg or no Wittenberg, the Here and Now that is the only scene of Marlowe's delights *and* torments. And it is the *poetry* that says so. Its erotic *tremolo* is unmistakable. It conjures up an Inferno that is closer to young Werther's Hell than to that of the Last Judgment, closer to the Hell of a Faustus who has been enchanted and then deserted by Helen of Troy than to the Hell of a ministering Angel who has betrayed his divine employer. In brief, it is the poetic Hell of Christopher Marlowe, not the theological Hell of St. Augustine or St. Thomas. Without outraging the sensibility of Marlowe's poetry, we may even discern in *Doctor Faustus* anticipatory echoes of Zarathustra's voice as in the second part of Nietzsche's work ("On the Islands of Bliss") he exclaims: *"If* there were gods, how could I endure not being a god?! *Therefore* there are no gods." Religious? Undoubtedly. But at a remove of "ten thousand hells" from the Christian pieties of the first Faust-book.

Hell when he feared to make known his discovery of how to stay under water for long stretches of time, and decided to keep it to himself because men would only use it for making machines with which to carry their wicked designs into the seas.[15]

Yet such timely reflections are still no answer to our question: Is the alternative of salvation or damnation still meaningful? Indeed, the atomic Armageddon would not bring home— home?—the ancient meaning of damnation. It would be, on the contrary, the consummation of absolute meaninglessness—of a meaninglessness which may have acquired demonic properties on its journey from the laboratories of science to the arsenals of power; but if so, then this demonic acquisition could not affect the proud theological meaninglessness of the scientific "truths" in whose pursuit the demons were begotten. For Dr. Faustus, once bitten, soon discovered means with which to overcome any theological shyness: in the war between Heaven and Hell he declared himself a neutral and claimed that the works of his mind were supremely irrelevant to the theological status and destiny of man's soul. He became the "objective observer" of creation and finally of himself. But the genius of invention that possessed him played him a trick. In the long run he willy- /17/ nilly became the inventor of a new kind of Hell: of the dull inferno of a world without meaning for the soul, a world ruthlessly examined by the detached mind and confusedly suffered by the useless passions. If once Dr. Faustus had sold his soul to the Devil for the promise of success in his search for Truth, he now tried to annul the bargain by turning scientist and insisting that in his role as a searcher for Truth he had no soul. Yet the Devil was not to be cheated. When the hour came, he proved that this search, conducted behind the back of the soul, had led to a Truth that was Hell.

Let our Fausts of science, thought, and letters loudly protest against the Bomb! He need not be the Devil who asks: Are all their works testimony to the surpassing worth and sanctity of life, and a refutation and denunciation of anyone who might think life base and senseless enough to render its destruction a matter of irrelevance? Or are not most of their works demonstrations rather of life's ultimate senselessness? And he need not be the Devil who says: There is a connection between the threat of atomic annihilation and that spiritual nothingness with which the mind of the age has been fascinated for so long, between universal suicide and Dr. Faustus's newly discovered damnation—a universe which, as a philosopher who knew his science put it, is "a dull affair," "merely the hurrying of material, endlessly, meaninglessly." "However you disguise it," Whitehead wrote, "this is the practical outcome of the characteristic scientific philosophy which closed the seventeenth century"[16]—and which may close the twentieth, as we, alas, are bound to add, with a /18/ still more practical outcome of Dr. Faustus's witty enterprise to outwit the Devil by creating a Hell of his own.

Damnation or salvation—is there, then, any meaning left in the Faustian theological alternative? It would seem so; and it would not be perverse but only shocking to say that salvation and damnation have entered once again, albeit in unmythological guise, into the major philosophic speculations of the epoch, not to mention its exuberantly depressed and flamboyantly desperate art and literature, and not to give in to the temptation to see the profound and ingenious absurdities of our most recent physical sciences through the eyes of a Dr. Faustus, "theologically" embarrassed again at the end of his journey. Be this as it may, there can be little doubt that it was a quasi-theological apprehension that made Einstein in his old age look askance upon the post-Einsteinian theories in physics which his own discoveries had sent running amuck amid all traditional tenets of logic, reducing to an illusion man's belief that he can form a concrete idea of the physical world he inhabits. But confining ourselves to the philosophic thought of the times—to Heidegger's philosophy of Being, Jaspers's or Heidegger's or Sartre's philosophy of Existence, or Wittgenstein's philosophy of Language—we shall not miss the urgency with which, explicitly or implicitly, they are concerned with man's relatedness or, as the case may be, unrelatedness to

---

[15]Leonardo da Vinci: *Manuscripts,* Codex of the Earl of Leicester (Milan, 1909), folio 22.

[16]A. N. Whitehead: *Science and the Modern World* (Cambridge, 1964), 69.

what truly *is*. Is man, their questioning goes, through any of his innate powers, whether of logical reasoning, feeling, intuition, will, or language, *at one* with the nature of Being, or absurdly estranged from it? Or is he altogether mis- /*19*/ led by his desire to "be" in a meaningful universe, and deluded by his language which, throughout the centuries, has persuaded him that he "is" in a world that makes sense in the manner that logic, grammar, and syntax do? Was Nietzsche right when he suspected that he who spoke of "meaning" was the dupe of linguistic convention? "I fear," he said, "we cannot get rid of God because we still believe in grammar."[17]

Is it so far a cry from such extremities of the human mind to the question of salvation and damnation? Not farther, perhaps, than from a shock to an insight. Those questions of the philosophers are instinct with the sense of an ultimate fate of souls. For what else is salvation if not the fulfillment of a destiny in the integrity of Being, what else damnation if not the agony of a creature without destiny, forever unreachable, in monstrous singularity, by any intimations of a surpassingly sensible coherence, and forever debarred, in his short, uncertain, anxious, and perishable life, from any contact with something lasting, sure, serene, and incorruptible? And if he lives, in this sense, upon his chances of salvation, upon which of his varied and conflicting faculties is this hope founded? Where and when and how *is* he?

In the Christian centuries preceding the appearance of the first Faust-book, there could hardly be any doubt concerning the answer. Man's hope rested upon obedience to the revealed will of the Creator, upon faith in Him, and upon the love of Him. And Reason? Yes, upon Reason too; and some of the Doctors of the Church even believed, not quite unlike Socrates, in the natural propensity /*20*/ of Reason to prove, through the unfolding of its inherent logic, the existence of a supreme guarantor of meaning: God. But this was, for them as much as for Socrates, a Reason which, like the gift of Love, had to be guarded jealously against the ever-present menace of betrayal, corruption, and

sin; for Reason, just like Love, could become a harlot, and, goaded by curiosity and not restrained by wisdom, could enter into complicity with evil. Nicholas of Cusa, the German theologian knew this[18]—two centuries before the scientist Pascal, at the climax of the "scientific revolution," accused the scientific, the "fair Reason," of having corrupted everything with its own corruption;[19] and more than a century before the German Faustus said to the Devil: "But I will know or I will not live, you must tell me."[20]

2

Ever since the villainous Dr. Faustus had been elevated by Marlowe to the rank of a tragic hero, the notion of a possible sin of the mind gradually disappeared. In this, above everything, was the New Age new. What hitherto had been regarded as a satanic temptation, was now felt to be the bait of God; for it was through his mind, his whole mind, that man was blessed. His Reason was the guarantee that he existed in a state of pre-established Harmony with the divine Intelligence which had created the world: the more man knew, the better he knew God. This was the revolutionary theology of the /*21*/ great scientific explorers in the sixteenth and seventeenth centuries. If there was, perhaps, a measure of protective diplomacy in the theological pronouncements of the astronomers, they were yet abundantly sincere, and if they tried to catch the conscience of the Church, they yet expressed the consciousness of the age. "Thanks be unto you, my Lord Creator, for granting me the delight of beholding your creation. I rejoice in the works of your hands. Look down upon my work, the work that I have felt called to do: I have employed all the powers of mind you have given me. To those men who will read my demonstrations, I have revealed the glory of your creation, or as much of its infinite riches as I could comprehend within the narrow limits of my reason." Thus Kepler, concluding the ninth chapter of the fifth book of

[17]Friedrich W. Nietzsche: *Gesammelte Werke*, Musarion-Ausgabe, 23 vols. (Munich, 1922–29), XVII, 73.

[18]Nicholas of Cusa: *Wichtigste Schriften,* ed. and trans. into German by F. A. Scharpff (Freiburg, 1862), 492.
[19]Blaise Pascal: *Pensées,* No. 294 in the numbering of Léon Brunschvicg's edition (Paris, 1897).
[20]Scheible, II, 966.

his *Harmonices mundi.* For the Cartesian age of the *Cogito ergo sum* is now upon us: it is by virtue of thought, by the power of Reason and all its gifts, that I truly exist, truly *am,* integrated into *Esse,* into the Reality of Being.

The greatness of a philosopher does not rest upon the beauty and cogency of his reasoning alone. Unless his grain of truth falls upon ground made ready to receive it by the season of history, it may grow, if grow it will, in pale obscurity. But Descartes reasoned upon the instruction of an approaching summer; and therefore he reasoned so greatly, so vehemently, and so effectively, uninhibited by the flaws easily detectable in all great, vehement, and effective reasoning once the reapers have done with it. He proclaimed that God was no deceiver: God gave us our reason and the instinct that makes us look upon our reason /22/ as the instrument of Truth. Can it have been His will to lead us astray through our rationality? Can we credit Him with such scandalous deception? It was History, it was the disposition and rational credulity of the age, and not pure Reason, that lent persuasiveness to the Cartesian argument. For Reason would suggest that, if this God of the philosophers had dealt so honestly with us in giving us Reason and Descartes, He deceived us grievously with the confounding gift of our passions or indeed with the heart's desire for a peace that passes understanding. Such blasphemies against the rational philosophy were even uttered at the time: by Pascal. For the honest creator of Descartes had capriciously created also the man who would not believe in the God of the rational philosophers, insisting upon the God of Abraham, Isaac, and Jacob. But Pascal's protests remained all but inaudible to the *Zeitgeist,* bent as it was upon its rational enlightenment. *"Cette belle raison corrompue a tout corrompu,"*[21] wrote Pascal; but who would believe that fair Reason, the Cartesian anchor of Being, was corrupt, infecting everything with its corruption? *Doctor Faustus* was done for: the fable, that is; the man was saved. For with his desire to know, he was rooted in the ground of everything that was: in the mind of God. *Cogito ergo sum:* it might be translated "But I will know

or I will not live"—the first Dr. Faustus's injunction to the Devil.

The history of literature was in a mischievous and jesting mood when, in the heyday of the Cartesian empire of the mind, in the middle of the enlightened eighteenth century, it allowed Lessing to try his hand at writing a /23/ *Faust.* We do not know how far he advanced the enterprise. The story goes that he entrusted the finished manuscript to a coachman who never delivered it at the address Lessing gave him. Very likely he was in the service of Satan; for this was, we are told by friends of Lessing's, the first *Faust* that, of course, ended with the Devil's defeat and Faust's salvation. One of its scenes is preserved. In it Faust asks seven spirits of Hell who of them is the speediest, and allots the prize to the little demon who boasts that he is as quick as is the transition from good to evil.[22] Clearly, this scene would be more to the point if the speedy change were from evil to good; for, according to the report, Lessing had turned the wicked Faust of the legend into a mere phantom with which the Lord teased the Devil. The real Faust was immune from human weakness and knew no passion save one: an unquenchable thirst for science and knowledge. And so it came as no surprise to the age of the Enlightenment that at the moment when the hellish hosts were about to dispatch the phantom Faust to Hell, a voice from Heaven enlightened the poor devils about the divine deception: "No, you have *not* triumphed; you have not prevailed over humanity and scholarship: God has not planted the noblest of instincts in man merely in order to make him wretched for ever. He whom you have made your victim is nothing but a phantom."[23]

Perhaps the absconding coachman was a benevolent man, after all. He may have helped Lessing's reputation as a dramatist by the miscarriage of his *Faust.* It was hard enough for Marlowe to come to grips with the subject /24/ of Faust; but to recast it in the mold of the Enlightenment was about as promising as it would have been for the French Revolution to

---

[21]Pascal, *op. cit.,* No. 294.

[22]Included in the seventeenth of Gotthold E. Lessing's *Briefe, die neueste Literatur betreffend,* February 16, 1759.

[23]Letter of von Blankenburg, May 14, 1784. In Lessing's *Gesammelte Werke* (Leipzig, 1858), I, 367 f.

adapt *Macbeth* to the belief that the murder of monarchs was supremely desirable. Lessing himself seems to have recognized this later in his life when, on the occasion of Maler Müller's literary excursion into Faustian territory, he spoke of the impossibility of being in earnest about the story. "Anyone," he said, "who today should attempt to represent such a subject in order to awaken serious belief in it . . . would be courting failure."[24]

This was in 1777; but more than half a century later, in 1831, Goethe, at the age of eighty-two, brought such precarious courting to one of the most celebrated consummations in the history of literature: he sealed a parcel that contained the manuscript of the at last concluded Part II of his *Faust*. The *"Hauptgeschäft,"* the main business of his life, as he was in the habit of referring to it during his last years, was done; or rather, Goethe willed that it should be done: the seal was to protect it above all from his own persistent scruples and dissatisfactions. As death approached, he was determined not to meddle any more with this *Sorgenkind,* this problem-child of his. Also, the parcel was not to be opened for the time being because, as Goethe wrote five days before his death, the hour was "really so absurd and confused" that he was convinced his "long and honest effort in building this strange edifice" would be ill-rewarded. "It would drift, fragments of a shipwreck, towards barren shores and lie buried in the sandy dunes of time."[25] Yet once, during the last /25/ two months of his life, he broke the seal again to read from the manuscript to his beloved daughter-in-law, and afterward promptly confided to his diary that this reading had made him worry once more: should he not have dealt at greater length with "the principal themes"? He had "treated them, in order to finish it all, far too laconically."[26] Touching words! Goethe felt he had been in too much of a hurry when he disposed of his "main business"—over which he had spent more than sixty years. It would almost seem that Lessing was right in suggesting that the age itself did not allow anyone to succeed in writing *Faust;* and Goethe's fears were, of course, justified. Indeed, the "absurd and confused" epoch did not know what to make of his *Faust II,* but this was not altogether the fault of the readers: Goethe's rendering of the "principal themes" was certainly not innocent of confusion.

In many a letter, written during his last months, he warned his friends not to expect too much of the withheld manuscript, above all not to look forward to "any solutions." He referred to his *Faust II* as "these very serious jests," and said that as soon as one problem appeared "to have been solved in it, it revealed, after the manner of the history of world and man, a new one demanding to be puzzled out."[27] True enough; for we are left with no end of puzzles when the curtain comes down upon Faust's entelechy, his immortal self, saved, not without the intervention of the inscrutable grace of God, through having kept his promise to strive eternally and never to content himself with any achievement on earth. But has he really fulfilled the famous condition of his salvation? Not quite, /26/ if we consult the plot; for there it would seem that Faust has been smuggled into Heaven, like precious contraband, by angelic choir boys who have snatched his soul from the Devil, the legal winner, while distracting his attention with their seductive beauty. But if we allow the surpassing poetry of the final scene to make us forget the letter of the wager, then again it would appear as if Faust had merely struggled in vain throughout his life to be rid of what was, regardless of his activities, his inalienable birthright in Paradise. Even by uttering the fatal words of ultimate contentment which, according to the Mephistophelian bet, were to commit his soul to eternal damnation; even by declaring himself satisfied with the last gift of the Devil— the magic transformation of pestiferous swamps into fertile land upon which he would found a republic of free men—he could not prevail upon the Upper Spheres to let him go to Hell. The damning utterance, with which in the end he renounces his eternal striving, is gleefully registered by Mephistopheles, tasting the fruit of victory; but it must have fallen upon deaf ears in Heaven: up there it is held that he has striven eternally all the same, and is therefore,

[24]R. Petsch: *Lessings Faustdichtung* (Heidelberg, 1911), 45.
[25]Letter to Wilhelm von Humboldt, March 17, 1832.
[26]Goethe: *Tagebuch,* January 24, 1832.

[27]Letter to Count Karl Friedrich von Reinhard, September 7, 1831.

with a little helping of divine grace, worth saving.

This, of course, is callous and blasphemous talk. It is unseemly to speak like this about Goethe's *Faust*, which justly has survived the blatant inconsistencies of its plot as one of the greatest poetic creations of the world. But it is a legitimate way of speaking about the *dramatic* and *theological* pretentions of the work. Part II is no drama whatever; and for Goethe to persist—and against what /27/ inhibitions!—in bringing it to a kind of dramatic and theological conclusion was a decision of quixotic heroism. In one sense Lessing stood a better dramatic chance with his abortive *Faust* than Goethe. Lessing's hero was single-mindedly dedicated, against all phantom appearances, to the pursuit of Knowledge and thus was an obedient servant to the God of the philosophers.

But Goethe's Faust? The complexities of his moral character are unresolvable. He is an ungovernable theological problem-child, and presents no simple alternative of good or evil to the Goethean God, who, far from being the God of the philosophers, seems not even to know his own mind. At one point the Devil, who ought to be familiar with God's ways, speaks of the divinity as if indeed the divinity were Lessing:

> *Verachte nur Vernunft und Wissenschaft,*
> *Des Menschen allerhöchste Kraft,*
>
> .   .   .
>
> *So hab ich dich schon unbedingt—,*[28]

meaning that Faust will be his, the Devil's, easy prey through the very contempt in which he holds man's supreme faculties: reason and scholarship. Yet is it true to say that Faust despises knowledge? Have we not learned from his first monologue that, despairing of all merely human knowledge, he has called upon black magic to help his ignorance and initiate his mind into the innermost secret of the world:

> *Dass ich erkenne, was die Welt*
> *Im innersten zusammenhält.*[29] /28/

[28]["Only look down on knowledge and reason
The highest gifts that man can prize,

   .   .   .

And then I have you, body and soul." (see ll. 1416–20 of *Faust*).]
[29]["May grant me to learn what it is that girds
The world together in its inmost being." (see ll. 30–31 of *Faust*).]

However, at many another point it would seem that not only has he done with the pursuit of knowledge, but, contrary to the Devil's enlightened judgment, pleases God by nothing more than his unwillingness ever to be weaned from his *"Urquell,"* the very source of his unreasoning and restless spirit—that spirit which prompts him, in translating the Bible, to reject *logos* as the principle of all things, nurtures in his soul the desire to be cured of all *"Wissensdrang,"* the urge to know, and drives him from his quiet study into the turbulent world to suffer in his own self, unimpaired by knowledge, all the sorrows allotted to mankind, and to rejoice in all its joys. True, as he enters Heaven, the chant of the cherubic boys welcomes him as their teacher; for he has learned much:

> *Doch dieser hat gelernt,*
> *Er wird uns lehren.*[30]

But it is with some concern for the celestial peace of the blessed children that one contemplates the possible substance and manner of his instruction.

Despite all these perplexities and confusions, Goethe's *Faust* is incomparably closer to the original Faust-book than would have been Lessing's. Despite the perplexities? Because of them! For Lessing's *Faust* would have been the generous and nobly simple-minded reversal of the Lutheran writer's morality of knowledge: the sixteenth century's damnation was salvation to the eighteenth. The Devil? Black magic? Bizarre souvenirs, picked up in some unclean exotic place by Reason on its grand tour through History. Goethe was incapable of such enlightenment. His /29/ morality of knowledge was infinitely complex, tangled up as it was, inextricably, with his moral intuition that man was free to commit sins of the mind: he could be lured toward the kind of "truth" that was deeply and destructively at odds both with his true nature and the true nature of the world—a moral offense against the order of creation. And this, surely, is a belief which Goethe shared with the author of the ancient legend of Dr. Faustus. Goethe had the historical impertinence to oppose Newton; and he said, and tried to prove, that Newton was wrong. What he truly meant was that New-

[30]["He will instruct us, instructed before us." (see ll. 964–65 of *Faust*, Part II.)]

tonian physics was false to human nature; and this is what he did say when he was not proudly determined to beat the physicists at their own game. Truth, for him, was what befits man to know, what man is *meant* to know; and he was convinced that the dominant methods of scientific inquiry were "unbecoming" to man, a danger to his spiritual health and integrity because they reduced the phenomena of nature to a system of abstractions within which their true being vanished, yielding nothing to man except empty intellectual power over a spiritually vacuous world: a power that was bound to corrupt his soul. And therefore Goethe said, outrageously: "As in the moral sphere, so we need a categorical imperative in the natural sciences."[31] Provocatively and significantly, he even had the courage to play the crank by expressing uneasiness about microscopes and telescopes: "They merely disturb man's natural vision."[32] And when his Wilhelm Meister for the first time gazes at the stars through a telescope, he warns the astronomers around him of "the morally bad effect" these instru- /30/ ments must have upon man: "For what he perceives with their help . . . is out of keeping with his inner faculty of discernment." It would need a superhuman culture "to harmonize the inner truth of man with this inappropriate vision from without."[33]

3

The perplexities of Goethe's *Faust* are due, firstly, to Goethe's inability—which he had in common with the sixteenth-century writer of the first Faust-book—to divorce the problem of knowledge from the totality of man's nature, to separate the aspiration of his mind from the destiny of his soul; and they are due, secondly, to Goethe's inability—which he had in common with his own age—unambiguously to demonstrate this totality and this destiny, that is to say, to *define Human Being*. This is why his Faust, so confusingly, is now a man who has embarked upon a desperate quest for knowledge, now a man who curses knowledge as a futile

distraction from the passions' crying out for the fullness of life, and now again a man who reaches his *"höchster Augenblick,"* his highest moment, in the renunciation of his search for both knowledge and passionate self-fulfillment, in the resigned acceptance of his social duty to further the commonwealth of man. Because Goethe was the profoundest mind of an epoch dispossessed of any faithful vocabulary for the definition of Human Being, he was possessed by two overpowering and paradoxical intuitions: that man's *being* was definable only through his incessant striving to be- /31/ come what he was not yet and was yet *meant* to be; and that in thus striving he was in extreme danger of losing himself through his impatient and impetuous ignorance of what he was. Therefore, Faust's soul was an unfit object for any clearly stated transaction between Heaven and Hell, and the definitive bargain of the first Faust-book had to be replaced by a wager whose outcome was left in abeyance. If Faust ceased to strive, he would be damned; but he would also be damned if, in his ceaseless quest for himself and his world, he overstepped the elusive measure of his humanity. Yet in the drama itself, Faust could only be damned *or* saved. Thus Goethe had to reconcile himself to the dramatic absurdity of a salvation merited both by the endlessly uncertain voyage and the contented arrival at an uncertain destination. An uncertain destination: for the Faust who believes he has arrived is a blind and deluded man, taking for the builders of a great human future the diggers of his grave. It is as if the honesty of Goethe's precise imagination had forced him in the end to disavow, with terrible poetic irony, the imprecision of the dramatic plot. And indeed, had it not been for the grace of God, or for the Promethean youth who designed the plot of *Faust*, Goethe, in his old age, might well have damned his black magician. For it was the man of eighty-two who wrote the scenes (as if at the last moment to obstruct the workings of salvation) where Faust's involvement in the satanic art is truly black and satanic: the scenes in which his mad lust for power and aggrandizement kills the very goodness and innocence of life, this time without a trace of that saving love which, long ago, /32/ had left him with a chance of ultimate forgiveness even in his betrayal of Gretchen.

[31]Jubiläums-Ausgabe of *Goethe's Works*, 40 vols. (Stuttgart and Berlin, n.d.), XXXIX, 72. (Abbreviated J.A.)
[32]*Ibid*. IV, 229.
[33]*Ibid*. XIX, 138 f.

When, after all the paraphernalia and phantasmagoria of imperial politics and high finance, of science laboratories, classical incantations and mystical initiations, of which most of *Faust II* is composed, the last act begins, we seem to be back, unexpectedly, in the world of Gretchen: in the shadow of linden trees, at the little house and chapel of a faithful old couple, Philemon and Baucis, contentedly living near the sea on what is now Faust's estate. Just then they are visited by a mysterious wanderer whom many years ago they had hospitably put up and helped after the shipwreck he suffered in the nearby shoals. Now he has come to thank them once again and to bless them. Through this scene we enter the realm of inexhaustible ambiguity in which Faust's end and transfiguration are to be enacted. The neighborhood of the two old people's cottage has been much improved by Faust's land-winning enterprise. Where once the stranger had been cast ashore, there stretch now green fields far into what used to be shallow sea. This certainly seems to be to the good, and Philemon, the husband, praises the change lyrically and admiringly; but his wife views it with misgivings. Surely, it was a miracle, but one that was performed in godlessness. Floods of fire were poured into the ocean and human lives recklessly sacrificed in order to construct a canal. Moreover, Faust, the owner of the new land, seems to be, for no good reason, intent upon driving them from their house and garden; and so they all enter the chapel, ring its bell, and kneel down to pray. And /33/ as Faust, in the park of his palace, hears the bell—the very same "silvery sound" which had once announced to the lost traveler on the beach the closeness of his rescuers (and it was, we should remember, "the celestial tone" of church bells that on a certain Easter morning had called Faust back from desperation and made him withdraw from his lips the suicidal cup of poison)—as Faust now hears the sound of simple piety ring out from the hill, he curses it as a reminder of the petty limits imposed upon his power, and in a senseless rage commands Mephistopheles to remove the couple to another place. They and their guest perish as Faust's order is carried out, and house and chapel go up in flames.

Yet while Faust's most damnable crime is being committed, the scene changes to the tower of his palace where the watchman Lynceus intones the song that is one of Goethe's most beautiful lyrical creations:

Zum Sehen geboren,
Zum Schauen bestellt . . .[34]

ecstatically affirming the beauty of everything his eyes have ever seen—"whatever it be":

Ihr glücklichen Augen,
Was je ihr gesehn,
Es sei, wie es wolle,
Es war doch so schön![35]

It is hard to imagine profounder depths for poetic irony to reach than it does at this moment of change from that show of absolute evil to this absolute affirmation. And what vast expanses of irony are compressed into /34/ the brackets which Goethe inserted after the exultant celebration of the world's beauty—a beauty which no evil can diminish. "Pause" is written between those brackets. Pause, indeed! For the watchman's recital continues with the observation that his duties on the tower are not only "aesthetic" in nature; and instantly he registers "the abominable horror" threatening him from out of "the darkness of the world":

Nicht allein mich zu ergetzen,
Bin ich hier so hoch gestellt;
Welch ein greuliches Entsetzen
Droht mir aus der finstern Welt!—[36]

from out of that dark world where Faust's servant, Mephistopheles, in the course of executing his master's megalomaniac orders, unthinks, as it were, the very thoughts of charity, compassion, and peace, shattering the luminous sphere whence, by Goethe's symbolic design, had once emerged the shipwrecked stranger. It is as if the "whatever it be" of that absolute affirmation had not been meant to include the evil of a world ravished by the black magic of godless power. And as in the whirls of smoke that drift from the burning house, the demons of human failure form—like avenging Erinyes appointed by the slain wanderer—and as one of them, the spirit of Anxiety, approaches Faust to strike with

[34][See text, Part II, ll. 242–43.]
[35][See text, Part II, ll. 254–57.]
[36][See text, Part II, ll. 258–61.]

blindness him who had "run through life blindly," his eyes are at last opened; and he utters a wish that is not a magic conjuration but almost a prayer: /35/

Könnt' ich Magie von meinem Pfad entfernen,
Die Zaubersprüche ganz und gar verlernen . . .[37]

If only he could rid himself of magic and utterly forget how to invoke it! There is more consistent drama in the brief sequence of these scenes than emerges from the bewildering totality of the poem, more dramatic occasion for either damning Faust because of his evil-doing as a magician, or for saving him because of his desire to abandon the evil practice.[38]

It is the theme of black magic through which Goethe's *Faust* is linked, in almost a sixteenth-century fashion, with Goethe's morality of knowledge. What, we may well ask, can black magic mean to Goethe's sophisticated mind? The black magic of *Faust* is the poetically fantastic rendering of Goethe's belief that evil arises from any knowing and doing of man that is in excess of his "being." Man aspiring to a freedom of the mind fatally beyond the grasp of his "concrete imagination," seeking power over life through actions that overreach the reaches of his soul, acquiring a virtuosity inappropriately superior to his "virtue"—this was Goethe's idea of *hubris,* his divination of the meaning of black magic. Absolute activity, activity unrestrained by the condition of humanity, he once said, leads to bankruptcy;[39] and everything that sets our minds free without giving us mastery over ourselves is pernicious."[40] He saw something spiritually mischievous, something akin to black magic, in every form of knowledge or technique that "unnaturally" raises man's power above the substance of his being. In his *Faust* black magic almost always works the perverse miracle of such "de-substantiation." /36/ Whether Faust conjures up the very spirit of Nature and Life, the *Erdgeist,* only to realize in distracted impotence that he cannot endure him; whether the body politic is being corrupted by insubstantial paper assuming the credit that would only be

due to substantial gold; whether Homunculus, a synthetic midget of great intellectual alacrity, is produced in the laboratory's test tube, a brain more splendidly equipped for thinking than the brains that have thought it out: the creature capable of enslaving his creators; or whether Faust begets with Helena, magically called back from her mythological past, the ethereal child Euphorion, who, not made for life on earth, is undone by his yearning for sublimity—throughout the adventures of his Faust, Goethe's imagination is fascinated, enthralled, and terrified by the spectacle of man's mind rising above the reality of his being and destroying it in such dark transcendence. This, then, is black magic for Goethe: the awful art that cultivates the disparity between knowledge and being, power and substance, virtuosity and character; the abysmal craft bringing forth the machinery of fabrication and destruction that passes understanding.

4

In the last two *Fausts* of literary history, Paul Valéry's and Thomas Mann's, the gulf, most dreaded by Goethe, between knowledge and the integrity of being, between virtuosity and the sanity of substance, has become so wide that even the Devil seems to be lost in it: for the human soul, in the hunt for which the Devil has always sought /37/ his livelihood, is in an extreme state of malnutrition. But the mind lives in formidable prosperity and has no need to raise loans from Hell for indulging even its most extravagant ambitions.

Valéry has called his sequence of variations on the ancient theme *Mon Faust;* and indeed his Faust is more *his,* more the possession of the author who has created the frigid paragon of aesthetic intellectuality, Monsieur Teste, than he is the Devil's. Yet this is by no means to the advantage of his spiritual prospects: these are as gloomy as can be. For if he does not lose his soul, this is only because he has none to lose. In the affluence of his intellectual riches, he *is* the lost soul, just as Mephistopheles is a lost devil in the face of a human world overflowing with self-supplied goods of the kind that was once the monopoly of Hell. The Hell-supplied wings of the eagle are in demand no more. As Ivan Karamazov before him, so Valéry's Faust shows the Devil that he is an anachronism: his exist-

[37][See text, Part II, ll. 258–59.]
[38]*Faust II,* Act V, Scenes "Offene Gegend," "Palast," "Tiefe Nacht," and "Mitternacht."
[39]J.A., IV, 225.
[40]*Ibid.* 229.

ence was based solely on the unenlightened be-lief that "people weren't clever enough to damn themselves by their own devices."[41] But those days have gone. "The whole system," Faust says to Mephistopheles, "of which you were the linch-pin, is falling to pieces. Confess that even you feel lost among this new crowd of human beings who do evil without knowing or caring, who have no notion of Eternity, who risk their lives ten times a day in playing with their new ma-chines, who have created countless marvels your magic never dreamt of, and have put them in the reach of any fool. . . ."[42] And even if Mephistopheles were not on the point of being starved out of the /38/ universe for want of human souls, this Faust would still have nothing to gain from a bargain with him. His intellec-tion is as strong as he could wish, and he knows what he does when he dismisses his hellish vis-itor as, after all, "nothing but a mind";[43] and therefore, he adds: "We could exchange func-tions."[44] It is as if he had said: *"Cogito ergo sum in profundis"*—"I think and thus I am in Hell already"; or "I know and therefore I will not live"—the uncanniest cancellation of the first Faust-book as well as of the Cartesian ontol-ogy. Moreover, the passion with which Goethe's Faust assails the innermost secret of the world is dissolved by Valéry in *ennui,* the unkeen ex-pectation of an emptily precise answer to be given by some Homunculus or electronic bore.

If Valéry's Mephisto, the "pure mind," has become unemployable as a seducer in a society of satiated intellects and emasculate souls, Thomas Mann has found a role for him which brings the literary history of Dr. Faustus to a conclusion that is definitive in its perversity: the Devil is now the giver of a soul. It is he who supplies feeling and passionate intensity to a Faustian genius whose soul and being had been frozen into rigidity by the *cogitare,* the chill of intellectual abstraction, and whose art was, therefore, the art of purely speculative virtu-osity. The musician Leverkühn, Thomas Mann's Dr. Faustus, has, like the epoch whose music he

composes, despaired of any pre-established har-monies between the human mind and the truth of the world; and having lost any such faith, he exists in a state of total despair. Not for him the music of "subjective harmony," the music of souls sup- /39/ ported by the metaphysical as-surance that in their depths they mirror the eter-nal and sublime verities of Creation. For Lever-kühn, life, to its very core, that is, to its innermost void, is absurd and chaotic; and if the human mind goes on, absurdly and yet stub-bornly, to insist upon some semblance of order, this order has to be constructed from nothing by the sheer obstinacy of the abstractly logical im-agination. Therefore, this imagination reflects only itself and not some dreamt-of consonance between the self and cosmic harmonies. Beetho-ven was mistaken; and so Leverkühn announces his desperate plan to compose a piece of music that would take back, "unwrite," the greatest of all musical celebrations of the "subjective har-mony," the Ninth Symphony: the Ninth Sym-phony is not true, or true no more. But if it is not true, then neither is Goethe's *Faust,* the poetic equivalent in subjective harmony to that choral dithyramb; and just as Thomas Mann makes his composer revoke the Ninth Symphony, so he himself revokes Goethe's *Faust* by writing the book of Faust's damnation. For Goethe's *Faust,* despite its unresolvable doubts and am-biguities, and despite its holding back, confusing, and obstructing redemption until it can only be had in a riot of poetic contradictions— Goethe's *Faust* yet embodies the faith that Faust is saved: for he aspires to that self-realization through which, by metaphysical necessity, he loyally realizes the will, order, and ultimate pur-pose of the cosmos itself. It is by virtue of the "subjective harmony" that Faust's infinite en-thusiasm, time and again confounded, must yet triumph in the end over Mephisto's /40/ ironi-cal, cold, and logical mind—the supremely de-tached mind that on one great theological occa-sion had won its detachment, once and for all, by denying the design of Creation.

Precisely such a mind is owned by Leverkühn; and therefore the music he writes is detached, ironical, cold, and logical, composed within a mathematically austere system which has been ingeniously calculated to conceal, or transcend,

[41]Paul Valéry: *Plays.* Trans. by David Paul and Robert Fitzgerald in the *Collected Works,* 13 vols., Bollingen Series (New York, 1960), III, 41.

[42]*Ibid.* 39.

[43]*Ibid.* 30.

[44]*Ibid.* 29.

or hold at bay, the chaos within and without, the subjective dissonance that has taken the place of the subjective harmony. Indeed, it is a soul-less music; and the most scandalous idea in Thomas Mann's scandalously profound book is this: a soul is finally bestowed upon this music by the Devil. When Mephistopheles calls on the composer to ratify the pact long since concluded in Leverkühn's embrace of the prostitute who gave him the "disease of genius," the visitor from Hell remarks: "They tell me that the Devil passes for a man of destructive criticism." It is, of course, Goethe who has made him believe this by portraying Mephistopheles as cynicism incarnate, out to distract Faust's enthusiastic inspiration. But now the Devil emphatically disclaims this reputation: "Slander and again slander. . . . What he wants and gives is triumph over it, is shining, sparkling, vainglorious unreflectiveness!"[45] And he does fulfill his promise: Leverkühn's last and greatest work, "The Lamentation of Dr. Faustus," the choral work he composes on the verge of madness and in protest against the Ninth Symphony, using as his text the first German Faust-book, is even stricter in form and more ingenious in calculation /41/ than his preceding compositions; and yet it is, for the first time, abandoned self-expression, an ecstasy of desperation, a panegyric of the inner abyss. "Subjective harmony," the lost soul of music, is recovered—a soul without hope. For the re-established harmony is now fixed between the subject and that dispensation by which he is unredeemable. "Being" has been returned to "doing," and substance to virtuosity: but "being" means being damned, and the substance is the stuff of Hell. This music is the mystical consummation of distraught godlessness, the emergence of a soul from the alchemy of its negation. "After all," says Thomas Mann's Devil, "I am by now [religion's] sole custodian! In whom will you recognize theological existence if not in me?"[46]

Thus ends the eventful story that has led from the damnation of Dr. Faustus through his liberation to his damnation. It was Goethe's desire to arrest it in the middle of its journey by teaching the "insatiable Speculators" his morality of knowledge. His failure deserves the most thoughtful attention.

Goethe would have found much to love in the story, written 2,500 years ago, of a Chinese sage who once met a simple man, his better in wisdom. The sage, seeing how the man watered his field in a very primitive manner, asked him: "Don't you know that there is a contraption called a draw-well, a kind of machine that would enable you to water a hundred such little fields in one day?" And he received this reply: "I have heard my teacher say: He who uses machines, conducts his business like a machine. He who conducts his business like a machine, will soon /42/ have the heart of a machine. He who has the heart of a machine has lost all certainties of the spirit. He who has lost the certainties of the spirit must needs sin against the meaning of life. Yes, I do know such machines as you speak of, but I also know why I shall not use them."

Undoubtedly, Goethe would have applauded the wisdom of this story. Yet the "modern man" in him would also have known that he could not live by its lesson. After all, he greeted with enthusiasm the plans for the Panama Canal and found no more fitting symbol for Faust's renunciation of magic than his assuming the position of a welfare engineer. The ambiguities of his *Faust* provide the measure of his lasting dilemma, a dilemma that is bound to stay with us. But the refusal to contemplate it on a level beyond the expediencies of science, technology, and statesmanship would deny the essential freedom in which we may still—no, not resolve the tension but sustain it without despairing. Where nothing can be done, the deed is in the enhancement of being. If, as even Goethe's *Faust* might teach us, grace cannot be merited by man, he may yet try to earn his hope. Goethe's intuition of the "categorical imperative" that is needful in the pursuit of knowledge can be articulated but vaguely. Yet this is no reason for preferring the exact prospect opened by that scientific earnestness and moral frivolity which would hear nothing of the inexact morality of knowledge. For that exact prospect is monstrous in its exactitude: a race of magician's apprentices who, as

[45]Thomas Mann: *Doctor Faustus,* trans. from the German by H. T. Lowe-Porter (New York, 1948), 237.
[46]*Ibid.* 243.

the one in Goethe's poem *"Der Zauberlehrling,"* are about to perish in the floods they themselves have released by the magic formula; /43/ a horde of cave-dwellers, their souls impoverished by machines and panic helplessness, sheltering themselves from the products of their titanically superior brains.

It is a vision from the first German Faust-book. Dr. Faustus was taken to the place he had bargained for and, so we read, "thereafter it became so sinister in his house that no one could live in it."[47] /44/

[47]Scheible, II, 1068.

Hans Egon Holthusen

The World Without Transcendence

> One of the finest and most splendid gifts of God is music. Satan is very hostile to it. With it many a temptation can be repelled.
> —Martin Luther

Thomas Mann's new novel, entitled "Doctor Faustus. The Life of the German Composer Adrian Leverkühn, Related by a Friend," is based on motifs that connect the following groups of themes: theology, demonology, and music; the problem of music with the problem of the figure of Faust and the latter again with the psychology of "the German"; the problem of genius with the motif of selling one's soul to the devil and this in turn with the essence of music on the one hand and the problematic nature of the German soul and German history on the other. "If Faust is to be the representative of the German soul, he ought to be musical," the author said in a speech delivered at the Library of Congress in Washington in 1945. At once he went on to say, with reference to the latest catastrophe of German history: "such musicality of the soul is dearly bought in another sphere—the political, the sphere of human living together." In the baleful light of the Third Reich's descent into hell, Faust's pact with the devil becomes, for the speaker, a metaphor of the real meaning of German history; and nothing can inhibit him from declaring to his American listeners with the most complete candor that "today"—that is, in the spring of 1945—"the devil is literally bearing away the soul of Germany."

What meaning, what character, what positional value (*Stellenwert*) does the statement have, that contains the intellectual germ, the basic notion of this book—the statement that Faust really ought to be musical? To what region of cognition, what order of the knowable shall we assign it? When genius dips its hand into the water of truth, it forms a sphere, as it did in the pure hand of the Hindu woman in Goethe's "Pariah" trilogy:[1] a creative idea is born. Goethe's "graven form that develops as it lives," his *"Ur*-plant," his "primal phenomenon"[1] —those are "ideas." /123/ Schiller's "freedom," Leibniz's "monad," Pascal's "argument of the wager"—those are ideas. But the statement that Faust really ought to be musical is an *aperçu,* a bon mot, a feat of witty association. Like everything else which the thinker Thomas Mann has produced, it comes under the category of cultural criticism. Even the assumption, agreed upon as a matter of course, that Faust is the symbol of the German soul, is a thesis of cultural criticism of a very relative, perspectivist sort. It may well have obtained for only a few decades; it has become almost a vulgar preconception today; and moreover, it loses every shred of meaning when it is applied to National Socialism and its brainless deviltries. Neither for Marlowe nor for Valéry can the Faust material have had a specifically "German" character; nor for Goethe either. He would have been the

[1]The "Pariah" trilogy is a lyric of Goethe's; a "primal phenomenon" is an archetype.

last to interrupt the process of transforming personal experiences into universal symbols of humanity by reflections about nationality. Only the literary historian and critic of culture can derive a national psychology from the German tradition of the Faust motif.

The Faust figure of the old chapbooks, that was seized upon, consumed, and transformed by Goethe's immense imaginative power and reborn as the vessel of Goethean ideas, is an abstract mythic pattern for Thomas Mann; he draws his analytical, psychological, essayistic circles around it, just as he did around the figure of Goethe in *The Beloved Returns* and the Biblical narrative in the Joseph novels. Of the "genuine" Faust nothing remains but a late-medieval-Lutheran, demonological-neurotic atmosphere. The true crystallization point is the aforesaid notion of the cultural critic, with which he ingeniously connects the notion of the Germans' characteristic musicality. Faustian atmosphere is mingled with musical atmosphere. Thus a typical Mannian work results: for it has always been the forte of his insinuating talent to dissolve traditional ideas of such concepts as are "in the air" into atmosphere, or as he once called it himself, "atmospherialia"; to reduce everything to one level by psychologizing; and then, ironically or emphatically, to link everything up with everything else. This is the secret of his stylistic brilliance in general and his famous ironies—set in the subjunctive—in particular: for example, the secret of Naphta, the Jesuitical-Jewish terrorist, who proclaims the proletarian *civitas dei,* or Gregorian Marxism. It is a style of thinking and writing whose conspicuous features may be characterized as *interesting:* the style of an omnipresent intellect, restlessly experimenting, combining and pondering, most subtle, most responsive to stimuli—indeed dependent on stimuli and at times so much at their mercy as to lose all autonomy.

From the beginning the theme of music occurs in Thomas Mann's work like a leitmotif. In *Buddenbrooks* it plays a decisive role, as in the *novella* "Tristan" and the *Reflections of a Nonpolitical Man.* It is inherent in the "Schopenhauerian" triad—"music, pessimism, humor" — /*124*/ that young Thomas Mann likes to strike in defining the mood of his own life, and in the sense of "the Cross, death, and the grave" that he shares with young Nietzsche and occasionally conjures up, in the name of suffering and morality, against Renaissance aestheticism and the brutal or hectic glorification of life. As Wagnerian music it simultaneously represents the principles of modernity and of conservatism, it stands for a chromatic, analytic way of thinking, a thinking in enharmonic changes and atmospheric mixtures, and for a gloomy nonpolitical and anti-democratic stance. In *Buddenbrooks* little Hanno's musicality moves into a sphere of decadence, alienation from the burgher's world, illness, dissolution, and death. In the *Reflections,* at the occasion of the famous analysis of *Palestrina,*[2] music appears as a Pfitznerian "sympathy with death," a motif that is united simultaneously with a German-romantic sort of nationalism, affording the author the opportunity to cite, with emphasis, a "defiant" dedication of Pfitzner's to Grand Admiral von Tirpitz.[3] In the same book certain Faust-motifs related to music are already to be found: above all the linking of music to theology, religion, and the spirit of Luther and the Reformation. "The musical education of the German," we read there, "began with Martin Luther, a pedagogue challengingly national in his basic character, theosophist, religious teacher, and musician in one; and so very much so, that in his case musicality and religiosity can hardly be kept separate, that one is equated with the other in his soul—as has been characteristic of the Germans from that time on." Typical sentiments of the reformer are cited, this one for instance: "Music I have always been fond of. It is a fine, hearty gift of God and closely related to theology." And the remark that this art is "a semidiscipline and taskmaster, making people milder and more gentle, better behaved and more reasonable."

Theology and religion, closely linked to music as they are, are viewed at the time (1917) in the light of a well-disposed conservatism, even though their contents, however opposed to nationalism Mann's intention was, appear diluted or volatilized by an extreme rationalism. "Religion," we read, "the place of worship, this sphere of the extraordinary, sets free the human

[2][An opera by Hans Pfitzner, first performed in 1917.]

[3][Chief of the German navy in the first World War, and an outspoken imperialist.]

element and makes it beautiful"; and elsewhere occurs the fantastic sentence: "Belief in God is the belief in love, life, and art." As to the Reformation, the forty-year-old Thomas Mann discovers that he is induced "to revere an event of genuinely German majesty" in it, which taught the German "to bear metaphysical freedom more universally." What French history lacks is nothing but a Reformation at the right time, and the revolution of 1789—here the author follows Carlyle's view—is "only the vengeful return of Protestantism, which had been rejected two hundred years before." For "freedom" here is not on the side of the Jacobins and the political West, but on that of Luther, Goethe, and /125/ Bismarck, whom Thomas Mann calls a "second Luther, a really great event in the history of German self-experience, a gigantic German fact, defiantly set off against European antipathy." "Freedom" means here a musical, reformational, antipolitical frame of mind, that insists on "denying the correspondence between the spirit and political life, or rather, recognizing the noncorrespondence of the two."

Music then, to return to the beginning of this labyrinthine and infinitely extensible chain of motifs, is the opposite of Enlightenment, "progress," politics, the attitude of the "eggheads of civilization" (*Zivilisationsliteratentum*),[4] and democracy. It is the German antidote to the rhetorical bourgeois of 1789, to revolutionary "virtue," to the "renascence of the Jacobin," and the "moralizing racket (*Moralbonzentum*) of the sentimental, terroristic, republican type." It is the "image and artistic-spiritual reflection of German life itself. "Music" is the quintessence of all German superiority, the battle cry of an enthusiastic nationalism. In its name Thomas Mann, inspired by warlike patriotic ardor, raises the Germans to the state of transfiguration—the same Germans whom, according to his testimony thirty years later, the devil will bear away. On the one hand he glorifies them in the image of Eichendorff's Ne'er-do-well,[5] who is a symbol of

"pure humanity, humanely romantic humanity, to say it again: of the German"; while he encourages them on the other hand to stride forward, armed with Krupp cannons, "on the imperial path," bravely affirming their own aggressiveness. "The world-people of the spirit, having attained exuberant physical power, had drunk a long draught of the fount of ambition; it desired to be a world-people if God called upon it, *the* world-people of reality[6]—by means, if it had to be (and obviously it had to) of a breakthrough by sheer force."

"Music is a daemonic realm," the speech on Germany asserts (in 1945); "it is the most calculated order and chaotic antireason at once, rich in gestures of conjuration and incantation; it is the magic of numbers,[7] simultaneously the art farthest from reality and yet the most passionate, abstract, and mystic." Music is "calculation raised to mystery"; it is "energy per se, energy itself," as young Leverkühn once remarks, "but not as an idea, but in its reality. I would point out to you that that is almost the definition of God," he adds, without observing that he is irresponsibly overinterpreting a purely formal analogy, merely to create a "theological" mood. Kierkegaard's essay on Don Juan is mentioned, both in the speech referred to and in *Faustus* itself, but it is only the /126/ theological-erotic "demonologic" *atmosphere* of this work which Thomas Mann makes use of, while its subtle and severe dialectic, its system of exactly distinguished categories fades into vagueness. "A highly theological affair, music," the devil says in his long discussion with Leverkühn, which is the nucleus of the book, "just as sin is, as I am." To put it briefly and bluntly, music is possessed by the devil. Leverkühn is driven to the peak of his musical genius by the devil, who has stolen into his entelechy via a syphilitic infection. Music, which Mann expressly praised in the *Reflections,* using Luther's words, as a "gift of God," has been stealthily transformed to a gift of the devil. It is he who gives the hero "a whole hourglass full of the devil's creative time, yes, who even presents him with particular melodies to fulfil his obligations under the pact. At

---

[4]A term coined by Thomas Mann early in the First World War to express his bitter rejection of those German liberal or leftist intellectuals, above all his brother Heinrich, who took a pro-Western position.

[5]The charming wanderer whose sobriquet appears in the title of the romantic novella, *Aus dem Leben eines Taugenichts* (1826).

[6]*I.e.,* the dominant world power.

[7]Mann was fascinated by numerology throughout his life. Here he refers to the mathematical relations between various notes of the scale.

one point, while reflecting on his beloved friend, the chronicler of Adrian's life asks himself: Was it one of those melodic illuminations, to which he was—I'd almost say—exposed in those days, and through which powers of whom I wish to know nothing kept their word . . . ?" Music therefore, which the author still loves passionately, now as in other days, is in league with the Evil One. Music, of which Luther said that "Satan was very hostile" to it; music, to which men have always ascribed the power to calm, make blissful, bear them upward; music, which the most ancient wisdom and mythology of mankind has quite decidedly associated with the spirit of joy, with piety and love, with the "harmony of the spheres," with the cosmogonic Eros. Was not music always the smile of the soul? Were not even the wild beasts calmed by Orpheus? Did he not move the *underworld,* "humanize" it, make it responsive to his amorous complaint?

Something "daemonic," something reminiscent of Goethe's Earth-Spirit, amoral in its natural might, does no doubt inhere in every created power, in all energies and drives of man, in all feeling, loving, and knowing, and especially in all artistic productivity. But if one wishes to understand the concept in that fashion, then the demonic is innocent, sheer existent force and vital power, and one cannot simply equate it arbitrarily with evil by blurring the boundaries between the various categories. On the other hand, if one wants to subsume under it certain enervating, intoxicating effects, hostile to discipline and filling timid moralists with dismay, the concept may perhaps be applicable to Wagner, Strauss, or certain effects of Bruckner's brasses which stir up nervous ecstasies; but it cannot be extended to Beethoven's joyous allegros and certainly not to the "Goldberg Variations," to the "St. Matthew Passion," to Mozart.

If finally the term demonic is intended to have reference to the general "irrationality" of music, its free-floating (*gegenstandslos*) passionateness and emotional power, its sweet, supermoral tenderness, its "bovine warmth," as Thomas Mann puts it, then suspicion is cast on its relation to love, its character as love; love is made demonic or even diabolical. /127/ On this point too, as will appear, Thomas Mann has not been inconsistent. Here a problem arises which can perhaps

best be characterized by the question: "Has reason alone been baptized? Are the passions heathen?" Kierkegaard, who used this quotation from Young as a motto for his *Either-Or,* in his hypersensitivity about the tension between the ethical and aesthetic pole of his thinking, characterized the "sensual brilliance," the "uninsulated eroticism" of music as demonic: a most brilliant contribution to the thorough understanding of the problem of Don Giovanni. One should however counter Kierkegaard's notion with a certain amount of the medieval realist's fidelity to the Creation and joy in sheer existence, unless one is willing to let love itself and music in general appear in a bad light.

Regarding Thomas Mann's concepts, it is easy to sink into a bottomless pit if one wants to fix, circumscribe, and place one of them. His concepts have no definite boundaries, no locus, no region where they obtain without ambiguity. As concepts they are not to be taken at all seriously, they are to be understood only as continuously varying atmospheric values and psychological stimulants. Mann, with his enormous stylistic energy, devotes great care to combining them, reworking them, and employing them effectively. A sort of superessayism is at work with an unbounded, unscrupulous lust for making new associations or combinations, an ambiguous and subtle art of distorting and confusing concepts, of arranging them in a montage. Thus it is possible that, according to the mood of the author, music appears at one time as "a gift of God," at another as black magic; the nature of the Germans at one time appears transfigured, in the light of a humane romanticism, at another as miserably abandoned to the pact with the devil.

Music, theology, the Reformation, and the problem of the German are again combined in a chain of motifs, and only in this context does the "demonism" of music reveal its entire meaning. Luther, the "musical theologian," "a gigantic incarnation of the German character (*Wesen*)," still has quite the same importance as before, but now the accent lies in the other aspects of his character: the "choleric and churlish," and his passionate, immediate relation to Satan. As evidence of his spirit we get to hear, this time, only violent phrases that leave the content of his theology completely obscure: "The devil's sow, the Pope," and similar things.

His modern parody and caricature is Ehrenfried Kumpf, professor of theology at Halle, a foul-minded "man of the people" and a devil of a fellow, who hurls a roll at a nonexistent Old Nick, roaring out *"Apage!"* He is an "all-out nationalist of the Lutheran type," who raves to his students about "Hell and its pit" in a strangely mannered, very crude Old German with sixteenth-century reminiscences, and replaces theology with demonology. The meaning of Lutheran exorcism is perverted and reversed by deleting the God-concept of Luther's impassioned prayers and leaving Satan as the only "theological" figure. /*128*/

Side by side with Kumpf teaches Eberhard Schleppfuss, the *Privatdozent*[8] in the psychology of religion, an even more cunning champion of the idea of the devil. He has settled upon the psychological aspect of religious life—more precisely, the sexual, neurotic aspect—as his field; he senses in the objects of his discipline "only the almost irresistible provocation to defilement," only "the stimulus to blasphemy which emanates from the sacrosanct," and ostentatiously relates unpleasant and sadistically erotic tales about the witch-burning period. In this case the science of divine matters has become spiritual lewdness. All interest in theology seems to be born of bitter resentment against what is holy. The devil is more interesting than God, and the Satanic Nay is more stimulating intellectually than the triumphant Yea of Creation and Revelation. The lower element is mobilized against the higher; psychological knowledge supplants ontological and metaphysical knowledge. Sigmund Freud is proven correct, over against the mighty tradition of occidental theology from Augustine and Thomas Aquinas to Luther, Pascal, and Kierkegaard. Transferred to a critique of moods, this attitude means: melancholy is truer than joy; when melancholy one perceives things as they are.

All this, devised most slyly and with great technical competence and insinuatingly presented, amounts to theology's being compromised as a diabolic science, which then in turn involves music's being made suspect as an art very close to theology and the demasking of the Germans as a people especially vulnerable to theology and music. The element of the German character evoked in the cosmos of *Doctor Faustus* is not the "classic" which rejoices in reason and form, the bright, the humane: not Mozart[9] and Goethe, not Kant, Schiller, Lessing, or Hölderlin. Nor was it the lovably romantic, the element which appeals to the inwardness of one's nature: Eichendorff, Schubert,[9] Caspar David Friedrich,[10] and Mörike have no part in it. The strength and grandeur, devotion and ardor of the German Middle Ages play no part. Not a word is said of all this. But the element of violent immensity, of fatal *hubris* and perilous temptation is conjured up: everything which could be by hook or crook connected with Satan —thus the "Faustian," thus Luther, certain of Beethoven's traits, above all Nietzsche, whose career has to serve, even in many details, as a pattern for the biography of Adrian Leverkühn. Here "German" connotes above all the atmosphere of late Gothic architecture and of the age of the Reformation—to be sure without the concept of God of those periods—a world full of apocalyptic unrest, hysterical eccentricity, and syphilitic infection. These things are "German": "the urgent pilgrimage to the Holy Blood at Niklashausen in the Tauber valley, children's crusades and bleeding Hosts, famine, the Peasants' /*129*/ Revolt, war and the pestilence in Cologne, meteors, comets, and significant omens, stigmatized nuns, crucifixes . . . A fine time, devilishly German time!"

On this occasion it is not Weimar that is "German," but Kaisersaschern, Leverkühn's home town, Lübeck[11] transfigured, a Lübeck shifted to the region of Naumburg, the landscape of Nietzsche, Bach, Händel, and Thomas Münzer;[12] it is a town psychoanalytically understood, of which it is said: "In the air there was still something of the attitude of the human spirit in the last decades of the fifteenth century, the hysteria of the dying Middle Ages, something of a latent psychological epidemic." And further: "Symptomatic of such archaic, neu-

---

[8]Roughly the equivalent of an American assistant professor.

[9]Austrian, not German.

[10]A romantic painter, 1774–1840.

[11]Thomas Mann's birthplace.

[12]A German Anabaptist, much to the left of Luther during the Reformation; beheaded after the defeat of the Peasants' Revolt.

rotic depths and the secret psychological disposition of a town are the many 'originals,' ec-
centrics, and harmless half-crazy types who live
within its walls and make up the image of the
place, as it were, like the old buildings."

Against this atmosphere, where Luther, music,
and the devil are at home, where Nietzsche-
Leverkühn grew up, the classical philologist
Serenus Zeitblom protests in the name of Thomas
Mann, just as the author himself, in his speech
about Germany, protests against Luther in the
name of Giovanni de Medici. Zeitblom represents a humanism without brilliance, aged, and
a bit Philistine; he is the philological element in
Nietzsche, which connected him with Erwin
Rohde and Jacob Burckhardt;[13] he is the spirit
of Weimar if one thinks of this translated into
the realm of pedantry and gloom. Therefore, in
the puzzling game of concepts, the values
"Goethe" and "Luther," "Humanism (*Humani-
tät*)" and "music" have dissociated themselves
and become mutual enemies. If moreover in
former times the spirit of Mazzini, of political
devotion to ideology and to the French Revolution appeared as the quintessence of horror and
a prodigy of inhumanity, things have become
thoroughly different now. "Democracy" and
"humanism" have been united, and the classical
philologist and humanist Zeitblom is also a little
Settembrini—without his Italian fieriness, to be
sure.

Seen in this perspective, the Reformation inevitably loses much of its "genuinely German
majesty." "The renewal through reform of a
religion which was already withering away, already regarded with general indifference" necessarily causes profound displeasure. "And a man
of my type," Zeitblom writes, "may well ask
himself whether these ever-recurring rescues of
an element already on the point of perishing are
actually to be welcomed from the cultural point
of view; whether the Reformers are not rather
to be viewed as reactionary types, harbingers of
misfortune." Yes, yes, the Thirty Years War! If
one re- /130/ gards world history as a bowling
alley on which everything automatically follows
a predetermined course, and where specific political catastrophes necessarily ensue, every time,

from specific intellectual causes, then the Thirty
Years War "necessarily" grew from Luther's actions, as National Socialism did from Hegel and
Nietzsche and the Bolshevik Revolution from
Hegel and Marx. Such a way of viewing matters
mostly results in the distortion of history and in
ideological montage. It disregards the element of
freedom in all history, the mystery of spontaneity
in every moment of history. It ignores the element of "translation," which mediates between
the idea and actuality. It underrates the irrationality of matter-of-fact reality, the obscure, in-
calculable way things operate in the geologic
movement of historical masses and forces.

Thomas Mann himself, in his speech about
Germany, carries Zeitblom's resentful rejection
of the Reformation to its extreme when he remarks: "Its results for Germany were the Thirty
Years War, which depopulated it, caused a
disastrous cultural retrogression, and probably,
through its immorality and pestilences, made
something different and worse of German blood
than it was perhaps in the Middle Ages." Then
the German classic and romantic movements,
our music, our philosophy, are products of inferior blood? A truly despicable sentence, a fantastic indiscretion! But with these characteristics,
I admit, the "devilishly German period" of the
Reformation retains hardly a trace of any good
quality. The author has taken over everything
from Dürer's picture "Knight, Death, and Devil"
except the figure of the knight. Luther himself,
once praised in a challenging tone as a godly
musician and the man who educated his people
to attain metaphysical freedom, now appears,
with his mouth full of crude invectives, as the
deathly foe of real, that is political, freedom and
the prime example of all our political doltishness.
"He was a hero of freedom," says Thomas
Mann, "but in the German manner, for he understood nothing about freedom. I'm not referring now to the 'Freedom of a Christian Man,'[14]
but to the political freedom of the citizen—that
not only left him cold; its stirrings and demands
were profoundly repugnant to him."

It is remarkable that Mann's way of setting
up political and "culture-critical" problems has
not changed since 1917; it has remained on the

---

[13]Actually neither of these scholars was a mere
philologist, or lacked brilliance.

[14]Title of Luther's famous tract, 1520.

same plane and is orchestrated in the same taste and style of thinking and with the same stock of concepts and motifs. What has changed is the position of the writer, his political "opinion." What has changed is the distribution of plus and minus signs, the recipes for arranging, polarizing, and accenting values, master images, and concepts. The disparity between the intellectual and political life of the Germans: here it appears again, but regarded critically and from without. In those days evidence of German maturity and superpolitical humaneness (*Hu-* /*131*/ *manität*), it is the opposite today: namely stubborn provincialism, "romantic counterrevolution," peevish imperviousness to the ideas of the "European religion of humanity." The "quintessentially German divergence between *national* impulse and the ideal of political *freedom*" (Thomas Mann, 1945) corresponds exactly with the assertion that the German authoritarian state of the Bismarckian type was the citadel of true freedom and social progress, and with the polemical protest (of 1917) against the "baldly abstract" concept of freedom held by the political West, against the "system of parliaments and parties, that affects all of a nation's life like a pestilence." In 1945 we read: "The Reformation, like the rising against Napoleon later, was a *nationalistic* movement towards freedom"; for the Reformation (that had as much connection with nationalism as Robespierre's "virtue" with the Gospel) has slid in the meantime over to the side of German liabilities. The French Revolution, formerly seen as an unsuccessful attempt to make up for the lack of a reformation, an attempt that very quickly degenerated into ideological terrorism, has now become the epitome of political freedom, although, we are told, it actually brought forth the concept of the nation.

"The 'nation,'" Mann now states, "was born in the French Revolution; it is a revolutionary and libertarian concept that includes the human; its domestic policy is freedom, its foreign policy is —Europe. All the attractiveness of the French political spirit is due to this fortunate unity." The whirligig of concepts is functioning splendidly. For now it is Napoleon whose "policy is Europe," while the Germans, otherwise of so cosmopolitan and European a disposition, were so morally stupefied by music that they actually committed a "nationalistic" revolt against Europe when, allied with England, Russia, and Austria, they freed Europe from Napoleon's domination. For "the German idea of freedom is 'folkish' and anti-European, always very close to barbarism." With this, the bastard ideas of Hitler and Rosenberg are blithely projected upon the totality of our political and intellectual history; and phenomena like the Storm and Stress, Schiller, Kant, Beethoven's *Fidelio,* Stein, Marx, Uhland and the Forty-Eighters[15] are ignored in the most cavalier way. Thus, for better or for worse, he reaches the following conclusion: "A people which is not inwardly free and responsible to itself does not deserve external freedom; it has no say about freedom and when it does use that sonorous word, it uses it falsely. The German concept of freedom was always directed outward. . . ." Outward—to be understood as the "breakthrough by main force" to becoming the "world people of reality." In 1917 it was Thomas Mann who so brilliantly instrumented the ideological musical accompaniment to that attempted breakthrough. /*132*/

[15]Here the author is listing movements, men, and so forth, all of which were products of the decades between 1760 and 1850. Nearly all of them were liberal, indeed libertarian.

Erich Kahler

Thomas Mann's Doctor Faustus

"Terminal Work" of an Art Form and an Era

The great novels of the 20th century, its essential books, are without exception *terminal* books, apotheoses of the narrative form. Proust's *À la recherche du temps perdu,* Gide's *Faux-Monnayeurs,* Joyce's *Ulysses,* Kafka's great parables, Musil's *Mann ohne Eigenschaften,* Broch's *Das Tod Vergils,* Sartre's *Nausée,* Camus' *Étranger*—each, in theme, is an inventory of our spiritual holdings, a moral, aesthetic, and metaphysical reckoning-up of our human estate; some of them, in form, carry abstraction to a point beyond which further evolution seems impossible. A deep, ultimate seriousness runs through them all, a seriousness which their ever-present irony increases rather than diminishes. Indeed, what is irony but the transcendence of self, a chain reaction of transcendence? Today, the spiritual, the artistic, the human itself balances on the highest peak of danger, "exposed on the mountains of the heart." So much has called it into question—how could it help questioning itself?

And indeed art has come to question its own existence—cannot escape doing so. The last veils of fiction, the last pretense of a divine plaything, are gone; the real thing invades the work of art; bare reality, of more dimensions than the individual artist can cope with, decomposes and shatters the novel. How can the artist hope to reach the central, innermost condition of our world—which is his ultimate function—without going into its formidable factual and technical processes? How can he hope to master its growing complexity without a corresponding increase in density and abstractness of presentation, without speculative analysis and exegesis?

Thus the story loses its value as a special event and becomes a parable of the human condition; the individual character becomes a type, the symbol a model. The artist today must load the tangible with so many levels of meaning that the complete work really becomes an orchestral score requiring a conductor—and indeed have single works of art ever before enlisted so many program notes and interpretations?

"When I hear about hearing . . ." says Adrian Leverkühn in *Doctor Faustus.* "When I read about reading . . ." would be a legitimate paraphrase: the reader cannot "follow" the theme without going one level of abstraction beyond it to embrace the entire structure, for the structure has in fact become the theme—the "what" ends up as the "how."

The traditional art forms have grown problematic through external, social, and cultural evolution, as well as through internal evolution, evolution of technique; art has become its own subject matter. And since the function of the artist and the intellectual /*348*/ has been called into question by the moral and social events of our epoch, the artist himself is drawn into a kind of polyphonic soliloquy on his role in our world.

It is just here that we have the content of Thomas Mann's entire work, which as a whole, bears the distinguishing traits of the great terminal books of our epoch. But in his work the terminal quality does not appear all at once; it may be watched as a process, evolving through decades.

Thomas Mann's development as a novelist comprises the whole development of modern narrative prose. He began his career with a book that, though marked by the destiny of modern art, still resembled the traditional realistic novel. Indeed, he has gone on using the comfortably circumstantial, digressive manner of the 19th-century novel right up into the latest, "structuralist" stages of his work—even in this last summing-up, his *Faust*. Yet what a long way from *Buddenbrooks* to *Doctor Faustus*. All that has happened to us, to the world, to art, during the last half-century, can be read in the course of this journey.

Mann's whole *oeuvre,* we have said, must be regarded as a single, consistent creation because, throughout, there may be felt in it an unconscious or semi-conscious tendency toward a structural unity of the whole. It is a dynamic macrocosm, a more and more dense and comprehensive complex of developing motifs, exhibiting as a whole a fugal character such as is otherwise found only in single novels or works of art. Just as each work gains increasing symbolic richness by the use and intensification of a leitmotif and the fusing of several leitmotifs, so on a larger scale the work as a whole exhibits the progressive exfoliation and metamorphosis of one single, all-pervasive theme. Mann himself, in his autobiographical sketch, has pointed, not without surprise, to the relationships within the magic square: *Buddenbrooks, Tonio Kröger, The Magic Mountain,* and *Death in Venice.* Yet exact correspondences of this sort are to be found throughout his entire work.

The lifelong central theme of Mann's books has been an inquiry into the function of art and the artist, of culture and the intellectual in modern society. This cluster of problems had its origin in the 19th century, rising out of the Industrial Revolution and the political changes attendant on it, out of the mechanization, collectivization, standardization of our world, and the increasing alienation of the artist from his society.

At first the artist took a stand for threatened culture: defensively in romanticism and aestheticism; aggressively in dandyism and insolent eccentricity. But gradually, almost insensibly, his attitude began to change: his own position, the nature of art and culture themselves, became problematic to him.

It was not that his attitude toward bourgeois society changed, but that he no longer supported culture unequivocally. Instead he began to lean more and more toward a new barbarism.

Even before Nietzsche we see signs of such a development. Leconte de Lisle wrote *Poèmes Barbares,* Théophile Gautier proclaimed: *"La barbarie vaut mieux que la platitude."* With Nietzsche the problem becomes broadly apparent, and later developments branch out in many directions. One way leads directly through the brash extremism of the Futurists' of Spengler, Klages, and Jünger, to the *trahison des clercs;* another leads to the savagely defiant vagrancy of Knut Hamsun and D. H. Lawrence's glorification of the vital urges; a third leads to the ambivalent scepticism in matters cultural of tired aristocrats such as Hermann Bang and Eduard Keyserling; the last and most far-reaching way leads to the bold investigations of the contemporary novel.

Thomas Mann had an initial advantage as compared with other great novelists of his generation, an advantage without which he could not have covered the vast distance between realism and structuralism. The problem fundamental to the modern novel—the role of the intellectual within his society, a problem that, in the last analysis, /349/ is the problem of man generally, of the individual surviving precariously in a technological, collective, incommensurate world—was not a problem Mann had to realize and experience intellectually; it was given to him in his cradle as his primary experience of himself. He himself *was* the problem, by virtue of the contrasts of his origin, the conjunction of the bourgeois and the artistic. From childhood he bore within himself that tension which impels the basic theme of our era.

His earliest stories introduce this theme. They are all studies of outcasts: the misshapen or unfortunate, like little Herr Friedemann, the lawyer Jacoby (*Little Lizzie*), Tobias Mindernickel, Lobgott Piepsam (*The Way to the Churchyard*); the invalid, like Albrecht van der Qualen (*The Wardrobe*); the man set apart by religious exaltation, like the monk Hieronymus (*Gladius Dei*), the archetype of Savonarola (*Fiorenza*); and already, as early as *The Dilettante* and Spinell (*Tristan*), the outcast as literary man, the would-be-artist in his illegitimate, tragi-comic opposition to life and to the social norm. Incidentally, in both *The Wardrobe* and *Tristan* we find the germ of the motif of *The Magic Mountain:* the peculiar removal from life, the isolation and insulation that goes with illness and the atmosphere of healing. The sanitarium in *Tristan* almost strikes us as a sketch for the one in *The Magic Mountain*. Even so early as this Thomas Mann was in possession of the outlines of a work that was to be precipitated by an entirely different, unforeseeable experience, his sojourn at Davos.

These stories, as well as *Buddenbrooks*, are all what is commonly called realistic fiction. They are realistic in a cruel, often painful way that points to the influence of the great Russian novelists; they seem to result from a deliberate discipline in sustaining with exact imagination the minutest circumstances of human suffering, perverted emotion, painful embarrassment. But —and this is a wholly modern aspect of Mann's style, distinguishing it from that of the Russian novelists—all these eccentric facts have been pushed to an extreme of precision, a point of caricature, where they turn into transcendent ironies. The experience of reality has become superintensive, ironically intensive. At the same time this irony has the property of creating symbols. A perfect example is the situation in *The Way to the Churchyard:* the contentious drunkard, Piepsam, tries to push the blond, young cyclist (life) from his bicycle. Later examples are Tonio Kröger in the *Moulinet des Dames;* the carious teeth of the Buddenbrooks and the consul's collapse head-first into the gutter; Mario and the magician; and so forth. These are all extreme, vicious, ironic contrasts, and their extreme irony is what makes them symbolic. They have their root in an archetypal conflict, the ironic constitution of the artist himself.

The style of every genuine artist is originally a style of personal experience; this is true of Thomas Mann in a very special sense. There is hardly another literary *oeuvre* that bears so clear an autobiographical stamp. Mann himself has told us, for instance, in his autobiographical sketch, that every single detail in *Death in Venice* is authentic, none of it fictitious. All that happens to any individual endowed with a truly personal style of experience seems to converge into an organic system of symbols and to assume an apparently inevitable relationship to his nature. This phenomenon is particularly marked in Thomas Mann, whose fundamental problem was shaped by the circumstances of his birth. Since he experiences everything under the sign of the primary tension of his being, the raw material of life almost immediately assumes for

him a symbolic character. The reciprocal irony of his psychological situation, and that further irony which transcends it, sharpen the symbolism still more. This peculiar disposition, this instinctive tendency to organize all experience symbolically, seems to account for the unique organic inter-relatedness, the fugal character of Mann's entire work.

Even the works of his early, realistic period evidence a very personal system of /350/ symbolic coordinates, an irony that creates distance and transcendence. Both in *Buddenbrooks* and in *Tonio Kröger,* the fundamental, personal problem is developed almost autobiographically, in the first, genealogically, from the bourgeois standpoint, in the second, individually, from the standpoint of the artist. Bourgeois and artist, each turns his gaze and inclination toward his counterpart: there is an exact correspondence between the consul Thomas Buddenbrook, who finds solace in Schopenhauer, and Tonio Kröger, with his nostalgia for the normal, blond, and respectable.

Already culture and intellect are represented as decadence, love is associated with decline; the artist is seen as a pariah from the start, iridescent with suspect hues, shading into the daemon, the invalid, the social outcast, the adventurer, the criminal; already he is stranded in the ironic situation of expressing a life he himself is unable to live. And already the multiple variations the basic theme is to undergo in the later books become discernible. Tonio Kröger's identification, somehow felt by him to be legitimate, with the swindler, foreshadows Felix Krull, swindler-by-extravagance-of-fantasy, and the blasphemous hoax of the paraphrase of *Dichtung und Wahrheit* in Krull's diary. A single metaphor of Tonio's ("mufti's no use . . .") furnishes the germ of *Royal Highness,* the outcast "upward," the sublime clown who keeps directing a performance that is being enacted without him.

From here on the motifs split and ramify and re-join, form new variations, change keys. In *Death in Venice* the conflict that had earlier appeared as an external friction between art and life is internalized; it is within the artist, indeed, within art itself: a conflict between daemon and discipline. Discipline is what preserves the artist, what justifies art and keeps it in the framework of social responsibility. Once discipline slackens, the daemon, the *eros,* breaks loose, and in the maelstrom of debauchery both art and artist are swept into sickness and death. The active counterpart of the passive Aschenbach is the magician Cipolla (*Mario and the Magician*), another outcast, deformed, but one who compensates and overcompensates his deformity—a deeper image of the artist seen as the irresponsible puppeteer of souls who uses his magic to cast people into the most unholy ecstasies. At this point the artist passes over into the demagogue, the dictator. He too is swept into perdition by his daemon, but not because of mere passivity but because of *hubris:* unlike Aschenbach, Cipolla does not let himself go or drift, but on the contrary exercises all his powers. He is a virtuoso of the will, a fiend for the sheer joy of conquest. He does not yield to his daemon but allies himself with it, indeed identifies himself with it, challenges it, incites it.

The Magic Mountain projects Aschenbach's psychic split into the world at large. The powers of the psyche widen out into whole landscapes. Magic expands into the magic mountain, into the sphere of an intellectual, morbid, irresponsible dissociation from life, where culture and nursing merge, and where the dissolution of dying overintensifies the stimuli of life. Discipline becomes the valley of duties, of normal, responsible action. But these too—the duties, the responsibilities, the active, normal life—lead into war and final collapse.

Here we come upon an alteration in the fundamental motif. The normality of the normal is no longer secure. Before this, Mann's work had been dedicated to the problem of life's boundaries: by means of his various outcasts he had delimited an area of healthy, normal, insouciant life. Now he discovers signs of decay on both sides of the boundary—in the world of action as well as up there on the magic mountain. Dying is part of living as living is part of dying.

The ambivalence, the paradox of all living things is at last revealed. *The Magic Mountain* opens out into an unanswered question: What *is* life anyway? What is normal? What is man and where does he stand? What is the norm of man and his measure? Goethe's question is raised once more (in a world terribly changed) —the /*351*/ question of *Tasso,* of *Iphigenie,* of the *Elective Affinities,* of *Faust.* . . .

In all of Thomas Mann's books after *The Magic Mountain,* there runs through the persistent motif of conflict between the abnormal and the supposedly normal, an anxious question as to the being and becoming of man. The *Joseph* novels open up the remotest layers of our mythical, totemistic past, which are at the same time the darkest layers of our psyche, the underworld of savage urges, lying ever in wait within us. Joseph rises out of these regions in a long, precarious process of sublimation, and there rises with him, within him, the sublimated, spiritualized God-image—he being the prefiguration of Jesus. He too bears a stigma from the beginning, the stigma of Grace. Grace again is full of abysses and wiles, and great discipline is required of its possessor. But, for one supreme moment, the norm seems to have shifted to spiritual man. For one moment. Joseph's counterpart was to appear, the Antichrist, the man stigmatized by the curse of spirit: Faustus.

The presentation of the Apollonian genius in *Lotte in Weimar* forms the transition. The image of Goethe emerges intact, "great, serene, and wise," as "a sacrifice—and bringer of sacrifice"; genius is preserved as an object of our reverence, sublimated as "simply the face of man." All this is still in the vein of Joseph. But behind it we see the cost, the full measure of Goethe's, of the artist's sacrifice: not only the mastering of a world increasingly packed with factual material, of days crowded with labor, and of a refractory audience, but also the ruining of many people, among them those closest to him, and the abandoning of his own everyday humanity. Discipline once more, distance, alienation, and the chill of an uncanny, transcendent irony. This brings us to Faustus, who is entirely governed by this coldness.

I have called *Faustus* the final chapter of a terminal *oeuvre.*

To start with, it gathers together all the variations and filiations of the fundamental motif, relates them in a new way, tests one against the other, and reduces them all in magnificent concentration to the old dominant theme. For what else is this Faustus but a cosmic Tonio Kröger, a Tonio Kröger expanded to his ultimate epochal and human significance? Faustus represents the extreme, the most mature fruit of the arch-problem, the arch-experience. The psychological split is portrayed through two characters: Adrian Leverkühn and Serenus Zeitblom —the intellectual adventurer and the "healthy" bourgeois.

The character who lives a normal life writes the biography of the one who, in the simple, human sense, is not allowed to have a life. In Adrian, Tonio Kröger's primary alienation from life, his ironic detachment from it, is pushed to its metaphysical limits. Aschenbach's daemon, which operates through love and sickness, and Cipolla's daemon, which operates more subjectively as *hubris* and defiant self-aggrandizement, are united in Adrian's devil. Daemon and discipline are no longer seen as opposites, but discipline comes to serve the daemon. Between daemon and discipline, impulse and reason, death and life, there goes on the same mystical dialectic, the same reciprocal intensification that we found in *The Magic Mountain*. Besides, Adrian is really Joseph's counterpart, his spiritual kin. Adrian's elevation leads to perdition, whereas the "Pit" leads Joseph to glory; the sublimation which in Joseph's case is an act of God, in Adrian's case is an act of the Devil. From a different point of view Adrian, the Dionysian musical genius, is a counterpart of Goethe, the Apollonian, visual genius. Here too the opposites betray affinity, for both are in each: in Goethe the dark, romantic, Faustian impulse; in Adrian the lucid, visual, rational grasp of the whole. But in the last analysis the blessing and the curse seem to be contained in the contrast between word and sound, poetry and music.

Faustus is also a terminal book in point of style, the ultimate precipitation of Thomas Mann's artistic discipline. I have already intimated how this discipline, which is of /352/ North German, Hanseatic, Prussian provenance, developed through artistic filiations and the irony of an inner tension into a symbol-creating property. Discipline in art must necessarily express itself in a sharpened sense of form, an intensive striving for organic wholeness, and that means to see things symbolically.

From without, from Richard Wagner and Tolstoy, came the suggestion of the leitmotif, which in *Tonio Kröger* already is transferred from characters to ideas. Mann tells us that in *Tonio Kröger* he for the first time conceived of narrative composition as a texture of ideas woven of various themes, as a musical nexus— his affinity to music was very strong from the outset. Out of such a musical conception grows the fugal character of the later works and of his *oeuvre* as a whole.

But *Faustus* can hardly be compared any longer to a fugue; it is almost—if we may apply musical terms to a literary composition—what Adrian calls a "strict movement." It is a structure in which each detail has an exact symbolic reference, a structure of utter complexity, in which not only the various dimensions and layers, but within these each sub-motif and minor variation, is related to the rest and back to the fundamental motif. In spite of the semblance of ease in both invention and narrative, nothing here is accidental, nothing stands for itself alone; everything refers to everything else, each detail is determined by the whole. Correspondences run backwards and forwards, between beginning and end, upper and lower levels, in a kind of labyrinthine mathematics. From Buchel to Pfeiffering; from the father's "speculating on the elements" to the son's *Symphonia Cosmologica* and his fantastic excursions into the galactic and submarine spheres; from his actual mother Elsbeth to Mother Manardi and the ultimate mother Schweigestill; from Stallhanne to the maid Walpurgis; and from the laughing dog Suso, through the black swine at the entrance of the devil-house in Palestrina, to the dog Kaschperl (one of the devil's nicknames); from the dog's laugh to Adrian's bent for laughter and the tendency of his music to parody and "sardonic deviltry"; from the clear-wing moth to the whore; from the "greedy drop" and the osmotic, heliotropic pseudo-creatures to the pathological lumbar migrations of the spirochetes and to the mannikins of the *Gesta Romanorum;* from Dürer's "Apocalypse" to Kleist's *Puppet Show;* from the destiny of Adrian's doctors to that of the Rogge sisters; and from the divines of Halle to the intellectuals of Munich who smirk at the bankruptcy of the intellect—among all these a net of converging relationships is woven, and one rational and daemonic system contains them all. Even the most casual incident has its place: an emerald ring is engraved with a plumed serpent whose tongue is feathered like an arrow; an outing into the Bavarian mountains leads to Linderhof, the castle of a mad, possessed king.

The great drama of Tonio Kröger as Faustus, the drama of modern art and Germany, mirrored by the humble scribe Serenus—the impotent subject and onlooker—truly images the deeply involved Thomas Mann, ever present in the background. It is enacted simultaneously on all levels, no less in the theoretical discussions and spiritual ventures of musical technique than in syphilis, murder, and madness. The same disquieting suspense informs the descriptions of musical scores and the biographical sections; indeed the climactic boldness of the musical compositions comes to stand for the biographical climax.

We need not be surprised if readers shake their heads over the minute descriptions of a kind of music that has never been written and perhaps never could be written. People will ask: Is this necessary? Is this possible? It was necessary, and it has been done. It is both legitimate and necessary. A reader who wishes to be spared the reading of the theoretical discussions and technical details may as well spare himself the reading of the book altogether; there is no other way of penetrating to its innermost meaning. The time is past when writers could give credibility to artist-characters by letting them /353/ work for years at some monumental literary idea in color or sound and then having them perorate about the work, as Hauptmann and even Ibsen did with their artist-characters. While this procedure has always been false and threadbare, today it has become quite impossible. The progression of man today, the progression of mind, is through technical processes, and it is through them that we must seek it and understand it.

Thus the channelling of events through technical processes is not a sign of weakness or arbitrariness, not mere caprice, but an imperative requirement of the total structure giving the literary work its power of persuasion. For at the center of this book lies the problem of the destiny of artistic genius and of art itself.

But what happens in and to Adrian comprises not only the fate of modern art and the intellectual; it comprises also the tragedy of Germany that is enacted in the background, the transgression of the German character, of which Adrian partakes; it comprises the general crisis of our world. The narrative takes place within three overlapping time-spans: the time-span of Adrian, 1885 to 1941, which is extended backwards into the historical depths of medieval Germany and the German Reformation by means of the spiritual climate of Kaisersaschern where Adrian spent his childhood and by means of the humanistic-pietistic university town of Halle where he studied; the time-span of the Third Reich, whose period of incubation coincides with Adrian's prime, and whose triumph and fall Zeitblom witnesses with horror even as he writes the story of Adrian's life; finally, our own epoch, which has given birth to the crisis of modern art and of the intellectual, and which is continuing even as we read.

All these time-strata are not only homologous but also variously interconnected. Thus the chronicle of German political events, inserted at intervals by Zeitblom into his biography of Adrian, is sometimes cross-connected with that biography, as in the discussions of the students at Halle and of the Munich intellectuals, or in the appearance of the impresario Fitelberg, who confronts Germanism with Judaism.

At the same time the book is interwoven with strands of Thomas Mann's personal history; there are long passages that are more nakedly autobiographical than any other writing by this author, who throughout his career has drawn so largely on his own life. Kaisersaschern, its form and atmosphere, the "witches" in its streets, point toward Mann's native city, Lübeck; Palestrina is the place where, under virtually identical circumstances, Thomas Mann wrote his *Buddenbrooks*. Pfeiffering and Munich both evoke familiar scenes. Mann's family, his friends and acquaintances have been introduced into the story barely disguised, in some cases without change of name, in the fashion of montage.

This bold and rather disturbing procedure—apart from the lure and significance of parody—has the character of a radical confession of self. It is as though Thomas Mann wished to emphasize that he belongs in the story, is a part of it, that the destinies of Leverkühn and Zeitblom as well as of Germany, the intellectual, and modern art, deeply involve him. This *pro domo* applies not only to the author but also to the work. The compulsive tendency toward irony and parody in Adrian's creation; his rejection of make-believe and the "divine game" which leads to the self-abolition of art; the "never-relaxed, perilous playing of art on the edge of impossibility"; its "pilgrimage on peas"; its "strict counterpoint"; "the highest and strictest organization, a planetary, cosmic norm"; the "universal unity of dimensions"; the "calculation raised to mystery"; and finally the "thrust from intellectual coldness into the adventure of new feeling," the desire for "an art without suffering, psychologically sound, far from solemn, serenely intimate," "an art on terms of closest familiarity with mankind," and the conviction that the spirit "even in its most daring sallies, researches, and ventures, which seem to remove it from the common taste, can nevertheless count on serving humanity, and, in the end, in a very /354/ roundabout way, even actual people. . . ."—all this is the self-projection not only of the author, it is the self-projection and self-reflection of the book. If we listen closely we may even catch in the cruel narrative that *vibrato* of the voice attributed to Adrian when he speaks with a half-modest, half-haughty casualness of the artist's ultimate familiarity with mankind.

It is Serenus Zeitblom who serves to strengthen confessional to the point of self-interpretation. True, he is the author's other half, the Overbeck of the Nietzschean Adrian, a second-remove ironic reflection of the normal on the abnormal, but his true function goes far beyond all this. He is the mediator between the various spheres, not only between Adrian and life, but also between the book and the world. He is a loose personification of the author's symbolic conscience, the commentator whose fears and forebodings, queries and meditations furnish the necessary cross-references—perhaps too many and too explicit for the acute reader, yet still hardly enough for those obtuse to symbolism. It is he who provides the additional experience of the German tragedy and integrates it with the rest; who, with his numerous reservations and confidences, makes the highly wrought craftsmanship

seem easy and unobtrusive, and effects the transition to human emotion.

The creation of this character enabled Thomas Mann to maintain his highly synthetic Adrian, this cosmic figure, within the context of humanity, to make of him a real and moving character, though this is accomplished a little at the expense of Zeitblom, who often feels and expresses things that are actually outside his pale. However, the author has tried in advance to give psychological credibility to these deviations—and, indeed, man is an unstable, vibrant substance whose hidden depths may be stirred to unforeseeable effects by certain crises and stimuli. Furthermore, in this book psychology no longer counts. Zeitblom is a voice, ultimately the author's voice: "I am too close to my subject . . . but when things become serious art is left behind. . . ." Of course this itself is artifice, but it passes over into truth.

This monumental undertaking is terminal also in that it truly represents the contemporary version of the Faust problem. Valéry's *Faust,* which plays with very similar ideas, is but a fascinating existentialist idyll compared with this. Thomas Mann brings this representative symbol, not only of German but of Western culture, up to date. He treats it with finality, secularizing it and its daemon, and integrating it in a purely mundane cosmos. Redemption here has become synonymous with integration. This means that the Faustian drama is revealed as the dialectical predicament of every creature, the inborn paradox of life.

This process permeates all levels of the book. Adrian's Faustian character is constitutional. The daemon resides *within him* from the start, in his migraine, in his enormous intelligence which rapidly assimilates all that can be known. Thence ennui, the challenge to the ever more sublime, ironic transcendence, risibility, and a coldness both somber and blasé. The daemon also surrounds him, in the father who "speculates on the elements," in the medieval German climate of Kaisersaschern, in the latent polyphony of the vast collection of musical instruments in his uncle's warehouse and the growing lure of the mathematical magic of music. The genius of the stammering organist Kretschmar and the example of Beethoven carry him further, further still the theological studies at Halle, which Adrian chooses partly out of ascetic conceit, partly as a supreme feat of self-mastery, a braving of the highest powers.

For theology is a highly charged, daemoniac field of force. It survives in our modern world as a last island of medieval spirituality, a twilight area of magical dialectics and dialectical magic. This accounts for its deep affinity with mathematico-magical music. The daemon takes on greater reality in two professors of divinity, Kumpf and Schleppfuss. The baroque and blustering Kumpf, after the manner of Luther, /355/ throws bread rolls at the devil lurking in the corner of his room. But Schleppfuss, who proves by slippery, keen logic the interdependence of good and evil and the verity of witchcraft, represents, as his appearance and name indicate, the Evil One himself.

In Leipzig, whither Adrian goes later to pursue his musical studies—the attraction of music proving more concrete and immediate—the daemon finally assumes an active and decisive role and starts intervening, from within as well as from without. Adrian's proud superiority, his sensitive intellectuality and primal alienation are associated with an extreme chastity, a chastity more innocent because more naive than the pious and shrewd chastity of Joseph. It contains both a touching childlikeness and an element of cold pride.

It is just this kind of rarefied innocence that invites the deepest humiliation by sex and a consequent involvement in guilt. Indeed this presumptuous intellectuality, this ironic transcendence, constitutes in itself the Fall. The porter in Leipzig who guides Adrian to a brothel instead of a restaurant is merely an instrument of the inner daemon. Love flares up at the most casual physical contact, the purest love—with a whore, love returned even from the swamp, and this love, love from the first closed to the genius, contains the poison, the demoniac involvement, the Mephistophelian pact—that in reality was concluded from birth.

Original Sin has its way; the love-poison is consumed, consciously, despite all warnings. The pact is sealed, partly out of a genuine commitment to love, partly out of proud defiance, the innate urge to self-enhancement, to the supreme act of challenge. This monstrous union of the highest with the lowest, the most solitary with

the most promiscuous, of genius with *vulgus,* this union—fulfilment and treason in one—constitutes one of the most moving love stories in world literature. It also contains in germ the manifold meaning of this powerful book.

From here on tragedy takes its predestined course. The wanton, ghastly dialogue with the Devil in Palestrina, while ostensibly the center of the book, only expresses what has been clear from the beginning: "Thou shalt not love."

And another thing it makes utterly clear is the primary determinance, the biological conditioning of the spiritual drama. "You see me," says the Devil, "therefore I exist for you. Is it worth while asking whether I really exist? Is not that which acts actual? Is truth not that which is felt and experienced?" Thus hallucination and reality have equal validity, and the fellow lolling on the sofa speaks both from within and from without. The coldness that emanates from him is nothing else than the reflection of the spiritual coldness of Adrian, of that white heat that feels like ice to the touch; and the Mephistophelian wit is nothing else than Adrian's own irony. It is the same with all subsequent events: the ruin of the amorous friend whom Adrian, at once bashful and diabolic, sends as his suitor to the girl they both love; the girl's recoil; and, in his house, the death of his little nephew, the dearest of all to him, the last, tenderest Eros; set over against these, the spiritual closeness of the woman who instinctively keeps herself at a distance, whom he never sees—concord only between strangers: it is all emanated by force of that inner magic in a person which has the property of creating destiny all around itself.

Adrian's Faustian drama is set entirely within the being of spiritual man. The old cosmic drama between Heaven and Hell has been transferred into the human heart. Even the voyages into the stellar system and the submarine world are phantasmagoria nourished by science. The theological conflict is secularized; God and the Devil are secularized and made to dwell in a single body.

How naively chaste, how allegorically pure was Goethe's tragedy by comparison! There the theological element pervaded the whole cosmic scene, good and evil were neatly separated, and man was endowed with free choice. This contemporary *Faustus* is likewise full of theology, but theology has /356/ become a small, atavistic residue, a medieval remnant, revealed as a deeply suspect region where God and Devil fluidly merge, are mutually dependent, where the good is a *fleur du mal* and vice versa.

The Faustian man has stepped over into the secular realm of art, and his fate becomes the very fate of modern art, the fate of the alien intellectual in our mechanized world. His fate is inherent in his intellectuality and insofar as he is what he is, and does not deny himself, he has no longer any choice. In his very attempt to realize what is creatively true he finds himself today, together with art, together with all that is essentially human, in a diabolical plight, in the state of alienation, of the Fall—the Fall by rising, by ironic transcendence. What is good, what is bad? Sound or sick? What is innocence, if the purest—the spirit—is sin? Where lies the norm? All this has become difficult to resolve. Concepts and values are no longer immune, but have become tainted by each other.

Thus the drama is reduced to a point; event becomes stasis, becomes existence. Life's ambiguity, life's paradox, is revealed. The Devil resides in God and God in the Devil. Sublimest chastity becomes the easiest prey of the whore.

The German character, "threatened with being wrapt up in itself like a cocoon," with "the poison of solitude," beset with longings, with the urge to break into the world, is beguiled into a grab for world power that brings it nothing but the world's hatred, and suffering. The nation whose power of abstraction is the highest, whose spirituality is the most perfectly and perilously detached, the nation of Kant, Schiller, Hölderlin, plunges ahead of the rest into a sub-animal condition. This is the nation that has created the model of a modern secularized hell, where the incredible actually happens, "without any accounting," in sound-proof cellars, where torment and lust are commingled.

And what of modern art? What of this terminal book, this extreme document? Do we not find the same symptoms here? Magic has developed into the strictest structural norm, and the strictest norm—in science, too—leads back into magic. Ultimate irony, the chain reaction of transcendence, mixes with the elements and becomes deadly serious. From the furthest, cosmic, objectivity we are thrust into utter subjectivity, the confessional.

In paradoxes such as these, indeed throughout the crisis of our age, we sense the motif of Kleist's *Puppet Show:* "Thus once again we must eat of the Tree of Knowledge in order to fall back into the state of innocence." The entire effort, the supreme effort, of the contemporary spirit is directed toward this: to eat once again of the Tree of Knowledge, to make possible the impossible, redemption through union, through closest familiarity of climactic spirit with mankind. And the last hope of spirit, "the hope beyond hopelessness," "transcendence of despair," is the paradox of Grace, that salvation comes only of utter desperation. /357/

Bernhard Blume

from *Aspects of Contradictions: On Recent Criticisms of Thomas Mann*

This "truth content" is the matter at stake in a basic, radical attack launched against Thomas Mann by a distinguished essayist, Hans Egon Holthusen.[6] He too complains again and again

[6]Hans Egon Holthusen, "Die Welt ohne Transzendenz," *Merkur*, III (1949), 38–59 and 161–80. Also published as a brochure (Hamburg, 1949).

about Mann's political beliefs, deploring now his partisan rigidity, now his inconsistency. Here he continually plays off the *Reflections of a Nonpolitical Man* (1918) against "Germany and the Germans" (1945) and *Doktor Faustus.* Yet one is inclined to apply to Holthusen's own work what he says of the "thematic arrangement" of *Doktor*

Faustus as "cultural criticism": that is, it is most rewarding when it avoids political matters. Above all, philosophical (*weltanschauliche*) defects provoke him: what he cannot find in Mann's work is truth. But what is the "truth" of a creative writer? Well, in Mann's case, as Holthusen says, it is "something transitory, nonbinding, and highly suspect. It is conceived of without 'eternity' and quite without objectivity." He cites from the *Reflections* a remark of Mann's to the effect that all truths are relative to a given time. "The intellect," Mann writes, "is the courtier of the will, and the needs . . . of a time present themselves as 'insights,' as 'truths.' " Obviously this derives from Nietzsche. Holthusen also stresses it, a bit condescendingly, as a "discovery of the era of Schopenhauer and Nietzsche, now pretty dated." Here it "is being popularized in a *feuilletonistic* way," as he puts it. Now Thomas Mann was not the first *feuilletonist*, after all, to popularize Nietzsche's doctrines; the "consistent relativism" which Holthusen so categorically censures in Mann is a basic characteristic of the age.[7] /*160*/ "There are no definitive statements any longer," Wilhelm Emrich has declared in an analysis of the contemporary novel, "neither in Kafka, nor Musil nor Thomas Mann, since the multiplicity of possible reflections and insights approaches infinity."[8] This is precisely the point, and Emrich accordingly does not waste his time by informing us whether he welcomes or deplores this situation, but rather indicates how this multiplicity of possible reflections and insights necessarily produces new artistic forms and "structural models." Thomas

Mann's tendency "to connect everything with everything else," which bothers Holthusen so much, rises from his awareness of this situation; and when Holthusen states that Mann's concepts have "no definite boundaries, no locus, no sphere in which they are valid without ambiguity," he will be contradicted on one point only: that is, in his conclusion that therefore they are "not to be taken seriously." The much-cited irony, the "ambiguity" of Mann's style and attitude, is by no means only the result of changes in his mood, as Holthusen seems to assume. Rather, it is the necessary expression of an artistic view in which there is nothing unambiguous, but only perspectives which endlessly cross and intersect one another.[9] Inevitably, anyone who expected to find the "simple statement of great wisdom"—the absence of which Holthusen deplores—in art of this type will be frustrated. In general, concepts like "wisdom" or "eternal truth" are equally unusable as aesthetic criteria; for, as Hofmannsthal put it as a young man: "the value of a poem does not depend on its meaning (otherwise it would be wisdom, say, or learning) but its form."[10] Still sharper is Nietzsche's formulation: "To be an artist, man pays the price of experiencing the element which all nonartists call 'form' as *content*, as 'the thing itself.' "[11] Just this is the price Thomas Mann paid to be an artist. It is an inescapable fact that such an artistic existence is problematic. Just how problematic it is appears in Nietzsche's sentence which follows the aphorism just quoted: "Thus, to be sure, one becomes part of an *inverted world,* for content becomes something merely formal—and this includes one's own life." Undoubtedly Mann was aware of /*161*/ these profound problems; the pact which Leverkühn concludes with the devil is evidence of this. We remember the condition the devil makes: "Thou shalt not love!" Basically it is superfluous, for Leverkühn has always fulfilled it. Actually he *cannot* love, his purely formal existence in which everything becomes art makes this impossible.

[7]Holthusen has no difficulty in defending himself when the charge he made against Mann is turned on him. Thus: "Someone asked how it came about that I awarded the laurel to the Catholic philosopher Haecker at one time, and at another to the nihilist Benn. For after all, a man's intellectual world must be unambiguous, a definitely bounded system. . . .

"I accepted the challenge, put the word 'truth' in the plural and asked in return why it should not be possible to owe fealty to different, even opposed truths in the same degree, if not at the same time, if one affected my consciousness no less strongly and centrally than did the other.

". . . I distinguished between a truth 'for me' and a truth 'per se' . . . ." *Ja und Nein* (München, 1954), p. 267.

[8]"Formen und Gehalte des zeitgenössischen Romans," *Universitas,* XI (1956), 51.

[9]Compare also Max Rychner's statement: "The concept ambiguous . . . means . . . in Thomas Mann that a phenomenon partakes of two antithetical spheres of meaning." *Die Neue Rundschau,* 1955, Heft 3, p. 270.

[10]*Loris. Die Prosa des jungen Hugo von Hofmannsthal* (Berlin: Fischer, 1930), p. 265.

[11]*Der Wille zur Macht* (Leipzig, 1930), p. 552.

This is his guilt, tragic guilt if you will, for it is presupposed in his own being. As we know, Mann encountered it in his own existence. From the beginning, "ironic distance" from life has been regarded as a basic theme of his personality and his creative work. In the last analysis, even his political emigration can be regarded as the logical continuation of an attitude whose decisive trait has always been "not being involved." It is not meant in a completely positive way but still stated with respect when Hans Paeschke declares: "Indeed, it is no laughing matter when a man who was an outsider all his life . . . an emigrant from life even before his emigration, is finally sought out by his most essential archetype as Leverkühn was by the devil."[12] (Paeschke's critique of Mann, in this as in other matters, is distinguished by his objective mode of argumentation.) Thomas Mann himself called *Doktor Faustus* "a penance for having been away."[13]

By citing this "being away" some writers have tried, *tout court,* to deny Mann any right at all to treat a theme like that of *Doktor Faustus.* In a negative discussion of the book, Walter Boehlich declares that the author lacked "the soil to which he owes all"—German soil, that is —when he was writing *Doktor Faustus,* and therefore the novel inevitably had to "fail." "To the degree to which he no longer understood Germany he had to misunderstand the symbol of Germany [that is, Faust]." For far from Germany, on American soil, no such symbol can be forged, for America "a country without a great literature, without a poetic tradition, without vital criticism . . . seems not to be a country in which symbols can flourish." Also it is difficult, Boehlich holds, to describe such matters as the developments in Germany from 1933 to 1945, unless one has "experienced" them; by "experience" he means physical presence, "being there." At the close Boehlich reaches a sarcastic climax in alluding to a famous remark[14] of

Goethe's: "It was an epoch of world history, and Thomas Mann can say that he was not there."[15]

It is delightfully ironic that the most valid reply to Boehlich's claims comes from Holthusen. On the question of "experience" and "being there" he declares: ". . . it is not 'experience' that makes the creative writer, but imagination." Further explaining his position, he writes: "I /162/ have read bundles of poems that were written in concentration camps, and there was barely one of them which could not have been written by a third-class, sentimental lyricist of the school of Emanuel Geibel.[16] On the other hand, two or three pages by an important writer, who never saw a concentration camp from within or without, seem to me the best, as literature, that I have read on this topic."[17] These remarks of Holthusen follow almost immediately after Boehlich's article in the same journal. To be sure, they do not refer to it nor to Mann, but that does not prevent them from being relevant.

But quite apart from the question of how Thomas Mann may have conducted himself in life, distance from life, "coldness in life" is one of the great themes of his *work.* At the end it undergoes a grandiose heightening (*Steigerung*) in the figure of Leverkühn and in his pact with the devil. Yet parting from life and renouncing love make up only one side of the diabolic pact. The other is the alliance with illness. Here it is not simply that intellectual heightening is linked to the weakening of vitality, genius with degeneration, as occurs again and again in Mann's work from *Buddenbrooks* on. Now it is rather that this linking is consciously engineered. What Leverkühn is ready for, what he desires in the depth of his being, is heightening of productivity at the price of self-destruction. Basically, the spirochetes are only the drastic expression of a condition which under certain circumstances could also be brought about by drugs. "Illumination" as a toxic frenzy, inspiration reached at such a price, is a crime, a pact with the devil. Holthusen makes his strongest objections to the pact with the devil as the intellectual center of the novel—

[12]Christian E. Lewalter and Hans Paeschke, "Thomas Mann und Kierkegaard. Ein Briefwechsel über den *Doktor Faustus* und sein Kritiker," *Merkur,* III (1949), 933.

[13]"Die Aufgabe des Schriftstellers," *Neue Zeitung,* 26 September, 1947.

[14][Goethe's remark was made after the army of revolutionary France checked the invading allied forces at Valmy in 1792.]

[15]Walter Boehlich, "Thomas Manns *Doktor Faustus,*" *Merkur,* II (1948), 588–603.

[16][Nineteenth-century writer; here a symbol of derivative mediocrity.]

[17]"Exkurs über schlechte Gedichte," *Merkur,* II (1948), 605.

and thus appears again in the ranks of Mann's opponents. If one makes the countervailing point that the appearance of the devil must be regarded as a dialogue imagined by Leverkühn (which Holthusen obviously failed to see) it is correct as long as one remains in the psychological and rational sphere.[18] This is the sphere of Zeitblom, the fictive narrator of the story, whom Holthusen continually confuses with Mann.[19] Erich Brock, with his statement that the devil of *Doctor Faustus* is "one of those ambiguous marginal concepts which cannot exist and yet must exist," comes closer to the paradoxical complexity of this figure. He is, Brock says, "the most extreme element of our self, and precisely for this reason he is wholly alien to us."[20] In this sense it could be maintained that the devil in *Doctor Faustus* simultaneously exists and does not exist, that Mann does and does not believe in him. That is not simply ironic am- /*163*/ biguity; basically the situation of Goethe's Mephisto is very similar. But precisely by comparing *Doctor Faustus* with Goethe's *Faust* Holthusen attempts to depreciate the novel. In Goethe, he declares, the devil is "finally overcome by the Yea of eternal love. In *Doctor Faustus* he has become autonomous and no longer has a divine opponent to fear." Or, as Holthusen says elsewhere, the "idea of God" is "not to be perceived" in Mann's works. Even if that were the case, it would not indicate anything about the actual value of Mann's novel. But quite aside from that, when the devil appears in a novel and God does not, that still does not mean that God is not present. It is well known that there are countless stories in which the devil appears and God is not even mentioned; this does not weaken their Christian character. In this case the term "negative the-

ology" has rightly been used. No one would derive from this the statement that Thomas Mann "believes" literally in the figures of Christian mythology. That the Evil One exists may reasonably be doubted; not that evil exists.

The pact with the devil in *Doctor Faustus* signifies that aesthetic existence is viewed under the aspect of *guilt*. Yet it does not mean that music, regarded in the *Reflections* as a gift of God, is now, as Holthusen puts it, "briefly and crudely put, possessed by the devil." Rather, it partakes of both realms; music is an instrument which belongs to the higher and lower powers and therefore is ambiguous; everything depends on the spirit of the man it serves. These thoughts are not as wholly new and unheard-of, as wholly off the track, as Holthusen's objections might lead one to believe. There is that *Kapellmeister* Berglinger whom Wackenroder imagined in order to exorcise the doubts and anxieties in which his passionate love for music involved him. When Berglinger speaks of the "criminal" innocence of music, of its "terrible obscurity, ambiguous as an oracle,"[21] when his author says of him that the "mere *health* of the soul did not satisfy"[22] him, when he himself declares: "My lustful artist's joys are poisoned deep in the very germ; I wander about, sick in my soul, and from time to time poison pours through my veins,"[23] those are turns of phrase in which the themes of *Doctor Faustus* are already sounded, as it were in a prelude. The author, Wackenroder, had a soul of childlike purity and piety. No one has ever doubted it, but precisely in unlimited abandonment to the divine beauty of art he saw the temptation to stray from the path of living up to the Christian and moral demands of life. . . . /*164*/

[18]Lewalter, *loc. cit.*, p. 925.
[19]Compare Hanns Braun, "Welt ohne Transzendenz? Zu einer Kritik an Thomas Manns *Faustus*," *Hochland*, XLI (1949), 597.
[20]"Die ideengeschichtliche Bedeutung von Thomas Manns *Doktor Faustus*," *Trivium*, VII (1949), 123.

[21]Wilhelm Heinrich Wackenroder, *Werke und Briefe*, ed. Friedrich v.d. Leyen (Jena, 1910), I, 194.
[22]*Ibid.*, p. 127.
[23]*Ibid.*, p. 274 (by Tieck). On the figure of the demonic musician in the romantic period, cf. also Korff's discussion of Berglinger, in his *Geist der Goethezeit*, III (Leipzig, 1949), pp. 60 ff. and of Kreisler, vol. IV (Leipzig, 1953), pp. 544 ff.

Topics for Writing and Research

SHORT PAPERS ON THE SOURCES

1. Show through statements from the *Faustbuch* that it was intended as a warning to Protestant readers.

2. Working from the letters and other documents relating to the *historical* Faust, construct an account of Faust's life that you consider historically sound.

3. Show what materials relating to the historical Faust appear in the *Faustbuch*.

4. What clearly supernatural materials appear in the *Faustbuch?*

5. Describe Helen of Troy as she is portrayed in the *Faustbuch*.

SHORT PAPERS ON THE INDIVIDUAL WORKS

6. Summarize the subplot of Marlowe's play —the scenes dealing with the clowns and their imitations of Faustus.

7. Discuss elements of the morality play in Marlowe's *Dr. Faustus* (the good and evil angels, the old man). Check on moralities in the library.

8. Describe the appearance and personality of Mephistopheles in Goethe's *Faust*.

9. Make a study of the archaic language in the chapter from Thomas Mann's book. What words are used that are not in current usage? What turns of phrase or expression appear that do not conform to modern grammatical practice? It should be noted, of course, that the archaic expressions only approximate those in the German original.

10. Describe Wagner as he is portrayed by Goethe.

11. Describe the experiences of Faust on Walpurgis Night in Part One of Goethe's *Faust*.

12. Marlowe's Faustus has been called a Renaissance man. Discuss his characterization in this light.

13. Why does Shapiro end his poem with an atomic explosion? How does this conclusion relate to the history of Faust given in the poem?

14. Describe Faust's encounter with the Seven Deadly Sins in Marlowe's play. How does this scene relate to the overall story of Faustus as Marlowe tells it?

15. Show how Shapiro's poem utilizes materials deriving from the Faust tradition as a whole.

SHORT PAPERS ON THE INDIVIDUAL CRITICAL ESSAYS

16. Ornstein justifies the inclusion of the comic scenes in *Dr. Faustus*. Agree or disagree with his argument.

17. Show how, according to Ornstein, Marlowe's Faustus degenerates until he is no better than the comic characters in the subplot.

18. Clemen argues that Marlowe shows his own spiritual wrestlings in *Dr. Faustus*. Either uphold this view or contend that the play is an objective work and does not reveal Marlowe's personal views.

19. Clemen is interested in the development of thought in *Dr. Faustus* as revealed in the speeches and soliloquies of Faustus. Show how Marlowe's play marks an advance over its predecessors.

20. Barber argues that Marlowe's portrayal of Faustus is based on Protestant attitudes. Carefully read the section on the play concerning Communion (pages 160–61) and the scene with the Pope (pages 58–61). Evaluate Marlowe's attitude toward Catholicism.

21. Barber attempts to show that the love of Marlowe's Faustus for Helen is a kind of blasphemy. Agree or disagree with Barber's argument.

22. According to Barber, the sin of gluttony is heavily stressed in Marlowe's play. Locate all references to gluttony in either a physical or a spiritual sense and summarize your findings.

23. Lange quotes Goethe to establish that there is no single, simple idea underlying *Faust*. What, according to Lange, is Goethe's purpose?

24. Trace the developments in *Faust,* Part Two, as Lange summarizes them.

25. Heller recounts the history of the Faust theme in recent years. Is the theme as important as he indicates?

26. Restate Heller's argument that Goethe is less optimistic than Lessing.

27. Holthusen's title indicates that in Mann's novel the supernatural forces in the *Faustbuch*, for example, become projections of the personality of the hero. Summarize the main points of Holthusen's argument.

28. Kahler, like Holthusen, discusses the fact that Mann turns the supernatural into aspects of personality. But Kahler is especially interested in *Doctor Faustus* as a terminal work. Considering the other terminal works mentioned and his discussion of Mann's work, state what Kahler means by the term.

MEDIUM–LENGTH PAPERS INVOLVING COMPARISONS BETWEEN THE WORKS

29. What problems did Marlowe and Goethe face in adapting the Faust materials to the stage?

30. Compare the attitudes of Marlowe, Goethe, and Mann toward the damnation or salvation of Faust. Before writing this paper, read Mann's novel as a whole.

31. Show the similarities and differences in plot and structure between Marlowe's *Dr. Faustus* and Goethe's *Faust*.

32. Compare Marlowe's Wagner and Goethe's Wagner.

33. Contrast the characterization of Mephistopheles in Marlowe with that of Mephistopheles in Goethe.

34. Compare the characterization of Faustus in Marlowe to that of Faust in Goethe.

35. To what extent is the character of Leverkühn in Thomas Mann's novel comparable to that of Faust in Goethe?

36. Shapiro's poem is a concise narrative of the Faust story. What advantages or disadvantages does this approach have as contrasted with the dramatic approach of Goethe?

MEDIUM–LENGTH PAPERS INVOLVING COMPARISONS BETWEEN THE CRITICAL ESSAYS

37. Ornstein does not insist that Marlowe wrote the comic scenes in *Dr. Faustus;* however,

he argues that they form an integral part of the play. Clemen considers Marlowe's authorship of these portions "very questionable." Consider the arguments of both in relation to the play and draw your own conclusions as to the importance of these scenes in the work and whether Marlowe wrote them.

38. Compare the evaluations of Goethe's work by Lange and Heller. Decide which approach you consider superior and explain why.

39. Barber states that Marlowe's *Dr. Faustus* can be read either as a play about a modern man rebelling against limitations or as the story of the damnable Faustus. Uphold one view or the other.

40. Holthusen criticizes Thomas Mann rather harshly. Blume comes to Mann's defense. Read Mann's novel as a whole and evaluate the conclusions of these two critics.

41. Compare Heller's evaluation of Mann's book with that of one of the other critics.

42. Marlowe called his play *The Tragicall Historie of Doctor Faustus,* and Goethe called his work a tragedy. Utilizing the critical essays and some additional readings on the theory of tragedy, show in what ways the two works can be considered tragedies.

43. Kahler and Holthusen agree on the complex nature of Mann's novel, but they disagree on its value. Read the novel and uphold one or the other in a paper.

MEDIUM–LENGTH PAPERS INVOLVING APPLICATIONS OF THE CRITICAL ESSAYS TO THE WORKS

44. Ornstein evaluates the importance of the comic elements in Marlowe's play. Decide if these elements are as important as he suggests and either uphold his point of view or develop an alternative argument, citing evidence from the play.

45. Clemen suggests that Marlowe shows development in Faustus's thinking as he speaks. Study several of the major speeches and either agree or disagree, giving reasons and illustrations.

46. Evaluate Heller's argument that Marlowe's poetry is not in harmony with his plot.

47. Analyze the changes that Goethe makes

in the Faust story in terms of Lange's commentary.

48. Lange argues that the usual interpretation of Goethe's *Faust* is overly optimistic. Justify or oppose this point of view from your reading of the work, especially of the conclusion.

49. Kahler says of Mann's Adrian Leverkühn, "The old cosmic drama between Heaven and Hell has been transferred into the human heart." Gather evidence from the chapter of Mann's book included here to prove that the devil is actually a part of Adrian's own nature.

TOPICS FOR LONG RESEARCH PAPERS

50. Analyze the relationship between the plot and the subplot in Marlowe's *Dr. Faustus.*

51. Discuss the use of verse and prose in Marlowe's *Dr. Faustus.* What type of scene is in prose? in verse? What is the relationship between the use of prose or verse and the characters and mood in the scene?

52. What is the attitude toward Catholicism in Marlowe's play? Relate the portrayal of Catholic officialdom in the play to the position of the Catholic church in Elizabethan England.

53. What evidence of intellectual pride can be found in Marlowe's Faustus? Is the sin of pride the cause of Faustus' damnation? Prepare a paper on this subject after referring to a good encyclopedia for a discussion of the seven deadly sins and especially the sin of pride.

54. Analyze *Faust* as an expression of Goethe's philosophy. Does Goethe present a coherent philosophy in the play? See the discussion of Goethe in Santayana's *Three Philosophical Poets,* as well as in the essays by Lange and Heller.

55. Show how Mann utilizes traditional Faust materials in new ways to make them suitable in the twentieth century.

56. Consider the secularization of religious elements in Mann's novel. Note, for example, that the devil is portrayed in such a way as to suggest that he is a projection of Leverkühn's personality.

57. Consider the problems of presenting Goethe's *Faust* on the stage. Do some research in the library on various stagings of the first part and of the two parts together in developing this paper.

58. In the various portrayals of Faust, trace the movement from Renaissance exuberance to eighteenth-century enlightenment, nineteenth-century pessimism, and twentieth-century analysis and searching for meaning.

59. Trace the Faust tradition in Germany. Utilize the *Faustbuch,* Goethe's *Faust,* Mann's *Doctor Faustus,* and the criticism of these works. Some library research will be helpful.

60. The correlation between the rise of Protestantism and the great popularity of the Faust story in the sixteenth and seventeenth centuries has often been noted. We find, for example, material critical of Catholicism in the *Faustbuch* and Marlowe's play. Utilizing materials in the library, try to explain the relationship between the Faust tradition and Protestantism.

61. Write a paper on magic and necromancy in Elizabethan England and its relation to Marlowe's *Dr. Faustus* and the *Faustbuch.*

62. Trace the history of Faust in music. The Faust story has been utilized in operas and other works by Berlioz, Gounod, Liszt, and others. Listen to recordings of these works and see performances or films if possible, in addition to doing library research on the history of Faust in music.

63. Trace the history of Faust in English literature. The chief works are by Marlowe and Byron, but there are numerous lesser examples. A recent contribution is the novel *The Magus,* by John Fowles.

64. Show how the conditions of Elizabethan theatrical performance explain various differences between Marlowe's *Dr. Faustus* and Goethe's *Faust.*

65. Show how one of the works reflects its author's life and character.

66. Write a brief paper on one of the following:

a. Berlioz's *La Damnation de Faust.*

b. Gounod's *Faust.*

c. Boito's *Mefistoféle.*

d. Simon Magus.

e. The magi in New Testament times.

f. Thomas Mann's interest in music.

g. The devil on the Elizabethan stage.

h. Karl Shapiro's poetry.

67. Describe two or more twentieth-century productions of Marlowe's *Dr. Faustus* and the critical reactions to them.

68. Cite evidence that Goethe's work has not been particularly successful on the stage.

69. Discuss the reputation of Goethe's *Faust* from its writing to the present time.

70. Discuss the Faust story as a puppet play.

71. Show the connections between the Faust tradition and the Don Juan tradition.

72. Compare and contrast the librettos of Gounod's *Faust* and Berlioz's *The Damnation of Faust*. Compare one or both with Goethe's *Faust*.

Suggestions for Further Reading

Students who desire to explore further the sources of the Faust tradition will find an excellent collection of materials, both legendary and historical, in *The Sources of the Faust Tradition from Simon Magus to Lessing* by Philip Mason Palmer and Robert Pattison More (New York: Oxford University Press, 1936). A reliable study of the whole tradition from its origins in magic and religion through the Simon Magus period to twentieth-century versions of the Faust story was written by E. M. Butler in three interesting and highly readable volumes, *The Myth of the Magus* (1948), *Ritual Magic* (1949), and *The Fortunes of Faust* (1952), all issued by Cambridge University Press. *The Fortunes of Faust* traces the main literary treatments of the theme to 1947.

The Faust theme has been a rich subject for comparative studies. The student interested in such study should devote some attention to the quarterly publications *Comparative Literature* and *The Journal of the History of Ideas*.

Further commentary or Marlowe's work is readily available in a paperback edited by Irving Ribner, *Christopher Marlowe's Dr. Faustus: Text and Major Criticism* (New York: Odyssey Press, 1966). Students should note especially the article "Science Without Conscience" by Harry Levin, which also appears in *The Overreacher* (Cambridge, Mass.: Harvard University Press, 1952). Thomas Mann's *Doctor Faustus* is available in most libraries; students interested in a modern treatment of the Faust theme should read the novel as a whole. Additional critical aids for students of Marlowe and Thomas

Mann can be found in the collections of essays by Clifford Leech and Henry Hatfield listed below.

Those who wish to read Part Two of Goethe's *Faust* in its entirety will find many translations. An inexpensive paperback version of *Faust, Part Two*, translated by Philip Wayne, is available from Penguin Books (Baltimore, Md., 1949).

BIBLIOGRAPHY

Bakeless, John, *The Tragical History of Christopher Marlowe*, 2 vols. Cambridge, Mass., Harvard Univ. Press, 1942.

Bergsten, Gunilla, *Thomas Mann's Doctor Faustus*. Bonniers, Sweden, Svenska Bökforlaget, 1963. This study relates incidents in Mann's novel to materials in the *Faustbuch*.

Boas, F. A., *Christopher Marlowe: A Biographical and Critical Study*. Oxford, Clarendon Press, 1940.

———, ed., *The Tragical History of Doctor Faustus*. New York, Gordian Press, 1932 (reprinted 1966).

Campbell, Lily B., "Dr. Faustus: A Case of Conscience." *Publications of the Modern Language Association*, Vol. LXVII (1952), pp. 219–39.

Davidson, Clifford, "Doctor Faustus of Wittenberg." *Studies in Philology*, Vol. LIX (1962), pp. 514–23.

Emerson, Ralph Waldo, "Goethe, or the Writer," in *Representative Men*. Boston, Houghton Mifflin, 1876, pp. 261–90.

Enright, D. J., *Commentary on Goethe's Faust*. New York, New Directions, 1949.

Fairley, Barker, *Goethe as Revealed in His Poetry.* New York, Ungar, 1963.

———, *A Study of Goethe.* Oxford, Clarendon Press, 1967.

Fowles, John, *The Magus.* Boston, Little, Brown, 1965. The most recent full-scale literary treatment of the Faust theme. A large novel, it presents a thoroughly modernized psychological study of the motif.

Frye, R. M., "Marlowe's *Doctor Faustus:* The Repudiation of Humanity." *South Atlantic Quarterly,* Vol. LV (1956), pp. 322–28.

Gray, Ronald D., *Goethe: A Critical Introduction.* London, Cambridge Univ. Press, 1967.

Greg, W. W., ed., *Marlowe's Dr. Faustus, 1604–1616.* Oxford, Clarendon Press, 1950. A study of parallel texts.

———, "The Damnation of Faustus." *Modern Language Review,* Vol. XLI (1946), pp. 97–107.

Haile, H. G., *The History of Doctor Johann Faustus, Recovered from the German.* Urbana, Univ. of Illinois Press, 1965.

Hatfield, Henry, ed., *Thomas Mann: A Collection of Critical Essays.* Englewood Cliffs, N. J., Prentice-Hall, 1964.

———, *Goethe, a Critical Introduction.* Cambridge, Mass., Harvard Univ. Press, 1964.

Heilman, Robert B., "The Tragedy of Knowledge, Marlowe's Treatment of Faustus." *Quarterly Review of Literature,* Vol. II (1946), pp. 316–32.

Heller, Otto, *Faust and Faustus: A Study of Goethe's Relation to Marlowe.* Language and Literature Series, No. 2. St. Louis, Mo., Washington Univ., 1931.

Kahler, Erich, *The Orbit of Thomas Mann,* to be published by Princeton University Press, Princeton, N. J., in 1969.

Kirschbaum, Leo, "Marlowe's Faustus." *Review of English Studies,* Vol. XIX (1943), pp. 225–41.

Kocher, Paul H., *Christopher Marlowe: A Study of His Thought, Learning, and Character.* Chapel Hill, Univ. of North Carolina Press, 1946.

Leech, Clifford, *Marlowe: A Collection of Critical Essays.* Englewood Cliffs, N. J.: Prentice-Hall, 1964.

Leppman, Wolfgang, *The German Image of Goethe.* Oxford, Clarendon Press, 1961.

Lewes, G. H., *The Life and Works of Goethe.* Boston, Mass., Ticknor and Fields, 1856.

Lunacharski, A. V., *Faust and the City,* trans. by L. A. Magnus, in *Three Plays of A. V. Lunacharski.* New York, Dutton, 1923.

Mann, Thomas, *The Beloved Returns: Lotte in Weimar.* New York, Knopf, 1940. A novel about the life of Goethe.

———, *Essays of Three Decades.* New York, Knopf, 1947. This volume contains three excellent essays on Goethe and *Faust.*

———, ed., *The Permanent Goethe.* New York, Dial Press, 1956.

Mason, Eudo C., *Goethe's Faust, Its Genesis and Purport.* Berkeley, Univ. of California Press, 1967.

Mizener, Arthur, "The Tragedy of Marlowe's *Doctor Faustus.*" *College English,* Vol. V (1943), pp. 70–75.

Peacock, Ronald, *Goethe's Major Plays.* New York, Hill & Wang, 1959.

Robertson, John George, *The Life and Work of Goethe.* London, Routledge & Sons, 1932.

Santayana, George, *Three Philosophical Poets.* Cambridge, Mass., Harvard Univ. Press, 1922. This discussion of philosophy and poetry links the work of three poets: Lucretius, Dante, and Goethe.

Simpson, Percy, "Marlowe's *Tragicall History of Doctor Faustus.*" *Essays and Studies,* Vol. XIV (1929), pp. 20–34.

Smith, John C. "Marlowe's Dr. Faustus." *Scrutiny,* Vol. VIII (1939), pp. 36–55.

Stawell, F. M., and G. Lowes Dickinson, *Goethe and Faust, an Interpretation.* London, Bell & Sons, 1928.

Steane, J. B., *Marlowe: A Critical Study.* Cambridge, Cambridge Univ. Press, 1964.

Strich, Fritz, *Goethe and World Literature,* trans. by C. A. M. Sym., New York, Hafner Publishing, 1949.

Swinburne, A. C., "Christopher Marlowe," in *The Age of Shakespeare.* New York, A. M. S. Press, 1908 (reprinted 1965), pp. 1–14.

Westlund, Joseph, "The Orthodox Christian Framework of Marlowe's *Faustus.*" *Studies in English Literature,* Vol. III (1963), pp. 191–205.

White, Andrew, *Thomas Mann*. New York, Grove Press, 1965. This study contains a valuable brief summary of Mann's life and works and a helpful bibliography.

Wilkinson, E. M., and L. A. Willoughby, *Goethe, Poet and Thinker*. New York, Barnes and Noble, 1962.